WITHDRAWN

Treatment Choices for Alcoholism and Substance Abuse

Treatment Choices for Alcoholism and Substance Abuse

Edited by

Harvey B. Milkman, Ph.D.
Metropolitan State College, Denver, Colorado

Lloyd I. Sederer, M.D.
McLean Hospital, Harvard Medical School

Lexington Books
D.C. Heath and Company/Lexington, Massachusetts/Toronto

Library of Congress Cataloging-in-Publication Data
Treatment choices for alcoholism and substance abuse / edited by
  Harvey B. Milkman, Lloyd I. Sederer.
      p.   cm.
    Based on presentations at a regional conference sponsored by the
  Alcohol and Drug Abuse Division, Colorado Dept. of Health, June 3–4,
  1988 at Denver, Colo.
    ISBN 0-669-20019-0 (alk. paper)
    1. Alcoholism—Treatment—Congresses. 2. Substance abuse—
  Treatment—Congresses. I. Milkman, Harvey B. II. Sederer, Lloyd
  I. III. Colorado. Division of Alcohol and Drug Abuse.
    [DNLM: 1. Alcoholism—therapy—congresses. 2. Substance Abuse—
  therapy—congresses.   WM 274 T7845 1988]
  RC565.T745   1990
  616.86'06—dc20
  DNLM/DLC
  for Library of Congress   89-13192
                                                                  CIP

Copyright © 1990 by Lexington Books

All rights reserved. No part of this publication may be reproduced or transmitted in any form or by any means, electronic or mechanical, including photocopy, recording, or any information storage or retrieval system, without permission in writing from the publisher.

Published simultaneously in Canada
Printed in the United States of America
Casebound International Standard Book Number: 0-669-20019-0
Library of Congress Catalog Card Number: 89-13192

The paper used in this publication meets the minimum requirements of American National Standard for Information Sciences—Permanence of Paper for Printed Library Materials, ANSI Z39.48-1984. ∞™

Year and number of this printing:

90 91 92 10 9 8 7 6 5 4 3 2 1

Dedicated to our families and friends

Contents

Figures xiii
Tables xv
Preface xvii
  Harvey B. Milkman
Introduction xix
  Harvey B. Milkman

Part I Biological Factors 1
  Prologue 3
  Boris Tabakoff

1. **A Review of Genetic Influences on Psychoactive Substance Use and Abuse** 7
   Allan C. Collins and Christopher M. de Fiebre

   Some Questions 7
   Genetic Influences on Human Substance Abuse 14
   Genetic Influences on Substance Use–Related Behaviors
     in Animals 19
   Summary 20
   References 21

2. **Harnessing Brain Chemicals: The Influence of Molecules on Mind, Mood, and Behavior** 25
   Stanley G. Sunderwirth

   Hypocrisy and the Need for Mood Alteration 26
   Activities, Molecules, and Mood 27
   Molecules, Neurotransmission, and Mood 28
   Arousal and Synaptic Chemistry 30
   Synaptic Homeostasis 32
   Relaxation and Synaptic Chemistry 34

Food for Your Mood   35
Exercise and Endorphins   38
Summary   39
References   40

3. **Biological Approaches to Addiction Treatment   43**
   John A. Renner, Jr.

   Opiates   43
   Alcohol   48
   Cocaine   54
   Benzodiazepines   58
   Nicotine   62
   Polydrug Abuse   65
   References   67

4. **Nutrition and Recovery from Alcoholism   73**
   Lee Ann Mjelde Mossey

   Alcoholic Malnutrition   74
   Specific Nutrient Deficiencies   78
   Deficiencies and Relapse   81
   Nutritional Assessment   83
   Treatment   84
   Evaluation   84
   Conclusion   85
   References   86

Part II   Prevention and Early Intervention   89
Prologue   91
Robin Room

5. **Prevention and Early Intervention of Addictive Disorders   95**
   Peter E. Nathan

   Some of the Dimensions of Abuse in the United States   95
   Outcomes of Treatment for Long-Term Alcohol Dependence   97
   Alternatives to Treatment: Prevention and Early Intervention   98
   References   105

6. **The Assessment and Treatment of Alcohol- and Drug-Related Traffic Offenders   109**
   David S. Timken

   The Legislation   109
   The Law   109
   The Evaluation Process   110
   Classification and Referral   114

Education and Therapy Programs   115
Monitoring Clients   117
Program Evaluation   118
Conclusion   119
References   119

Appendix 6–A: Classification Criteria

7. **Prevention and Intervention in Schools   123**
   Mary VanderWall

   Policy   126
   Curriculum   126
   Staff Development   127
   Alternatives for Students   128
   Parent and Community Involvement   129
   Intervention   129
   Evaluation   132
   Conclusion   132
   References   132

   Appendix 7-A: Hawkins-Stafford School Improvement Act PL 100-297 Title V—Drug Free Schools and Communities Act   135
   Appendix 7-B: Sample DFSCA Three-Year Action Plan   137
   Appendix 7-C: Sample DFSCA Three-Year Action Plan   139
   Appendix 7-D: School District Contacts   141

8. **Employee Assistance Programs as an Early Intervention Strategy for Substance Abuse   143**
   Carol L. Hacker

   Employee Assistance Programs   144
   Prevention, Intervention, and Treatment   148
   The EAP as an Information Resource   153
   The Future   155
   References   156

Part III   Multiproblem Patients   159
   Prologue   161
   William A. Frosch

9. **Mental Disorders and Substance Abuse   163**
   Lloyd I. Sederer

   Models of Dual Diagnosis   164
   Concurrent Axis I and Substance Abuse Disorders   166
   Concurrent Axis II and Substance Abuse Disorders   170

Discussion 174
References 178

10. **Alcohol and Drug Problems in Women: Old Attitudes, New Knowledge** 183
    Sheila B. Blume

    The Drinking or Drug-Taking Woman as Victim 185
    Implications for Prevention 186
    Barriers to Chemical Dependence Treatment 187
    Special Problems of Chemically Dependent Women 190
    Codependence Issues 193
    Treatment Outcomes 194
    Summary 195
    References 196

    Appendix 10–A: DIS Questionnaire 199

11. **Elements of Recovery: A Longitudinal Analysis** 201
    George E. Vaillant

    Why Does Addiction Occur? 202
    Why Does Relapse Occur? 204
    Why Do People Not Relapse? 205
    Pathways to Recovery 206
    Summary 207
    References 208

Part IV   Treatment and the Law   209
   Prologue 211
   Norman E. Zinberg

12. **The Prosecutor's Goals Beyond Conviction** 217
    Alexander M. Hunter and *Robert A. Pudim*

    Conviction and Punishment 218
    Reasons for Punishment 219
    References 224

13. **Treatment Strategies for Juvenile Delinquents to Decrease Substance Abuse and Prevent Adult Drug and Alcohol Dependence** 225
    Susan L. Stein, Carol J. Garrett, and *Dave Christiansen*

    Theoretical Model 226
    Treatment Components 227
    Project Clients 228

Evaluation Plan   230
References   232

14. **Rehabilitation of Multiple DUI Offenders: An Innovative Model   235**
    Phillip G. Sidoff, Carole Christianson, Steven P. Merrefield, and *Judy Brown*

    Background   235
    The Existing System in Colorado   237
    The Melding of Treatment and Corrections   238
    The Colorado Model for Rehabilitation of Multiple DUI Offenders   241
    Clinical and Programmatic Observations   244
    Summary and Future Applications   245
    References   246

Part V   Treatment Alternatives   247
   Prologue   249
   Howard J. Shaffer

15. **Alcohol Treatment Alternatives: What Works?   253**
    William R. Miller

    Five Myths of Treatment   254
    Specific Treatment Modalities   256
    Client-Treatment Matching   259
    Conclusions   260
    References   262

16. **Cognitive-Behavioral Treatment of Problem Drinking   265**
    Chad D. Emrick and *Gregory A. Aarons*

    Theory   266
    Treatment   275
    Conclusion   282
    Notes   283
    References   283

17. **Affective Modes in Multimodality Addiction Treatment   287**
    Robert Vaughn Frye

    Treatment Planning   287
    Change and Recovery   289
    Affective Modes   290
    Conclusion   304
    References   305

18. **Family Therapy Approaches to Substance Abuse with a Special Focus on Alcohol Issues**   309
   Victor A. Harris

   Typology of Treatment Approaches   311
   A Model for Type 3 Family Therapy   315
   Summary   318
   Annotated Bibliography   318
   Notes   319
   References   319

   Appendix 18–A: Codependence Project Protocol for Therapy Sessions   323

19. **Therapy with Families of Adolescent Substance Abusers**   329
   M. Duncan Stanton and *Judith Landau-Stanton*

   Family Life Cycle Issues   330
   Dealing with the Parental Subsystem   333
   Sibling Factors   336
   Grandparents   336
   Other Systems   338
   References   338

20. **Interventions with the Substance-Abusing Nurse**   341
   Vernice Griffin Hills.

   Patient Dynamics and History   342
   Treatment   345
   Results   348
   Conclusion   349
   Suggested Readings   349
   References   350

Epilogue: Integrating Treatment Choices   351
   Howard J. Shaffer and Blase Gambino
Appendix: Counseling Interest Inventory   377
Index   381
About the Contributors   391
About the Editors   397

Figures

1–1. Frequency distributions of risk of substance abuse due to genetic and environmental factors.   11

2–1. Structural similarity between norepinephrine and amphetamine.   27

2–2. Chemical transmission of a nerve impulse.   29

2–3. Effect of cocaine on the reabsorption of excitatory neurotransmitters (norepinephrine) into the presynaptic membrane.   32

2–4. Conversion of tryptophan to serotonin in the brain.   36

2–5. Conversion of tyrosine to norepinephrine in the brain.   37

3–1. Phases following a cocaine binge.   56

7–1. Relationship between health education experience and health-related behavior.   125

9–1. Differential diagnosis.   175

18–1. Flowchart of delivery design/treatment protocol.   317

20–1. Primary drugs of abuse.   344

20–2. Noncontingency versus contingency patients.   348

Tables

3–1. Standard Benzodiazepine Dosing Schedule 51
3–2. Bromocriptine Regimen for Cocaine Withdrawal 57
3–3. Benzodiazepines in Common Use 59
5–1. Estimated Number of Deaths Attributable to Alcohol in the United States, 1980 96
9–1. Models of Dual Diagnosis 164
9–2. DSM III-R Axis I Disorders: Clinical Syndromes 166
9–3. Psychoactive Substance-Induced Organic Mental Disorder: Alcohol 167
9–4. DSM III-R Axis II Disorders 171
9–5. DSM III-R Axis II Disorders: Personality Traits and Disorders 171
9–6. Importance of Identifying Dual-Diagnosis Patients 174
9–7. Effects of Substance Abuse on Recovery from Psychiatric Disorder 176
11–1. Outcome of One Hundred Heroin Addicts at Three Points in Time after Index Hospital Discharge 203
11–2. Outcome of One Hundred Alcohol-Dependent Individuals at Three Points in Time after Index Hospital Discharge 203
11–3. Factors Associated with Absence of Relapse for a Year or More 206

13–1. Prevalence of Drug Use among 1986 Committed Juveniles   229

13–2. Characteristics of Drug Use   230

13–3. Delinquency Factor Assessment   232

14–1. Admission Criteria for Colorado Multiple DUI Offender Program   243

Preface

Harvey B. Milkman

The Addictions: Multidisciplinary Perspectives and Treatments, edited by H. Milkman and H. Shaffer, was first published in 1985. Disparate clinical observations, research findings, theoretical formulations, and treatment approaches were consolidated to promote a unified perspective on addiction. Our intent was to reduce the trend of unidimensional reductionism and simplistic explanation in a field beset by complexity. By March 1989, the book had reached its seventh printing.

Treatment Choices for Alcoholism and Substance Abuse represents the next generation of an evolving interdisciplinary approach to addictive phenomena. As we enter the last decade of the twentieth century, it is clear that improved treatment outcomes can occur if remedial efforts are prescriptive. Clinicians must develop the skills to organize individually tailored treatment strategies around the constellation of biological, psychological and social factors that shape each person's unique style of chemical dependence and associated dysfunction.

This volume is intended as a conceptual bridge between individual differences in patterns of substance abuse and effective strategies for their change. We adhere to a philosophy that rational clinical practice follows scientific theory that is solidly grounded in research. In recognition of the multifactorial nature of addiction, the text is organized around a continuum of issues that affect clinical practice: biological factors; prevention and early intervention; multiproblem patients; treatment and the law; and treatment alternatives. A thought-provoking commentary is provided at the beginning of each section, orienting the reader to the broad philosophical and scientific issues that surround particular treatment strategies. We then present germane theoretical perspectives, followed by papers that address specific applications in clinical practice. In other words, the text for each section moves from the general to the specific, from the theoretical to the applied.

This book is based in good part on presentations at Treatment Choices in Substance Abuse, a regional conference sponsored by the Alcohol and Drug Abuse Division, Colorado Department of Health, 3–4 June, 1988. We are indebted to the division staff: Robert B. Aukerman and Harold "Bud" Meadows, director and associate director, for supporting a multifactorial approach to a conference on addiction treatment; Danelle Young, director of treatment services, and David S. Timken, Ph.D., clinical services coordinator, for helping to conceptualize and implement the broad scope of this project.

We are deeply grateful to the many authors who have entrusted their clinical, research, and theoretical expertise to this publication. I am especially thankful to Howard Shaffer, Stanley Sunderwirth, and William Frosch for their collaborative contributions and continued support during the past two decades. We are thankful to the late Norman Zinberg for his contribution to this volume and recognize his unique leadership in the development of an interdisciplinary model for addiction. He has bestowed upon us a wider view.

I would like to thank Greg Aarons for his collaboration and for coining the term *treatment choices* and Imelda Mulholland for her referencing assistance. I also would like to thank Ed Karnes, chairperson, and Jack Hesson, professor, Department of Psychology, Metropolitan State College, for their friendship and encouragement throughout my academic career. Finally, this work would not have been possible without the quarter century of intellectual stimulation and camaraderie provided by Lloyd Sederer.

Introduction

Harvey B. Milkman

> Brain circuitry permits momentary ecstasy or prolonged pleasure
> ... sustained ecstasy is neurophysiologically impossible."
> —Sidney Cohen, M.D., *The Chemical Brain*

The complications that may arise from exposure to psychoactive substances vary in response to combined influences from drug, set, and setting (Zinberg 1984). Rather than a unitary disorder, substance abuse problems are multidimensional, with great variation among individuals. Consequently, no treatment is optimal for all patients. In fact, research findings do not support the efficacy of most popular substance abuse interventions (Miller and Hester 1986).

If remedial efforts are to be more successful, treatment must be prescriptive. Clinicians are obliged to discover the purpose and meaning of substance abuse for each patient. They must then select, from the panoply of systems available, interventions that are compatible with patient need.

Shaffer and Neuhaus (1985) clarified the process of eclectic treatment planning by offering a multidimensional model for assessment and diagnosis. Assessment efforts should be directed toward understanding the causes and consequences of substance abuse from biological, psychological, and sociocultural perspectives. While biological factors are clearly a substrate for addictive phenomena, single-minded attention to the influence of molecules on mind, mood, and behavior have not yielded positive results. "Bewildered by the diversity of philosophical positions and theoretical perspectives, the less experienced practitioner, in particular, is apt to retreat to a narrow, restricted model that does not allow for individual patient differences" (Shaffer and Neuhaus 1985).

Any discussion of treatment choices for alcoholism and substance abuse must consider—yet not overly rely on—the biological factors that may predispose an individual toward chemical dependence or exacerbate the complications of chemical consumption. There is widespread agreement that addiction involves a genotype by environment mix. Rather than nature versus nurture, heredity and society collaborate in the determination of an individual's vulnerability to substances. In Boris Tabakoff's commentary for part I, "Biological Factors," he insightfully compares the scientific study of social influences to the principles of thermodynamics. The behavior of a volume of gas subjected to various physical influences (for example, pressure or temperature) can be sufficiently explained without offering a clue to the unique behavior of any given molecule. An individual's genetic constitution must be considered to understand how a particular molecule will react.

In chapter 1, "A Review of Genetic Influences on Psychoactive Substance Use and Abuse," Collins and de Fiebre discuss clear evidence that demonstrates heritable factors in alcoholism. This information has been obtained in studies of identical twins, reared together or apart, in family studies, and in adoption studies. The findings indicate that if a given child has an alcoholic parent, that child is much more likely than the population norm to experience severe problems with alcohol sometime during his or her life. Although not as well studied, evidence exists that tobacco use also is genetically influenced. Little can be said, however, about precisely what aspect of substance use or abuse is genetically controlled. Animal studies show that initial sensitivity to drugs, drug self-administration, degree of tolerance, and severity of withdrawal are all influenced by genetic factors. For alcohol, these differences may be explained by genetically regulated variations in interactions between ethanol and cell membranes. For nicotine, there may be individual differences in the number of brain receptors for nicotine and in the ability of these receptors to desensitize or inactivate when nicotine binds to them. Understanding the genetic factors that regulate substance use and abuse may ultimately result in early identification of potential abusers and more focused treatment approaches.

Although still imprecise, molecular biology has developed useful models to explain the familiar patterns of increased craving and loss of control associated with continued use of psychoactive substances. In chapter 2, "Harnessing Brain Chemicals: The Influence of Molecules on Mind, Mood, and Behavior," Sunderwirth likens the brain to computer hardware that can be programmed to achieve various moods depending on the software used. The brain may be programmed via "user-friendly" software, such as those molecules produced by activities, or may run programs that are not completely compatible. Although noncompatible software (psychoactive substances) will run certain programs (mood changes), eventually this software has the potential to cause damage to the hardware (brain). Thus, we are guided to advocate natural highs (Milkman and Sunderwirth 1989), encouraging the use of life-enhancing activities to achieve the mood alterations essential for a fulfilling life. This view is entirely consistent with Tabakoff's suggestion in the prologue to part I that understanding the "diverse biological and environmental influences [on substance abuse] . . . will allow for the use of natural environmental variables to orchestrate the genetically influenced body chemistry and thereby reduce the reliance on exogenous chemical modifiers of mood and behavior."

Through the pursuit of "unnatural highs," chemical changes that are not readily reversible can occur in the brain. Sunderwirth compares these to a metal spring that can be stretched thousands of times without losing strength or flexibility. If, however, the spring is stretched beyond a certain limit, it will lose its ability to rebound to its original condition. If the brain, this overextension by the use of mood-altering drugs is manifested in an overreaction to the drug (through changes in enzyme levels in the region of the synapse), which is not readily reversible. It is this alteration of enzyme levels with corresponding changes in neurotransmission that is partially responsible for the addictive process.

Exponential growth in scientific understanding of the neurochemical substratum for craving and addiction guides contemporary approaches to treatment. In chapter 3, "Biological Approaches to Addiction Treatment," Renner provides a state-of-the-art overview of mechanisms of action and biological interventions for the substances most commonly abused in modern society: opiates, alcohol, cocaine, benzodiazepines, nicotine, and polydrug combinations.

Chemical substitutes may be prescribed for narcotics detoxification, and pharmacologic stabilization may be achieved through methadone maintenance. Chemical treatments for alcoholism and tranquilizer abuse include medication for detoxification, substitution and aversion therapy, and biochemical treatments for psychiatric complications. Cocaine pharmacotherapy may involve detoxification and management of acute withdrawal through noneuphoriant dopamine agonists, along with treatment for concurrent psychiatric disorders. Renner describes nicotine as an addictive central nervous system (CNS) stimulant with devastating health effects. He reviews withdrawal in terms of immediate and long-term behavioral effects and delineates medications that have been found useful in diminishing symptoms associated with smoking cessation.

Psychoactive substances not only interfere with delicate neurochemical processes that affect mood and performance, but they also may compromise nutritional reactions that influence physical health. In chapter 4, Mossey demonstrates the need for assessment of the alcoholic's dietary needs as a routine part of alcoholism treatment. Prolonged use of alcohol is an accepted cause of malnutrition and is especially critical in population groups already at risk for poor nourishment (for example, the elderly and adolescents). The high caloric value of alcohol provides quick energy without supplying essential nutrients, and the body prefers it to those essential energy sources. Alcohol also interferes with the body's absorption of whatever nutrients the alcoholic may ingest. Any assumption that the alcoholic can postpone diet therapy until later in recovery is as flawed as an assumption that nutritional status does not influence psychological or cognitive functioning. Specific nutrient deficiencies that have been associated with depression, for example, include iron, B_6, thiamine, B_{12}, and folic acid. Left untreated, a biochemically based depression could precipitate a return to alcoholic drinking. Nutritional assessment and an ongoing regimen to facilitate optimum nutritional status are basic to the recovery process.

Karl Menninger (1963) noted that "treatment depends on diagnosis.... One does not complete a diagnosis and then begin treatment; the diagnostic process is also the start of treatment" (p. 333). Obviously, early problem identification and incisive prevention is at the forefront of effective intervention. In the prologue to part II, "Prevention and Early Intervention," Robin Room distinguishes traditional prevention strategies based on service provision—that is, something is being done for or to a client by a human services specialist—from approaches that are more or less self-enforcing or self-financing. The latter approaches include market controls, environmental change, and deterrence. Since short-term demand for alcohol and tobacco is relatively inelastic, governments can profit from raising taxes while also having some effect on reducing consumption. Environmental changes may include federal regulation of smoking on airplanes, training bartenders in peaceable methods of refusing service, and making sterile needles available to intravenous drug users. The literature on deterrence differentiates general deterrence (the effect of a measure in preventing a prohibited act) from specific deterrence (the effect of a measure in stopping those who have been caught committing the act from doing it again). While specific deterrence tends to be very costly because of the requirement of intensive service provision (such as police and prison guards), general deterrence, such as countermeasures to drunk driving (including immediate driver's license suspensions), is often more effective.

The value of increasing effort toward self-enforcing approaches to prevention is echoed in chapter 5, "Prevention and Early Intervention of Addictive Disorders." Having reviewed the literature extensively, Nathan finds that we are a good deal better able to prevent some of the consequences of alcohol misuse, such as alcohol-related car crashes and fetal alcohol syndrome, than chronic alcohol abuse itself. He notes that "year after year nine out of ten alcoholics and drug addicts are not treated in this country. Chances are an even lower percentage of women, minorities, youths, and elderly persons are treated, largely because most treatment programs are designed to meet the needs of the prototypic white, middle-aged, male alcoholic." Nathan reports that restrictions on the availability of alcohol, by raising both taxes and minimum age of purchase (market control), have yielded real changes in both consumption and the consequences of consumption by youth. The question of whether such measures affect the heaviest drinking 20 percent of our population, those who consume 80 percent of the beverage alcohol, remains unanswered. According to Nathan, in 1988, the overall cost to society for alcohol abuse was approximately $150 billion; the drug toll was estimated at $70 billion.

One apparent reason for the moderate success of drunk driving prevention efforts has been the emergence of specialized programs designed for individuals who are found guilty of driving while under the influence of alcohol or drugs. In chapter 6, "The Assessment and Treatment of Alcohol- and Drug-Related Traffic Offenders," Timken describes the Colorado system, which has been recognized by the U.S. Department of Transportation as providing state-of-the-art assistance to drinking drivers in the areas of screening, referral, treatment, and monitoring of offenders. The Colorado system categorizes offenders into three types: (1) problem drinker or drug user, (2) incipient problem drinker or drug user, and (3) nonproblem or social drinker or drug user. Of Colorado's 300,000 alcohol- or drug-related driving cases between 1980 and 1988, only 18 percent were classified as not having a problem with alcohol or drugs. A 1988 study of overall program effectiveness analyzed the driving records of nearly 29,000 randomly selected offenders who were initially evaluated between May 1984 and June 1985. The study clearly showed that recidivism was consistently higher among offenders who failed to complete the education and therapy requirements of the program.

Although the success of service provision approaches to substance abuse prevention is difficult to document, a number of researchers have reported early intervention strategies that have resulted in dramatic reductions in problem drinking in young adults (Sanchez-Craig and Wilkinson 1987; Annis 1986; Miller 1978). A variety of behavioral techniques are used to teach clients self-control skills, which are then expected to help them make more appropriate choices about when, where, and how much they drink.

In chapter 7, "Prevention and Intervention in Schools," VanderWall discusses the effects of federal and state legislation on school-based prevention and early intervention efforts. Research and experience show that drug and alcohol education in schools should be far more comprehensive than a content-oriented curriculum. While most school programs promote prevention by providing age-appropriate cognitive preparation, skill development, and rehearsal, school-based intervention programs have been more difficult to initiate. Traditionally, intervention in a student's current drug or alcohol use has been a touchy legal issue, and there have been few available programs to serve as models. As school personnel have become more sophisticated about alcohol and drug abuse, early intervention has emerged as an important prevention device.

Another increasingly popular approach to service-oriented prevention is covered in chapter 8, "Employee Assistance Programs as an Early Intervention Strategy for Substance Abuse." According to recent estimates by the National Institute on Drug Abuse (NIDA), as many as 23 percent of all workers use drugs on the job and 5 percent have serious addiction problems. The tremendous costs in terms of productivity, safety, interpersonal relations, and personal health are estimated to be in the $70 billion range. The extent of government and industrial alarm is registered by the number of Americans who are now subject to mandatory urine testing as a condition of employment. Some experts currently estimate the numbers of employees subject to urine testing to be in the range of five million. The distinct possibility exists that during the early 1990s, 80 percent of all companies will be testing their employees for drug abuse (Trebach 1987).

In addition to detection and deterrence of drug abuse through urine testing, employers have become increasingly committed to treatment as a viable alternative to suspension or firing. Employee assistance programs (EAPs) are assessment and treatment services financed by an employer for employees who have problems. As supervisors and employers have become aware that employees need help with a range of problems, EAPs have evolved from employee alcoholism programs to employee assistance programs. These broadbrush efforts assist troubled employees with problems such as marital conflict, family issues, financial or legal needs, child care, elderly parents, or medical needs. There are two major EAP models: in-house (internal) and contract services (external). In the internal model, EAP personnel are hired by the employer for assessment, referral, and limited treatment services. The external model provides employee assistance services by contracting with an EAP provider independent of the employer organization. The contributions of EAPs to the treatment of substance abuse and chemical dependence are affirmed by the increase in their numbers. In 1972, 25 percent of the Fortune 500 companies had EAPs; seven years later, in 1979, 57 percent of these companies had such programs. By 1985, there were more than eight thousand EAPs nationwide (Chiabotta 1985; McClellan 1982).

Paralleling the realization by alcohol assistance programs that employee problems are considerably more extensive than those engendered by alcoholism and drug abuse, the mental health community has begun to focus on an increasingly complex view of individuals who abuse substances. The prologue for part III, "Multiproblem Patients," provides a particularly enlightening metaphor for a more sophisticated appreciation of patients who abuse substances as distinct individuals rather than as general types. Frosch explains how one of the important contributions of DSM III has been the introduction of multiple axes, forcing us to think of personality as well as disease, of physical illness as well as mental illness, of external stressors and functional abilities.

In chapter 9, "Multiproblem Patients: Mental Disorders and Substance Abuse," Sederer first tackles the clinical reality of people who present for treatment with more than one psychiatric condition—namely, substance abuse and a mental disorder. A description of various models for understanding dual-diagnosis patients is followed by a discussion of three clinical syndromes that tend to coexist with substance abuse disorders: (1) substance abuse–induced organic mental disorders, (2) the major mental illnesses that psychiatrists treat (schizophrenia, affective disorders, and anxiety disorders), and (3) adult or residual attention deficit disorder (ADD). Sederer then addresses the extent to which differentiations can be made among the different substances of abuse as they interact with personality disorders (borderline, narcissistic, and antisocial). The importance of identifying dual-diagnosis patients extends to differential diagnosis (the capacity to differentiate disorders from one another), the course and prognosis of psychiatric illness, the potential efficacy of treatment efforts, the qualifications of the staff needed for treatment, and the staging of treatments provided to the dually diagnosed.

In chapter 10, "Alcohol and Drug Problems in Women: Old Attitudes, New Knowledge," Blume discusses some of the special problems encountered by women who abuse alcohol. Nearly half the population of women who are treated for alcoholism have additional psychiatric disturbances, which may include substance use or abuse, phobias, major depression, or personality disorders. Not only do women present with more complicated psychiatric profiles, but they also must endure special obstacles to treatment. While female alcoholics bear the pernicious stigma of being sexually promiscuous, nearly two-thirds of the female alcoholics in a recent study reported that they were victims of unwanted sexual contact as a child by an older person (Fillmore 1985). Although there is a 2 to 1 ratio of males to females who suffer from alcoholism, women are underrepresented in treatment by a ratio of 4 to 1. Largely due to social disapproval, women may be described as the hidden alcoholics. They are more likely to drink alone, their problems are more likely to be denied by themselves and their families, and there often has been a long history of sexual abuse and victimization of many kinds.

In chapter 11, "Elements of Recovery: A Longitudinal Analysis," Vaillant deals with the question "What are the essential factors that enable patients to recover from alcoholism?" After ten to fourteen years of tracking one hundred alcoholics with an average history of ten years of alcohol abuse before hospitalization, Vaillant found at the time of the most recent follow-up that 38 percent of the alcoholics had been abstinent for a year or more. Why?

Vaillant found that unlike heroin addicts, who are typically unstable prior to becoming addicted, alcoholism *causes* occupational and relationship instability. Once an individual is an alcoholic, alcohol becomes the dominant form of gratification. The more structured an alcoholic's life, the less prone he or she is to relapse. The prognosis is clearly better for people who are married, have been employed for at least four years, and were raised in their parents' culture. Vaillant illuminates four pathways from alcoholism to recovery: (1) new relationships, (2) compulsory supervision, (3) substitute dependence, and (4) joining an inspirational group.

Although the alcoholic may stumble upon these pathways accidentally or through costly treatment regimens, perhaps the easiest way is through Alcoholics Anonymous (AA). To be sure, AA is by far the most common element in treatment approaches in the United States. Although reported correlations between AA attendance and abstinence are common, causal interpretation is difficult. Is AA essential to recovery, or do people who relapse simply drop out of AA? In Miller's survey of research that has addressed the efficacy of AA treatment strategies (chapter 15), he reports that not one of the four studies that qualify as controlled trials of AA strategies have found a beneficial treatment effect.

In accord with Vaillant's findings that structure in the addict's life is central to the recovery process, the criminal justice system has attempted to coerce stability through external controls. In Norman Zinberg's thoughtful prologue to part IV, "Treatment and the Law," he explores the complex, interactive relationship between intoxicant use and crime. Although it is commonly assumed that drugs are a gateway to crime, 50 percent of those currently convicted with histories of intoxicant use had difficulties with the law *before* they were users. Therefore, cleaning up the addicted individual, as suggested by the intoxicant-to-blame theory, would be quite insufficient as a treatment strategy for a great number of criminal addicts. Perhaps more realistically, if one considers a vicious cycle theory, treatment should involve a more comprehensive effort, albeit more expensive and time-consuming, at social rehabilitation. Zinberg notes: "In all likelihood, the original social antagonism, further unleashed by the chronic disorientation of heavy intoxicant use, became more fixed and less amenable to a rational relationship with society in general and the criminal justice system in particular."

In chapter 12, "The Prosecutor's Goals Beyond Conviction," Hunter and Pudim pursue a core notion that treatment for substance abuse problems is a necessary part of rehabilitation. Studies of the relationship between drugs and criminal activity repeatedly show that up to 80 percent of all state prison inmates were under the influence of an intoxicant at the time they committed the crime for which they were imprisoned. According to the U.S. Bureau of Justice (1988), half of those serving sentences for robbery, burglary, and theft were daily users of some illegal drug.

When one considers the fact that harsh punishment does not serve as a deterrent to crime, Zinberg notes in his prologue, "the need for reeducation and treatment other than incarceration or punishment alone is inescapable." Outcome studies of a small number of programs, many taking place in prison and continuing with care after release, appear to reduce participants' involvement with drugs and crime (Wexler, Lipton, and Johnson 1985).

In chapter 13, "Treatment Strategies for Juvenile Delinquents to Decrease Substance Abuse and Prevent Adult Drug and Alcohol Dependency," Stein, Garrett, and Christiansen describe an innovative program for treating delinquents. The theoretical underpinning for the Colorado Office of Substance Abuse Prevention (OSAP) project is that blocked or limited opportunity (strain) is related to bonding with delinquent peers and subsequent drug use.

The Colorado OSAP project uses skill-based education and vocational training to increase the probability that youths will have the ability to reach conventional goals. The OSAP program involves four distinct components: (1) an *assessment* to ensure the timely referral of eligible youths into the project; (2) a *wilderness* component to provide an esteem-building drug-free outdoor experience; (3) a *residential* and vocational stage lasting up to six months to provide skill-based rehabilitation; and (4) a *community* transition component with a significant other to maintain and reinforce skills in a home community.

A particularly visible group of criminal offenders are those with several drunk or drugged driving arrests. Typically, the multiple driving under the influence (DUI) or driving while ability impaired (DWAI) offender passes through an overburdened legal system several times and is sent to an outpatient program focusing on alcohol education and therapy. While these intervention systems have proven effective for the first offender (see chapter 6), there is a uniformly low success rate for the multiple DUI offender. Recidivism continues to occur regardless of whether the reoffender is sentenced to monitored use of Antabuse, AA, or residential alcohol treatment. The final outcome for the repeat offender is often a long-term sentence to penal institutions, where substance abuse problems typically remain unaddressed. In chapter 14, "Rehabilitation of Multiple DUI Offenders," Sidoff, Christianson, and Brown first review the literature on multiple DUI programs and then describe an innovative treatment/rehabilitation project tailored to meet the special needs of this criminal/addict population.

From the spectrum of student/client/patient/offender issues covered in this brief introduction, it is apparent that no single treatment approach is optimal for all or even most people with alcohol or drug problems. Instead, there exists a range of promising options. In Howard Shaffer's prologue to part V, "Treatment Alternatives," he discusses how theories or models of substance abuse determine the nature of treatment. Theory also determines whether a given substance abuser will accept help. Shaffer notes, "Because . . . theoretical models identify the nature of potential solutions, treatment alternatives are either accepted or rejected by prospective patients and their lay explanation of addiction." Shaffer finds that in spite of an array of available treatment options, clinicians often do not make contact with their patients and uniformly apply a rote set of treatment strategies.

It is no wonder that research findings do not support blanket reliance on popular substance abuse treatment interventions. Treatment must be prescriptive—that is, therapy should be geared toward specific patient needs—if clinical efforts are to be more successful. In chapter 15, "Alcohol Treatment Alternatives: What Works?," Miller discusses common beliefs about alcoholism treatments that are not substantiated by scientific fact. He reports that a substantial number of alcoholics recover without ever undergoing treatment. This is consistent with the research finding that long-term recovery is much less influenced by treatment events than by experience and conditions in the individual's life following treatment. Miller debunks the widely held belief that the hospital is the only (or most effective) way to address alcohol problems. He finds "no reasonable support" for this notion among the controlled studies on treatment outcome. There appears to be no overall advantage for residential, intensive, or longer treatment over less expensive alternatives. Those with more severe alcohol problems and limited support systems, however, may fare better with an abstinence goal and may have increased benefit from intensive treatment.

Although no one treatment has been shown to work for all patients, a number of positive studies to date indicate that the most successful methods consist of techniques to help clients suppress their drinking (and perhaps their urge to drink) and interventions to alter other life problems that could lead to relapse. Programs that have combined both types of strategies have shown strong treatment effects.

In chapter 16, "Cognitive-Behavioral Treatment of Problem Drinking," Emrick and Aarons present an alcoholism intervention model that offers a distinct alternative to the traditional disease concept. In contrast to the disease model's primary emphasis on avoiding the complications from either preexisting or evoked biological determinants, the cognitive-behavioral therapist considers the patient to be suffering from distorted cognitions and environmental contingencies that can be corrected through behavioral skills training and education directed toward developing effective cognitive strategies for coping with life's challenges. The therapist's role is primarily as an educator who expects clients "to set their own standards, monitor their own performance, and reward or reinforce themselves appropriately" (Brickman et al. 1982).

Cognitive-behavioral treatment is predicated on a thorough analysis of the cognitive, social, and behavioral factors involved in the maladaptive behavior to be modified. Once the initial assessment has been completed, therapists select only those cognitive behavioral strategies that seem to address the identified problems best. Training in social skills and affect regulation can be conducted using established behavior therapy procedures such as in vivo desensitization, problem solving, meditation, relaxation, and aerobic exercises.

In chapter 17, "Affective Modes in Multimodality Addiction Treatment," Frye discusses the role of improved affect regulation as an integral adjunct to a cognitive-behavioral treatment regimen. Clients may be trained in achieving an affective experience that may alter consciousness and awareness and produce positive changes in emotion, mood, and temperament. Such states may be considered natural highs and may help fill the void caused by abstinence from psychoactive substances. Affective modes may include stress management training such as deep relaxation and meditation; covert conditioning;

biofeedback; charismatic therapy; creative therapies that use dance, music, art, movement, and drama; suggestion; and group marathon therapy. Like psychoactive chemicals, these experiences create self-induced changes in neurotransmission (Milkman and Sunderwirth 1983). Unlike the use of psychoactive substances, these experiences are less apt to result in harmful consequences, but they afford relief from discomfort and stress.

Multimodality treatment as suggested by Frye is gaining increasing research support under what might also be termed *broad-spectrum approaches*. These strategies focus on life problems other than drinking that may be related to drinking problems. Their core notion is to promote recovery by helping the individual cope successfully with a range of difficulties that might otherwise encourage relapse. In chapter 18, "Family Therapy Approaches to Substance Abuse with a Special Focus on Alcohol Issues," Harris outlines three related, yet conceptually different, models for family intervention. The conflict between behavioral and disease concepts of alcoholism and its effect on family therapy may be understood by classifying family therapy approaches according to the primary focus of the therapist. Harris views Type 1 and 2 approaches as similar in that the primary focus is on the needs of the alcoholic. Their differences are that for Type 1, the therapist is only secondarily concerned with family issues, while Type 2 theories consider family needs in conjunction with the needs of the identified patient.

Type 3 approaches to alcoholism problems differ from the other two in that the therapist is *not* concerned with alcoholism per se but with the consequences for the family of having or having had an alcoholic member. Type 3 practitioners find that typical alcohol treatment approaches tend to recreate the alcoholic family system: The alcoholic is the center of attention, the coalcoholic (spouse) is either the supporter or provider, and the children are neglected. The emphasis in this approach is not on the addict or alcoholic but on codependence. The individuals who compose the network around the alcoholic learn through therapy that they have their *own* process and goals and that they have value independent of the alcoholic family member.

In chapter 19, "Therapy with Families of Adolescent Substance Abusers," Stanton and Landau-Stanton present eloquent clinical examples of how family involvement—even surrogate (foster parents or relatives) or symbolic (the network of health care workers who have taken a role in the adolescent's treatment)—is critical to positive treatment outcomes. Grandparents are often particularly important in augmenting the treatment process. The authors suggest that it is always necessary to evaluate the substance-abusing adolescent and his or her family within their context. This includes other systems with which they commonly interact: school, peer group, church, court, welfare system, and self-help groups such as AA or NA (Narcotics Anonymous). Such systems have their own agendas, which need to be coordinated with family therapy efforts. By joining with these systems, the therapist may empower parents and other family members to make constructive changes on behalf of the adolescent substance abuser.

In chapter 20, "Interventions with the Substance-Abusing Nurse," Griffin deals with the thorny issue of treating the impaired health professional. The American Medical Association (AMA) estimates that one physician in ten is in some way impaired (Arana 1982). An estimate of alcohol and drug dependence among nurses is 8 to 10 percent of a total number of 1.7 million nurses in the United States (Buxton, Jessup, and Landry 1985). Griffin presents outcome data for a contingency contracting approach to treatment. The focal point of this technique is a contract whereby the substance-abusing nurse agrees to surrender his or her license to the state board of nursing if at any time during treatment an obtained urine specimen contains an illicit drug. This leveraging device, in conjunction with more traditional therapy, has enabled a significant number of patients to remain abstinent while continuing their careers as health professionals.

At present, the number of impaired or addicted substance abuse counselors remains unknown. Perhaps those most committed to relieving the suffering of alcoholics or drug addicts should take heed of the ancient biblical directive: "Thou hypocrite, first cast out the beam out of thine own eye; and then shalt thou see clearly to cast out the mote out of thy brother's eye" (Matthew 7:5).

In the epilogue, "Integrating Treatment Choices," Howard Shaffer and Blase Gambino move beyond the traditional disease model for treating alcoholism and drug abuse. They present a stage change model that describes the basic process of recovery from any harmful lifestyle, with or without formal treatment.

The first stage—the emergence of addiction—is characterized by initial use followed by an epicycle in which the addictive behavior continues to provide positive effects while simultaneously producing adverse consequences that begin to weigh more heavily. At this level, addicts may be described as having a focused delusional system. They remain grounded in a realistic world view with one noticeable exception: They are blind to accepting a causal association between their addiction and the life problems they have had to endure.

For those who recover (including natural quitters and patients), a distinct turning point marks the beginning of the second stage—the evolution of quitting. Adverse consequences enter the addict's awareness, and he or she no longer clings to the view that his or her life problems are the result of external events. The acceptance of personal responsibility is an essential feature of this stage. This cognitive shift may then be followed by marked behavioral change and lifestyle reorganization. New drug-free activities become elevated to a position of increased priority. The integration of these competencies into regular day-to-day behavior is the essence of relapse prevention.

Prescriptive treatment choices for alcoholism and substance abuse should be based on accurate assessment of a given patient's position on the stage of change continuum. At the end of the first stage, for example, when adverse consequences still remain unconnected to the acceptance of personal responsibility, confrontation and clarification are the most useful clinical interventions. Family systems and group treatments offer the greatest utility in penetrating the unwitting collaboration of enablers and codependents in keeping the negative effects of the addict's style of coping out of awareness.

At the turning point (the beginning of the second stage), when the addict wants to stop, psychodynamic treatments can be very helpful. The patient is ready to commence making sense out of chaotic emotions and unresolved childhood conflicts. Behavioral treatment remains premature until the patient becomes sufficiently organized to consider actively changing. At this point, behavior, psychodynamic, family, and group therapies can all be effectively applied depending on the match between the patient's basic beliefs about the nature of his or her addiction and the therapist's preferred style of intervention. *The Counseling Interest Inventory* (Appendix A) is useful in matching patients to styles of intervention that are compatible with their underlying beliefs and life philosophies. Throughout the lifelong period of recovery that ideally occurs during the latter portion of the second stage, behavioral approaches help patients to cope with risky situations and to avoid negative thoughts, while psychodynamic techniques are valuable in gaining mastery over negative emotional states.

Practitioners have now reached a turning point in the evolution of treatment choices. The efficacy of substance abuse interventions will show dramatic improvement as we become increasingly sophisticated in prescribing levels and types of patient care to match specific dimensions of patient need.

As the twentieth century comes to a close, we anticipate a diminution in the need for alcoholism and substance abuse treatments. There will be a greater emphasis on detailing the social factors that promote or reduce the use of intoxicants. Understanding the mechanisms by which social and cultural processes influence behavioral change will result in successful promotion of natural means to alter consciousness, providing increased pleasure, meaning, and fulfillment throughout the life cycle—the era of *Natural Highs*.

References

Annis, Helen M. 1986. "Is Inpatient Rehabilitation of the Alcoholic Cost-Effective? Con Position." *Advances in Alcohol and Substance Abuse* 5:179–190.

Arana, G.W. 1982. "Treatment and Management of the Impaired Physician." *Hospital Progress*, May, 60–63.

Brickman, P., V.C. Rabinowitz, J. Karuza, D. Coates, E. Cohn, and L. Kidder. 1982. "Models of Helping and Coping." *American Psychologist* 37:368–84.

Buxton, M., M. Jessup, and M. Landry. 1985. "Treatment of the Chemically Dependent Health Professional." In *The Addictions: Multidisciplinary Perspectives and Treatments*, edited by H. Milkman and H. Shaffer, Lexington, Mass.: Lexington Books, 131–144.

Chiabotta, B. 1985. "Evaluating EAP Vendors." *Personnel Administrator* 30 (8):39–43.

Fillmore, K.M. 1985. "The Social Victims of Drinking." *British Journal of Addictions* 80:307–14.

McClellan, K. 1982. "An Overview of Occupational Alcoholism Issues for the 80's." *Journal of Drug Education* 12 (1):1–27.

Menninger, K. 1963. "The Vital Balance: The Life Process in Mental Health and Illness." New York: Viking Press.

Milkman, H., and S. Sunderwirth. 1983. "The Chemistry of Craving." *Psychology Today*, October, 36–44.

———. Manuscript on Natural Highs. In preparation.

Miller, W.R. 1978. "Behavioral Treatment of Problem Drinkers: A Comparative Outcome Study of Three Controlled Drinking Therapies." *Journal of Consulting and Clinical Psychology* 46:74–86.

Miller, W.R., and R.K. Hester. 1986. "Inpatient Alcoholism Treatment: Who Benefits?" *American Psychologist* 41:794–805.

Sanchez-Craig, M., and D.A. Wilkinson. 1987. "Brief Treatments for Alcohol and Drug Problems: Practical and Methodological Issues." Paper presented at the Fourth International Conference on Treatment of Addiction Behavior, Beyen, Norway, August.

Shaffer, H.J., and C. Neuhaus. 1985. "Testing Hypotheses: An Approach for the Assessment of Addictive Behaviors." In *The Addictions: Multidisciplinary Perspectives and Treatments*, edited by H. Milkman and H. Shaffer, Lexington, Mass.: Lexington Books, 87–104.

Trebach, A.S. 1987. The Great Drug War. New York: NY. Macmillan.

U.S. Bureau of Justice. 1988. "Profile of state prison inmates, 1986." US Bureau of Justice Statistics. Washington DC: USGPO, 1986.

Wexler, H.K., D.S. Lipton, and B.D. Johnson. 1985. "Prison and Drug Treatment: The Critical 90 Days of Re-entry." Report prepared for the American Society of Criminal, San Diego, November.

Zinberg, N.E. 1984. *Drug, Set and Setting: The Basis for Controlled Intoxicant Use*. New Haven: Yale University Press.

Part I
Biological Factors

Prologue

Boris Tabakoff

The use of psychoactive substances by humans predates any historical record, and the circumstances attendant to the initial use of exogenous chemicals to modify mood or behavior are subjects for imaginative speculation. The available records of use of psychoactive compounds such as alcohol, marijuana, and opiates indicate that concern regarding the untoward effects of the substances on the individual and society also are not novel occurrences. For instance, as early as 1700 B.C., the Code of Hammurabi placed restrictions on the sale of wine and on riotous gatherings in the houses of the Babylonian wine merchants (Harper 1904). At the beginning of the Christian era, the Brahmans attempted to control cannabis use in India, restricting it to religious ceremonies (Nahas 1973). And in fourteenth-century Egypt, the ruling emir attempted to reverse the untoward social consequences of hashish use by ordering all cannabis plants uprooted and condemning all users to have their teeth extracted (Nahas 1973).

Given the societal concern about the pathologic use of alcohol and other psychoactive drugs over centuries, one wonders what factors have maintained this use so that it is as prevalent today as it was in earlier history. One would expect that if alcohol and drug use were inherently disadvantageous to individual survival or societal vigor, the trait would not be maintained and would be eliminated by genetic selection. The purported intellectual insights and increased creativity provided by psychoactive drug use have been, at times, widely touted but difficult to demonstrate when assessed under stringent experimental conditions. For instance, the claims in the 1960s and 1970s of increased insight and prophetic vision under the influence of compounds such as mescaline and LSD (Huxley 1963) are reminiscent of earlier experimentation with volatile anesthetics. Oliver Wendell Holmes, who was intimately involved with the early use of ether in surgery, also used the substance himself for its mind-altering properties. He was enamored of what he considered to be the profound wisdom attained during his intoxications, and he decided to commit his wisdom to paper. Upon his recovering from intoxication and examining his writings, however, the only thing he found legible was the statement "A strong smell resembling turpentine prevails throughout" (Holmes 1871).

We are currently unaware of the total explanation of the factors that maintain alcohol and drug use in individuals and in various societies, but we can be assured that these factors are diverse. The diversity arises from both the biology of an individual and the surrounding environment. One has to consider that different scientific approaches will need to be applied and different "laws" developed to explain both the individual and societal factors that lead to use and abuse of psychoactive substances. By analogy, the laws of thermodynamics can explain the behavior of a volume of gas subjected to various perturbations, such as changes in pressure or temperature, without explaining the behavior of any individual molecule of the gas within that volume. Some have considered that only the studies of society (the whole "volume" of individuals) can provide the laws by which we can diminish or freeze alcohol or drug use. However, the observed disproportionate relationships among individual and societal responses introduces an added complexity requiring that the focus of science be placed on *both* the individual and his or her environment. In this approach, the factors that initiate, as well as those that maintain, drug use are amenable to explanation. For instance, it may well be the influence of peers and the availability of alcohol and certain drugs that promote initial drug use by an individual, but the progression to compulsive use (addiction) may be the result of the pharmacologic properties of the substance acting on the genetically determined characteristics of that individual's nervous system.

We are inherently attracted to parsimonious or all-encompassing explanations of phenomena such as drug abuse, but there is also a beauty in a collage of diverse elements that bring enlightenment to a subject. The debate on whether nature or nurture is the prime determinant of risk for alcoholism continues to consume significant energy of the proponents of both viewpoints. This controversy was recently highlighted by the case of *Traynor v. Turnage,* which was argued in the U.S. Supreme Court (Traynor v. Turnage 485 U.S. Supreme Court). This case revolved around the issue of whether alcoholism was a debilitating disease or willful misconduct. In chapter 1, Collins and de Fiebre review the interactions between genetics and environment that influence drug use. The formula that needs to be remembered is

$$V_P = V_G + V_E$$

This formula indicates that the phenotypic variance (V_P), which is a measure of the differences in the characteristics of individuals in a population, is a result of the *sum* of the environmentally determined variance (V_E) and the genetically determined variance (V_G) in the characteristic of interest (drug use). In other words, both environment (nurture) and genetics (nature) are involved.

Some of the environmental factors that contribute to the desire to take mood-altering drugs and the non–drug-related behavioral methods for altering brain chemistry and drug-taking mood are discussed by Sunderwirth in chapter 2. In chapter 4, Mossey adds the consideration of nutritional factors to the list of natural means of altering brain chemistry and attendant mood and behavior. One must, however, expand this list further to keep in mind the importance of the relationships among the individual, his or her actions, and the surrounding environment. Clearly important in drug-taking behavior and treatment of substance abuse are learning and conditioning factors, which can maintain drug use and lead to relapse in abstinent individuals. An example of such conditioning is the severe craving that opiate addicts can experience when exposed to drug paraphernalia, friends, and situations previously associated with drug use.

What will be important to unravel in the future is the relationship between the sensory stimuli, generated by the environment or one's own activity (such as, exercise), and the body chemistry that produces changes in mood and/or leads to a craving for alcohol and drugs. The framework provided by knowledge of the endogenous opioids, the endorphins and enkephalins, is serving to generate further knowledge of other molecules naturally present in the brain and important for determining mood and drug use. A well-described receptor system in the brain is the one that responds to benzodiazepines (such as Valium), barbiturates, and possibly alcohol. This receptor system is controlled by the amino acid–derived compound gamma-aminobutyric acid (GABA), and the system acts to reduce neuronal excitability. Recently, a novel peptide (DBI) has been isolated from the human brain. DBI may modulate the activity of the GABA receptor by binding to the same site as the benzodiazepines. DBI's effects are opposite those of the benzodiazepines, however. Instead of producing calming effects and reducing anxiety, DBI increases anxiety in animals. Currently there is little evidence of how environmental factors or commonly abused drugs interact with the production or actions of DBI in humans, but it is already clear that the receptor system on which DBI is postulated to act is a heterogeneous entity. This receptor heterogeneity is genetically determined and can translate into differences in sensitivity of an animal (or human) to drugs such as alcohol and other sedatives. Differences in the character of an individual's GABA receptors also may contribute to that individual's responses to his or her environment.

To understand a human's desire to take drugs, and to be able to rationally intervene and treat drug abuse, we need to understand a number of diverse biological and environmental influences. It is hoped that this understanding will allow for the use of natural environmental variables to orchestrate the genetically influenced body chemistry and thereby reduce the reliance on exogenous chemical modifiers of mood and behavior.

References

Harper, R.F. 1904. *The Code of Hammurabi, King of Babylon.* Chicago: University of Chicago Press.
Holmes, O.W. 1871. *Mechanism in Thought and Morals.* Boston: James R. Osgood.
Huxley, A. 1963. *The Doors of Perception and Heaven and Hell.* New York: Harper & Row.
Nahas, G.G. 1973. *Marihuana: Deceptive Weed.* New York: Raven Press.
Traynor v. Turnage, 485 U.S. Supreme Court, 99 L.Ed 2d 618, 108 S. Cr. 1372 (1988).

1
A Review of Genetic Influences on Psychoactive Substance Use and Abuse

Allan C. Collins
Christopher M. de Fiebre

The modern world is complex and, in many cases, stressful. Perhaps not surprisingly, many individuals use one or more psychoactive substances, often on a daily basis, in an attempt to deal with life and life's problems. Not everyone, however, finds psychoactive substance use pleasurable or helpful, and consequently not everyone ends up using or abusing psychoactive substances. This chapter summarizes some of the recent findings that may explain why some people use and abuse psychoactive substances and why others do not. Special emphasis is placed on reviewing some of the literature indicating that genetic factors contribute to drug use, misuse, and abuse. A discussion of studies of genetic influences on drug use by humans is accompanied by brief discussions of animal studies that may ultimately prove useful in identifying precisely what the genetically determined factors may be. Such knowledge may prove useful in developing rational therapies for drug abuse and, of greater importance, in identifying specific individuals who are at risk for developing drug misuse and abuse problems.

Some Questions

What is a drug? Almost everyone has his or her own definition of what a drug is. For the purposes of this discussion, we will use the definition that a drug is any substance that increases or decreases the rate at which a normal physiological or biochemical process occurs. This definition is relatively unrestrictive in that any substance can be considered a drug. It is restrictive in that it focuses on consequences of drug action: A drug speeds up or slows down normal physiological and biochemical processes, but it does not make the body do something that it is totally incapable of doing.

Presumably, virtually all drugs work by specific mechanisms. For example, they inhibit or activate enzymes, inhibit or activate hormone or neurotransmitter receptors, and block ion channels. All of these processes are regulated by genetic factors. Individuals differ in the amount and types of enzymes (isoenzymes) they have, and they also probably differ in the number and affinity of hormone and neurotransmitter receptors and in ion channels. Thus, individuals would be expected to differ in sensitivity to specific drugs based on preexisting differences in the enzyme, receptor, or ion channel that the drug affects. They also may differ in their rates of metabolism of drugs. It may be that some of the genetically regulated differences in drug misuse and abuse relate to genetically determined differences in the sites of drug action or to genetically determined differences in rates of drug metabolism.

What is drug dependence? Recent years have seen a significant reconsideration of what drug abuse is all about. For many years, the term *addiction* was used to describe the excessive use of psychoactive substances. In recent years, this term has been discarded because no universally agreed on definition could be obtained. *Drug dependence* is now used in its stead. A working definition of drug dependence includes primary and secondary criteria. Primary criteria that must be met for a substance to be viewed as having dependence liability include the following:

- Highly controlled or compulsive use must be present.
- The substance must have psychoactive effects.
- The drug must reinforce certain behaviors that facilitate drug acquisition and use.

Secondary criteria include the following:

- The use of the substance becomes ritualistic or stereotypic (the drug is used in the same way, at the same times of day, in the same place, and so on).
- Continued use is seen even though harmful effects on the person's health, job, or family occur.
- Relapse is seen following abstinence.
- Individuals suffer from recurrent desires (cravings) for the drug.

Although these criteria are almost universally seen as being descriptive of the dependence process and of drugs that produce dependence, they certainly are not sufficient. Agents can be misclassified using these criteria. For example, sugar fits almost all of the primary and secondary criteria with the possible exception that it lacks marked psychoactive effects, although some people experience a "sugar high." Consequently, sugar could be judged as being addicting with some degree of reasonableness. Indeed, it may be addicting, but only for some people. This logic should, we believe, be applied to all substances. Many substances probably have the potential for being abused, but it is the individual's physiology and biochemistry that determine whether he or she abuses the substance.

Several other properties of drugs with abuse potential should be kept in mind. Most notably, people develop a tolerance to the actions of most drugs of abuse. This tolerance often occurs for both desired and undesired effects. The undesired effects (toxicities) often limit drug use, while the desired effects (euphoria, less anxiety, and so on) promote use. The development of a tolerance to the toxic actions will allow an individual to increase his or her daily dosage and consequently facilitate abuse behavior.

Once adequate doses have been ingested for a long enough period of time, physical dependence may develop. Physical dependence is characterized by a withdrawal syndrome. In the past, withdrawal syndromes were classified as periods of hyperexcitability. Today, we use a broader definition in that a withdrawal syndrome is characterized by one or more behavioral or physiological responses that are opposite in nature to the effects elicited by the first dose of a given drug. Thus, withdrawal from a depressant drug (such as an opiate, alcohol, or a barbiturate) may be characterized by hyperexcitability and even convulsions, whereas withdrawal from a stimulant drug (such as an amphetamine or cocaine) is characterized by depression.

Tolerance and dependence arise as a consequence of continued exposure to the drug. In many cases, these phenomena may be due to changes in brain chemistry or physiology. Individuals appear to vary in their ability to develop tolerance and in the severity of withdrawal syndromes. These differences may be due to genetically determined differences in the ability of specific neurochemical systems to respond to chronic exposure to a drug. Thus, genetic factors may regulate the levels of specific biochemical factors (enzymes, receptors, and ion channels) that the drug affects, and genetic factors may also regulate the ability of neurochemical factors to adapt to the continued presence of the drug. Both these factors may contribute to the overall genetic influence on drug dependence.

Is there an environmental influence? Unfortunately, many individuals continue to think in terms of genetic influences or environmental influences. In all probability, very few traits are influenced solely by genetic factors or solely by environmental factors. This is true even for physical traits. For example, it is clearly established that height and weight are genetically determined, but it is just as clearly established that environmental factors play an important role. How else can one explain the observation that Japanese who were born and raised in Hawaii are three to four inches taller and twenty to thirty pounds heavier, on average, than their parents who were born and raised in Japan? Presumably, the more balanced diet enjoyed by Hawaiians promoted the growth spurt seen in first-generation Hawaiians of Japanese descent.

Geneticists have described the relationship between genotype and environment mathematically as follows:

$$G + E + (G \times E) = 1$$

Thus, the magnitude of any given trait is influenced by genetic (G) and environmental (E) factors as well as by genotype-by-environment interactions. For a trait such as height, there are genetic factors, environmental factors (diet, weather, and general health status), and genotype-by-environment interactions in which environmental factors regulate the expression of genes. Using the height example, Japanese raised in Hawaii are taller and heavier than their ancestors, but they are not nearly as tall or heavy, on average, as Scandinavians. In other words, the environment influences a trait, but the degree of influence is regulated by interactions with the genotype of the individual. The genotype, in a sense, sets a template or range over which a trait can be expressed. The exact level of expression is determined by environmental factors; that is, the environment fine-tunes the expression of the trait by interacting with the genotype.

How could genetic variability in drug abuse arise? If we assume the simplest of all cases, that addictability to a specific drug is due to a single gene that has two different forms (alleles) designated A and a, we will find within the population three different genotypes: AA, Aa and aa. If the A allele increases addictability and the a allele decreases addictability with equal strength (they are, in the words of the geneticist, codominant) within the population, there will be people with very high addictability (AA), others with average addictability (Aa), and still others with low addictability (aa). If the frequencies of A and a in the total population are 0.5, a three-peaked curve would result, with 25 percent having high risk, 50 percent average risk, and 25 percent low risk. If the gene frequency for A is greater than 0.5, the risk factor curve will be skewed toward the high-addictability range; if A is less than 0.5, the curve will be skewed toward low addictability.

It is highly likely that drug use is regulated by more than one gene, as most behavioral traits are polygenically regulated. Adding more genes will smooth the curve out. For some drugs, a bell-shaped genetic risk curve would be obtained; this would be expected for a drug with average addiction liability. For other drugs, the curve may be skewed toward the high-risk end; very few people would not find the use of this drug rewarding, and addiction liability would be high. If the genetic risk curve is skewed toward the low-risk end, only a small fraction of people would, because of genetic reasons, end up abusing this drug. Thus, as noted in figure 1–1, risk curves can be skewed to the left or right for any drug because of genetic reasons.

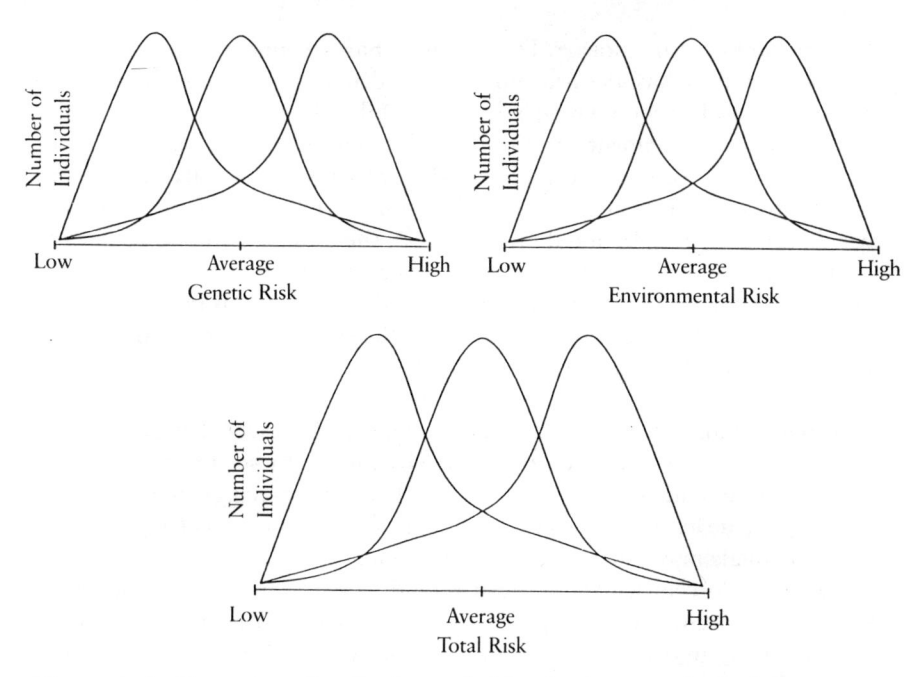

Figure 1–1. Frequency distributions of risk of substance abuse due to genetic and environmental factors. Total risk is determined by the sum of genetic, environmental, and gene-by-environment interaction risks.

Does environmental variation also exist? Clearly, different people live in different microenvironments. These differences in environment could affect drug use. It is more likely that an individual will experiment with a drug if it is readily accessible, and chronic use might be more likely if accessibility is accompanied by permissiveness or positive peer pressure. Drug use may increase under certain circumstances, such as the very stressful circumstances encountered by American military personnel in Vietnam. Alternatively, experimentation with a drug is less likely if access is limited, and chronic use is not likely if the environment does not support or encourage substance use. Thus, as noted in figure 1–1, risk curves can be skewed to the left or right for any drug because of environmental influences.

Do genetic and environmental factors interact to affect drug abuse? In our view, the $G \times E$ interaction term is likely to be the most significant factor in influencing substance use and abuse. It is not known why all people within a given type of environment do or do not use and abuse drugs. It may be that a specific environment promotes drug abuse in one individual and is without effect or inhibits it in another. For example, parents who are restrictive and regimented may reduce the use and abuse of drugs in one child and promote drug use in another child who is rebellious. Only when we begin to recognize that the same environment can influence different genotypes (people) in different ways will we begin to make marked progress in identifying environmental intervention strategies that will discourage experimentation with and chronic use of drugs. As noted in figure 1–1, the total risk (the sum of G, E, and $G \times E$) curves are likely to be bell shaped or skewed to the left or right for different drugs. Whether a specific individual ends up using and abusing a specific drug will depend on that individual's genetic loading and the precise environment in which the individual is placed.

What may be inherited? Drug abuse is a complex behavior that may be regulated by a number of factors. Included among these are drug avidity (whether an individual perceives a drug as being reinforcing), acute sensitivity, tolerance development, and withdrawal severity. Some evidence suggests that individuals may differ in each of these factors.

Drug reinforcement may differ from individual to individual. Some people may experience a euphoric response following drug administrations, whereas others may have a dysphoric response. This difference may be due to both genetic and environmental factors, but it seems reasonable to suspect that individuals who find a drug pleasurable are more likely to continue use, whereas individuals who find a drug unpleasant are less likely to continue use.

Acute sensitivity to the psychotropic and toxic effects of a drug may also affect abuse potential. It is well established for virtually every drug that individuals differ in sensitivity to both the pharmacologic and toxicologic action of the drug, and such differences could affect whether abuse develops. Schuckit and Gold (1988), for example, reported that sons of alcoholic fathers, who are more likely than are sons of nonalcoholic fathers to become alcoholic, are less sensitive to alcohol's actions as measured by overall drug effect—dizziness, nausea, and level of high—and in terms of biochemical markers such as prolactin and cortisol release. It may be that reduced sensitivity allows the individual to take larger doses of alcohol, which ultimately facilitates the development of alcoholism. Similarly, reduced sensitivity to toxic actions (nausea, tremor, or malaise) also would facilitate increased alcohol use.

The ability to develop a tolerance to the behavioral and toxic actions of drugs also may be important. If an individual slowly develops a tolerance to either the pleasant or unpleasant effects of a drug, the likelihood of increasing the dose used is minimized. In contrast, if a tolerance develops quickly, the dose used may increase quickly.

For many drugs, chronic use is accompanied by the development of physical dependence. Physical dependence is uncovered when drug use is decreased or stopped, as a withdrawal syndrome develops. Drug use may persist not because the individual is seeking the pleasurable effects elicited by the drug, as total tolerance to these effects may develop. Rather, drug use may persist because the individual is avoiding the discomfort associated with drug withdrawal. If individuals differ in severity of withdrawal, differences in persistence of drug use could ensue.

How is genetic influence detected? Certain traits, or phenotypes, are influenced by heritable factors (genetics). These factors are generally assessed by studying individuals who are closely related biologically. Individuals who are more closely related biologically should be more similar, with respect to the trait of interest, than are individuals who are more distantly related or unrelated. Thus, genetic influences are established by studying families, adoptees, twins, and twins reared apart.

Studies of Families. If a particular trait runs in a family, it may have a genetic basis. Traits such as height, weight, eye color, and skin color clearly run in families and likely have a genetic basis. Simply because a trait runs in a family, however, does not implicate genetic causation. It does not seem reasonable, for example, to conclude that the citizens of Milan speak Italian because of a genetic predetermination. If a trait runs in a family (that is, if children resemble their parents), the contention that genetic factors influence the trait would be supported. It would not, however, be proven that the trait is genetically regulated.

Studies of Adoptees. Studies of adoptees also is useful in assessing genetic or environmental causation. An Italian presumably speaks Italian because he or she grew up in a family that spoke Italian. If an Italian child who had been raised in an English-speaking family spoke Italian fluently and did not speak English, an argument could be made for genetic causation. Because such a child would speak English, an environmental influence on language must be invoked. Thus, if adoptees are studied and the adoptee resembles its biological parents, genetic factors are presumed to be primarily responsible for regulating the trait. If the adoptee resembles the adopting parents, environmental causation seems likely.

Studies of Twins. Twins come in two forms: identical, or monozygotic (MZ), and fraternal, or dizygotic (DZ). MZ twins arise from the splitting of a single fertilized egg, and each twin is exactly like its sibling at all genetic loci. DZ twins arise from the simultaneous fertilization of two different eggs. DZ twins are no more similar or different genetically than are any other sibling pair (they are identical at about 50 percent of all genetic loci), but they do share a more common environment than other sibling pairs. Twin studies usually measure concordance. If one twin exhibits a particular trait and the other twin also exhibits the trait, the twins are said to be concordant. If the twins differ, they are said to be discordant. If a trait is concordant to a higher degree in MZ twins than in DZ twins (for example, 90 percent of MZ twin pairs and 60 percent of DZ twin pairs are concordant), it is highly likely that the trait in question is genetically regulated. The MZ-DZ difference is a measure of genetic influence. If there is little or no difference between MZ and DZ twin pairs in concordance, the trait is probably influenced to a high degree by environment.

Studies of Twins Reared Apart. Twins, especially MZ twins, often have very similar environments, which confounds estimates of genetic influence. One of the more powerful research strategies used to assess genetic influence is to study concordance in twins reared apart. These twins are generally adopted shortly after birth and are raised in separate families. If MZ twins reared in different environments are concordant for a trait, the likelihood that the trait is regulated by genetic factors is high. If, however, MZ twins are discordant, environmental influences must be considered.

Genetic Influences on Human Substance Use

As might be expected, the most data concerning potential genetic influences on substance use and abuse in humans are available for alcohol and tobacco. Virtually every one of the research strategies outlined above has been used to explore potential genetic influences on alcohol use and abuse, and the consensus is that genetic factors influence alcoholism. A smaller data set, using fewer techniques, has been developed for tobacco use. Probably because use of other drugs such as cocaine and marijuana is illicit, information on potential genetic causes of use and abuse of these substances is virtually nonexistent. This lack of data should not be interpreted as meaning that there is not genetic causation; the lack of data is due to a lack of serious inquiry.

Genetics and Alcoholism

Family Studies on Alcoholism. The concept that alcoholism may run in families is certainly not new. Aristotle wrote that drunken women "bring forth children like themselves," and Plutarch suggested that "one drunkard begets another." Much of this early thought hinged on the possibility that the presence of alcohol at the time of conception seriously affected the drinking behavior of the child. While this concept has fallen into disfavor, the concept that alcoholism has a familial basis has not.

In the past eighty years, more than one hundred studies have shown that alcohol abuse is familial (Goodwin 1976). These studies indicate that approximately 25 percent of the first-degree male relatives of alcoholics become alcoholics. Cotton (1979) summarized data from thirty-nine studies conducted over the previous four decades and found that an average of one-third of any sample of alcoholics had at least one parent with an alcohol abuse problem. These findings are robust in that they clearly show an aggregation of alcoholism in families. Since many alcoholics do not have first-degree relatives who are themselves alcoholic, however, these findings show that nonfamilial factors also can influence whether or not alcoholism is seen.

It has been suggested that alcoholism can be classified as either familial or nonfamilial (Goodwin 1976). Under this classification, familial alcoholism would be characterized by a younger age of onset, more severe symptoms, and a more rapid progression. The underlying assumption of this classification is that familial alcoholism is genetically based, while nonfamilial alcoholism is an environmentally induced phenocopy (that is, the environment produces a syndrome that copies genetically based alcoholism). It is most likely that alcoholism is neither purely familial nor purely nonfamilial but is a result of a variety of gene-by-environment interactions. For some individuals, genetic factors may play a greater role in determining whether alcoholism is seen, but for other individuals, environmental factors may play a greater role. It is doubtful, in any one individual, that alcoholism results solely from genetic (familial) or environmental (nonfamilial) factors.

Adoption Studies on Alcoholism. The first adoption study on alcoholism was conducted by Roe in 1944. No differences were found between the drinking behavior of children of alcoholics and that of children of nonalcoholics. The sample size in this study was small, and no criteria were presented for the diagnosis of alcoholism.

Some of the most convincing data supporting the genetic influence on alcoholism come from adoption studies. As noted above, if an adoptee resembles his or her biological parents, genetic influence must be considered. If the child resembles his or her adopting parents, environmental influences are probably important in regulating the trait being studied.

In a study of half and full siblings, Schuckit, Goodwin, and Winokur (1972) found that having an alcoholic biological father correlated with alcoholism in sons. No correlation between alcoholism in sons and alcoholism in stepfathers was seen. This suggested that hereditary factors are more important than environmental factors in producing alcoholism.

Three adoption studies were conducted in the 1970s and early 1980s in Denmark, Sweden, and the United States (Goodwin 1985; Bohman 1978;

Cadoret, Cain, and Grove 1979). Genetic factors were clearly indicated in the etiology of alcoholism in all three studies. These studies found that sons of alcoholics are three to four times more likely to be alcoholic than are sons of nonalcoholics, and sons of alcoholics that are adopted by nonalcoholic parents are just as likely to be alcoholic as are sons raised by their alcoholic biological parents. The data on daughters of alcoholics are not as clear. Although the frequency of alcoholism was not as great in females as in males, two studies found a correlation between [adopted-out] daughters and their biological mothers (Bohman, Sigvardsson, and Cloninger 1981; Cadoret, Cain, and Grove 1979).

Twins Studies on Alcoholism. In the first study that examined alcoholism in twins, Kaij (1960) found that MZ twins were more concordant for alcoholism than DZ twins. Partanen, Bruun, and Markkanen (1977) found within a twin sample that there was no overall difference between MZ and DZ twins; however, among younger twins within the sample, a difference existed. Hrubec and Omenn (1981) found MZ twins more concordant for alcoholism than DZ twins, while Murray, Clifford, and Gurlin (1983) found no differences between MZ and DZ twins. In two of four studies, the data supported the notion that there is a genetic component to alcoholism. In one study, no genetic influence was supported, and in another, the results were equivocal.

The finding by Partanen, Bruun, and Markkanen (1977) that genetic factors are important in alcoholism in young twins but are less important in older twins deserves special mention. As will be discussed later, this also is true of smoking. As stated, drug abuse results from genetic factors, environmental factors, and the interaction between genes and environment. It might be that genetic factors are more important in influencing drug-taking behaviors in young persons and environmental factors are more important later in life. It is possible that the relative importance of environment in determining drug-taking behavior increases as people age because they are exposed to more environments, some of which promote substance use. A person's genome remains constant throughout life. Therefore, the relative importance of environment can increase with age as a person is exposed to more environments that can interact with his or her genome.

Genetics and Smoking

Unfortunately, not very many studies have attempted to assess genetic influences on smoking, and those studies that have been carried out have used limited methodologies, primarily the twin method. These studies simply investigated whether concordance for smoking behavior exists within MZ and DZ twin pairs. The authors of most of these studies have assumed that all smokers are addicted to tobacco or nicotine, which is, at least in our view, as patently absurd as is the assumption that all users of alcohol are alcoholics. Despite these problems, the conclusion that genetic factors regulate tobacco use seems obvious.

Fisher was the first to study the potential influence of genetic factors on smoking behavior (Fisher 1958a; Fisher 1958b). In these studies, he examined smoking behavior in male (Fisher 1958a) and female (Fisher 1958b) MZ and DZ twins. The male twins had been reared together, whereas nearly half of the female twins had been separated shortly after birth. He found that in both males and females, concordance for smoking behavior (both members of the twin pairs were smokers or nonsmokers) was higher in the MZ twins; rearing conditions did not affect the MZ-DZ differential. Several other studies (Todd and Mason 1959; Raaschou-Nielsen 1960; Dies et al. 1969) have subsequently replicated these findings.

A major flaw of most of the early twin studies is that subjects were classified simply as smokers or nonsmokers. Friberg et al. (1959); Cederlof, Friberg, and Lundman (1976); Crumpacker et al. (1979); and Kaprio et al. (1978) all attempted to break smoking status in twins into several groups. Groups such as light and heavy smokers and ex-smokers were used. Use of this strategy confirmed the previous observations: Genetic factors seem to regulate tobacco use.

Some of the more recent studies have attempted to obtain estimates of a parameter known as heritability. Heritability is an estimate of the fraction of the variance in a measure that may be ascribed to genetic influences. It may vary between 0 (no genetic regulation) and 1.0 (absolute genetic regulation). Williams, Crumpacker, and Krier (1981) reported a heritability estimate of 0.51 for ever/never smoking. Kaprio et al. (1978) obtained heritability estimates for smoking in discrete age groups. The heritability estimates varied between 0.55 for 18- to 20-year-olds to 0.11 for those over 60. This implies that genetic factors are very important in regulating smoking status in young people but environmental influences become the dominant factor with age. If it is assumed that the environment works by influencing gene expression, it would be expected that initial expression of a trait—smoking or nonsmoking in this case—would be set largely by genetic factors, but as time goes on, the environmental influences would fine-tune the expression of the trait. It should be noted that estimates of heritability for alcoholism also are considerably higher for younger people than are estimates for older people (Partanen, Bruun, and Markannen 1977).

Pedersen (1981) also studied heritability for smoking status in Swedish twins and obtained a heritability value of 0.84 in her total sample. She estimated heritability in male twins at 0.70 and in female twins at slightly greater than 1.00 for smoking status. These values seem very high because they approximate the heritability values calculated for height and weight in this same sample. Pedersen also calculated heritability estimates for the use of spirits

(0.28), coffee and tea (0.78), and tranquilizers (0.28). The heritability estimates for alcohol and caffeine-containing beverage consumption agree with estimates made by others (Gurling, Grant, and Dangle 1985).

Eysenck (1980) is the only investigator who has used more than the twin method to assess genetic influences on smoking. He examined twins and their extended families. His analysis included assessments of assortative mating, age-gene interaction, and sex differences. The combined twin and family heritability estimates for age of onset of smoking and for average consumption were 0.22 and 0.38, respectively. Eysenck also calculated the proportions that genetic and environmental factors contributed to the total variance. For age of onset of smoking, 60 percent of the variance was due to the specific environment of each twin, 11 percent was due to the common or shared environment, and 30 percent was additive genetic. When average daily consumption was studied, 50 percent of the variance was ascribed to specific environment, and 42 percent was additive genetic. In addition, persistence of smoking was analyzed. This analysis indicated that 68 percent of the variance was genetic. These results suggest that environmental factors are very important in promoting the initiation of smoking but genetic factors are most important in allowing it to persist; nonsmokers quit and smokers persist primarily because of genetic regulation.

Genetics and Polysubstance Use

It used to be a common belief that a given individual used only his or her drug of choice. A careful analysis of substance use indicates that this simply is not true. If an individual who is addicted to opiates cannot obtain his or her usual drug, other drugs may be substituted, most frequently alcohol. This observation has been made repeatedly and has led to the suggestion that an addictable personality may exist. As noted earlier, we know virtually nothing about genetic factors that may promote heroin, cocaine, or hallucinogen use and abuse. Consequently, we do not know if the addictable personality is influenced by genetic factors. There is reason to suspect, however, that such a study would be fruitful based on current knowledge of interactions between alcohol and tobacco.

The simultaneous use of alcohol and tobacco is very common. A host of studies (see, for example, Deher and Fraser 1967; Crowley et al. 1974; Griffiths, Bigelow, and Liebson 1976; Craig and Van Natta 1977) have demonstrated that as the use of one substance increases, so does the use of the other. Alcoholics tend to be heavy smokers (Deher and Fraser 1967; Walton 1972; Maletzky and Klotter 1974), and under laboratory conditions, access to alcohol clearly increased cigarette smoking in alcoholic men (Griffiths, Bigelow, and Liebson 1976). Interestingly, this increase in smoking when alcohol is present is seen in alcoholics but not nonalcoholics (Henningfield, Chait, and

Griffiths 1984). Conversely, for both males and females, smokers and ex-smokers are more likely than nonsmokers to drink greater amounts of alcohol (Carmody et al. 1985). Thus, a high association between alcohol abuse and tobacco use exists. Although the evidence supports the notion that genetic factors influence the development of alcoholism and tobacco use, we do not know whether the same genes are involved. Certainly this possibility must be considered.

Cocaine use has become epidemic in the United States, and 87 percent of cocaine abusers also abuse other psychoactive drugs, most commonly alcohol (Gold 1984; Smith 1986). As is the case with tobacco, it is not clear whether people use these two psychoactive agents because of common genetic influence, but this has been suggested. Smith (1986) notes, "Clinical experience at the Haight-Ashbury Free Medical Clinic indicates that a positive family history of alcoholism also increases the probability of cocaine addiction, when the susceptible host is exposed to cocaine." This comment is based on clinical experience, not on a well-designed study. If it is true that individuals with a positive family history of alcoholism are more susceptible to cocaine dependence, it may be that alcoholism genes are really substance abuse genes and the precise form of substance use and abuse that emerges depends on environmental factors such as availability and family, peer, or societal attitudes.

Genetic Influences on Substance Use–Related Behaviors in Animals

Studies of human psychoactive substance use and abuse may indicate that genetic factors regulate these processes, but very little beyond this conclusion is possible from studies with humans. Ethical considerations preclude most studies that might be of value in determining precisely what is being influenced genetically. Consequently, animal studies may be of value. In animal studies, questions such as the following can be asked: Does initial sensitivity to a drug influence addictability? A systematic search for biochemical and physiological mechanisms that regulate dependence processes also may be possible only in animal studies.

Most animal studies of genetic influences on substances of abuse have used laboratory mice or rats. These species are used for many reasons, not the least of which is that genetic control is possible. For example, many inbred mouse and rat strains exist. An inbred strain is similar to MZ twins in that all members of a strain are genetically identical to all other members. Any differences between individual members of a strain are due to environmental influences. Inbred strains of mice, for example, differ in sensitivity to a first dose of alcohol (Crabbe 1983), nicotine (Marks, Burch, and Collins

1983), cocaine (Ruth, Ullman, and Collins 1988), and many other drugs. Mouse strains also differ in the rate of development of tolerance to alcohol and other drugs (Crabbe et al. 1982; Marks, Stitzel, and Collins 1986) and in severity of withdrawal syndromes (Belknap 1980). Inbred mouse strains also differ in drug self-administration (Pickett and Collins 1975).

Another advantage of the use of animals in studying substances of abuse is that it is possible to selectively breed animals for specific traits. Selective breeding requires considerable time and expense, but once appropriate animal models have been developed, tremendous progress can be made in understanding the genetic factors that regulate the selected-for trait as well as the biochemical processes that the genes regulate. As might be expected, the selective breeding approach has been used most often to study alcohol actions. Researchers have successfully bred for differences in alcohol self-administration (Li et al. 1987), sensitivity to a single dose of alcohol (McClearn and Kakihana 1981), and severity of withdrawal following cessation of chronic treatment (Crabbe and Kosobud 1986; Crabbe et al. 1987). The fact that researchers have successfully developed lines of mice and rats that differ in these alcohol-related traits proves that these traits are regulated by genes. Of greater importance is the fact that studies of the biochemical actions of alcohol that regulate these traits are made easier once appropriate animal models are available.

The genetic approach has not been used nearly as much for the study of other drugs with abuse potential. Nonetheless, the technique has immense potential, and more and more animal researchers are beginning to use genetic strategies. An important outcome of this advance may well be an improved understanding of how genes might influence substance abuse in humans. In addition, because the environment of laboratory animals may be more readily controlled than the environment of humans, it may very well be that careful control of genetic factors also may allow for an improved understanding of environmental influences on substance use.

Summary

Clear evidence indicating that genetic factors regulate alcohol use and abuse is accumulating. These findings may ultimately prove useful in determining who is at risk for becoming an alcoholic. Similarly, it may be that genetic factors influence tobacco use. Environmental influences also are important, but it is highly likely that environmental factors stimulate substance use only in those individuals who have the correct genetic configuration. It may be that genetic factors regulate addictability to drugs in general and that the precise form of substance abuse that develops in those who have the correct genes is determined by factors such as accessibility and societal attitudes.

Additional data are needed before we can identify individuals at risk, but once this is possible, it may be possible to develop rational methods of environmental intervention that will be useful in treating alcoholism and perhaps other forms of substance misuse and abuse.

References

Belknap, J.K. 1980. "Genetic Factors in the Effects of Alcohol: Neurosensitivity, Functional Tolerance, and Physical Dependence. In *Alcohol Tolerance and Dependence*, edited by H. Rigter and J. Crabbe, 157–80. Amsterdam: Elsevier/North Holland.

Bohman, M. 1978. "Some Genetic Aspects of Alcoholism and Criminality: A Population of Adoptees." *Archives of General Psychiatry* 35:269–76.

Bohman, M., S. Sigvardsson, and R. Cloninger. 1981. "Maternal Inheritance of Alcohol Abuse: Cross-Fostering Analysis of Adopted Women." *Archives of General Psychiatry* 38:965–69.

Cadoret, R.J., C.A. Cain, and W.M. Grove. 1979. "Development of Alcoholism in Adoptees Raised Apart from Alcoholic Biologic Relatives." *Archives of General Psychiatry* 37:561–63.

Carmody, T.P., C.S. Brischetto, J.D. Matarazzo, R.P. O'Donnell, and W.E. Connor. 1985. "Co-occurrent Use of Cigarettes, Alcohol, and Coffee in Healthy, Community-Living Men and Women. *Health Psychology* 4:323–35.

Cederlof, R., L. Friberg, and T. Lundman. 1977. "The Interactions of Smoking, Environment and Heredity and Their Implications for Disease Etiology. *Acta Medica Scandinavica* 612(Suppl):1–127.

Cotton, N.S. 1979. "The Familial Incidence of Alcoholism: A Review." *Journal of Studies on Alcohol* 40:89–116.

Crabbe, J.C. 1983. "Sensitivity to Ethanol in Inbred Mice: Genotypic Correlations among Several Behavioral Responses. *Behavioral Neuroscience* 97:280–89.

Crabbe, J.C., J.S. Janowsky, E.R. Young, A. Kosobud, J. Stack, and H. Rigter. 1982. "Tolerance to Ethanol-Induced Hypothermia in Inbred Mice: Genotypic Correlations with Behavioral Responses. *Alcoholism Clinical and Experimental Research* 6:446–58.

Crabbe, J.C., and A. Kosobud. 1986. "Sensitivity and Tolerance to Ethanol in Mice Bred to Be Genetically Prone (WSP) or Resistant (WSR) to Ethanol Withdrawal Seizures." *Journal of Pharmacology and Experimental Therapeutics* 239:327–33.

Crabbe, J.C., A. Kosobud, B.R. Tam, E.R. Young, and C.M. Deutsch. 1987. "Genetic Selection of Mouse Lines Sensitive (COLD) and Resistant (HOT) to Acute Ethanol Hypothermia." *Alcohol and Drug Research* 7:163–74.

Craig, T.J., and P.A. Van Natta. 1977. "The Association of Smoking and Drinking Habits in a Community Sample." *Journal of Studies on Alcohol* 38:1434–39.

Crowley, T.J., D. Chesluk, S. Ditts, and R. Hart. 1974. "Drug and Alcohol Abuse among Psychiatric Admissions: A Multidrug Clinical-Toxicological Study." *Archives of General Psychiatry* 30:13–20.

Crumpacker, D.W., R. Cederlof, L. Friberg, W.J. Kimberling, S. Sorensen, S.G. Vanderberg, J.S. Williams, G.E. McClearn, B. Grever, H. Iyer, M.J. Krier, N.L. Pedersen, R.A. Price, and I. Roulette. 1979. "A Twin Methodology for the Study of Genetic and Environmental Control of Variation in Human Smoking Behavior." *Acta Genetica le Medicale et Gemellologiae* 28:173–95.

Deher, K.F., and J.G. Fraser. 1967. "Smoking Habits of Alcohol Out-Patients." *International Journal of the Addictions* 2:259–68.

Dies, R., M. Honeyman, M. Reznikoff, and C. White. 1969. "Personality and Smoking Patterns in a Twin Population." *Journal of Projective Technical Personality Assessments* 33:457–63.

Eysenck, H.J. 1980. *The Causes and Effects of Smoking*. London: Temple Smith.

Fisher, R.A. 1958a. "Lung Cancer and Cigarettes?" *Nature* 182:180.

———. 1958b. "Cancer and Smoking." *Nature* 182:596.

Friberg, L., L. Kaij, S.J. Dencka, and E. Jonsson. 1959. "Smoking Habits of Monozygotic and Dizygotic Twins." *British Medical Journal* 1:1090–92.

Gold, M.S. 1984. *800-Cocaine*. New York: Bantam Books.

Goodwin, D.W. 1976. *Is Alcoholism Hereditary?* New York: Oxford University Press.

———. 1985. "Alcoholism and Genetics: The Sins of the Fathers." *Archives of General Psychiatry* 42:171–78.

Griffiths, R.R., G.E. Bigelow, and I. Liebson. 1976. "Facilitation of Human Tobacco Self Administration by Ethanol: A Behavioral Analysis." *Journal of Experimental Analysis of Behavior* 25:279–92.

Gurling, H.M.D., S. Grant, and J. Dangl. 1985. "The Genetic and Cultural Transmission of Alcohol Use, Alcoholism, Cigarette Smoking and Coffee Drinking: A Review and an Example Using a Log Linear Cultural Transmission Model." *British Journal of Addiction* 80:269–79.

Henningfield, J.E., L.D. Chait, and R.R. Griffiths. 1984. "Effects of Ethanol on Cigarette Smoking by Volunteers without Histories of Alcoholism." *Psychopharmacology* 82:1–5.

Hrubec, Z., and G.S. Omenn. 1981. "Evidence of Genetic Predisposition to Alcoholic Cirrhosis and Psychosis: Twin Points by Zygosity among Male Veterans." *Alcoholics: Clinical Experimental Research* 5:207–15.

Kaij, L. 1960. *Studies of the Etiology and Sequels of Abuse of Alcohol*. Lund, Sweden: University of Lund.

Kaprio, J., S. Sarna, M. Koskenvuo, and I. Rantasalo. 1978. *The Finnish Twin Registry: Baseline Characteristics, Section II*. Helsinki: University of Helsinki Press.

Li, T.-K., L. Lumeng, W.J. McBride, and J.M. Murphy. 1987. "Rodent Lines Selected for Factors Affecting Alcohol Consumption." *Alcohol and Alcoholism* (Suppl 1):91–96.

Maletzky, B.M., and J. Klotter. 1974. "Smoking and Alcoholism." *American Journal of Psychiatry* 131:445–47.

Marks, M.J., J.B. Burch, and A.C. Collins. 1983. "Genetics of Nicotine Response in Four Inbred Strains of Mice." *Journal of Pharmacology and Experimental Therapeutics* 226:291–301.

Marks, M.J., J.A. Stitzel, and A.C. Collins. 1986. "A Dose-Response Analysis of Nicotine Tolerance and Receptor Changes in Two Inbred Mouse Strains." *Journal of Pharmacology and Experimental Therapeutics* 239:358–64.

McClearn, G.E., and R. Kakihana. 1981. "Selective Breeding for Ethanol Sensitivity: Short-Sleep and Long-Sleep Mice." In *Development of Animal Models as Pharmacogenetic Tools*, edited by G.E. McClearn, R.A. Deitrich, and V.G. Erwin, Monograph, no. 6. Rockville, Md.: National Institute on Alcohol Abuse and Alcoholism.

Murray, R.M., C. Clifford, and H.M. Gurlin. 1983. "Twin and Alcoholism Studies." In *Recent Developments in Alcoholism*, vol. 1, edited by M. Galanter, chapter 5. New York: Gardner Press.

Partanen, J., K. Bruun, and T. Markkanen. 1977. "Inheritance of Drinking Behavior: A Study of Intelligence, Personality, and Use of Alcohol of Adult Twins." In *Emerging Concepts of Alcohol Dependence*, edited by E.M. Pattison, M.B. Sobell, and L.C. Sobell, chapter 10. New York: Springer Publishing Co., Inc.

Pickett, R.A., and A.C. Collins. 1975. "Use of Genetic Analysis to Test the Potential Role of Serotonin in Alcohol Preference." *Life Sciences* 17:1291–96.

Raaschou-Nielsen, E. 1960. "Smoking Habits in Twins." *Danish Medical Bulletin* 7:82–88.

Roe, A. 1944. "The Adult Adjustment of Children of Alcoholic Parents Raised in Foster Homes." *Journal of Studies on Alcohol* 5:378–93.

Ruth, J.A., E.A. Ullman, and A.C. Collins. 1988. "An Analysis of Cocaine Effects on Locomotor Activities and Heart Rate in Four Inbred Mouse Strains." *Pharmacology, Biochemistry and Behavior* 29:157–62.

Schuckit, M.A., and E.O. Gold. 1988. "A Simultaneous Evaluation of Multiple Markers of Ethanol/Placebo Challenges in Sons of Alcoholics and Controls." *Archives of General Psychiatry* 45:211–16.

Schuckit, M.A., D.W. Goodwin, and G. Winokur. 1972. "A Half-Sibling Study of Alcoholism." *American Journal of Psychiatry* 128:1132–36.

Smith, D.E. 1986. "Cocaine-Alcohol Abuse: Epidemiological, Diagnostic and Treatment Considerations." *Journal of Psychoactive Drugs* 18:117–29.

Todd, G.F., and J.I. Mason. 1959. "Concordance of Smoking Habits in Monozygotic and Dizygotic Twins." *Heredity* 13:417–44.

Walton, R.G. 1972. "Smoking and Alcoholism: A Brief Report." *American Journal of Psychiatry* 128:1455–59.

Williams, J.S., D.W. Crumpacker, and M. Krier. 1980. Stability of a factor-analytic description of smoking behavior. *Drugs, Alcoholism and Dependency* 5:467–78.

2
Harnessing Brain Chemicals: The Influence of Molecules on Mind, Mood, and Behavior

Stanley G. Sunderwirth

> There was once a little girl
> Who had a little curl
> Right in the middle of her forehead
> And when she was good
> She was very very good
> But when she was bad she was horrid

How often have we dealt with people (including ourselves) whose erratic behavior leaves us frustrated, bewildered, and often angry? In recent years, we have begun to understand behavior in terms of molecules that are either produced by the brain or reach it through the blood-brain barrier. To avoid extreme alterations in mood, the brain must maintain a relatively homeostatic level of these mood-altering molecules.

The popular nursery rhyme is a good description of the consequences of the brain's inability to maintain a consistent level of the molecules that influence a person's mind, mood, and behavior. This chapter shows how the synaptic concentration of neurotransmitters is intimately involved in determining not only mood but total personality.

The widespread abuse of drugs is a consequence of an innate desire and possibly even need to change the way a person feels. Clearly, the girl in the nursery rhyme is not happy in her "horrid" phase and would like to return to her "very good" phase. Through the ages, people have experimented with and abused many chemical agents that have had the ability to produce a particular mood. Unfortunately, the use of these chemicals often is accompanied by undesirable consequences leading to compulsion, loss of control, and continuation in spite of harmful consequences.

This chapter explains how certain types of beneficial everyday activities may be substituted for substance abuse in order to bring about desirable mood changes. It shows how psychoactive molecules produced by certain activities bring about these changes and in general how synaptic chemistry affects mind, mood, and behavior.

Hypocrisy and the Need for Mood Alteration

In any text on treatment modalities for addiction, the most obviously desirable treatment is one that requires no treatment—that is, one in which there is no addiction to treat. The antidrug campaign "Just Say No" is based on this concept and is an updated version of the old adage "An ounce of prevention is worth a pound of cure." In spite of the media hype surrounding this slogan, however, there is some doubt whether this campaign has been as effective in curbing drug use among young people as was originally anticipated. There are several reasons why this approach may not slow the runaway train of drug abuse among youths. One reason is that the slogan itself must seem hypocritical to the sophisticated youngster who sees adults engaging in substance abuse on an unparalleled scale through the daily use of mind-altering drugs such as tobacco, alcohol, and prescription drugs. Indeed, it is hypocrisy for adults to tell a teenager "Just Say No" to certain mind-altering drugs when these same adults use other psychoactive drugs on a daily basis. Knowing the commonly touted figures that more than 350,000 adults die each year from tobacco-related illnesses and more than 100,000 die from alcohol-related illnesses further reinforces the youth's resentment against preaching about the dangers of drugs. These young people resent being told that their drugs are bad but those used by adults are good. As Robert Millman of New York Hospital–Cornell says, "If caffeine, nicotine, alcohol and prescription and over-the-counter depressants and stimulants are included, few people in the United States would be found who take no psychoactive drugs" (Gross 1986).

Equally significant but often misunderstood by the "Just Say No" campaigners is the basic human desire to alter our moods periodically in order to achieve a level of mental arousal or satiation consistent with the need to relieve stress. For example, people often search for ways to alleviate depression by seeking amusements such as movies, vigorous exercise, or the use of mind-altering drugs such as alcohol, tobacco, or prescription drugs. Even drinking his or her morning coffee is a conscious effort to alter a person's mood from drowsiness to a state of mental alertness. Andrew Weil (1986) believes that the human desire to alter consciousness periodically by a number of means is as normal as the hunger or sex drive. Serious problems arise not so much from the desire itself but from the means used to achieve alteration of consciousness. It is my belief that it is possible for humans to harness their own brain chemicals to achieve desirable mood changes without the use of drugs. For example, we know that certain activities dramatically alter people's level of arousal. Hang gliding off El Capitan in California or wrestling a Bengal tiger would certainly bring about a "high" not entirely unrelated to that experienced by amphetamine ingestion. This would include enhanced alertness, increased stamina, rapid heartbeat, and inability to sleep immediately following the experience.

The following sections discuss how various activities bring about the release of certain molecules in the brain and how these molecules affect the human state of consciousness.

Activities, Molecules, and Mood

In 1982, Milkman and Sunderwirth proposed that the neurochemical processes that occur as a result of certain arousal activities may be similar to the process that occurs when stimulant drugs are ingested. In fact, it appears quite likely that these drugs actually mimic the natural neurochemistry that occurs in the brain during fight or flight activities. That this proposal may be true is supported by the similarity of the chemical structure of the stimulant drug amphetamine and the chemical norepinephrine (Figure 2–1), which occurs naturally in the brain and is thought to be one of the chemicals responsible for mental arousal during fight or flight.

Milkman and Sunderwirth also proposed that opiate ingestion mimicked the neurochemistry experienced by the release of endorphins during relaxation or satiation activities. As might be expected, exogenous opiate molecules have a structural similarity to naturally occurring endorphins produced by the brain. They later proposed (1987) that the use of fantasy to reduce stress is neurochemically related to the use of psychedelic drugs. Although some of these mood-altering activities have the potential for addiction, many of them are life enhancing and are necessary for a person's overall well-being.

It therefore seems logical that we should be able to use the molecules produced in the brain to achieve the mood alterations that we not only desire but actually need if we are to lead happy and productive lives. We refer to those moods brought about by such beneficial activities as *natural highs*.

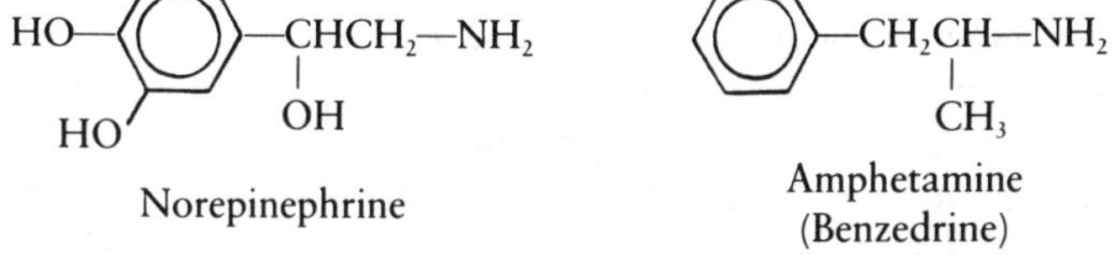

Norepinephrine

Amphetamine (Benzedrine)

Figure 2–1. Structural similarity between norepinephrine and amphetamine.

The relationships that exist between the brain, endogenous chemicals produced through activities, and powerful mind-altering drugs may be understood using an analogy of a computer and two different brands of software. In this analogy, consider the brain as the hardware, which can be programmed to achieve various moods depending on the type of software used. A person may program his or her brain by using compatible software, such as those molecules produced by activities. Alternatively, a person may choose to use software that is not completely compatible. Although the incompatible software (amphetamine, cocaine, or heroin) will run certain programs (various mood changes), extended use of this software has the potential to cause serious damage to the hardware (brain). For this reason, the emphasis on natural highs encourages the use of life-enhancing activities to produce the molecules needed to achieve the mood alterations so essential to human life.

Although it is somewhat reductionistic to say that molecules rule human lives, the truth is that they have an enormous influence over the way people think, the level of their moods, their behavior, and most other aspects of their lives. To understand how molecules can exert such control, we need to consider how the brain functions. This is not meant to be an intricate discussion of neurochemistry, but simply a review of fundamental concepts necessary to understand the influence of molecules on human life.

Molecules, Neurotransmission, and Mood

The brain is composed of billions of nerve cells (neurons), which interconnect with each other to form trillions of connections. Interestingly, none of these trillions of interconnections involve actual contact between the individual neurons. It is this lack of "hard wiring" that enables molecules, both endogenous and exogenous, to play such a dominant role in people's lives. To understand this role, we must first understand how messages are passed from one neuron to the other, since the brain is not hard wired. This is best summarized in a statement by Avram Goldstein (1982): "The language of the brain is chemistry."

The impulse that carries the message from one neuron to another is chemical, and the chemical messengers are organic molecules known as neurotransmitters. This term is very descriptive, since these molecules transmit the message between neurons. Figure 2–2 illustrates two neurons in close proximity separated by a gap called the synaptic junction or synapse. When a nerve impulse arrives at the presynaptic nerve terminal, channels in this terminal are opened and calcium ions (Ca^{++}) flow into the cell. This triggers a process in which neurotransmitter molecules (diamond shaped) are released from the terminal into the synapse. The neurotransmitters then cross the synapse and attach themselves to specific receptor sites embedded in the post-

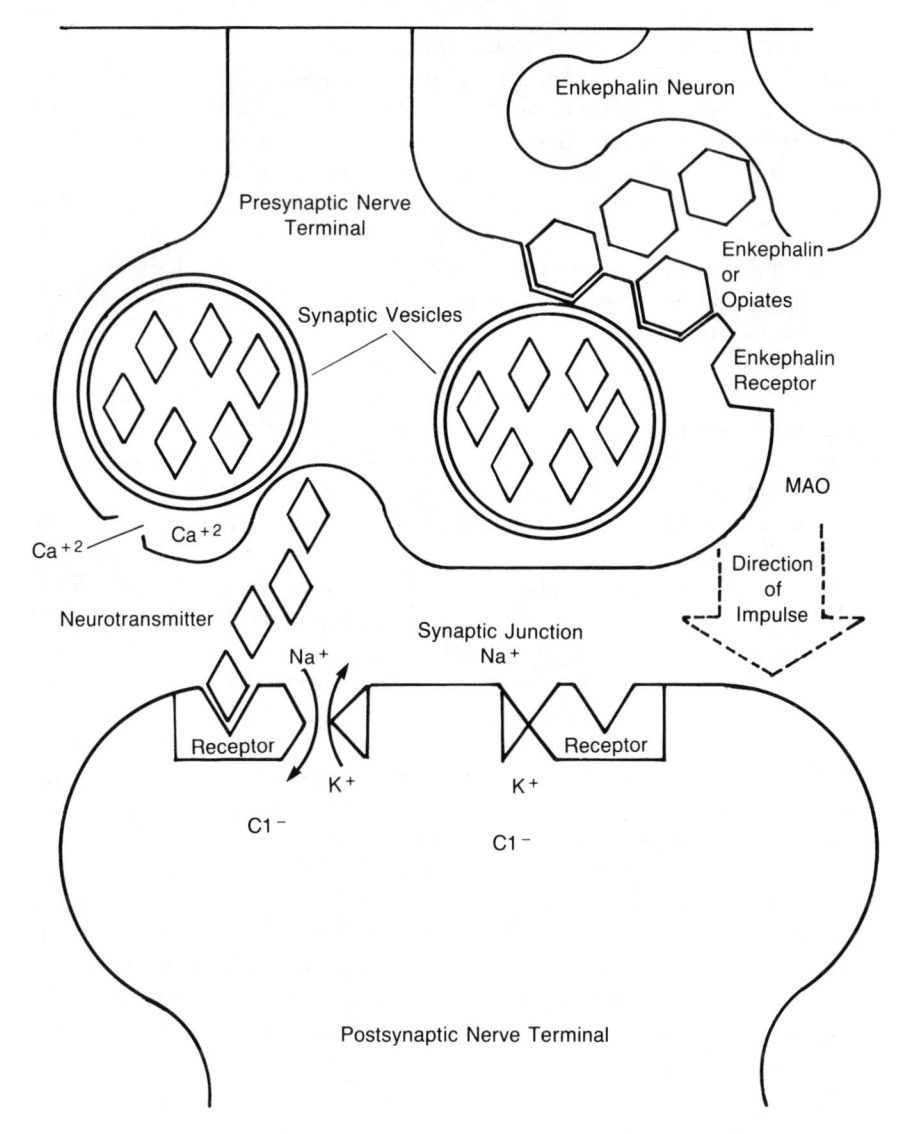

Figure 2–2. Chemical transmission of a nerve impulse.

synaptic nerve terminal. It is important to note that the shapes of the receptors must complement the shapes of the neurotransmitters. That is, only specific neurotransmitters will fit into the receptors of a given postsynaptic nerve terminal. It is this attachment of a sufficient number of neurotransmitters to receptors that is responsible for the condition of a nerve impulse from one neuron to another.

To understand how this neurotransmitter-receptor interaction may result in transmission of the impulse, it is important to understand the normal polarization of the postsynaptic membrane. The postsynaptic membrane is negatively polarized internally due to more intracellular negative charges (Cl^-, PO_4^{-3}, and so on) than positive charges (K^+, Na^+). This is partially due to the tendency of potassium ions (K^+) to move from the interior of the cell to the extracellular fluid, leaving behind a net negative charge within the cell. The attachment of a neurotransmitter to a receptor site opens channels in the receptor that allow a "rush" of positive ions (mostly Na^+) into the cell. This momentarily (for approximately one millisecond) reverses the polarity of the membrane. The rapid influx of sodium ions into the postsynaptic cell more than offsets the departure of potassium ions, resulting in a reversal of polarity (or depolarization), which then generates an action potential that sends the impulse to the next neuron, where the process starts over. As implied earlier, it is only when a sufficient number of receptor sites are occupied by neurotransmitters that the process described above results in depolarization of the postsynaptic membrane.

For the messages or impulses to continue passing through this neuronal pathway, the postsynaptic membrane must be repolarized. This is initiated by the release of the neurotransmitters from the receptor sites. The neurotransmitters must then cross the synapse and return to the original presynaptic terminal, where they may be stored awaiting their release following the arrival of a new impulse. Upon the release of the neurotransmitters from the postsynaptic membrane, the channels in the receptor sites close. Negative polarization of the membrane is reestablished through the removal of intracellular sodium ions by means of very efficient ion pumps, which force these ions out of the cell. This entire process, from the arrival of the impulse at the presynaptic neuron to the repolarization of the postsynaptic membrane, is called neurotransmission and is the mechanism by which molecules are able to exert control over a person's mind, mood, and behavior. [For a summary of neurotransmission, see Bloom, Lazerson, and Hofstadter (1985).] Obviously, this process must be very rapid, with the discharging and charging of the postsynaptic membrane occurring many times each second.

Arousal and Synaptic Chemistry

Let us now consider how synaptic chemistry determines a person's moods. Once again, the important concept to remember is that the postsynaptic neuron will "fire" only when a sufficient number of receptor sites have been occupied by neurotransmitters. Any process that increases the number of neurotransmitters in the synapse decreases the time required for a sufficient number of receptors to be occupied and thus the time for the neuron to fire. Thus, the rate at which a given neuron fires is directly related to the number of neurotransmitters in the synapse.

The importance of this concept is apparent when we consider the effect of neuronal firing on a person's level of arousal. In general, as the rate of firing increases in a given neuronal pathway, the activity for which that pathway is responsible increases. For example, if a particular pathway is responsible for mental alertness, an increase in the number of neurotransmitters in the synapses of that pathway will result in an increased rate of neurotransmission with a corresponding increased mental alertness. A general rule to follow is that if other conditions are the same, the number of neurotransmitters in the synapse determines the rate of neurotransmission. It also follows that the rate of neurotransmission in excitatory pathways in the central nervous system (CNS) determines a person's level of arousal.

Let us now consider the previous example of hang gliding off El Capitan. As the pilot approaches the edge of the cliff and then soars into space, there is a rush of excitatory neurotransmitters into the synapse, which brings about an immediate increase in the rate of neuronal firing (neurotransmission) and in turn results in an elevation of mood, an increased alertness, and a complete elimination of either drowsiness or depression.

The neurochemistry of this natural process can be mimicked by either cocaine or amphetamines. The presence of cocaine in the synapse blocks the reabsorption of the excitatory neurotransmitters back into the presynaptic junction (Figure 2–3), with a resultant increase in the number of neurotransmitters in the synapse. These neurotransmitters are then available for binding to receptor sites. As indicated earlier, the postsynaptic neuron will fire only when a sufficient number of receptor sites are occupied. An increase in the number of neurotransmitter molecules in the synapse due to cocaine will therefore decrease the time needed for this critical number of receptor sites to be occupied. Amphetamines enhance the release of neurotransmitters from the presynaptic neuron, which also increases the number of neurotransmitter molecules in the synapse. In both cases (cocaine and amphetamines), the firing rate of the neuronal pathway is increased, with the resulting temporary elevation of mood similar to that caused by hang gliding off El Capitan or wrestling a Bengal tiger.

I have used the rather extreme example of hang gliding or tiger wrestling to dramatize the concept that people can achieve mood changes without the use of powerful drugs and to underscore that these drugs mimic the natural neurochemistry of the brain. Assuming that the pilot of the hang glider does not have an accident, his or her experience represents a life-enhancing activity, which I refer to as a natural high. Programming the brain by using incompatible software such as cocaine or amphetamines, although temporarily gratifying, has the potential for serious damage to the hardware (the brain), including compulsion, loss of control, and continuation in spite of harmful consequences.

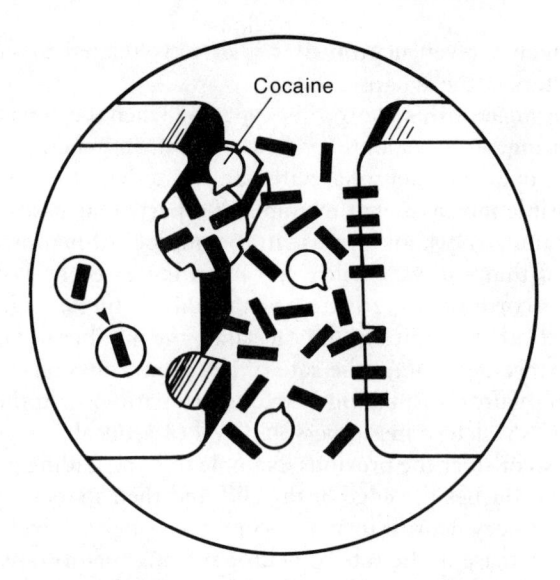

Figure 2–3. Effect of cocaine on the reabsorption of excitatory neurotransmitters (norepinephrine) into the presynaptic membrane.

Source: "Scientific American," *New York Times*, 22 March 1983.

As this chapter has shown, a person's moods are determined to a large degree by the level or concentration of neurotransmitters in the synapse. In fact, a person's very personality, intelligence, and consciousness are reflections of the synaptic concentration of neurotransmitters. Those attributes that people consider distinctly human are a result of the chemistry of the synapse. As Steven Rose (1973) has said, "It is not too strong to say that the evolution of humanity followed the evolution of the synapse!" (p. 176).

Synaptic Homeostasis

The survival of any organism depends on that organism's ability to maintain dependable and predictable behavior. Unpredictable and aberrant behavior can only decrease the organism's overall chances for survival. Since behavior is so closely linked to neurotransmission, it is imperative that the brain have mechanisms to restore neurotransmission to a baseline level (homeostasis) following any activity that upsets normal neurotransmission. The mechanisms by which the brain regulates neurotransmission are a combination of enzymatic and other changes. These mechanisms work together to maintain homeostatic neurotransmission through a combination of actions, including one known as the enzyme expansion theory, which was proposed by Goldstein and Goldstein (1968).

In addition to various enzymatic changes, the receptors on the postsynaptic neuron exhibit a self-regulatory capacity that enables them to alter their sensitivity to neurotransmitters during periods of either excessive or minimal neurotransmitter concentration (Cohen 1988). Any activity that increases the level of neurotransmitters in the synapse is countered by biological mechanisms that attempt to minimize the effect of this altered neurotransmitter level. In a similar manner, activity- or drug-induced decreases in the level of neurotransmitters in the synapse are countered by mechanisms that tend to raise the level of neurotransmission back to a pre-activity or pre-drug baseline level. For this reason, any activity that alters a person's moods through a change in neurotransmission must be repeated if he or she wishes to obtain the desired altered state of consciousness. If the activity is abuse of powerful mind-altering drugs, the brain's natural tendency to regulate neurotransmission can lead to tolerance, dependence, and addiction. With activities that bring about only a moderate fluctuation, however, the brain usually restores homeostasis without any serious problems.

The danger of becoming addicted by using life-enhancing activities to alter moods is minimal compared to that of using powerful mood-altering drugs, which put a severe strain on the brain's ability to maintain homeostasis. As a result, changes occur in the brain that are not readily reversible. This can be compared to a metal spring that can be stretched thousands of times without losing its strength or flexibility. If the spring is stretched beyond a certain limit, however, it will lose its ability to rebound to its original condition. In the brain, this overextension by the abuse of mind-altering drugs is manifested in an overreaction to the drug through changes in enzyme levels that are not readily reversible. It is this alteration of enzyme levels that is partially responsible for the addictive process.

Unfortunately, some imbalances in the synaptic concentration of neurotransmitters are not caused by activities, including mind-altering drugs. Occasionally the brain, even without activity-induced fluctuations, will lose control of synaptic homeostasis, with dreadful results. Perhaps nowhere is this loss of neurotransmitter homeostasis more evident than in disorders such as schizophrenia, mania, depression, Tourette's syndrome, Parkinson's disease, and Huntington's chorea, which are the result of either chemical imbalances in the synapse or degeneration of the neurons containing these synapses. For example, abnormally high levels of dopamine in the synapse have been associated with schizophrenia, and imbalances in the synaptic concentrations of norepinephrine are associated with mania (high levels) and depression (low levels). The case for the ability of neurotransmitter molecules to influence mind, mood, and behavior could not be more manifest than in these tragic examples.

Relaxation and Synaptic Chemistry

Obviously, not all people wish to alter their moods by hang gliding or engaging in other arousal activities. Many people prefer to seek relaxation or satiation rather than arousal. As we have seen, arousal can be achieved through those activities that increase the concentration of excitatory neurotransmitters such as dopamine and norepinephrine in the synapse. It would therefore seem logical that relaxation could be achieved through activities such as opiate ingestion, which decreases the level of these neurotransmitters in the synapse and therefore decreases the rate of neurotransmission in excitatory pathways. This opiate-induced decrease in the rate of neurotransmission is responsible for both the analgesia and the euphoria produced by these drugs.

It has long been suspected that the body is capable of producing its own pain-killing and euphorogenic chemicals, since certain activities seem to decrease pain and produce a sense of well-being or contentment. The brain chemicals responsible for this decrease in synaptic concentration of excitatory neurotransmitters were discovered in 1974 by Hughes and Kosterlitz (Hughes et al. 1975). These compounds are a series of related molecules called endorphins (endogenous morphine) and enkephalins (in the head) that have been dubbed "The Keys to Paradise," since they are believed to be responsible for moods associated with joy and happiness. Literally thousands of articles have appeared in both the popular and the scientific press extolling the virtues of endorphins. Everything pleasurable from runner's euphoria to warm chicken soup has been attributed to the release of endorphins. Janet Hopson (1988) has called endorphins the primary chemicals in the "biochemical bandwagon of the 1980's". Although the media hype is undoubtedly exaggerated, there is evidence that certain activities can release endorphins to relieve pain and bring about feelings of euphoria and well-being. For example, eating is soothing as well as analgesic. Who has not experienced relief from the misery of a headache or a cold by eating a favorite food?

As in the case of opiates, endorphins function by decreasing the concentration of excitatory neurotransmitters in the synapse. This is accomplished by a mechanism that retards the release of these neurotransmitters from the presynaptic terminal into the synapse. The mechanism involves the attachment of the endorphin molecules to receptor sites on the presynaptic terminal (Figure 2–2). The inhibition of the release of excitatory neurotransmitters into the synapse is governed by the number of enkephalin receptor sites that are occupied. Most pleasurable activities, such as meditation, listening to music, and eating pleasant-tasting food, release enough enkephalins to bring about a sense of well-being without overstretching the "synaptic spring" and can therefore be repeated frequently without fear of permanent overextension. Drugs such as heroin, however, stretch the synaptic spring too far, resulting in a strain on the brain's restoring mechanism, which may not be immediately restored. Put another way, the brain is made to deal with the alterations in the synaptic concentration of neurotransmitters brought about by moderate activities but may be unable to cope with the severe alterations brought about by powerful drugs.

As in the case of drugs that dramatically increase the synaptic concentration of excitatory neurotransmitters, those drugs that bring about a decrease in excitatory neurotransmitters are met head-on by the brain's internal mechanism, which attempts to restore a homeostatic level of neurotransmission. As mentioned earlier, the restoring mechanism involves substantial enzymatic changes in the postsynaptic neuron that are not readily reversible even if the drug is removed. Once again, it is these enzymatic changes that are partially responsible for the tolerance and dependence that are the hallmarks of addiction.

Food for Your Mood

For years people believed that the brain was impervious to assaults from junk food and other atrocious diets. This attitude persisted in spite of folk legends extolling the powers of certain foods to alter the functioning of the brain. Such foods included fish (brain food), oysters (aphrodisiac), and milk (to help bring on sleep). In 1974, however, Fernstrom and Wurtman published a major article describing their research with the ability of ingested tryptophan to increase the level of serotonin in the brains of laboratory rats. In addition, they showed that a diet high in carbohydrates also increased the brain's level of serotonin, a neurotransmitter associated with sleep. Although the carbohydrates themselves contain no serotonin, their inclusion in the diet enhances the ability of the amino acid tryptophan already present in the blood to cross into the brain, where it is converted to serotonin by the chemical reactions shown in figure 2–4. For many years, people also have believed that warm milk induces sleep when ingested before bedtime. This is entirely plausible, since milk contains a sizable amount of tryptophan, which may cross the blood-brain barrier and be converted into serotonin. In an analogous manner, a meal rich in meat protein, which contains the amino acid tyrosine, would be expected to increase the level of norepinephrine by the metabolic scheme shown in figure 2–5.

Wurtman (1982) described the conditions under which neurotransmitter precursors such as tyrosine can cross from the blood into the brain to form neurotransmitters, or norepinephrine. This increase in synaptic norepinephrine would be expected to be accompanied by an increased arousal state. Therefore, it should be possible for a person to exert some control over his or her level of arousal by selecting certain types of food. Certainly it is unwise to eat a high-carbohydrate meal for breakfast or lunch if a person wants to

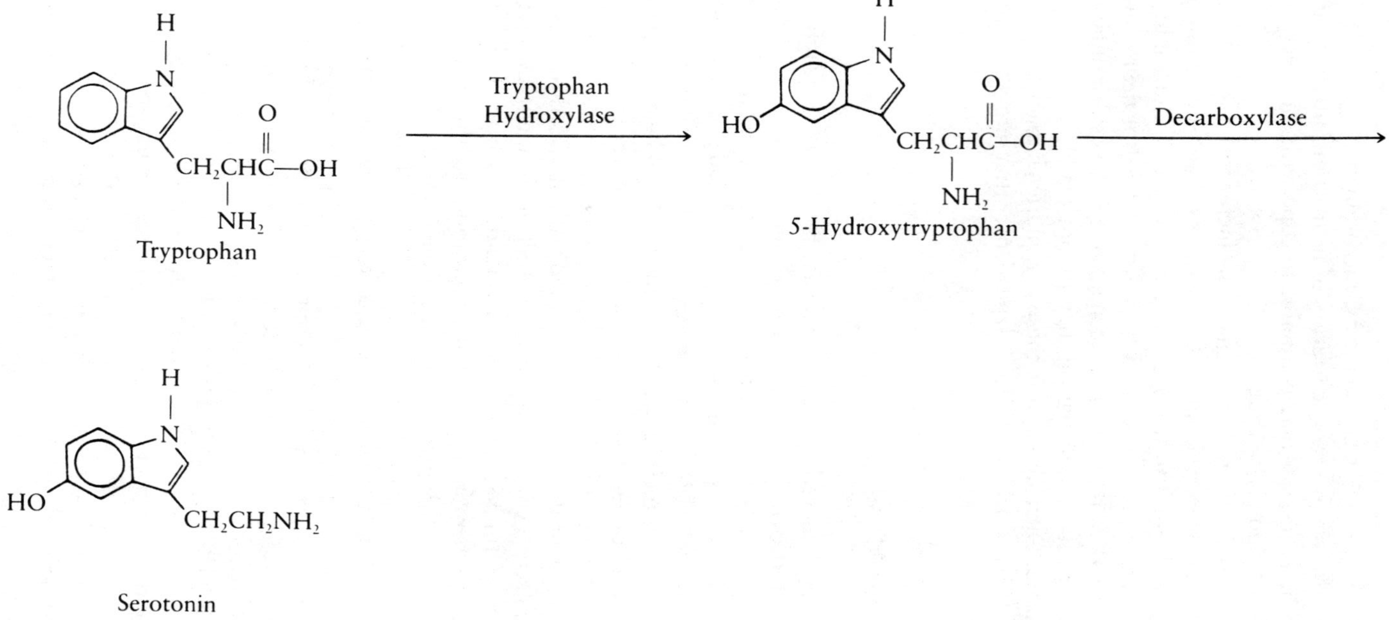

Figure 2–4. Conversion of tryptophan to serotonin in the brain.

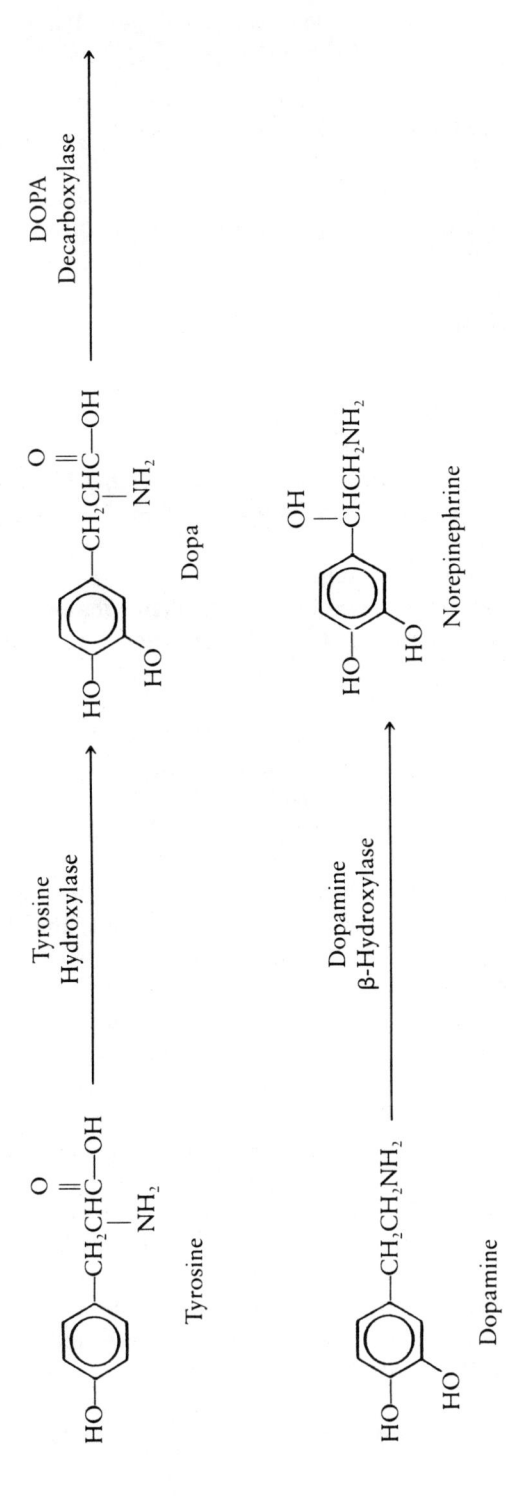

Figure 2–5. Conversion of tyrosine to norepinephrine in the brain.

remain alert throughout the day. Lunch especially should consist of a sufficient amount of protein to maintain a synaptic level of norepinephrine consistent with the need to avoid postlunch drowsiness. However, those wishing to obtain a good night's sleep would do well to consume complex carbohydrates in order to increase the level of serotonin in the brain.

Exercise and Endorphins

For the past several years, we have been bombarded by claims of "runner's high," "exercise euphoria," and other benefits attributed to the effects of vigorous exercise. Exercise has been associated with a reduction of anxiety (Morgan 1984a, 1984b), antidepression (Griest et al. 1979), enhanced sleep patterns (Fielding 1982), and a reduction of stress (Cooper, Gallman, and McDonald 1986). Dishman (1985) provides a comprehensive summary of the psychological effects of exercise.

Following the discovery of endorphins and enkephalins by Hughes et al. (1975), exercise-induced altered states of awareness were attributed in many cases to the release of these endogenous opiates. There is a considerable volume of research on the relationship between vigorous exercise and the release of plasma endorphins (Steinberg and Sypes 1985; Rahkila et al. 1987; Goldfarb et al. 1987). Since endorphins should bring about analgesic effects as well as euphoria, it would be expected that if vigorous exercise produces endorphins, their presence would be manifested by a decrease in pain sensitivity. This was found to be the case by several investigators, including Berk et al. (1981), and Haier, Quaid, and Mills (1981). These and other studies have shown that "an increase in the peripheral plasma levels of beta-endorphin in humans after exercise has been noted by all investigators to date" (Farnell 1984).

Farnell and others have noted, however, that in animal studies, there does not seem to be an accompanying increase of endorphins in the brain in most investigations to date. This is because most peptides, such as endorphins, do not cross from the blood into the brain. This is a rather serious flaw in the runner's high–endorphin connection, since to cause any alteration in state of consciousness, the endorphins would need to get into the brain from the blood or be generated in the brain. There is some evidence that both of these mechanisms may be operative under certain conditions. Barta, Yashpal, and Henry (1981) found that there was a decrease of endogenous opiates in the pituitary and an increase of these substances in the limbic system of rats subjected to the stress of cold-water swimming. In addition, Pert and Bowie (1979) and Sforzo et al. (1986) found that subjecting rats to cold water swimming brought about an alteration of opiate receptor occupancy. Also, Orlova et al. (1988) found that there was an increase of beta-endorphin and enkephalins in the brains of rats following long-term swimming training. While these results cannot be directly correlated with altered endorphin levels in the brains of humans following vigorous exercise, there is at least the potential for this correlation.

There is also some evidence that under conditions of stress, the blood-brain barrier may become weakened. For example, it has been shown that trypan blue will cross the blood-brain barrier under certain conditions (McArthur 1985). While this lack of convincing scientific evidence for the direct correlation of the increase of endogenous opiates in the brain with exercise euphoria is disappointing, the beneficial psychological effects of exercise have been documented and summarized in a report from a conference held at the National Institutes for Mental Health (Morgan 1984b). These benefits clearly outweigh any doubts or concerns about the exercise-endorphin relationship.

Summary

It is important to realize that all people have both an occasional need and a desire to alter their state of consciousness in order to deal with life's many stresses. One important mechanism by which mood alterations are produced involves a change in the level of neurotransmitters in the synapse, which in turn alters the rate of neurotransmission, with a corresponding alteration in mood. Synaptic changes in neurotransmitter concentrations may be brought about by the use of exogenous substances such as heroin or cocaine. These drugs bring about such a dramatic alteration in the level of neurotransmitters that the brain's ability to maintain homeostatic neurotransmission may be taxed to the point where synaptic alterations in enzymes and receptor sensitivity are not readily reversible, resulting in tolerance and dependence.

Since certain activities besides drug abuse also can alter synaptic neurotransmitter levels, it should be possible to seek out these activities that are compatible with our desired altered state of consciousness in order to achieve desirable alterations in neurotransmission. Risk taking and other exciting activities bring about an increased level of neurotransmission without the deleterious effects inherent in cocaine or amphetamine use. Certain relaxation activities are believed to bring about a release of endorphins, which act as internal opiates to decrease neurotransmission and thereby satiate moods. In recent years, a great deal of literature (both scientific and popular) has appeared extolling the virtues of using those internal opiates to achieve relief from stress, depression, anxiety, pain, and many other ills associated with undesirable neurotransmission. Nowhere is this literature more prominent than in the study of exercise and its effect on endorphin levels. However, not everyone can run in order to achieve the desired altered state, nor is this activity necessarily the most efficient way to achieve natural highs. People can undertake many activities to alter the concentration of neurotransmitters in the synapse and thus to produce the desired mood without the use of drugs. Some of these, such as creative efforts, falling in love, running, meditation, participating in sports, listening to music, reciting poetry, playing with grandchildren, or cuddling a pet, are healthful and beneficial life-enhancing activities.

To ensure that people use their internal neurochemistry to reach desirable altered states, Hopson (1988) suggests living an "unfettered natural life. Laugh! Cry! Thrill to music! Reach puberty! Get pregnant! Get aerobic! Get hungry! Eat!" (p.33). However, not all mind-altering, drug-free activities are without some risk of addiction, characterized by compulsion, loss of control, and continuation in spite of harmful consequences. Activities such as crime, gambling, promiscuous sex, and constant danger can be as damaging and addicting as drugs. These are very powerful mind-altering activities, and the rush of excitatory neurotransmitters into the synapse during these activities creates a stress on the brain's ability to restore homeostasis. It is, therefore, important to seek out moderate activities that create a pleasant mood change without placing an undue burden on the brain's ability to restore synaptic homeostasis.

References

Barta, A., K. Yashpal. 1981. "Regional Redistribution of Beta-Endorphin in the Rat Brain: The Effect of Stress." *Progress in Neuropsychopharmacology.* 5:595–598.

Berk, L.S., S.A. Tan, C.L. Anderson, and G. Reiss. 1981. "-EP Response to Exercise in Athletes and Non-Athletes." *Medicine and Science in Sports and Exercise* 13:131.

Bloom, F., A. Lazerson, and L. Hofstadter. 1985. *Brain, Mind and Behavior.* New York: W.H. Freeman.

Cohen, S. 1988. *The Chemical Brain: The Neurochemistry of Addictive Disorders.* Irvine, Calif.: Care Institute.

Cooper, K.H., J.S. Gallman, and J.L. McDonald, Jr. 1986. "Role of Aerobic Exercise in Reduction of Stress." *Dental Clinics of North America* 30(Suppl. 4):133–42.

Dishman, R.K. 1985. "Medical Psychology in Exercise and Sport." *Medical Clinics of North America* 69. (1): 123–43.

Farnell, P.A. 1984. "Exercise and Endorphins—Male Responses." *Medicine and Science in Sports and Exercise* 17 (1): 89–93.

Fernstrom, J.D., and R. Wurtman. 1974. "Nutrition and the Brain." *Scientific American* 230 (2): 84–91.

Fielding, J.E. 1982. "Effectiveness of Employee Health Improvement Program." *Journal of Occupational Medicine* 24:907–16.

Goldfarb, A.H., B.D. Hatfield, G.A. Sforzo, and M.G. Flynn. 1987. "Serum Beta-

Endorphin Levels during a Graded Exercise Test to Exhaustion." *Medicine and Science in Sports and Exercise* 9 (2): 78–82.

Goldstein, A. 1982. Oral Presentation at the Sixth Annual Summer Institute on Drug Dependence, Colorado Springs, Colo.

Goldstein, A., and D.B. Goldstein. 1968. "Enzyme Expansion Theory of Drug Tolerance and Physical Dependence." *Research Publications of the Association for Research in Nervous and Mental Disease* 46:265–67.

Griest, J.H., M.H. Klein, J.F. Eischens, A.S. Gurman, and W.P. Morgan. 1979. "Running as Treatment for Depression." *Comprehensive Psychiatry* 20:41–53.

Gross, A. 1986. "Addiction: Quitting is the New High," *Vogue*, August, 330.

Haier, R.J., K. Quaid, and J.S.C. Mills. 1981. "Naloxone Alters Pain Perception after Jogging." *Psychiatry Research* 5:231–32.

Hopson, J. 1988. "A Pleasurable Chemistry." *Psychology Today*, July/August, 29–33.

McArthur, J.W. 1985. "Endorphins and Exercise in Females: Possible Connection with Reproductive Dysfunction." *Medicine and Science in Sports and Exercise* 17 (1): 82–88.

Milkman, H., and S. Sunderwirth. 1983. "The Chemistry of Craving." *Psychology Today*, October, 36–44.

———. 1987. *Craving for Ecstasy*. Lexington, Mass.: Lexington Books.

Morgan, W.P. 1984a. "Affective Beneficence of Vigorous Physical Activity." *Medicine and Science in Sports and Exercise* 17 (1): 94–100.

———. 1984b. *Coping with Mental Stress: The Potential and Limits of Exercise Intervention*. Bethesda, Md.: National Institutes of Mental Health.

Orlova, E.K., M.G. Pshennikova, A.D. Demitriev, and F.Z. Meerson. 1988. "Increased Level of Immunoreactive Opioid Peptides in the Brain and Adrenals of Rats as Affected by Adaptation to Physical Loading (in Russian)." *Biulleten Eksperimentalnoi (Muskova) Biologii I Meditsiny (Moskva)* 105 (2): 145–48.

Pert, C.G., and D.L. Bowie. 1979. "Behavioral Manipulation of Rats Causes Alterations in Opiate Receptor Occupancy." In *Endorphins in Mental Health Research*, edited by E. Usdin, W.E. Bunney, and N.S. Kline, 93–104. New York: Oxford University Press.

Rahkila, P., E. Hakala, K. Salminen, and T. Laatikainen. 1987. "Response of Plasma Endorphins to Running Exercises in Male and Female Endurance Athletes." *Medicine and Science in Sports and Exercise* 19 (5): 451–55.

Rose, S. 1973. *The Conscious Brain*. New York: Alfred A. Knopf.

Sforzo, G.A., T.F. Seeger, C.B. Pert, and C.O. Dotson. 1986. "In Vivo Opioid Receptor Occupation in the Rat Brain Following Exercise." *Medicine and Science in Sports and Exercise* 18 (4): 380–84.

Steinberg, H., and E.A. Sypes. 1985. "Introduction to Symposium on Endorphins and Behavioral Processes: Review of Literature on Endorphins and Exercise." *Pharmacology, Biochemistry and Behavior* 23 (5): 857–62.

Weil, A. 1986. *The Natural Mind*. Boston: Houghton Mifflin.

Wurtman, R. 1982. "Nutrients That Modify Brain Function." *Scientific American* 246 (4): 50–59.

3
Biological Approaches to Addiction Treatment

John A. Renner, Jr.

Opiates

Medical records indicate that opium was used to control pain as early as the first century A.D. The first abuse of opium was observed in China after the technique of opium smoking developed in the seventeenth century. Addiction to tincture of opium occurred secondary to the use of patent medicines in the nineteenth century. With the isolation of morphine from the opium poppy in 1803 and the invention of the hypodermic needle in 1840, factors were in place that permitted the intravenous administration of a highly potent opiate and ushered in the modern era of opiate addiction.

Mechanism of Action

It is now known that there are specific opiate-binding receptors in the central nervous system (CNS). These receptors are most highly concentrated in the limbic system, that part of the brain that is thought to regulate the emotions. Pheiffer and Herz (1982) identified subtypes of these opiate receptors that differ in their affinity for opioid peptides and various opiates. The discovery of the endorphins, naturally occurring morphine-like substances in the brain, has led to a theory explaining opiate addiction. Endorphins are known to moderate pain and block opiate withdrawal, and they may well explain the effectiveness of acupuncture. The endorphin receptors in the brain are the same binding sites for opiates. Enkephalin, one of the endorphins, has a very high affinity for the delta opiate receptor. It has been postulated that an individual may be predisposed to opiate addiction because of an endorphin-mediated biochemical defect in the brain.

The discovery of the endorphins in the 1970s provided a useful model for understanding the addictive process. It proved a fascinating corollary to the theory proposed in 1965 by Dole, Nyswander, and Kreek to explain the success of the first methadone maintenance program. They suggested that heroin addiction was a medical illness and that addicts had a metabolic deficiency that caused them to experience intense euphoria after using heroin. This permanent deficiency would cause them to crave the drug and hence justified lifetime treatment with methadone (Dole, Nyswander, and Kreek 1966).

Repeated use of opiates is thought to cause receptors to become hypersensitive and/or to cause a proliferation of receptor sites. When opiates are no longer available at the receptor or are displaced by opiate antagonists, the CNS responds with a state of extreme hyperactivity. This can occur after as little as one week of steady opiate use. The addict experiences a state of intense craving, along with the familiar withdrawal symptoms associated with autonomic disregulation (sweats, diarrhea, cramps, rhinorrhea, and tremors). Depending on the class of opiates used, these symptoms can last from seven to fourteen days. Morphine and heroin are relatively short acting drugs. Their associated withdrawal state is intense but clears within seven days. Long-acting opiates such as methadone produce less intense withdrawal symptoms that often last more than two weeks. Addicts often complain that these more prolonged states are worse and are harder to tolerate.

Detoxification

The easiest way to relieve the discomfort of the withdrawal syndrome is to reduce the daily opiate dose gradually over a period of days for those addicted to short-acting drugs such as morphine, or for weeks or months for those addicted to longer acting drugs such as methadone. For practical purposes, the most common practice is to switch the heroin addict to methadone, which is then gradually withdrawn. Methadone is the only drug that is legally approved for this purpose and has the major clinical advantage of being able to control withdrawal symptoms with a single daily oral dose. The use of methadone to treat opiate addiction requires that the hospital or clinic obtain federal and state licenses to dispense methadone for this purpose and that strict federal guidelines be followed (U.S. Department of Health and Human Services 1980).

In inpatient settings, methadone is usually reduced by 20 percent each day from the initial stabilizing dose. The process is completed in 10 to 14 days, although the addict may continue to experience insomnia and mood disturbances for several weeks. Current federal regulations permit use of methadone for 30 days for outpatient detoxification. This may be extended up to 180 days if the program physician determines that the addict cannot tolerate a 30-day detoxification and that he or she is likely to relapse to heroin use (U.S. Department of Health and Human Services 1987).

The first step in evaluation of the patient is to obtain baseline vital signs, a urine drug screen for all the common drugs of abuse, and a history of previous drug use. Treatment with methadone should not begin until a state of opiate withdrawal has been established based on a physical examination. This must include evidence of an increase in pulse, respiration, blood pressure, and temperature. Other common findings include lacrimation, rhinorrhea, dilated pupils, gooseflesh, tremors, and recent track marks. Addicts also will present with many subjective complaints such as cramps, anxiety, nausea, chills, insomnia, and weakness. Detoxification should never be initiated on the basis of subjective complaints alone. No methadone should be dispensed until there is physical evidence of withdrawal.

The initial starting dose should not exceed 20 milligrams orally. Less may be given for a young addict with a smaller habit. An additional dose of 5 or 10 milligrams may be given if the vital signs have not begun to return to normal within two hours of the initial dose. It is rarely necessary or wise to exceed a dose of 40 milligrams during the first twenty-four hours. Once a dose that adequately controls the patient's withdrawal symptoms has been established, the detoxification process can begin.

A pharmacologic alternative to this standard approach has been the use of clonidine, an alpha-two-adrenergic agonist that suppresses the autonomic symptoms of withdrawal. Since it does not reduce the subjective symptoms of withdrawal, as methadone does, it may be unacceptable to some addicts. It is best to stabilize the addict first on methadone and then to reduce the dose to 20 milligrams per day. At that point, clonidine can be substituted for the methadone. Kleber has recommended a dose of 5 micrograms per kilogram per day. In any case, the dose should not exceed 0.6 milligrams per day (0.2 milligrams orally three times a day). Patients should be monitored closely for side effects of clonidine, including hypotension and sedation. Clonidine can be reduced to zero in seven days in inpatient programs; outpatient detoxification with clonidine should be spread over two to four weeks (Charney et al. 1981).

Detoxification has proven to be useful primarily in those cases where the addict is immediately transferred into a long-term residential drug treatment facility. For addicts unwilling to accept residential care, or for those followed only with outpatient counseling, short-term detoxification rarely leads to successful rehabilitation. Despite the high frequency of relapse in such cases, detoxification is an option that should always be available to the addict.

Pharmacologic Stabilization

The concept of the medical maintenance of opiate addicts dates back to the nineteenth century, when many American physicians regularly prescribed opiates to addicted patients (Musto 1973). Prior to World War I, there were forty-four Morphine Maintenance Clinics located across the United States. This pharmacologic treatment for addiction was made illegal in 1914 with the passage of the Harrison Act.

In 1964, the contemporary era in the medical management of addiction began when Dole, Nyswander, and Kreek initiated an experimental program using methadone to stabilize opiate addicts. They believed that chronic opiate use created a permanent neurochemical deficit in the CNS and that opiate addicts would need lifetime pharmacologic treatment. They compared this situation to the diabetic's lifetime need for insulin. Initial evaluations of the first methadone maintenance were highly optimistic and led to a nationwide series of maintenance clinics (Gearing 1971). Twenty-four years of experience with methadone has tempered the initial optimism (Renner 1984), but no other treatment has proven to be a more effective alternative for opiate addicts. More recent evaluations of drug treatment programs have demonstrated the value of this approach, particularly when coupled with skilled psychotherapy and other psychiatric services (McLellan et al. 1983).

Dole, Nyswander, and Kreek (1966) believed that high doses of methadone (80 to 120 milligrams per day) were needed to block the craving for opiates. Later, double-blind studies of varying doses demonstrated that many addicts could be successfully maintained on lower doses (Garbutt and Goldstein 1972). Today, most maintenance patients are on daily doses in the 50- to 60-milligram range. This dose is adequate to prevent the development of withdrawal symptoms and thus to provide the pharmacologic stability that makes it possible for addicts to participate in other rehabilitative activities.

For opiate addicts with no other serious psychopathology, methadone maintenance programs have been highly successful. Addicts with other major psychiatric disorders do well on methadone only if given intensive ancillary psychiatric treatment (McLellan et al. 1983). For individuals with severe antisocial personality disorders, therapeutic communities based on the Synanon model are probably the best treatment alternative (Yablonsky 1969).

Federal regulations have defined methadone maintenance as any form of treatment of opiate addiction with methadone that extends beyond thirty days. These federal guidelines restrict maintenance to addicts with a documented one-year history of addiction and evidence of a current state of physiological dependence. Dosing should not begin until there is evidence of withdrawal, as described in the previous section on detoxification. Methadone can be increased gradually until the patient feels stable. Doses of 100 milligrams per day cannot be exceeded without special permission from the Food and Drug Administration (FDA), which oversees methadone programs.

Treatment should continue for three to five years before attempting to detoxify the patient from methadone. Detoxification should not begin until the patient has shown major progress in rehabilitation by the elimination of all antisocial behavior and illegal drug use. If patients are unable to handle detoxification without a relapse to opiate use, more prolonged maintenance is an appropriate alternative.

One useful option to methadone is a longer acting derivative, Levo-alpha-acetylmethadol (L-AAM). This drug suppresses opiate withdrawal symptoms for forty-eight to seventy-two hours and thus permits patients to be dosed on a three day per week schedule, eliminating the need for take-home doses (Ling et al. 1984). Despite more than eighteen years of clinical trials, this drug remains in an investigational category and is not generally available to addicts. While some addicts do not seem to adjust to L-AAM, it does have some practical advantages over methadone and would greatly simplify the operation of methadone clinics by eliminating staff-patient conflict over medication take-home privileges.

Opiate Antagonists

An alternative approach to the pharmacologic stabilization of addiction is the use of drugs that block opiate receptors and hence block any sense of euphoria, as well as preventing the development of physiological dependence. By blocking the reinforcing effects of the opiates, it is postulated, the addict's drug-seeking behavior will be gradually extinguished.

Two drugs of this type have proven to be clinically useful. Naloxone is commonly used in emergency rooms to reverse opiate overdoses. Because of its short duration of action (two to four hours), this antagonist is of no practical use for the long-term management of addiction.

A more useful alternative is naltrexone. A single oral dose of 50 milligrams provides a blocking effect for twenty-four hours and lends itself to long-term outpatient use. Alternatively, patients can be dosed on a three times weekly schedule of 100 milligrams on weekdays and 150 milligrams on weekends. Use of this drug is contraindicated in patients with acute hepatitis or liver failure, since doses of 300 milligrams per day have been associated with signs of hepatic toxicity (Jaffe 1981). Patient compliance has been a major problem with naltrexone, with most clinic patients dropping out of treatment within six weeks (Ginsberg 1986). It seems to work best with highly motivated patients who have good family support, established careers, and no significant history of antisocial behavior. For practical purposes, very few addicts have been able to use this treatment approach successfully.

Treatment of Concurrent Psychiatric Disorders

There is a high lifetime incidence of psychiatric disorders in opiate addicts. These include affective disorders (74 percent), antisocial personality (27 percent), alcoholism (35 percent), and anxiety disorders (16 percent) (Rounsaville et al. 1982). In recent years, cocaine abuse also has become a major problem in methadone maintenance patients. While it has been difficult to prove the effectiveness of antidepressants in opiate addicts, some studies have shown that doxepin may be helpful (Kleber et al. 1983; Woody, O'Brien, and Rickels 1975). Patients who are schizophrenic or manic depressive have responded well to treatment with major tranquilizers or lithium. The use of benzodiazepines for complaints of anxiety has been highly problematic, since these drugs potentiate the euphoria produced by opiates and are readily abused by patients with this complaint. Disulfiram has been tried with methadone maintenance patients who continue to abuse alcohol. While methadone and disulfiram can be taken concurrently, it has been difficult to prove that this approach is more successful than methadone plus a placebo (Ling et al. 1983).

Alcohol

Mechanism of Action

Ethanol is a short-chain alcohol and is the primary active component of beverage alcohol. It is a potent CNS depressant that is lipid soluble and rapidly penetrates the blood-brain barrier. In social settings, it is used to produce a mild sense of relaxation and well-being. With increasing blood ethanol levels, drinkers experience a state of disinhibition, followed by a progressive loss of coordination and muscular control. After passing through a further stage of CNS hyperstimulation and agitation, the drinker eventually becomes sedated. At much higher blood levels, ethanol can produce coma and then death secondary to depression of the respiratory centers in the brain stem.

Unlike all of the other common psychotropic drugs, there appears to be no specific CNS receptor for ethanol. Ethanol is thought to produce its physiological effects by interacting with specific areas of neuronal membranes. This interaction increases the fluidity of cell membrane lipids, affecting the activity of various membrane-bound proteins—that is, enzymes, receptors, and ionophores (Tabakoff and Hoffman 1987). Since the neural membrane is the primary regulator of the transmission of impulses from one nerve to another, anything that alters neuronal transmission can have a profound effect on the function of the CNS.

Ethanol specifically seems to inhibit calcium uptake into synaptosomes, thus inhibiting the release of neurotransmitters (Leslie et al. 1983). This effect on calcium uptake probably produces the sedative-hypnotic effect of ethanol. It also appears that ethanol affects the gamma-aminobutyric acid (GABA)–benzodiazepine receptor–chloride complex (Hoffman and Tabakoff 1985). There is also evidence that ethanol affects ligand binding to some of the opiate receptors in the brain; it seems to decrease receptor affinity for those opiate receptors that have the greatest affinity for enkephalin (Pheiffer and

Herz 1982; Khatani et al. 1987). Thus, despite the absence of a specific ethanol receptor in the brain, there are clearly many highly specific effects on neurotransmitters and neuromodulator systems.

The development of tolerance to ethanol is due to effects on brain norepinephrine (NE), serotonin, and the neuropeptide vasopressin (Khanna et al. 1981; Hoffman 1987). The mechanisms causing physical dependence on ethanol are less well known but probably involve muscarinic cholinergic receptors and changes in the NE systems in the brain (Tabakoff, Munoz-Marcus, and Fields 1979).

Ethanol is high in calories but devoid of other essential nutrients such as vitamins, protein, and minerals. Chronic ethanol consumption leads to malnutrition and specific vitamin deficiency syndromes (Feldman 1982). Ethanol is metabolized only in the liver and cannot be stored in any body tissue. Excessive consumption of ethanol puts a major strain on hepatic function, eventually leading to a state of chronic inflammation termed *alcoholic hepatitis*. Ethanol and its major metabolite, acetaldehyde, have a direct toxic effect on brain cells, hepatic cells, and the myocardium.

Detoxification

Mild alcohol withdrawal can sometimes be successfully managed with rest and adequate nutrition; hospitalization and medication are not always required (Whitfield et al. 1980). In many cases, however, it is necessary to detoxify the alcoholic by administering another sedative-hypnotic. Ethanol itself, barbiturates, benzodiazepines, chloral hydrate, and paraldehyde all will effectively suppress the ethanol withdrawal syndrome. Because of their safety and efficacy, benzodiazepines are now the preferred drug for the management of this condition (Jaffe 1981; Sellers and Kalant 1982). They produce little cardiovascular or respiratory depression and act without depressing rapid eye movement (REM) sleep. This permits more rapid dream recovery following the prolonged dream suppression caused by heavy drinking. The patient is initially given enough medication to rapidly eliminate withdrawal symptoms and establish a state of very mild sedation. The drug is then gradually withdrawn over three to seven days.

The most common drug used for alcohol detoxification is chlordiazepoxide. This benzodiazepine, with its long-acting metabolites, is an ideal choice for routine uncomplicated alcohol withdrawal because of its low incidence of side effects, low abuse potential, and slow elimination from the body. After three to five days of administration, the drug self-tapers, producing a gradual, smooth drop in blood level over the next ten to fourteen days. Thus, chlordiazepoxide is preferred in public detoxification facilities where patients may often be discharged in three to five days or where there is a risk that the patient will leave the hospital prematurely. It is also the drug of choice for

fication, a procedure that can be recommended only for relatively stable patients following a brief drinking episode. Diazepam has similar pharmacokinetics because of its long-acting metabolites and is an appropriate alternative to chlordiazepoxide. However, diazepam should be avoided in those alcoholics known to abuse it.

It is now common practice in many inpatient settings to use short-acting benzodiazepines such as lorazepam or oxazepam for ethanol detoxification. These drugs require closer monitoring and adjustment of the patient's medication status and require a setting with adequate nursing support. Because of their more rapid elimination from the body, a smooth detoxification requires that the patient be dosed somewhat longer and that the dose be gradually tapered. This seems to work best in settings where the patient can remain in the hospital for two to three weeks following detoxification and where there is adequate structure and emotional support to help him or her remain abstinent.

The short-acting benzodiazepines are particularly helpful in the management of patients with other complicating medical problems, such as severe liver disease, or for elderly patients on multiple medications who present problems because of the risk of oversedation or unexpected drug interactions. Lorazepam has the added advantage that it is effective orally, intramuscularly, and intravenously.

For alcoholics who are also heavy smokers, higher doses of benzodiazepines may be needed because nicotine appears to increase the metabolism of benzodiazepines.

It has been suggested that the detoxification process can be facilitated and shortened by using ancillary medications that act to moderate the hyperactivity of the autonomic nervous system (Baumgartner and Rowen 1987; Rozenbloom 1988). Beta-blockers, such as propranolol, as well as alpha-adrenergic agonists, such as clonidine, have been reported to normalize vital signs rapidly and have been suggested for use alone, or in combination with benzodiazepines, to reduce the length of stay in hospital for detoxification. This procedure cannot be recommended, since these drugs do not suppress the underlying CNS hyperactivity and thus may mask the development of delirium tremens, a potentially life-threatening event.

The appropriate prevention for delirium tremens is adequate sedation with benzodiazepines. Diphenylhydantoin has been used routinely as a part of the treatment of ethanol withdrawal. This practice should be avoided unless there is a history of seizures unrelated to ethanol withdrawal. If the patient develops hallucinosis that is unresponsive to adequate doses of benzodiazepines, a dopaminergic blocker such as haloperidol (1 to 2 milligrams intramuscularly) should be given (Sellers and Kalant 1982).

Outpatient detoxification can be considered in those situations where the drinking episode has been brief, the patient is well known to the physician,

Table 3–1
Standard Benzodiazepine Dosing Schedule

Initial Loading Dose
Chlordiazepoxide, 100 mg PO q.h. 2 until mildly sedated
Diazepam, 20 mg PO q.h. until mildly sedated
Lorazepam, 2 mg PO q.h. until mildly sedated
Oxazepam, 30 mg PO q.h. until mildly sedated

Detoxification Dose

	Day 1	Day 2	Day 3	Day 4
Chlordiazepoxide 100 mg	q. 6 h.	q. 8 h.	q. 12 h.	q. 12 h.
Diazepam 20 mg	q. 6 h.	q. 8 h.	q. 12 h.	q.h.s.
Lorazepam 2–3 mg	q. 6 h.	Varies with patient's status*		
Oxazepam 30 mg	q. 4 h.	Varies with patient's status*		

Note: mg = milligrams; PO = by mouth, orally; q.h. = hourly; q. 6. h. = give every 6 hours; q.h.s. = give dose at bedtime.

*Gradual detoxification with the short-acting benzodiazepines should be spread out over ten to fourteen days.

and there is an adequate and supportive home environment, no history of seizures, no prior episodes of delirium tremens, and no evidence of polydrug abuse. Chlordiazepoxide is preferred for outpatient detoxification because of its low abuse potential and its long duration of action. Table 3–1 lists the standard benzodiazepine dosing schedule.

Inhibitors of Ethanol Metabolism

Drugs that interrupt the metabolism of ethanol also have been used as therapeutic agents in the treatment of alcoholism. The normal hepatic metabolism of ethanol involves three steps:

1. The oxidation of ethanol to acetaldehyde, which is catalyzed by the enzyme alcohol dehydrogenase
2. The oxidation of acetaldehyde to acetic acid, which is catalyzed by aldehyde dehydrogenase
3. The metabolism of acetate of CO_2 and H_2O

In attempts to discourage drinking by deliberately linking the ingestion of ethanol to an unpleasant reaction, two drugs have proven useful because of their ability to inhibit the enzyme aldehyde dehydrogenase. Disulfiram and carbimide both disrupt the metabolism of ethanol and cause a rapid elevation of acetaldehyde in the blood. Were an alcoholic to drink while on these drugs, blood levels of acetaldehyde would go up quickly, causing nausea, vomiting, facial flushing, dizziness, pounding in the chest, and an acute sense of respiratory distress. While generally nonlethal as long as drinking stops immediately, the experience can be quite frightening and acts as a strong adversive conditioner against further drinking.

Since effective blood levels of disulfiram can remain in the system for two to seven days after the drug is taken, it can be useful as a deterrent against impulsive drinking. Carbimide is much shorter acting and must be taken twice a day, requiring a high degree of patient motivation and compliance for effective treatment.

Studies have generally shown that disulfiram is ineffective when prescribed outside of an ongoing treatment relationship or an otherwise structured rehabilitation program (Gerrein, Rosenberg, and Manohar 1973). In large, multicenter double-blind studies, it has been difficult to prove that disulfiram is any more effective than a placebo in the treatment of alcoholism (Fuller et al. 1986). Many clinicians, however, prescribe it on a regular basis and are convinced of its benefit in selected cases. It must be remembered that placebos can sometimes be powerful adjuncts to treatment, particularly when both the patient and the physician believe that it will be helpful. In conditions that can be as difficult to manage as alcoholism, it may be foolish to ignore such a potentially useful medication.

Another drug used to produce conditioned aversion to alcohol is emetine. This drug causes nausea and vomiting and is given along with the patient's favorite beverage so that the alcoholic begins to associate the unpleasant effects of the emetine with the alcohol. Lithium also has been used as an emetic in some successful aversion conditioning programs. One recent experiment showed 36 percent abstinence in experimental subjects at a six-month follow-up versus 12 percent abstinence in controls (Jaffe 1987).

Control of Craving

Clinicians have long sought a drug that would eliminate the desire to drink and thus theoretically "cure" the patient's alcoholism. Many psychotropic medications have been tried, with little evidence of success. In those cases where it was clear that the patient was using alcohol to self-medicate some underlying psychiatric disease, effective treatment of the primary problem has sometimes eliminated the drinking. In most alcoholics, however, the drinking takes on a life of its own, regardless of any underlying psychopathology, and usually continues regardless of the presence or absence of the initial precipitant.

It is difficult to define the nature of craving. Is it a strong preference for the taste of alcohol? Is it a desire to escape from some chronic state of dysphoria or a low-level depression? Is it an effort to relieve a chronic anxiety state or an adult form of attention deficit disorder (ADD)?

Lithium is the only standard psychotropic medication that has shown some promise as a control of the craving for alcohol. In placebo-controlled double-blind studies in normals and recently detoxified alcoholics, lithium was found to reduce the desire to drink and to blunt the sense of intoxication produced by alcohol (Judd and Huey 1984). Many of the other studies of lithium in alcoholics have had methodologic difficulties and have not provided solid proof that there is any clinically significant reduction in drinking. At present, lithium appears to be most helpful in depressed alcoholics who are compliant with medication and maintain lithium levels greater than 0.4 milliequivalents per liter (Fawcett et al. 1984). There is no clear evidence that it is helpful in the treatment of nondepressed alcoholics.

Treatment of Concurrent Psychiatric Disorders

There is a high incidence of psychiatric symptomatology in detoxified alcoholics. Most complaints of depression, anxiety, and insomnia are part of the withdrawal syndrome and will clear during the course of detoxification. These complaints do not require specific treatment unless they continue beyond four weeks after the alcoholic attains sobriety. Since it is clear that some alcoholics may also abuse other sedatives, tranquilizers, stimulants, and even antidepressants, caution must be used when prescribing any psychoactive drugs (Hyatt and Bird 1987).

Up to 15 percent of alcoholics report significant levels of depression even after several weeks of sobriety. While such patients are commonly treated with tricyclic antidepressants, there is little evidence to document their efficacy, even in alcoholics with a major depression that clearly predated their drinking (Schuckit 1986). It is now recognized that chronic alcohol ingestion induces hepatic microsomal activity that results in lowered plasma levels of tricyclic antidepressants. Most studies of the efficacy of these drugs in alcoholics have used doses that were probably inadequate. However, there has been one study of doxepin and one study of amitriptyline that reported improvement in depression in selected alcoholics (Jaffe and Ciraulo 1985). Other work also has suggested that desipramine in high doses may be effective (Ciraulo, Barnhill, and Jaffe 1988). In treating depression in alcoholics, it is important to monitor blood levels of tricyclics to ensure that the drug is being given at therapeutic levels.

Alcoholics with bipolar affective disease should be treated with lithium, using standard doses. Effective control of mood swings can be expected to reduce drinking in manic patients, who often use alcohol to moderate their highs. There is some evidence that lithium also reduces the overall desire to drink (see the previous section).

Complaints of anxiety and insomnia may continue for months after the completion of detoxification. Because of their concern about using any drug likely to cause dependence, most clinicians prefer to manage these complaints without medication. While benzodiazepines are standard medications for these symptoms, no well-designed studies document their efficacy in the alcoholic. It remains to be proven whether some sober alcoholics can sustain sobriety through the controlled, nonabusive long-term use of benzodiazepines. Because active drinkers are notorious for their abuse of such medications, such use should not be encouraged. Evaluations have suggested, however, that fewer than 2 to 3 percent of sober alcoholics prescribed benzodiazepines actually abuse such drugs (Krypsin-Exner and Demel 1975). Sober alcoholics who are on stable doses of benzodiazepines but are unable to eliminate their use voluntarily should not be forced to detoxify unless there is clear evidence that they are abusing the medication.

Cocaine

Mechanism of Action

Cocaine is a naturally occurring local anesthetic that also acts as a powerful CNS stimulant. The initial euphoric effect is caused by activation of the dopamine (DA) reward centers in the midbrain. Dopamine pathways are stimulated because cocaine blocks the reuptake of DA at the synapse (Wise 1985). Cocaine also may act like tricyclic antidepressants by blocking the reuptake of NE (Dackis and Gold 1988). In addition to the sense of euphoria, the increased levels of DA and NE at the synapses trigger the classic "fight or flight" response of the sympathetic nervous system, with increased alertness, heart rate, respiration, blood pressure, and temperature. There is also a reduced need for food and sleep.

With chronic cocaine use, there is a general depletion of DA and NE levels in the brain. It is suspected that this occurs because chronic reuptake blockade prevents the recycling of free DA, which is then destroyed by metabolic processes at the synapse. The resulting depletion of DA in reward centers in the brain is hypothesized to cause the symptoms of cocaine withdrawal and the craving for continued cocaine use. Chronic depletion of brain NE is thought to explain the symptoms of depression seen during the withdrawal crashing phase; this produces sleep disturbances, suicidal ideation, loss of energy, anhedonia, and loss of interest in sex.

Management of Acute Withdrawal

A cocaine binge is usually terminated when the supply of the drug (or money) is exhausted. After several hours of intense craving for more cocaine, associated with extreme agitation, insomnia, and depression with possible suicidal ideation, the user goes into a period lasting for two to four days during which there is no craving and a gradually increasing desire to sleep that leads into a period of hypersomnolence (Gawin and Kleber 1986). During the next one to three weeks, moods and sleep patterns are stable, and there is little interest in cocaine use. During the next two months, however, the former user experiences a strong craving for cocaine and complains of anhedonia—a lack of pleasure or gratification from any of the normal activities of his or her life. Figure 3–1 illustrates the phases following a cocaine binge.

Since the acute withdrawal period is brief and not life threatening, there has generally been little interest in pharmacologic treatment. However, our growing understanding of the neural mechanisms that underlie the withdrawal process has led to various pharmacologic interventions geared to reducing the craving for cocaine. Different drugs have been tried based on their capacity to affect the DA and NE systems in the brain. The DA agonists bromocriptine, L-dopa, and amantadine have been used with some apparent success (Dackis, Gold, and Pottash 1987). They are thought to activate postsynaptic DA receptors. Bromocriptine had been used primarily to treat Parkinson's disease. It produces a fairly prompt clinical response during cocaine withdrawal, with improved mood and reduced craving. However, it appears to lose its effectiveness after ten to fourteen days. Table 3–2 lists the bromocriptine regimen for cocaine withdrawal.

The antiviral drug amantadine hydrochloride also has anti-Parkinson activity, but it seems to be less effective than bromocriptine in controlling symptoms related to cocaine withdrawal.

Various tricyclic antidepressants also have been used to treat the acute withdrawal state because of their ability to potentiate NE neurotransmission. Desipramine (up to 200 milligrams per day) has been thought to be the most effective in relieving postcocaine depression; it is also thought to help normalize DA levels. The main disadvantage of the tricyclics is their delayed onset of clinical effect. The worst feelings of depression and the greatest risk of suicide occur during the first two to three days following the end of the cocaine run. Desipramine does not begin to have significant antidepressant effects until ten to fourteen days after the start of treatment. For these reasons, it has been recommended that bromocriptine and desipramine be started on admission. The bromocriptine provides more immediate symptomatic relief; it can be stopped after two weeks, when the desipramine should begin to produce an antidepressant effect and to reduce craving (Extein and Gold 1988).

Phase 1
Crash
9 Hours to 4 Days

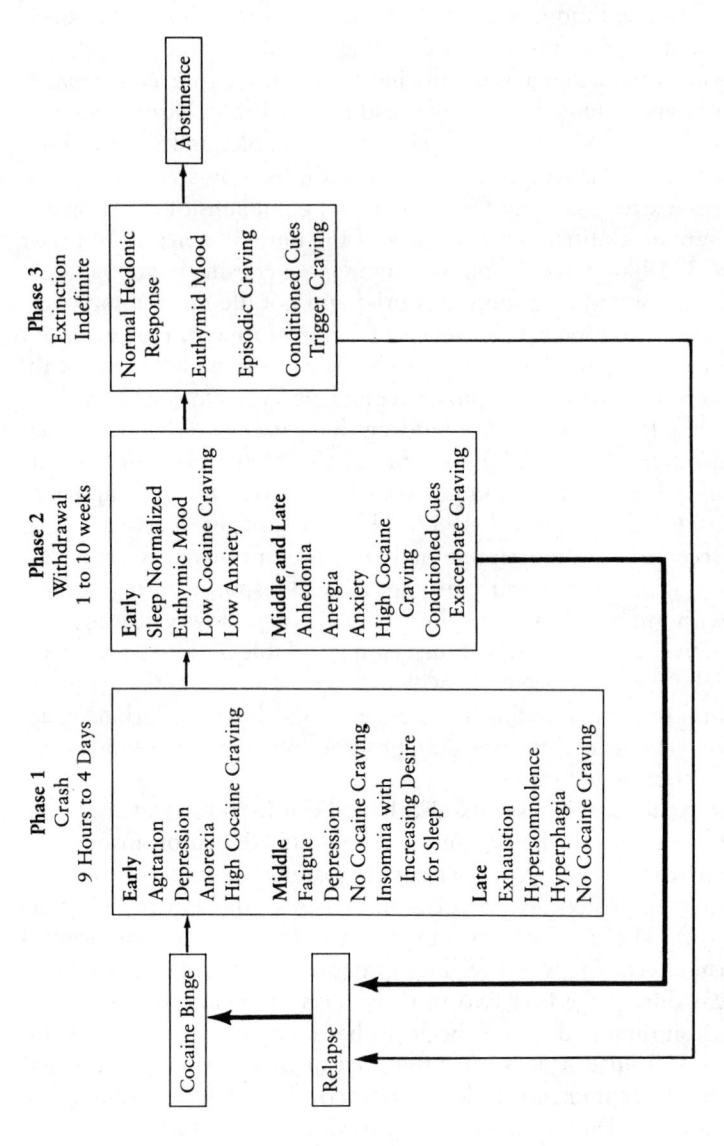

Early
Agitation
Depression
Anorexia
High Cocaine Craving

Middle
Fatigue
Depression
No Cocaine Craving
Insomnia with Increasing Desire for Sleep

Late
Exhaustion
Hypersomnolence
Hyperphagia
No Cocaine Craving

Phase 2
Withdrawal
1 to 10 weeks

Early
Sleep Normalized
Euthymic Mood
Low Cocaine Craving
Low Anxiety

Middle and Late
Anhedonia
Anergia
Anxiety
High Cocaine Craving
Conditioned Cues Exacerbate Craving

Phase 3
Extinction
Indefinite

Normal Hedonic Response
Euthymid Mood
Episodic Craving
Conditioned Cues Trigger Craving

Cocaine Binge → Relapse → Abstinence

Figure 3–1. Phases following a cocaine binge. The duration and intensity of symptoms vary depending on the binge characteristics and coexisting psychiatric diagnoses.

Source: Gawin, F.H. and H.D. Kleber. "Abstinence Symptomatology and Psychiatric Diagnosis in Cocaine Abusers," *Archives of General Psychiatry* 43:110 (1986).

Table 3–2
Bromocriptine Regimen for Cocaine Withdrawal

Day	Bromocriptine Dose	Frequency
1–2	1.25 mg	b.i.d.*
3–4	1.25 mg	t.i.d.**
5–6	2.5 mg	b.i.d.
7–11	2.5 mg	t.i.d.
12–14	5 mg	b.i.d.
15–20	Decrease by approximately 50% every two days.	

Source: C.A. Dackis and M.S. Gold, "Psychopharmacology of Cocaine," *Psychiatric Annals* 18: 529 (1988).
Note: Titration of the dose is necessary with anticraving and antiwithdrawal effects weighed against possible side effects. Lower doses than listed above are often sufficient. Maintenance bromocriptine treatment may be necessary if symptoms recur after discontinuation.
*Twice a day.
**Three times a day.

Long-Term Management

Two to three months after the end of a period of cocaine use, patients begin an extended period where moods are normal but there is still periodic craving. They remain vulnerable to recurrent use, particularly in response to conditioned environmental clues (see figure 3–1).

There has been very little solid research on the long-term pharmacotherapy of cocaine abuse. Most of the reported studies have followed patients on medication for only eight to ten weeks, and they provide little information on the possible longer term efficacy of bromocriptine, desipramine, and other medications (Gawin 1986).

Treatment of Concurrent Psychiatric Disorders

The most common psychiatric disorders found in cocaine abusers are major depressive disorder (30 percent), bipolar or cyclothymic disorder (15 percent), and ADD (3 to 6 percent) (Gawin 1986). As noted previously, there is little information on the long-term use of antidepressants in this population.

Similar problems exist regarding treatment with lithium. There have been few well-controlled studies of lithium in this population, but the general impression is that lithium is of no benefit except in those cocaine abusers who also present clear evidence of bipolar disease (Gawin 1986). There is little evidence that lithium is effective against primary cocaine dependence. However, all cocaine abusers should be screened carefully for bipolar affective disease and should be treated with lithium whenever indicated.

Three to four percent of cocaine addicts have a history of residual type ADD. ADD also has been associated with a dopamine-deficient state, and dopamine agonists have provided effective treatment (Wender 1975). In cocaine abusers with ADD, it has been reported that methylphenidate is useful in reducing craving and preventing relapse (Khantzian 1983). Other clinicians have reported improvement in ADD and decreased cocaine abuse in these patients when treated with bromocriptine (Cocores et al. 1987).

Benzodiazepines

Mechanism of Action

Benzodiazepines are widely prescribed because of their effectiveness in reducing anxiety. Unlike barbiturates and meprobamate, they have a wide margin of safety when taken in overdoses, have less severe and fewer side effects, and thus have generally replaced these drugs as antianxiety medications.

Specific benzodiazepine binding sites have been found in the CNS, particularly in the cortical and the limbic-forebrain areas. Benzodiazepines have a very high affinity for these sites; the affinity of a given benzodiazepine generally parallels its pharmacologic activity in humans and animals (Greenblatt, Shader, and Abernethy 1983). This binding to the receptor enhances the inhibitory function of the neurotransmitter GABA by increasing chloride permeability, which hyperpolarizes (inhibits) the neuron (Paul, Crawley, and Skolnick 1986). Because this effect on GABA-mediated neurons reduces brain excitation, all benzodiazepines (in increasing levels of dose and brain concentration) act as anxiolytics, sedative-hypnotics, and anticonvulsants. Long-term treatment with benzodiazepines reduces GABA activity. If the drug is stopped abruptly, there is a rebound hyperactivity assumed to be caused by low levels of GABA production (Snyder 1981). This rebound hyperactivity causes the symptoms associated with benzodiazepine withdrawal.

At least two different benzodiazepine receptors have been identified. Type I receptors are thought to mediate the antianxiety effect, and Type II receptors mediate the sedative effect. Clinical experience has demonstrated that tolerance develops to the sedative effect but rarely to the antianxiety effect, thus supporting the dual receptor hypothesis (Snyder 1981; Hollister et al. 1981). Cross-tolerance exists between the benzodiazepines and other CNS depressants such as alcohol and barbiturates. Combinations of these drugs have an additive effect and can be lethal in overdose situations.

It was initially thought that benzodiazepines did not produce dependence. However, dependence has been observed with high doses of all the benzodiazepines and also can occur when average therapeutic doses are taken over long periods of time (Lader 1983). Patients taking two to five times the prescribed dose have developed dependence within three weeks (Woody, O'Brien, and Greenstein 1975; Relkin 1966). For long-term patients on regular, nonescalating doses, 27 to 45 percent can be expected to show symptoms of withdrawal (Tyler, Rutherford, and Huggett 1981). Withdrawal symptoms are of the classic sedative-hypnotic type and include anxiety, insomnia, irritability, depression, tremor, nausea or vomiting, anorexia, blurred vision, and, rarely, psychotic manifestations (paranoid reactions and visual hallucinations) and seizures (Lader 1983; Hollister, Motzenbecker, and Degan 1961). Withdrawal symptoms have been similar in quantity and quality in both high- and low-dose patients (Hallstrom and Lader 1981). Since many of these symptoms are the same as the complaints for which the patient was initially treated, it is often difficult to distinguish withdrawal (rebound anxiety) from the original symptoms. Withdrawal symptoms, however, generally abate within one to two weeks.

Among the commonly prescribed benzodiazepines, it has been suspected that those drugs with a more rapid onset of effect have a greater abuse liability, since this feature is highly valued by drug abusers. Thus, diazepam has been found to be abused more frequently than oxazepam (Griffiths and Sannerud 1987). Similarly, it has been suggested that the longer acting, self-tapering benzodiazepines will be less likely to produce severe withdrawal and will therefore be less abused. At present, there is no information to confirm this hypothesis (Ciraulo 1985). Table 3–3 lists the benzodiazepines in common use.

Table 3–3
Benzodiazepines in Common Use

Generic Name	Proprietary Name	Common Use
Long-acting benzodiazepines		
Chlordiazepoxide	Librium	Tranquilizer
Clonazepam	Klonopin	Anticonvulsant
Clorazepate	Tranxene	Tranquilizer
Diazepam	Valium	Tranquilizer
Flurazepam	Dalmane	Insomnia
Halazepam	Paxipam	Tranquilizer
Prazepam	Verstran Centrax	Tranquilizer
Temazepam	Restoril	Insomnia
Triazolam	Halcion	Insomnia
Short-acting benzodiazepines		
Lorazepam	Ativan	Tranquilizer
Alprazolam	Xanax	Tranquilizer
Oxazepam	Serax	Tranquilizer

Detoxification

When patients are detoxified from benzodiazepines, they should be warned to expect a temporary increase in symptoms of anxiety as part of the withdrawal process. Unless these symptoms continue for more than four weeks, they should not be considered manifestations of a primary psychiatric condition. Since the course of many anxiety disorders is intermittent, there is no reason to expect that all patients will continue to be symptomatic or require ongoing medication.

The self-taper approach has been the most common way to manage benzodiazepine detoxification. For long-acting benzodiazepines, the dose should be reduced 5 milligrams per week; for short-acting benzodiazepines, the dose should be reduced 2 milligrams per week. During the initial dose cuts, the patient may experience no symptoms. Symptoms usually appear after a few cuts in dose, however. At that point, the rate of tapering should be slowed, and symptoms caused by each dose reduction should be allowed to clear before instituting the next cut. The final cuts may be the most difficult for the patient and should be carried out as slowly as is necessary to minimize withdrawal symptoms. For highly psychologically dependent patients, an extended taper using very small doses given every other day is recommended (Noyes et al. 1988).

An alternative approach is to switch the patient from short-acting drugs to long-acting benzodiazepines prior to starting the taper. Chlordiazepoxide is preferred because it is less likely than diazepam to produce euphoria. There is less fluctuation in blood level, and patients can be easily managed on a single daily dose at the end of the taper.

In some cases, it has been difficult to switch from some of the high-potency, short-acting benzodiazepines such as alprazolam to long-acting drugs without some acute withdrawal symptoms. This can be controlled by switching to clonazepam, a high-potency, long-acting drug (Herman, Rosenbaum, and Brotman 1957) or by using high doses of diazepam. For control of the withdrawal symptoms from alprazolam, dose ratios of 1 milligram alprazolam to 24 milligrams diazepam have been required (Votolato, Batcha, and Olson 1987).

Adjunctive medication has been of little value in moderating benzodiazepine withdrawal. Buspirone has no cross-tolerance with the benzodiazepines and thus is not useful in controlling withdrawal symptoms. Alpha-adrenergic agonists (clonidine) and beta-adrenergic blockers (propranolol) have not been particularly effective. They may reduce the severity of some physiological withdrawal symptoms, but they do little to control the patients' subjective feelings of anxiety (Goodman et al. 1986; Tyler, Rutherford, and Huggett 1981).

For patients with a preexisting anxiety disorder or depression, concomitant treatment with a low dose of a sedating tricyclic antidepressant, such as doxepin or amitriptyline, or imipramine in standard doses may be useful. These tricyclics should be started two weeks before beginning withdrawal from the benzodiazepine; they are effective antianxiety agents and will help to control any underlying anxiety symptoms that might reemerge during withdrawal (Noyes et al. 1988).

Substitution Therapy

The long-term use of benzodiazepines is a controversial subject. There have been few studies documenting the efficacy of these drugs for the long-term control of anxiety. As noted above, tolerance does not develop to the anxiolytic action of the benzodiazepines, even though patients may develop physical dependence even on normal therapeutic doses (Snyder 1981; Lader 1983). Despite the concerns of many clinicians, most patients do not escalate their doses or otherwise abuse these medications. The primary abuse of these agents occurs among young adults, who take benzodiazepines specifically to get high. Even among sober alcoholics, the majority of patients maintained on long-term benzodiazepines do not abuse the drugs (Ciraulo, Sands, and Shader 1988). In fact, maintenance on such medication may be crucial to the maintenance of the patient's sobriety. While it is always preferable that patients be managed without medication, long-term benzodiazepine maintenance may often be preferable to recurrent bouts of alcoholism (Rickels 1987). The use of such medication in a recovering alcoholic should always be carefully monitored. However, only a small minority of patients will abuse anxiolytic agents. Those recovering alcoholics with appropriately diagnosed anxiety disorders can be safely treated if rational prescribing practices are followed (Ciraulo, Sands, and Shader 1988).

Many patients on long-term treatment with benzodiazepines are physiologically and psychologically dependent on the medication, but they do not escalate the dose, combine it with alcohol or other drugs, or otherwise show evidence of drug abuse. It is therefore inappropriate to consider these patients to be drug addicts. Careful longitudinal studies are needed to evaluate this long-term use of benzodiazepines. Regardless of the presence of psychiatric symptoms that justify the long-term use of medication, it may be impossible to detoxify some of these patients successfully. It may well be appropriate to legitimize the indefinite maintenance of such patients on these drugs. Even though clonazepam is the only benzodiazepine approved by the FDA for chronic use, this does not reflect the standard medical use of many other benzodiazepines.

Nicotine

Mechanism of Action

After almost twenty-five years of public debate, Americans have finally come to terms with the fact that nicotine is an addicting drug with devastating health effects. Tobacco, primarily through the action of nicotine, has a profound effect on the brain, the autonomic nervous system, and many other body tissues. It is primarily a CNS stimulant that produces a mild sense of euphoria and an experience of increased energy and alertness; it also improves the user's ability to concentrate. Performance is improved on tasks requiring concentration and recall. Following this initial sense of increased alertness, there is a sense of calm and relaxation; decreased muscle tone can be observed in the legs and arms, and there is a decrease in stomach contractions. At the same time, there is an increase in heart rate and blood pressure. These actions are probably mediated by both the direct effect of nicotine and the release of various neurotransmitters, such as epinephrine. All these effects can be highly reinforcing. The regular user also develops tolerance and requires increasing doses to maintain the same level of drug effect.

It has been reported that children who are depressed in high school are almost twice as likely to become heavy smokers as compared with their nondepressed peers (Kandel and Davies 1986). No similar connection was found between depression in adolescence and adult addiction to any other drug. Glassman et al. (1969) noted a high incidence of depression in adults seeking medical treatment to help stop smoking. Men have been found to be more successful in smoking cessation programs than women, and women have been reported to be more depressed. Depression was noted to be the greatest single predictor of failure in smoking cessation programs.

When nicotine is stopped abruptly, the chronic user experiences withdrawal symptoms that begin within a few hours and last for several days. Symptoms can include craving for tobacco, restlessness, inability to concentrate, anxiety, headache, drowsiness, and gastrointestinal disturbances (American Psychiatric Association Staff, 1987). Sleep abnormalities can be demonstrated to include increases in sleep latency, REM, and total REM time. Abnormal sleep patterns may continue for months after stopping smoking, and craving for tobacco can continue for even longer periods.

It has also been suggested that smoking and nicotine withdrawal affect the neurotransmitter systems that are involved in major psychiatric disorders (Balfour 1984). Nicotine has been reported to alter the pharmacokinetics of various psychiatric medications; smoking appears to decrease the therapeutic effects of the tricyclic antidepressants, the benzodiazepines, and chlorpromazine (Dawson, Vestal, and Jusko 1984; Miller 1977; Pantuck et al. 1982). Heavy smokers may require higher than average doses of all of these medications. Since there is a very high incidence of smoking in chronic psychiatric patients (88 percent of schizophrenics and 70 percent of manic depressives), these findings have important implications for the management of large numbers of patients (Hughes and Hatsukami 1986; Gralnick 1988).

Detoxification

Most smokers find that the symptoms associated with the abrupt cessation of smoking are difficult to endure. There are two primary pharmacologic options to help moderate the withdrawal process. As with many other addictive drugs, a gradual detoxification may significantly reduce withdrawal symptoms. This can be done by having the patient gradually reduce the number of cigarettes used daily. This procedure may be enhanced by asking the patient to switch to his or her least favored brand of cigarettes or to a brand with lower nicotine content (nicotine fading).

If this approach is not successful, the smoker is told to immediately switch to nicotine gum. Each stick of gum contains 2 milligrams of nicotine bound to an ion-exchange resin. The gum should be held on the tongue and chewed gently over thirty minutes to avoid too rapid a release of nicotine. The patient also must be cautioned to avoid swallowing for at least one minute after a bout of chewing, to give the nicotine time to be absorbed through the oral mucosa. Since drinks with an acid pH such as alcohol, coffee, tea and soft drinks prevent nicotine absorption, the patient should wait for fifteen minutes after drinking such beverages before using nicotine gum. Twenty to thirty pieces of gum per twenty-four hours will generally be necessary for someone who has been smoking more than fifteen cigarettes per day (Schuckit 1988). The number of sticks of gum used is reduced gradually each day. This treatment approach should be avoided in patients with peptic ulcer disease, those with inflammations of the mouth, throat, or esophagus, and those with recent heart attacks or cardiac arrythmias.

Another pharmacologic option is the use of clonidine. Because of its capacity to reduce symptoms associated with overactivity of the autonomic nervous system, this drug has been used to moderate withdrawal symptoms associated with opiates, alcohol, and other sedatives. It has been reported to reduce craving for tobacco and to reduce symptoms of anxiety and restlessness during nicotine withdrawal. In one study, 27 percent of the subjects treated with clonidine were still not smoking at a six-month follow-up, compared with only 5 percent of the controls who were treated with a placebo (Glassman et al. 1969). At this time, there are still relatively few studies of the use of clonidine with tobacco addicts, and one needs to be alert to the development of side effects such as hypotension, sedation, and impotence (Schuckit 1988).

Nicotine addicts also should be carefully screened for depression or anxiety disorders. Because of the possibility that some smokers may be using tobacco as a form of self-medication, it may be helpful to initiate pharmacologic treatment for these disorders as an adjunct to the treatment of nicotine withdrawal.

Various supportive therapies and behavioral techniques also should be used. None of these pharmacologic treatments should be initiated outside of a more comprehensive "stop smoking" program (Goldstein et al. 1989).

Nicotine Replacement Therapy

It is apparent that some former smokers have become chronic users of other forms of nicotine. The degree to which other preparations, such as nicotine gum, will eliminate the health risks of cigarettes is unclear. It is possible that a significant black market could develop in these products. In their excellent review of the pharmacologic treatments for tobacco dependence, Jarvik and Henningfield (1988) noted that cigarette smoking can be reduced by nicotine gum, intravenous nicotine, buccal administration of nicotine in capsule form, nasal administration of nicotine in liquid form, and transdermal nicotine administration. Only the gum has been approved by the FDA, and it seems clear that the FDA's intent is that the gum be used exclusively for detoxification. It has not been recommended for replacement or maintenance therapy. Since some detoxification programs can extend over six months, however, it is not clear when detoxification ends and some form of maintenance (or replacement) begins.

Nicotine Antagonists

Several drugs are known to be nicotine antagonists, but only mecamylamine, which acts both centrally and peripherally, is functionally effective on patterns of cigarette smoking in humans. Antagonists that act only peripherally, such as pentolinium and hexamethonium, are less effective. In one study, mecamylamine plus counseling reduced craving in thirteen of fourteen subjects; half of the subjects quit smoking within two weeks (Tennant, Tarver, and Rawson 1984). At the time of quitting, the mean dose of mecamylamine was 26.7 milligrams per day. Despite being a nicotine antagonist, this drug also seems to have a sedative effect and to moderate withdrawal symptoms. This study needs to be repeated with placebo controls before the value of this treatment approach can be adequately assessed. Patient compliance will probably be a problem with this drug, as it is with the narcotic antagonists. Mecamylamine also has an anticholinergic antihypertensive effect that limits its use.

Pharmacologic Deterrents

Analogous to the use of disulfiram with the alcoholic, silver acetate taken in a gum preparation has been used to deter cigarette smoking. This compound reacts with the sulfides in tobacco smoke to produce sulfide salts that most people find extremely distasteful (Malcolm et al. 1986). Patient compliance is a problem with this approach. Each piece of gum is effective for only a few hours, and it must be taken repeatedly during the day. Until a longer acting deterrent is developed, it is unlikely that this approach will be of any major clinical significance.

Polydrug Abuse

Patterns of Use

One of the most striking changes in drug abuse patterns in the past two decades has been the growth of polysubstance abuse and a frequent pattern of a primary addiction coupled with recurrent ancillary drug use. It is becoming increasingly rare to find drug abusers who have used only one drug.

Alcohol and tobacco remain the most commonly used and abused drugs in our culture; it is not always clear which one serves as the common gateway into the drug world. Close behind is marijuana, which in 1983 was used on a regular basis by 27 percent of young adults (National Institute on Drug Abuse 1983). Twelve percent of this age group were also using heroin, cocaine, hallucinogens, or other psychoactive drugs each month, usually in combination with alcohol. In 1985, Galizio and Maistro reported that more than 80 percent of alcoholics below the age of thirty also abused at least one other drug, usually marijuana or cocaine.

Many of these drugs act to potentiate the high produced by drugs in other pharmacologic classes. It is generally appreciated that all of the sedative hypnotics have an additive effect and can be lethal, particularly in combination with alcohol. It is less widely known that the benzodiazepines potentiate opiates and that cocaine may cause the release of endogenous opioids, and thus augment the effect of heroin (Blumberg and Ikeda 1978). The pharmacologic interactions of these drugs and the intriguing complexity of some of the CNS receptors are only partially understood. Initially it was thought that ethanol and the barbiturates did not interact directly with the benzodiazepine binding site (receptor) in the CNS. It is now clear that the GABA–benzodiazepine receptor–chloride complex is affected by ethanol, barbiturates, other anxiolytics, and other anticonvulsant drugs (Paul, Crawley, and Skolnick 1986).

Problems in Patient Management

A detailed discussion of the management of acute polydrug overdoses is beyond the scope of this chapter. Nonetheless, all clinicians should be alert to identifying the special problems presented by these patients. Questions about multiple drug use must be included in all evaluations. Since patients frequently deny or minimize such behavior, a polydrug urine screen should be obtained on all drug program inpatients, on any applicants for methadone maintenance, and on any patients suspected of such drug use. Alcohol or drug programs that specialize in treating only one type of substance abuse should be particularly careful in identifying such patients. Multiple drug abuse should be suspected whenever a patient fails to respond to standard treatment approaches.

Anxiety and insomnia are common complaints during detoxification and withdrawal from most drugs of abuse. Patients often request ancillary medications for these complaints; this is to be avoided whenever possible. Slower detoxification or an increase in the dose of the primary medication are preferred ways to manage these complaints. Patients need to be reassured that the symptoms will gradually clear as long as they avoid other drugs. Proper sleeping habits should be encouraged, along with relaxation techniques or other behavioral interventions.

If complaints of insomnia persist during extended periods of sobriety, low doses of a sedating tricyclic antidepressant such as amitriptyline can be prescribed. Another option is L-tryptophan in doses of 2 to 4 milligrams at bedtime. Neither of these drugs is addicting, nor are they prone to abuse. However, some alcoholics have been reported to use large doses of amitriptyline (more than 500 milligrams) to potentiate the high of alcohol, so only moderate doses should be used (Hyatt and Bird 1987).

Methadone maintenance programs have had particular difficulty with patients who develop problems with alcohol, cocaine, or benzodiazepines once they realize that they can no longer get high on opiates. Behavioral controls, including frequent urine screens or breathalyzer checks, are helpful. Programs should always focus on total abstinence from all drugs as their primary treatment goal. If alcohol continues to be a problem, disulfiram, in combination with the methadone, can be given on a mandatory basis. As indicated earlier, there are few well-controlled studies to demonstrate the efficacy of this approach (Ling et al. 1983). Disulfiram is rarely helpful unless the patient also becomes active in a self-help program such as Alcoholics Anonymous or Narcotics Anonymous. Additional counseling and referral to Cocaine Anonymous should be mandatory for cocaine abusers, since there is no specific pharmacologic intervention for periodic cocaine use.

Polydrug abusers are more likely to have other psychiatric disorders than are individuals who abuse only one drug. Such patients should be evaluated carefully for major affective disorders, bipolar affective disease, and anxiety disorders. Appropriate pharmacologic treatment should be initiated as necessary. These patients can be difficult to treat and must be monitored closely because of their tendency to abuse all drugs, including those prescribed for concurrent psychiatric disorders. Pharmacologic intervention is not likely to be successful unless it is part of a comprehensive addiction rehabilitation program.

References

APA (American Psychiatric Association) staff. 1987. *Diagnostic and Statistical Manual of Mental Disorders, DSM-III-R.* 3rd, ed. Washington, D.C.: American Psychiatric Press.
Balfour, D.J.K. 1984. "The Effects of Nicotine on Brain Neurotransmitter Systems." In *Nicotine and the Tobacco Smoking Habit*, edited by D.J.K. Balfour, 61–74. New York: Pergamon Press.
Baumgartner, G.R., and R.C. Rowen. 1987. "Clonidine vs. Chlordiazepoxide in the Management of Acute Alcohol Withdrawal Syndrome." *Archives of Internal Medicine* 147:1223–26.
Blumberg, H., and C. Ikeda. 1978. "Naltrexone, Morphine and Cocaine Interactions in Mice and Rats." *Journal of Pharmacology and Experimental Therapeutics* 206:303–10.
Charney, D.S., D.E. Sternberg, H.D. Kleber, G.R. Heninger, and D.E. Richmond, Jr. 1981. "The Clinical Use of Clonidine in Abrupt Withdrawal from Methadone." *Archives of General Psychiatry* 38:1273–77.
Ciraulo, D.A. 1985. "Abuse Potential of Benzodiazepines." *Bulletin of the New York Academy of Medicine* 61:728–41.
Ciraulo, D.A., J.G. Barnhill, and J.H. Jaffe. 1988. "Clinical Pharmacokinetics of Imipramine and Desipramine in Alcoholics and Volunteers." *Clinical Pharmacology and Therapeutics* 43:509–18.
Ciraulo, D.A., B.F. Sands, and R.I. Shader. 1988. "Critical Review of Liability for Benzodiazepine Abuse among Alcoholics." *American Journal of Psychiatry* 145:1501–6.
Cocores, J.A., R.K. Davies, P.S. Mueller, and M.S. Gold. 1987. "Cocaine Abuse and Adult Attention Deficit Disorder." *Journal of Clinical Psychiatry* 48:376–77.
Dackis, C.A., and M.S. Gold. 1988. "Psychopharmacology of Cocaine." *Psychiatric Annals* 18:528–30.
Dackis, C.A., M.S. Gold, and A.L.C. Pottash. 1987. "Central Stimulant Abuse: Neurochemistry and Pharmacotherapy." *Advances in Alcohol and Substance Abuse* 6 (2): 7–21.
Dawson, G.W., R.E. Vestal, and W.J. Jusko. 1984. "Smoking and Drug Metabolism." In *Nicotine and the Tobacco Smoking Habit*, edited by D.J.K. Balfour, 210–15. New York: Pergamon Press.

Dole, V.P., M.E. Nyswander, and M.J. Kreek. 1966."Narcotic Blockade." *Archives of Internal Medicine* 181:304–9.

Extein, I.L., and M.S. Gold. 1988. "The Treatment of Cocaine Addicts: Bromocriptine or Desipramine." *Psychiatric Annals* 18:535–37.

Fawcett, J., D.C. Clark, R.D. Gibbons, C.A. Aageson, C.D. Pisani, and J.M. Tilkin. 1984. "Evaluation of Lithium Therapy for Alcoholism." *Journal of Clinical Psychiatry* 45:494–99.

Feldman, E.B. 1982. "Malnutrition in the Alcoholic and Related Nutritional Deficiences." In *Encyclopedic Handbook of Alcoholism,* edited by E.M. Pattison and E. Kaufman, 255–62. New York: Gardner Press.

Fuller, R.K., L. Branchey, D.R. Brightwell, R.M. Derman, C.D. Emrick, F.L. Iber, R.E. James, R.B. Lacoursier, K.K. Lee, and I. Lowenstam. 1986. "Disulfiram Treatment of Alcoholism." *Journal of the American Medical Association* 256:1449–55.

Galizio, M., and S.A. Maistro. 1985. *Determinants of Substance Abuse.* New York: Plenum Press.

Garbutt, G.D., and A. Goldstein. 1972. "Blind Comparison of Three Methadone Maintenance Dosages in 180 Patients." In *Proceedings of the Fourth National Conference on Methadone Treatment,* 411–14. New York: National Association for the Prevention of Addiction to Narcotics.

Gawin, F.H. 1986. "New Uses of Antidepressants in Cocaine Abuse." *Psychosomatics* 27 (Suppl): 24–29.

Gawin, F.H., and H.D. Kleber. 1986. "Abstinence Symptomatology and Psychiatric Diagnosis in Cocaine Abusers." *Archives of General Psychiatry* 43:107–13.

Gearing, F.R. 1971. "Evaluation of Methadone Maintenance Treatment Program." In *Methadone Maintenance,* edited by S. Einstein, 171–97. New York: Marcel Decker.

Gerrein, J.R., C.M. Rosenberg, and V. Manohar. 1973. "Disulfiram Maintenance in Outpatient Treatment of Alcoholism." *Archives of General Psychiatry* 28:798–802.

Ginsberg, H.M. 1986. "Naltrexone: Its Clinical Utility." In *Advances in Alcohol and Substance Abuse,* edited by B. Stimmel, 83–101. New York: Hawthorne Press.

Glassman, A.H., et al. 1988. "Heavy Smokers, Smoking Cessation, and Clonidine." *Journal of the American Medical Association* 259:2863–66.

Goldstein, M.G., R. Niaura, M.J. Follick, and D.B. Abrams. 1989. "Effects of Behavioral Skills Training and Schedule of Nicotine Gum Administration on Smoking Cessation." *American Journal of Psychiatry* 146:56–60.

Goodman, W.K., D.S. Charney, et al. 1986. "Ineffectiveness of Clonidine in the Treatment of the Benzodiazepine Withdrawal Syndrome: Report of Three Cases." *American Journal of Psychiatry* 143:900–3.

Gralnick, A. 1988. "Nicotine Addiction: Coping in the Psychiatric Hospital." *Carrier Foundation Letter.* 134:1–4.

Greenblatt, D.J., R.I. Shader, and D.R. Abernethy. 1983. "Current Status of Benzodiazepines." *New England Journal of Medicine* 309:354–58.

Griffiths, R.R., and C.A. Sannerud. 1987. "Abuse of and Dependence on Benzodiazepines and Other Anxiolytic/Sedative Drugs." In *Psychopharmacology: The Third Generation of Progress,* edited by H.Y. Meltzer, New York: Raven Press.

Hallstrom, C., and M.H. Lader. 1981. "Benzodiazepine Withdrawal Phenomena." *International Pharmacopsychiatry* 16:235–44.

Herman, J.B., J.F. Rosenbaum, and A.N. Brotman. 1987. "The Alprazolam to Clonazepam Switch for the Treatment of Panic Disorder." *Journal of Clinical Psychopharmacology* 7:175–78.

Hoffman, P.L. 1987. "Central Nervous System Effects of Neurophypophyseal Peptides." In *The Peptides*, vol. 8, edited by C.W. Smith, 239. New York: Academic Press.

Hoffman, P.L., and B. Tabakoff. 1985. "Ethanol's Action on Brain Biochemistry." In *Alcohol and the Brain: Chronic Effects*, edited by R.E. Tarter and D.H. Thiel, 19–68. New York: Plenum Press.

Hollister, L.E., F.K. Conley, et al. 1981. "Long-Term Use of Diazepam." *Journal of the American Medical Association* 246:1568–70.

Hollister, L.E., F.P. Motzenbecker, and R.O. Degan. 1961. "Withdrawal Reactions from Chlordiazepoxide." *Psychopharmacologia* 2:63–68.

Hughes, J.R., and D. Hatsukami. 1986. "Signs and Symptoms of Tobacco Withdrawal." *Archives of General Psychiatry* 43:286–94.

Hyatt, M.C., and M.A. Bird. 1987. "Amitriptyline Augments and Prolongs Ethanol-Induced Euphoria." *Journal of Clinical Psychopharmacology* 7:277–78.

Jaffee, J.H. 1987. "Pharmacological Agents in the Treatment of Drug Dependence." In *Psychopharmacology: The Third Generation of Progress*, edited by H.Y. Meltzer, 1605–16. New York: Raven Press.

Jaffe, J.H., and D. Ciraulo. 1985. "Drugs Used in the Treatment of Alcoholism." In *The Diagnosis and Treatment of Alcoholism*, edited by J.H. Mendelson and N.K. Mello, New York: McGraw-Hill.

Jarvik, M.E., and J.E. Henningfield. 1988. "Pharmacological Treatment of Tobacco Dependence." *Pharmacology, Biochemistry and Behavior* 30:279–94.

Judd, L.L., and L.Y. Huey. 1984. "Lithium Antagonizes Ethanol Intoxication in Alcoholics." *American Journal of Psychiatry* 141:1517–20.

Kandel, D.B., and M. Davies. 1986. "Adult Sequelae of Adolescent Depressive Symptoms." *Archives of General Psychiatry* 43:255–62.

Khanna, J.M., H. Kalant, A.D. Le, and A.E. LeBlanc. 1981. "Role of Serotonergic and Adrenergic Systems in Alcohol Tolerance." *Progress in Neuro-psychopharmacology and Biological Psychiatry* 5:459–65.

Khantzian, E.J. 1983. "An Extreme Case of Cocaine Dependence and Marked Improvement with Methylphenidate Treatment." *American Journal of Psychiatry* 140:784–85.

Khatami, S., B. Salasky, T. Shibuya, and P.L. Hoffman. 1987. "Selective Effects of Ethanol on Opiate Receptor Subtypes in Brain." *Nueropharmacology* 26:1503–7.

Kleber, H.D., M.M. Weissman, et al. 1983. "Imipramine as Treatment for Depression in Addicts." *Archives of General Psychiatry* 40:643–49.

Krypsin-Exner, K., and I. Demel. 1975. "The Use of Tranquilizers in the Treatment of Mixed Drug Abuse." *International Journal of Clinical Pharamacology Biopharmacy* 12:13.

Lader, M. 1983. "Dependence on Benzodiazepines." *Journal of Clinical Psychiatry* 44:121–27.

Leslie, S.W., E. Barr, et al. 1983. "Inhibition of Fast- and Slow-Phase Depolarization-Depenent Synaptosomal Calcium Uptake by Ethanol." *Journal of Pharmacology and Experimental Therapeutics* 225:571–75.

Ling, W., W. Dorus, W.A. Hargraves, R. Resnick, E. Senay, et al. 1984. "Alternative Induction and Crossover Schedule for Methadyl Acetate." *Archives of General Psychiatry* 41:193–99.

Ling, W., D.G. Weiss, V.C. Charuvastra, and C.P. O'Brien. 1983. "Use of Disulfiram for Alcoholics in Methadone Maintenance Programs." *Archives of General Psychiatry* 40:851–54.

Malcolm R., B.S. Currey, et al. 1986. "Silver Acetate Gum as a Deterrent to Smoking." *Chest* 10:107–11.

McLellan, A.T., L. Luborsky, G.E. Woody, C.P. O'Brien, and K.A. Druley. 1983. "Predicting Response to Alcohol and Drug Abuse Treatment." *Archives of General Psychiatry* 40:620–25.

Miller, R.R. 1977. "Effects of Smoking on Drug Action." *Clinical Pharmacology and Therapeutics* 22:749–56.

Musto, D.F. 1973. *The American Disease*. New Haven: Yale University Press.

National Institute on Drug Abuse. 1983. *Highlights from the National Survey in Drug Abuse: 1982*. DHHS pub. no. (ADM) 83-1277. Washington: GPO.

Noyes, R., M.J. Garvey, et al. 1988. "Benzodiazepine Withdrawal: A Review of the Evidence." *Journal of Clinical Psychiatry* 49:382–89.

Pantuck, E.J., C.B. Pantuck, K.C. Anderson, et al. 1982. "Cigarette Smoking and Chlorpromazine Disposition and Actions." *Clinical Pharmacology and Therapeutics* 31:533–38.

Paul, S.M., J.N. Crawley, and P. Skolnick. 1986. "The Neurobiology of Anxiety: The Role of the GABA/Benzodiazepine Receptor Complex." In *American Handbook of Psychiatry*, vol. 8: *Biological Psychiatry*, edited by P. Berger and H.K.H. Brodie, 581–96. New York: Basic Books.

Pheiffer, A., and A. Herz. 1982. "Discrimination of Three Opiate Receptor Binding Sites with the Use of a Computerized Curve-Fitting Technique." *Molecular Pharmacology* 21:266–71.

Relkin, R. 1966. "Death Following Withdrawal of Diazepam." *New York State Journal of Medicine* 66:1770–72.

Renner, J.A. 1984. "Methadone Maintenance: Past, Present, and Future." *Advances in Alcohol and Substance Abuse* 3 (1&2): 75–90.

Rickels, K. 1987. "Antianxiety Therapy: Potential Value of Long-Term Treatment." *Journal of Clinical Psychiatry* 48 (Suppl, 12): 7–11.

Rosenbloom, A. 1988. "Emergency Treatment Options in the Alcohol Withdrawal Syndrome." *Journal of Clinical Psychiatry* 49 (Suppl, 12): 28–31.

Rounsaville, B.J., M.M. Weissman, H.D. Kleber, and C. Wilber. 1982. "Heterogeneity of Psychiatric Diagnosis in Treated Opiate Addicts." *Archives of General Psychiatry* 39:161–66.

Schuckit, M.A. 1986. "Genetic and Clinical Implications of Alcoholism and Affective Disease." *American Journal of Psychiatry* 143:140–47.

Schuckit M.A. 1988. "Nicotine, Withdrawal, and Its Treatment." *Drug Abuse and Alcoholism Newsletter* 17 (6): 1–4.

Sellers, E.M., and H. Kalant. 1982. "Alcohol Withdrawal and Delirium Tremens." In *Encyclopedic Handbook of Alcoholism,* edited by E.M. Pattison and E. Kaufman, 147–66. New York: Gardner Press.
Synder, S.H. 1981. "Benzodiazepine Receptors." *Psychiatric Annals* 11:19–23.
Tabakoff, B., and P.L. Hoffman. 1987. "Biochemical Pharmacology of Alcohol." In *Psychopharmacology: The Third Generation of Progress,* edited by H.Y. Meltzer, 1521–26. New York: Raven Press.
Tabakoff, B., M. Muñoz-Marcus, and J.Z. Fields. 1979. "Chronic Ethanol Feeding Produces an Increase in Muscarinic Cholinergic Receptors in Mouse Brain." *Life Sciences* 25:2173–80.
Tennant, F.S., A.L. Tarver, and R.A. Rawson. 1984. "Clinical Evaluation of Mecamylamine for Withdrawal from Nicotine Dependence." In Harris, L.S. (ed.), Problems of Drug Dependence, *National Institute on Drug Abuse Research Monograph Series* 49 (Washington, D.C.: USGPO): 239–46.
Tyler, P., D. Rutherford, and T. Huggett. 1981. "Benzodiazepine Withdrawal Symptoms and Propranolol." *Lancet* 1:520–22.
U.S. Department of Health and Human Services. Alcohol, Drug Abuse and Mental Health Administration and Food and Drug Administration. 1980. "Methadone for Treating Narcotic Addicts: Joint Revision of Conditions for Use." *Federal Register* (21 CFR 291.505), 45(184):62694–709, September 19.
U.S. Department of Health and Human Services. Food and Drug Administration, National Institute on Drug Abuse. 1987. "Methadone in Maintenance and Detoxification; Joint Proposed Revision of Conditions for Use; Proposed Rule." *Federal Register* (21 CFR 291), 52(191):37046–61, October 2.
Votolato, N.A., K.J. Batcha, and S.C. Olson. 1987. "Comment: Alprazolam Withdrawal" (Letter to Editor). *Drug Intelligence and Clinical Pharmacy* 21:754–55.
Wender, P.H. 1978. "Minimal Brain Dysfunction: An Overview." In *Psychopharmacology: A Generation of Progress,* edited by M.A. Lipton, A. DiMascio, and K.F. Killaw, 1429–35. New York: Raven Press.
Whitfield, C. 1980. In *Phenomenology and Treatment of Alcoholism,* edited by W.E. Frann, I. Karacan, A.D. Pokorny, and R. Williams, 305–20. New York: Spectrum Publications.
Wise, R.A. 1985. "Neural Mechanisms of the Reinforcing Action of Cocaine." *National Institute on Drug Abuse Research Monogram Series* 50:15–35.
Woody, G.E, C.P. O'Brien, and R. Greenstein. 1975. "Misuse and Abuse of Diazepam: An Increasingly Common Medical Problem." *International Journal of the Addictions* 10:843–48.
Woody, G.E., C.P. O'Brien, and K. Rickels. 1975. "Depression and Anxiety in Heroin Addicts: A Placebo Controlled Study of Doxepin in Combination with Methadone." *American Journal of Psychiatry* 132:447–50.
Yablonsky, L. 1969. *Synanon: The Tunnel Back.* Baltimore: Penguin Books.

4
Nutrition and Recovery from Alcoholism

Lee Ann Mjelde Mossey

Alcoholism is one of the major causes of nutritional deficiencies in the United States today (Fahey and Boltri 1987; Graves 1985; Ryle and Thomson 1984; Shaw and Lieber 1983). Alcoholism and chronic alcohol abuse can cause, by direct or indirect effect, progressive degenerative damage to human tissue. This damage contributes to, or can result in, nutritional deficiencies (Lieber 1984a; Lieber 1985; Thomson 1985; World, Ryle, and Thomson 1985). These deficiency problems are compounded by the fact that alcoholics generally eat an insufficient diet (Thomson 1985; Wood 1984). In addition, alcohol-related tissue and organ damage requiring hospital and outpatient care have become one of the largest health care problems in the United States (Hataway, Raines, and Weinsier 1984; Shaw and Lieber 1983; Wood 1984; NIAAA 1987).

The weight of these problems has generated an abundance of scientific research and scholarly literature. This research is continually adding more and more data to our pool of knowledge. Nutrition as a cure for alcoholism, or as a main factor in etiology, has generated controversy but little result (Garrison 1984; Shaw and Lieber 1983) and is not a motivation for writing this chapter. What this chapter explains is that nutritional deficiencies, as a direct or indirect result of alcoholism, exist as a significant impairment in individuals with the disease of alcoholism and not just in some alcoholic individuals. I hope that the evidence presented here will help to create a situation in which more and more attention is given to this impairment. I also hope that nutritional assessment and therapy, along with medical care for tissue and organ injury, will become routine both in the primary treatment of alcoholism and in aftercare.

The issue of alcoholic drinking and its effect on an individual's overall health is a complex one. Thus, successful treatment requires as great an understanding as possible of these complexities. Keeping current with advances in knowledge is part of the medical treatment of any illness. Alcoholism merits the same aggressive treatment that any other medical illness would receive.

Aside from restoring the alcoholic to optimum physical health, the clinician must be concerned with cognitive, psychological, and behavioral consequences of malnutrition. These consequences can, in the right circumstances, sabotage or impair the patient's ongoing abstinence from alcoholic drinking. Garrison (1984) states unequivocally that "alcohol programs that do not incorporate nutrition as a fundamental component may be archaic and burdened with barriers to success." Others with a more conservative view suggest that symptoms associated with relapse could respond to nutritional therapy and that more research in the area is called for (Graves 1985). In one particularly startling study, a psychiatrist claimed a 90 percent rehabilitation rate after she arranged for daily hot meals to be supplied to a group of her patients (Leevy et al. 1985).

This chapter may be appearing at a vital time in the field of alcoholism. The vast majority of alcoholism treatment today is based on the concept that alcoholism is a potentially fatal disease. The American Medical Association (AMA) defines alcoholism as "an illness characterized by significant impairment that is directly associated with persistent and excessive use of alcohol. Impairment may involve physiological, psychological or social dysfunction" (Kirn 1986). There are some significant challenges to that definition in the United States today. Alan Marlatt, director of the Addictive Behavior Research Center at the University of Washington, along with some other researchers, is questioning whether alcoholism is a disease. He asks why a disease with a physical component seems to respond best to treatment with a spiritual approach, as in Alcoholics Anonymous (Kirn 1986).

In the wake of the U.S. Supreme Court ruling that the Veterans Administration can define alcoholism as "willful misconduct" rather than a disease (Traynor v. Turnage 1988), it seems an appropriate time to explore this area of malnutrition—tissue injury in the impairment of the alcoholic. The only successful way to treat these impairments is through medical care with nutritional support. This does not deny that the ancillary behavioral changes that facilitate abstinence and the ongoing support for those changes are indeed essential to recovery. Rather, I hope that a picture will emerge of how all these factors are interrelated and interdependent in the treatment of and the recovery from alcoholism.

I do not mean to suggest that nutritional therapy is a panacea or an indisputable method to ensure continuous abstinence. Instead, I suggest that the concept deserves investigation and implementation, as it seems to be an appropriate element of the medical treatment of alcoholism.

Alcoholic Malnutrition

The process by which an alcoholic becomes nutritionally deficient is complex. It is an end result of any combination of dietary deficiencies; an increased need for nutrients; the malabsorption, impaired use, excessive loss, and reduced storage of nutrients; and the progressive tissue injury with multiple effects on multiple organs caused by alcohol itself (Lieber 1984a; Lieber 1985; Thomson 1985; World, Ryle, and Thomson 1985).

Nutrients supply the body with energy and with substances to build and maintain tissue. The human biochemical processes that use nutrients are interrupted when alcohol is introduced. Alcohol provides a quick source of energy but has very little nutritional value (Antonow and McClain 1985a; Lieber 1985; World, Ryle, and Thomson 1985). Since the human system has no capacity to store alcohol's energy, it is given preferential treatment in the liver, to the displacement of other essential nutrients. Thus, the alcoholic may be getting enough energy but without the necessary substances to maintain health (Thomson 1985; World, Ryle, and Thomson 1985). These empty calories also displace other nutrients, with a reduced appetite and insufficient diet as a result (Bjorneboe 1986; Shaw and Lieber, 1983; Westerfield and Schulman 1959).

Alcohol itself has an enormous range of intricate effects on the human system (NIAAA 1987). Tissue injury results from cumulative biochemical insult, which, if occurring separately, might not be critical. It can take a surprisingly long time for significant organ damage to become apparent. Indeed, if tissue injury is discovered in time, it can sometimes be prevented or retarded. Added to tissue injury are the effects of malnutrition, which leads to gradual changes in body composition and progressive damage to organs. Thus, this progression of damage potentiates a continuum of injury to the whole human system (Thomson 1985).

This assault of alcohol creates the need for more nutrients, although the body may be receiving fewer due to poor diet (Dreyfuss 1983; Ryle and Thomson 1984). Ultimately, the alcoholic begins to suffer weight loss due to generalized malnutrition. With the rate of nutrient supply insufficient (due to malutilization or malabsorption), the body must call on its nutrient reserves (Thomson 1985). This situation exists even in the presence of adequate caloric intake. Calories derived from alcohol have so little nutritional value that they have no value in terms of maintaining body weight or nutritional reserves. This late-stage loss of nutrient reserves creates a situation in which the capacity to withstand further nutritional challenge is dangerously low (World, Ryle, and Thomson 1985).

Severe generalized malnutrition, with the accompanying weight loss, hair loss, open sores, or deformed bones, takes time to develop. Instead, we generally see a continuum of progressive decline in tissue and organ function and of progressive malnutrition. The alcoholic who enters treatment may be at any point on the continuum and show only subtle overt indications of malnutrition. By definition, a specific nutritional deficiency must be subclinical before it becomes clinical or visually apparent (Blachley and Knochel 1987; Ryle and Thomson 1984; Thomson 1985; Wood 1984). It would be wise to conclude that malnutrition of some degree is occurring in all alcoholics.

Treating alcoholic malnutrition is more sensitive and complex than just a regimen of nutritious meals. Before nutrition can be introduced, it is necessary to have a thorough understanding of the organ systems involved in the human body's biochemical processes.

Liver

The liver is the largest organ in the body and is the site of countless chemical reactions daily. One of these functions is the detoxification of harmful substances. The metabolism of alcohol by the liver alters the organ and profoundly affects the metabolism of many nutrients. Alcohol alters the storage, mobilization, activation, and metabolism of nutrients in and by the liver. In turn, alcoholic liver disease itself is a primary contributor to malnutrition (Antonow and McClain 1985b; Leevy et al. 1985; Li 1983; Lieber 1983a; Lieber 1985; Lieber 1983b; Mitchell and Herlong 1986; Shaw and Lieber 1983; Sherlock 1984). Specific nutrient deficiencies linked to liver damage are folate, thiamine, niacin, vitamin B_6, vitamin B_{12}, zinc, vitamin A, protein, and amino acid imbalance (Leevy et al., 1985; Lieber 1985; Lieber 1983b; Shaw and Lieber 1983; Sherlock 1984).

It has generally been established that alcoholic liver injury is due mainly to the toxic effects of alcohol alone. In the presence of an adequate diet, however, alcoholic liver disease can still develop (Badaway 1985; Lieber 1983a; Lieber 1985; Lieber 1983b; Mitchell and Herlong 1986). Nonetheless, the primary malnourishment of a poor diet and secondary malnutrition of malutilization of dietary nutrients is a contributing factor in alcoholic liver disease (Badaway 1985; Leevy et al. 1985; Lieber 1985; Lieber 1983b; Sherlock 1984). It has been estimated that fewer than 30 percent of alcoholics develop irreversible liver disease (Leevy et al. 1985). In its progression to this irreversible state, earlier stages of liver injury may not be detected by clinical tests (Carlen et al. 1986). This undetected liver injury may coexist with subclinical nutritional deficiencies.

For the alcoholic with liver disease, abstinence alone will not halt the progress of the injury. In the absence of appropriate therapy for nutritional problems, alcoholic liver damage may continue (Antonow and McClain 1985a; Lieber 1983b). Recognized in the treatment for alcoholic liver disease is an assessment of nutritional status, an analysis of the extent of injury, and the appropriate nutritional therapy to forestall further immediate damage or a continuation of progressive organ decline. Inappropriate nutrition can exacerbate the injury (Antonow and McClain 1985b; Badaway 1985; Lieber 1983b; Mitchell and Herlong 1986; Sherlock 1984). What is apparent is that there is a cycle of injury (with cause and effect) that may continue until a combination of medical care, abstinence, and nutrition therapy intervenes.

Pancreas

Alcoholic pancreatic disease leads to malabsorption of fatty acids, fat-soluble vitamins, and calcium (Sherlock 1984). Reduced pancreatic function is thought to be caused by insufficient dietary protein rather than just the excessive use of alcohol. Pancreatic deficiency may occur in as many as 44 percent of patients who have diets low in protein and have been drinking heavily (World, Ryle, and Thomson 1985).

Diet also is an accepted factor in carbohydrate tolerance and can occur in alcoholics with or without liver disease (Leevy et al. 1985). A study of twenty-two chronic alcoholics found that alcohol withdrawal did not rapidly reverse the impairment of glucose tolerance and insulin release. The alcoholics who maintaned a diet containing only the nonalcoholic calories (which they had been eating before the withdrawal of alcohol) showed no improvement in either glucose tolerance or insulin release. Recovery of glucose tolerance and insulin release after alcohol withdrawal was associated with a diet that included the appropriate amount of calories (Pezzarossa et al. 1986).

Gastrointestinal Tract

Nutritional imbalance is often compounded in chronic alcoholism by the effects that ethanol has on gastrointestinal function, with maldigestion and malabsorption contributing to secondary malnutrition (Lieber 1985; World, Ryle, and Thomson 1985). After oral ingestion, alcohol is rapidly absorbed by diffusion from the small intestine. It is less rapidly absorbed by the stomach (Li 1983; Lieber 1985). Thus, alcohol inhibits the absorption of nutrients, an effect that may be fundamental to specific nutritional deficiencies (Kirschman and Dunne 1984; World, Ryle, and Thomson 1985). Alcohol also damages the stomach and intestine so that food eaten is often not adequately absorbed, thereby causing an increasing state of malnutrition (Thomson 1985). Malnutrition can occur even in the presence of an adequate diet (Lieber 1984a). The end result of malabsorption may be severe functional impairment or tissue damage in other organs, most notably the liver and the brain, as a consequence of specific nutrient deficiencies (World, Ryle, and Thomson 1985).

Gastrointestinal tract problems may need to be treated carefully with nutrition (Lieber 1984b), as intestinal absorption in a given patient cannot be predicted accurately (Leevy et al. 1985).

Central Nervous System/Brain

The central nervous system can be affected by improper or inadequate nutrition in the absence of alcoholism. However, the most common nutritional disorder of the nervous system are a result of nutritional deficiencies caused by chronic alcoholism (Dreyfuss 1983; Graves 1985).

Chronic alcohol-related brain damage often is a direct result of nutrient depletion, particularly thiamine, niacin, vitamin B_6, and vitamin B_{12}. Lesser degrees of brain damage are frequently unrecognized. By the time a vitamin deficiency syndrome has developed and been diagnosed, irreversible damage may have occurred (Ryle and Thomson 1984). In an assessment of alcoholic brain damage to determine potential reversibility, it was found that liver disease can be clinically undetectable, although it may play a role in determining brain volume and density (Carlen et al. 1986).

In the development of tissue injury, dysfunction in one organ can trigger dysfunction in another. Evaluation of injury and malnutrition can become clouded by these interrelationships.

Specific Nutrient Deficiencies

A state of generalized malnutrition is common in alcoholic disease, but specific nutritional deficiencies also exist. The degree of deficiency and the specific nutrient are unique to each alcoholic. Specific nutritional deficiencies have particular symptoms that, if unrecognized and untreated, could have the potential to impair recovery from the active phase of alcoholism. What follows is a portion of what is known about those specific deficiencies.

Thiamine

Thiamine deficiency is probably the most widely known vitamin deficiency that can occur in alcoholism. The Wernicke-Korsakoff syndrome, which is a result of severe thiamine deficiency, is likely the most common psychological impairment associated with alcoholism (Bender 1984; Finlay-Jones 1986; Rosenthal and Goodwin 1985). Even so, nonalcoholic persons may develop the syndrome when they suffer from a severe thiamine deficiency (Reuler, Girard, and Cooney 1985).

Clinical manifestations of thiamine deficiency develop in only a small fraction of alcoholics. However, Wernicke-type pathology may be more common than is suspected clinically. Of fifty-one cases detected by autopsy, only seven were suspected during life. Most of those autopsied were alcoholics. Such evidence suggests that subclinical forms of the disease can affect cognitive function (Bender 1984; Reuler, Girard, and Cooney 1985; Rosenthal and Goodwin 1985). In the early stages of thiamine deficiency, symptoms that result are depression, insomnia, irritability, and impaired cognition (Abou-Saleh and Coppen 1986; Rosenthal and Goodwin 1985). Korsakoff's psychosis, whose worst effect is memory loss, is an essentially irreversible extension of Wernicke's disease (Abou-Saleh and Coppen 1986; Rosenthal and Goodwin 1985). It is important to note that thiamine does not cure all the symptoms of Wernicke's disease if deficiencies of other substances, such as magnesium ion, are present (Finlay-Jones 1986).

Folic Acid

The most common vitamin deficiency in alcoholism is that of folic acid, with low levels present in up to 90 percent of alcoholics with liver disease (Field 1985; Leevy et al. 1985; World, Ryle, and Thomson 1985). Increased folate excretion in the urine has been observed in four of five chronic alcoholic patients (Faizallah et al. 1986). In acute malnutrition, folate levels can change rapidly; therefore, laboratory evaluation of folate is difficult or unreliable (Rosenthal and Goodwin 1985).

Symptoms of folate deficiency are insomnia, forgetfulness, irritability, confusion, depression, macrocytic anemia, and impaired cognition (Abou-Saleh and Coppen 1986; Bender 1984; Fahey et al. 1987; Rosenthal and Goodwin 1985; Shaw and Lieber 1983). Several studies of depressed patients who were not responding to other forms of treatment showed improvement, and in one case complete remission, in treatment lasting from ten days to three months (Abou-Saleh and Coppen 1986). Even though folate deficiency symptoms respond to nutritional rehabilitation (Abou-Saleh and Coppen 1986; Bender 1984; Rosenthal and Goodwin 1985), considerable controversy exists concerning folate deficiency's effect on mental status, as no studies dealing specifically with this issue have yet been performed (Rosenthal and Goodwin 1985).

Vitamin B_{12}

Vitamin B_{12} malabsorption has been demonstrated in chronic alcoholism. Even when vitamin B_{12} serum levels are normal, the vitamin may be in a form that is not available for utilization (World, Ryle, and Thomson 1985). Body stores of vitamin B_{12} are so large than when intake or absorption is impaired, it still takes from one to two years to deplete the stores to a point where serum B_{12} levels fall below normal. It takes from two to six years more for full-blown deficiency symptoms to develop (Rosenthal and Goodwin 1985).

A complicating factor in diagnosing vitamin B_{12} levels is that deficiencies can be masked by an intake of folate. The patient can test normal for B_{12} while the deficiency is progressing. A person in this circumstance could develop profound psychiatric symptoms with no apparent B_{12} abnormalities on laboratory exam (Rosenthal and Goodwin 1985).

Signs of vitamin B_{12} deficiency are diverse. They progress from irritability, apathy, and somnolence to marked paranoid states, psychosis with delusions, and both visual and auditory hallucinations (Abou-Saleh and Coppen 1986; Fahey et al. 1987; Rosenthal and Goodwin 1985).

Niacin

The most severe effect of niacin deficiency is pellagra. Although pellagra is uncommon, it most frequently afflicts alcoholics and the elderly. The disease is produced by dietary insufficiency of tryptophan and niacin, but the full deficiency syndrome can develop in patients who shunt tryptophan into other metabolic pathways despite a normal diet (Rosenthal and Goodwin 1985).

The earliest psychological symptoms of pellagra are insomnia, fatigue, nervousness, irritability, depression, and memory loss. An acute confusional syndrome also may occur. This confusional state is reversible with niacin therapy (Abou-Saleh and Coppen 1986; Bender 1984; Rosenthal and Goodwin 1985).

Riboflavin

Riboflavin deficiency occurs in 17 percent of chronic alcoholics. Low dietary intake of riboflavin is the suspected mechanism for the deficiency (World, Ryle, and Thomson 1985). Deficiency symptoms are depression, impaired cognitive abilities, and hysteria (Bender 1984; Carney et al. 1982; Rosenthal and Goodwin 1985). Symptoms have been shown to respond to nutritional rehabilitation (Bender 1984).

Vitamin B_6

Vitamin B_6 deficiency occurs in a high proportion of alcoholics (Shaw and Lieber 1983; World, Ryle, and Thomson 1985). It can impair cognitive abilities and may play a role in depression (Bender 1984; Carney et al. 1982; Rosenthal and Goodwin 1985; Stewart et al. 1984). In recovery, it is best to avoid extreme supplementation of vitamin B_6, since megadoses have been known to cause a severe, sensory peripheral neuropathy (Fahey et al. 1987).

Zinc

Alcoholics with or without cirrhosis have been found to have an increased urinary zinc excretion (World, Ryle, and Thomson 1985). In a study of eighteen hospitalized alcoholic patients (five with liver disease and thirteen without), a significant reduction in the absorption of zinc was found in the study subjects compared with twelve normal controls. This impaired absorption occurred not only in the five subjects with liver disease but also in the thirteen subjects without clinical evidence of liver disease (Dinsmore et al. 1985a). Other evidence of an alcoholic zinc deficiency was found at autopsy of chronic alcoholics. The concentration of zinc was substantially and uniformly smaller in the brains and spinal cords of the chronic alcoholics than in the nonalcoholic controls. This finding reflects a genuine reduction in zinc in the alcoholics rather than a possible elevation of zinc in the controls (Kasarkis et al. 1985). Zinc supplementation has been shown to be beneficial in zinc deficiency.

Vitamin C

Another vitamin that is commonly deficient in chronic alcoholism is vitamin C. Some studies suggest that as many as 91 percent of chronic alcoholics are deficient in vitamin C (Faizallah et al. 1986; Field 1985). Studies also have shown that alcohol has an ascorbiuretic effect, even in healthy volunteers (World, Ryle, and Thomson 1985). The vitamin C is lost through excessive elimination in the urine after even modest amounts of alcohol (Faizallah et al. 1986). Symptoms of vitamin C deficiency include depression, hysteria, and confusion (Abou-Selah and Coppen 1986; Rosenthal and Goodwin 1985; Shaw and Lieber 1983). Severe vitamin C deficiency causes scurvy.

Magnesium

Magnesium deficiency occurs in alcoholics, probably due to decreased dietary intake and increased urinary losses (Blachley and Knochel 1987; Fahey et al. 1987; World, Ryle, and Thomson 1985). Depression is a common symptom of electrolyte deficiencies and is found in magnesium deficiency (Field 1985).

Deficiencies and Relapse

A relationship between alcoholism, organ dysfunction, malnutrition, and psychological and cognitive impairment exists. Controversy about the extent and significance of the relationship also exists, with little or no data available on the effects of ongoing abstinence from alcohol. The difficulties in establishing a clear link are obvious. It is possible that the implementation of nutritional assessment and therapy within the treatment of alcoholism will eventually provide a definitive conclusion.

Studies do exist, however, on diet and nutritional status and their relationship to psychological and cognitive function. In one thorough study of the effects of a specific two-week diet change in four subjects, it was found that the subjects had less emotional distress. The authors concluded that the relationship between diet and psychological dysfunction had not been delineated but that their study had succeeded in demonstrating that a relationship seems to exist (Christensen et al. 1985).

In another study of 260 healthy individuals over the age of sixty, it was found that nutritional status influenced cognition. A significant association between nutritional deficiencies and impaired cognition was detected. In testing results, lower scores were associated with lower blood levels of ascorbate, vitamin B_{12}, riboflavin, and folate. Correcting for education and income levels did not alter the degree of the association between performance on the cognitive tests and blood levels of the vitamins. The subjects were apparently healthy, active individuals whose cognitive impairment was detectable only by sophisticated testing (Rosenthal and Goodwin 1985). This study illustrates the challenge and the frustration of assessment and treatment. Subtle, difficult to determine deficits, impairments, and relationships may exist that require considerable time and effort to unmask.

One area in which there is a relationship between a symptom of nutritional deficiency and alcoholism is depression. Alcoholism and depression often occur together. Estimates of the incidence of major depression in an alcoholic population range from 28 to 59 percent (Zern et al. 1986). Distinguishing between primary and secondary depression is particularly difficult in alcoholics because the two conditions share several symptoms (MacMurray 1987; Zern et al. 1986). Physical illness and malnutrition also can cause depression (Field 1985). However difficult it may be, differentiating between the two types of depression is essential to selecting the proper treatment (Zern et al. 1986). A focus on the incorrect etiology will not alleviate the depression and might increase the severity of the symptoms (Field 1985). Specific nutrient deficiencies associated with depression include iron, zinc, vitamin B_6, thiamine, vitamin B_{12}, and folic acid. Biochemically based depression in an alcoholic could precipitate a relapse into alcoholic drinking if not treated appropriately. Granted, this could be a rare circumstance, and a majority of detoxified alcoholics appear free of significant depression after three to four weeks in an appropriate treatment program (MacMurray et al. 1987; Overall et al. 1985). But if even a small improvement in effectiveness of treatment is accomplished through nutritional therapy, it is important to use such therapy in providing care for such a large population (Finney and Moos 1986).

Anxiety also is related to depression and drinking. In some instances, anxiety may mask a depressive disorder (Field 1985). Anxiety is regularly described in the wide range of symptoms of nutritional deficiency. In studies of alcohol abuse and anxiety, alcohol has been shown to provide relief from anxiety. Furthermore, the onset of drinking commonly follows the onset of anxiety (Thyer et al. 1986).

Although a conclusive cause and effect relationship in nutritional deficiency and relapse may be lacking, this does not mean that it does not occur.

I hope that more attention will be given to this relationship as alcoholism treatment evolves.

Nutritional Assessment

The obstacles in assessing alcohol-related or alcohol-induced malnutrition are evident. How assessment will be achieved is the work ahead for medical and nutritional professionals. What follows is a discussion of some nutritional assessment tools and how they may be applied to alcoholics.

Body weight is one indicator of malnutrition. It has been suggested that a body weight of 60 to 80 percent of ideal is an indicator of moderate malnutrition. Body weights that drop below 60 percent of ideal indicate severe malnutrition (World, Ryle, and Thomson 1985). Since weight loss is often a later stage of malnutrition, its use as an assessment tool is limited. Malnutrition does not necessarily mean starving. The malnutrition that occurs in alcoholism may not have any such obvious symptoms (Field 1985; World, Ryle, and Thomson 1985).

Subclinical deficiencies, in which reserve stores are depleted but the entire deficiency syndrome has not developed, are difficult to diagnose (Graves 1985; Rosenthal and Goodwin 1985; World, Ryle, and Thomson 1985). The current state of the art in nutrition recognizes that individuals with subclinical malnutrition are at risk for a variety of pathologic processes and disabilities (Rosenthal and Goodwin 1985). The progressive nutritional deficiencies that occur in alcoholism are generally a whole grouping of various vitamin, mineral, and energy nutrient deficits, with each at a different point on a continuum and progressing at a different pace (World, Ryle, and Thomson 1985). Assessment for each deficit requires sensitive testing because the multiple deficiencies confuse and mask each other (Fahey et al. 1987; Lieber 1983b, Ryle and Thomson 1985).

Standard among dietary assessment tools is dietary intake. A history of a patient's intake can indicate the risk of a deficiency being present. The deficiency can then be confirmed by clinical testing (Rosenthal and Goodwin 1985; Ryle and Thomson 1984; World, Ryle, and Thomson 1985). Reliability of dietary histories given by alcoholics has been shown to be questionable, especially in their reports of protein intake. Alcoholics generally claim a higher intake than they actually had (World, Ryle, and Thomson 1985). In a thorough analysis of the number of days of food intake records required to confidently estimate individual nutrient intakes, Basiotis et al. (1987) found a wide range of days reported. The shortest time span averaged 31 days for food energy intake, and the longest averaged 433 days for vitamin A intake. The feasibility of using the dietary history of alcoholics is therefore limited at best. We can assume that generalized or specific malnutrition as a hallmark of alcoholism might be a more useful point of demarcation for a nutritional assessment.

Specific laboratory tests and procedures for evaluating alcoholics need to be developed in the field of medicine. An example would be in testing for anemia, which is a frequent and often nutritionally linked complication of alcoholism. Anemia has been found in 13 to 62 percent of chronic hospitalized alcoholics. In their study of 121 chronic alcoholics with a low hematocrit, Savage and Lindenbaum (1986) found multiple contributing causes of the anemia in most of the patients. They also found the sensitivity, specificity, and predictive values of certain laboratory tests used with nonalcoholic patients to be so limited in application to alcoholic patients as to question their usefulness. The direct and indirect effects of alcohol ingestion may affect standard tests used in the diagnosis of anemia because there are so many potential causes of low hematocrit in alcoholics. On the basis of their findings, these authors developed recommendations for the diagnosis of, and therapy for, anemia in alcoholics.

The benefits of sophisticated testing are great. For instance, the development of computerized psychometric tests may allow for earlier detection of brain injury related to malnutrition. This early stage injury could then be reversed with nutritional therapy before irreversible damage occurs (Ryle and Thomson 1984).

Treatment

Treatment of alcoholism that incorporates therapy for alcohol-related or alcohol-induced malnutrition must have a behavioral component. The overall nutrition program for each patient would incorporate medical assessment of tissue and organ injury, assessment of nutritional status, an individualized diet plan to restore optimum health, and motivation to care about his or her health by taking responsibility for his or her diet and for changing any negative eating patterns or behaviors. Treatment that is directed *at* the patient has limited effectiveness. To be motivational, the patient needs to become actively involved in the diet program from the beginning of treatment through aftercare.

Evaluation

The history of alcoholism treatment tells us that treatment for alcoholism per se is a fairly new phenomenon. Years ago, the only medical treatment available was for its complications. The advent of Alcoholics Anonymous in the late 1930s, marked the beginning of treatment for the disease of alcoholism.

Once medical care of alcoholism began, it became apparent that treatment needed to be evaluated for its effectiveness. Today patients, referral sources, and parties responsible for payment of alcoholism treatment are becoming more and more interested in specific outcomes of specific treatments (Miller 1986). The current industry norm is that 60 to 65 percent of those who complete treatment remain abstinent for at least one year following discharge (Kirn 1986). Even so, there is some controversy about desired outcome: Should it be abstinence; decreased volume and frequency of drinking; or less dysfunction in employment, family, social, or financial areas? There are proponents of various outcomes (Miller 1986).

In an extensive review of thirty-seven outcome evaluation studies published between 1976 and 1980 (Sobell et al. 1987), methodological advances as well as methodological problems are apparent. The five most notable deficiencies were as follows:

1. Insufficient reporting of subject background and drinking history variables
2. Inadequate description of treatment provided
3. Failure to gather pretreatment data for variables assessed in follow-up and failure to examine possible pretreatment differences among treatment groups
4. Drawing of conclusions in the absence of any statistical analysis
5. Failure to quantitatively assess drinking behavior

Bearing in mind the problems in effectiveness evaluation cited above and the growing interest of referral sources in program effectiveness, it is clear that any treatment program that incorporates an intensive nutrition component should also implement a viable effectiveness evaluation. The results of this evaluation would be an invaluable contribution to our knowledge of alcoholism treatment.

Conclusion

In my recent research on nutrition and its effect on the human aging process, I have been profoundly struck by the extent of the influence of nutrients on aging. The human body contains an exquisite balance of chemicals that deserves to be more clearly understood. The more that we can understand about alcohol and its effect on human biochemistry, the more hope there is for more effective medical treatment of alcoholism.

Two groups in our society are considered to be at risk for poor nutritional status, regardless of whether they are alcoholic or not. These are adolescents and elderly persons. Compounding the effects of an already poor diet with alcoholism or chronic alcohol abuse almost guarantees a state of malnutrition. These groups should be of special concern in the field of alcohol treatment.

A conclusive connection between alcoholism, nutrition, and abstinence remains to be established. There is enough evidence today, however, to merit continuing research in this area. We must recognize the root cause of a problem in order to alleviate or neutralize it. If that root cause is not appropriately identified and treated, the problem will remain and may increase in severity.

References

Abou-Saleh, M.T., and A. Coppen. 1986. "The Biology of Folate in Depression: Implications for Nutritional Hypotheses of the Psychoses." *Journal of Psychiatric Research* 20(2): 91–101.

Antonow, D.R. and McClain, C.J. 1985a. "Nutrition and Alcoholism." *Alcohol and the Brain* ed. Tarter, R.E. and Van Thiel, D.H. Plenum, New York.

———. 1985b. "Nutritional Support in Alcoholic Liver Disease." *Journal of Parenteral and Enteral Nutrition* 9(5): 566–67.

Badaway, A.A.B. 1985. "Nutrition and the Biochemical Pathology of the Alcohol-Induced Liver Injury." *Alcohol and Alcoholism* 20(2): 175–83.

Basiotis, P.P., S.O. Welsh, F.J. Cronin, J.L. Kelsay, and W. Mertz. 1987. "Number of Days of Food Intake Records Required to Estimate Individual and Group Nutrient Intakes with Defined Confidence." *Journal of Nutrition* 117(9): 1638–41.

Bender, D.A. 1984. "B Vitamins in the Nervous System." *Neurochemistry International* 6(3): 297–321.

Bjorneboe, G.E. 1986. "Effect of Alcohol Consumption." *American Journal of Clinical Nutrition* 44(5): 678–82.

Blachley, J.D., and J.P. Knochel. 1987. "Ethanol and Minerals." *Pharmacology and Therapeutics* 33(2–3): 435–48.

Carlen, P.L., R.D. Penn, L. Fornazzari, J. Bennett, D.A. Wilkinson, and G. Wortzman. 1986. "Computerized Tomographic Scan Assessment of Alcoholic Brain Damage and Its Potential Reversibility." *Alcoholism* (NY) 10(3): 226–32.

Carney, M.W.P., M.G. Ravindran, et al. (1982). "Thiamin, Riboflavin and Pyridoxine Deficiency in Psychiatric In-Patients." *British Journal of Psychiatry* 141: 271–72.

Christensen, L., K. Krietsch, B. White, and B. Stagner. 1985. "Impact of Dietary Change on Emotional Distress." *Journal of Abnormal Psychology* 94(4): 565–79.

Dinsmore, W.W., M.B. Callender, D. McMaster, and A.M. Love. 1985a. "Absorption of Zinc from a Standardized Meal in Alcoholics and in Normal Volunteers." *American Journal of Clinical Nutrition* 42(4): 688–93.

Dreyfuss, P.M. 1983. "Neurologic Disease." *Nutritional Support in Medical Practice.* Second Edition, ed. Schneider, H.A. and Anderson, C.E. et al. Harper and Row. New York.

Fahey, P.J., J.M. Boltri, et al. 1987. "Key Issues in Nutrition." *Postgraduate Medicine* 81(6): 123.

Faizallah, R.I., A.I. Morris, N. Krasner, and P.S. Walker. 1986. "Alcohol Enhances Vitamin C Excretion." *Alcohol and Alcoholism* 21(1): 81–84.

Field, W.E. 1985. "Physical Causes of Depression." *Journal of Psychosocial Nursing* 23(10): 6–11.

Finlay-Jones, R. 1986. "Should Thiamine Be Added to Beer?" *Australian and New Zealand Journal of Psychiatry* 20:3–6.

Finney, J.W., and R.H. Moos. 1986. "Matching Patients with Treatment: Conceptual and Methodological Issues." *Journal of Studies on Alcohol* 47(2):122–34.

Garrison, R.H. 1984. "Nutrition and Exercise as Neurochemical Modulating Factors in the Alcoholic Recovery Process." Paper presented at the *Ninth Annual California Conference on Alcohol Problems*, San Mateo, Calif., September.

Graves, J.R. 1985. "Role of Nutrition in the Treatment of Alcoholism." In *Progress in Alcohol Research*, vol. 1, edited by S. Parvez, Y. Burov, et al. 247–63. Utrecht: VNU Science Press.

Hataway, H., R.L. Raines, and R.L. Weinsier. 1984. "Nutrition: Its Ever-Increasing Role." *Family and Community Health* 7(1): 22–37.

Kasarskis, E.J., W.I. Manton, L.D. Davenport, J.B. Kirkpatrick, G.A. Howell, M.A. Klitenick, and C.J. Frederickson. 1985. "Effects of Alcohol Ingestion on Zinc Content of Human and Rat Central Nervous Systems." *Experimental Neurology* 90(1): 81–95.

Kirn, T.F. 1986. "Advances in Understanding of Alcoholism Initiate Evolution in Treatment Programs." *Journal of the American Medical Society* 256(11): 1405.

Kirschman, J.D., and L.J. Dunne, eds. 1984. *Nutrition Almanac*. New York: McGraw-Hill.

Leevy C.M., O. Frank, C.B. Leevy, and H. Baker. 1985. "Nutritional Factors in Liver Disease of the Alcoholic." *Acta Medica Scandinavica* 703(Suppl): 67–79.

Li, T.K. 1983. "Absorption, Distribution, and Metabolism of Ethanol and Its Effects on Nutrition and Hepatic Function." In *Medical and Social Aspects of Alcohol Abuse*, edited by B. Tabakoff, P.B. Sutker, and C.L. Randall. New York: Plenum Press.

Lieber, C.S. 1983a. "Alcohol, Protein Nutrition and Liver Injury." *Current Concepts in Nutrition* 12:49–71.

———. 1983b. "Interactions of Alcohol and Nutrition: Introduction to a Symposium." *Alcoholism: Clinical and Experimental Research* 7(1): 2–4.

———. 1984a. "Alcohol-Nutrition Interaction." *Alcohol* 1(2): 151–57.

———. 1984b. "Alcohol-Nutrition Interaction." *Journal of Dentistry for Children* 51(2): 137–40.

———. 1985. "Alcohol and the Liver: Metabolism of Ethanol, Metabolic Effects and Pathogenesis of Injury." *Acta Medica Scandinavica* 703(Suppl): 11–55.

MacMurray, J.P., D.G. Nessman, M.G. Haviland, and D.L. Anderson. 1987. "Depressive Symptoms and Persistence in Treatment for Alcohol Dependence." *Journal of Studies on Alcohol* 48(3): 277–79.

Miller, S.I. 1986. "Hot to Tell if Alcoholism Treatment Has Worked: Assessing Outcome Studies." *Hospital and Community Psychiatry* 37(6): 555–56.

Mitchell, M.C., and H.F. Herlong. 1986. "Alcohol and Nutrition: Calorie Value,

Bioenergetics, and Relationship to Liver Damage." In *Annual Review of Nutrition,* Darby, W.J., H.P. Broquist and R.E. Olson; eds. vol. 6. Palo Alto, Calif.: Annual Reviews, Inc.

Overall, J.E., E.L. Reilly, J.T. Kelley, and L.E. Hollister. 1985. "Persistence of Depression in Detoxified Alcoholics." *Alcoholism:* (NY) 9(4): 331–34.

Pezzarossa, A., C. Cervigni, F. Ghinelli, E. Molina, and A. Gnudi. 1986. "Glucose Tolerance in Chronic Alcoholics after Alcohol Withdrawal: Effect of Accompanying Diet." *Metabolism* 35(11): 984–88.

Reuler, J.B., D.E. Girard, and T.G. Cooney. 1985. "Current Concepts: Wernicke's Encephalopathy." *New England Journal of Medicine* 312(16): 1035–39.

Rosenthal, M.J., and J.S. Goodwin. 1985. "Cognitive Effects of Nutritional Deficiency." *Advances in Nutrition Research* 7: 71–100.

Ryle, P.R., and A.D. Thomson. 1984. "Nutrition and Vitamins in Alcoholism." In *Clinical Biochemistry of Alcoholism,* edited by S.B. Rosalki. New York: Churchill Livingstone.

Savage, D., and J. Lindenbaum. 1986. "Anemia in Alcoholics." *Medicine (Baltimore).* 65(5):322–38.

Shaw, S., C.S. Lieber, H.A. Schneider, C.E. Anderson, and D.B. Courson, eds. 1983. "Alcoholism." In *Nutritional Support for Medical Practice,* 2nd ed. New York: Harper & Row.

Sherlock, S. 1984. "Nutrition and the Alcoholic." *Lancet* 1984;1(8374): 436–39.

Sobell, M.B., S. Brochu, L.C. Sobell, J. Roy, and J.A. Stevens. 1987. "Alcohol Treatment Outcome Evaluation Methodology: State of the Art 1980–1984." *Addictive Behaviors* 12(2): 113–28.

Stewart, J.W., W. Harrison, F. Quitkin, and H. Baker. 1984. "Low B_6 Levels in Depressed Outpatients." *Biological Psychiatry* 19(4): 613–16.

Thomson, A.D. 1985. "Malnutrition and Tissue Injury." *Alcohol and Alcoholism* 20(2): 87–88.

Thyer, B.A., R.T. Parrish, J. Himle, O.G. Cameron, G.C. Curtis, and R.M. Neese. 1986. "Alcohol Abuse among Anxious Patients. *Behavior Research Therapy* 24(3): 357–59.

Traynor v. Turnage, 485 U.S. Supreme Court, . 99 L.Ed 2d 618, 108 S.Ct. 1372 (1988).

Westerfeld, W.W., and M.P. Schulman. 1959. "Metabolism and Calorie Value of Alcohol." *Journal of the American Medical Association* 170: 197.

Wood, B. 1984. "Alcohol and Nutrition." *Australian Alcohol/Drug Review* 3(2): 107–10.

World, M.J., P.R. Ryle, and A.D. Thomson. 1985. "Alcoholic Malnutrition and the Small Intestine." *Alcohol and Alcoholism* 20(2): 89–124.

Zern, M.A., U. Halbreich, K. Bacon, M. Galantee, B.J. Kang, and F. Gasparini. 1986. "Relationship between Serum Cortisol, Liver Function, and Depression in Detoxified Alcoholics." *Alcoholism (New York)* 10(3): 320–22.

Part II
Prevention and Early Intervention

Prologue

Robin Room

The chapters in part II are reflective of the current flood of activity in prevention and intervention for alcohol and drug problems in the United States. Broadly speaking, the 1986 omnibus drug bill marked a new push by the federal government into the support of youth education programs. In the 1988 bill, the balance of new money shifted from supply interdiction to treatment and intervention programs.

This new flood of activity is propelled more by fears and hopes than by rational decisions about resource allocations to proven strategies. Alcohol and drug use and abuse are intractable problems that defy any permanent solution—and for which the most effective solutions are often the least politically popular. The result, as Kettil Bruun put it, is that "the consistent frustrations concerning the relative lack of success in fighting [the problems make us] move compulsively from one model to another" (Bruin 1971). As we lunge around the restricted circuit of politically acceptable strategies, research findings from the last push in a particular direction are simply ignored or shoved out of the way. It seems that it is more important to maintain the illusion of progress and brand new beginnings than to learn from past experiences.

The focus in this part is on prevention and intervention strategies that involve service provision. Something is being done for or to a client by a professional or paraprofessional—a teacher, counselor, behavioral psychologist, or "alcohol and drug evaluation specialist." These may be distinguished from strategies that are potentially more or less self-enforcing or self-financing (Room 1980; Moore and Gerstein 1981) such as market controls, environmental changes, or deterrence. To provide a context for the chapters in this part, I briefly describe each of these strategies here.

Preparation of this commentary was supported by a National Alcohol Research Center grant (AA-05595) from the National Institute on Alcohol Abuse and Alcoholism to the Alcohol Research Group, Medical Research Institute of San Francisco, 1816 Scenic Avenue, Berkeley, CA 94709.

Market controls on licit commodities include regulation of the conditions and pricing of sales and recruit those in the legal business as watchdogs on illegal activities. More importantly, the legal entrepreneur has much to lose from contravening the control regulations. Alcohol control laws and controls on the dispensing of psychopharmaceuticals can thus be relatively effective at very little cost to the state. Since demand for psychoactive drugs such as alcohol is not very elastic in the short run, governments can benefit fiscally from raising taxes on them while also reducing consumption—including the consumption of heavy users, which is the main public health target (Kendell, de Roumanie, and Riston 1983; Room 1984). For presently illicit drugs, of course, the market control strategy involves the politically unthinkable cost of creating a legal market, however restricted. For licit commodities such as alcohol and tobacco, any increase in control must battle the opposition of those with vested interests in the existing market.

Environmental changes can be directed at the choice to use, at patterns of use, or at consequences of use. Federal regulation of smoking on airplanes is an example of an environmental measure directed at the decision to use. Training bartenders in peaceable methods of refusing service to the already intoxicated customer (server intervention training) is an example of a measure directed at patterns of use. Often the most effective way of preventing alcohol or drug problems is the direct prevention of consequences of use: making the world safer for (and from) heavy drinkers or drug users (Moore and Gerstein 1981). These strategies often run up against the political problems of predicating government actions on unpalatable facts—for instance, of acknowledging that some teenagers drink and use drugs. Examples of such measures include providing safe transportation home for people at parties, mandating air bags in cars to prevent traffic injuries, and making sterile needles available to intravenous drug users.

The literature on deterrence approaches distinguishes between general deterrence—the effect of a measure in preventing a prohibited act—and specific deterrence—the effect of a measure in stopping those who have been caught committing the act from doing it again. By its nature, specific deterrence tends to involve intensive service provision (counting police and prison guards as service providers). But to the extent that a measure operates through general deterrence, the service provision costs tend to be lower. Much recent research on countermeasures to drunk driving has focused on the deterrence effects of drinking-driver laws and regulations. Measures that involve a minimum of service provision—such as immediate driver's license suspensions—are often more effective than service-providing approaches such as drinking-driver reeducation (Sadler and Perrine 1984). Recent experience in Australian states has shown that a sustained high-visibility program or random breath-testing of motorists has had a large and continuing general-deterrence effect on drinking-driver casualties (Homel, Carseldine, and Kearns 1988). The main impediments to adopting such measures in the United States are political rather than fiscal.

Service provision strategies for dealing with alcohol or drug problems, however, have had a high and enduring popularity in the United States in the past thirty years. For decades, the main thrust of the alcoholism movement was the premise of building a publicly supported alcoholism treatment system. In a society that was in full reaction against the earlier view of the "liquor question" as an issue of public policy rather than private anguish, the tacit compromise between the movement and society was that attention should be confined to a narrow definition of *alcoholism*, caused by a "predisposing X factor" (Jellinek 1952). In this view, prevention of alcoholism awaited discovery of this mysterious factor (Room 1984). Illicit drug problems have a different history, with supply interdiction as the leading strategy for most of the present century and treatment policy subordinated to this effort. Since the beginning of the 1970s, however, there has also been a substantial increase in treatment provision in the illicit drug field.

Recent years have seen a substantial shift in the societal role of alcohol treatment. More and more, clients are in treatment as an alternative to incarceration, as has been true of drug treatment for much longer. Concomitantly, alcohol treatment programs have moved vigorously into intervention strategies that apply strong pressures to "break down the denial" of the "high-bottom" (less impaired) heavy drinkers. Increasingly, "early intervention" and "secondary prevention" have come to mean coerced treatment, as treatment services recruit new client populations in the struggle to maintain or increase their level of staffing and financing (Weisner and Room 1984). Service provision in the primary prevention field also has grown. For both alcohol and other drugs, outlays for educational service approaches have grown considerably in the past two decades.

The result of these policy developments has been the creation of a huge professional and semiprofessional constituency that is vocationally dedicated to reducing or eliminating alcohol and drug use. Cost constraints imply that the constituency cannot continue to grow indefinitely. Even at its present size, however, the existence of the constituency has become a factor in cultural change. In the past, when society has turned against recreational use of psychoactive drugs, it was in response to a massive mobilization of people committed to change—people who eventually tired of "moral suasion" approaches and moved to more coercive approaches (Blocker 1988). Most of those mobilized in past movements were contributing their time, rather than being paid for their work. In the era of the welfare state, perhaps a large and increasingly professionalized service-providing constituency is the way that such large cultural changes happen.

References

Blocker, J.S. 1988. *American Temperance Movements: Cycles of Reform.* Boston: Twayne Publishers.

Bruun, K. 1971. "Finland: The Non-Medical Approach." In *29th International Congress on Alcoholism and Drug Dependence,* edited by L.G. Kiloh and D.S. Bell, 545–59. Australia: Butterworths.

Homel, R., D. Carseldine, and I. Kearns. 1988. "Drinking-Driving Countermeasures in Australia." *Alcohol, Drugs and Driving* 4:113–44.

Jellinek, E.M. 1952. "Phases of Alcohol Addiction." *Journal of Studies on Alcohol* 13:673–84.

Kendell, R.E., M. de Roumanie, and E.B. Ritson. 1983. "Effect of Economic Changes on Scottish Drinking Habits 1978–1982." *British Journal of Addiction* 78:365–79.

Moore, M., and D. Gerstein, Eds. 1981. *Alcohol and Public Policy: Beyond the Shadow of Prohibition.* Washington, D.C.: National Academy Press.

Room, R. 1980. "Concepts and Strategies in the Prevention of Alcohol-Related Problems." *Contemporary Drug Problems* 9:9–47.

———. 1984. "Alcohol Control and Public Health." *Annual Review of Public Health* 5:293–317.

Sadler, D.D., and M.W. Perrine. 1984. *An Evaluation of the California Drunk Driving Countermeasure System.* Vol. 2: *The Long-Term Traffic Safety Impact of a Pilot Alcohol Abuse Treatment as an Alternative to License Suspensions.* Report CAL-DMV-RSS-84-90. Sacramento: California State Department of Motor Vehicles.

Weisner, C., and R. Room. 1984. "Financing and Ideology in Alcohol Treatment." *Social Problems* 32:167–88.

5
Prevention and Early Intervention of Addictive Disorders

Peter E. Nathan

This chapter reviews some of the data on the prevention of alcoholism and drug abuse. These data have led me to conclude that practitioners are a good deal better able to prevent some of the consequences of alcohol misuse, such as alcohol-related car crashes and fetal alcohol syndrome, than to prevent chronic alcohol abuse.

The chapter also considers treatment outcomes. Because of my focus on prevention and early intervention, I only summarize the rather disappointing data on outcomes of treatment of long-term alcohol dependence. I do, however, detail the more promising, though still preliminary, data on early intervention in the natural history of the disorder. I hope that sharing this information will provide additional perspective in preventing and treating the addictive disorders.

Some of the Dimensions of Abuse in the United States

As the following list illustrates, alcohol and drug abuse exacts a terrible and increasing toll on our society. That toll fully justifies our best efforts to prevent and treat these conditions.

- In 1983, the latest year for which these data are available, alcohol abuse cost the United States almost $117 billion. Of this amount, nearly $71 billion stemmed from lost employment and reduced productivity, while another $15 billion went to health care costs. The same figure in 1988 approached $150 billion (NIAAA 1987).
- In 1983, 48 percent of all persons convicted of crimes in the United States had been using alcohol when they committed the crime (NIAAA 1987).
- In 1980, alcohol use and abuse was either the main or a contributing cause in almost 100,000 deaths (table 5–1). In 20 percent of these deaths

Table 5–1
Estimated Number of Deaths Attributable to Alcohol in the United States, 1980

Cause of Death	Number of Deaths	Estimated Number Attributable to Alcohol	Percentage Attributable to Alcohol
Alcohol as the main cause (alcohol dependence syndrome, alcoholic cardiomyopathy, alcoholic cirrhosis of the liver, etc.)	19,587	19,587	100
Alcohol as a contributing cause			
Cancer of directly exposed tissues	31,955	7,269	20–25
Other diseases	150,280	11,679	5–25
Accidents (motor vehicle traffic accidents, accidental falls, drowning, suffocation, etc.)	96,987	37,849	10–50
Violence (suicide, homicide, etc.)	54,499	21,144	30–50
Total	333,721	77,941	5–50

Source: R.T. Ravenholt, "Addiction Mortality in the United States, 1980: Tobacco, Alcohol, and Other Substances," *Population and Development Review* 10:(1984).

(for example, in alcoholic cirrhosis and alcoholic cardiomyopathy), alcohol was the main cause. In an additional 40 percent (those that resulted from alcohol-related automobile and other accidents) alcohol was a contributing cause in that the death or deaths would likely not have occurred had alcohol not impaired judgment and driving ability. In the remaining 40 percent of the deaths, alcohol use accelerated an ongoing physical disease process (Ravenholt 1984).

- The economic cost of drug abuse to society was estimated to be at least $46.9 billion in 1980, the last year for which these data are available. Inflation had likely raised that figure to $70 billion or more by 1988. It includes both direct costs (for example, health care) and indirect costs (for instance, lost productivity) (Harwood 1984).

- Experience with illegal drugs in the early 1960s was confined to 2 percent or less of the U.S. population. By 1982, almost one-third of the population over the age of twelve had had at least some experience with these drugs. That percentage is probably higher today (APA Committee on Drug Abuse 1987).

- In 1983, 10 percent of violent crimes in the United States were drug related. One-third of all federal prisoners and more than one-half of all state prisoners were narcotics addicts (Goldstein 1985).

Outcomes of Treatment for Long-Term Alcohol Dependence

The data on outcomes of treatment for long-term alcohol dependence are sufficiently discouraging to justify a concentrated search for alternatives. Prevention and early intervention represent two of the best alternatives.

In any given year in this country, no more than 10 percent of those who meet accepted criteria for alcohol dependence are attracted to treatment. Figures for victims of drug dependence are even lower; probably no more than 5 percent of them enter treatment in any given year. These figures include persons whose treatment largely involves contact with self-help groups as well as those treated by professionals.

Thus, year after year, nine out of ten alcoholics and drug addicts are not treated in this country. Chances are an even lower percentage of women, minorities, youths, and elderly persons are treated, largely because most treatment programs are designed to meet the needs of the prototypic white, middle-aged, male alcoholic (Nathan and Skinstad 1987).

Moreover, as surveys of the treatment outcome literature dating from the early 1970s to the present continue to affirm, even when long-term alcohol-dependent persons are treated, treatment is only modestly effective (see, for example, Emrick 1974; Emrick 1975; Nathan and Skinstad 1987; Vaillant 1983).

Despite strong convictions that the treatment methods used are the ones that work best, the data indicate otherwise. They suggest that different treatment methods do not differ significantly in their effect on the ultimate outcomes of treatment for long-term alcohol dependence. In other words, differences in the theoretical underpinnings of the therapies, as well as in the techniques and procedures themselves, do not appear to be associated with differences in treatment outcomes (Emrick 1975; Polich, Armor, and Braiker 1981; Vaillant 1983).

Unexpectedly, the same seems to be true about locus and intensity of treatment. Whether treatment takes place in an inpatient or an outpatient setting and whether treatment lasts a week, a month, or a year have not been shown to affect outcomes (Miller and Hester 1986a). These findings are counterintuitive and unexpected.

In contrast, outcomes of treatment for long-term alcohol dependence apparently do vary with a number of the factors specific to the patient, including age; gender; marital, educational, and occupational status; drinking history and pattern; psychiatric status; and degree of motivation for treatment (Miller and Hester 1986b; Nathan and Skinstad 1987). Unfortunately, there is only so much that practitioners can do about the resources a patient brings to treatment.

Alternatives to Treatment: Prevention and Early Intervention

Given the modest results of the U.S. effort to treat long-term alcohol- and drug-dependent persons, it is not surprising that many practitioners have refocused their energies in two directions: (1) on the attempt to prevent alcohol and drug problems from developing in the first place, and (2) on the attempt to intervene earlier, before emerging problems with alcohol and drugs develop into intractable long-term dependence.

Prevention

Funding. Despite the widely known fact that alcohol and drug abuse are among the nation's most pressing health and social problems, federal and state authorities have not seen fit to allocate much money to the prevention of alcohol and drug use. In a recent and representative year, for example, only 4 percent of the federal funds expended on alcohol-related activities were allocated to prevention (NIAAA 1985). Despite the extraordinarily small size of this commitment ($24 million) in relation to the size of the problem, these funds made up 64 percent of the public funds that all federal, state, and local sources spent on alcoholism prevention.

Both the amount and the percentage of public funds allocated to prevention-related programs for alcohol and drug abusers have increased in response to the belated recognition that these conditions have reached epidemic proportions in this country. Nonetheless, the percentage of funds for prevention remains substantially less than 10 percent of the public funds earmarked for all alcohol- and drug-related purposes.

One reason funds for prevention increased in the late 1980s was to support the Reagan administration's attempt to restrict the supply of drugs by destroying them where they are grown and intercepting those who bring them into this country for distribution and sale. Two groups have soundly criticized these prevention methods: (1) the leaders of the countries where the drugs are grown, who fault the United States for failing to enforce its existing laws against the purchase and sale of drugs, and (2) American politicians, who claim that the profit margin associated with illegal drugs is so great that it guarantees an adequate supply regardless of any effort to restrict their importation.

Empirical research on the effectiveness of efforts to control alcohol and drug addiction by restricting the availability of the substances, reviewed a bit later in this chapter, supports the critics of the Reagan administration's approach to control. These data indicate that attempting to reduce alcohol and drug dependence by restricting availability is least effective for the very persons for whom these efforts are most important—those who are most heavily addicted (Levy and Sheflin 1983; Levy and Sheflin 1985).

Public Education Programs. Educational efforts to prevent alcohol and drug abuse have focused on public education and school-based programs. In both cases, results have been modest.

While public education, most often via the mass media, is generally acknowledged to have succeeded in increasing public awareness of the hazards of alcohol and drug misuse, it has probably had little effect on the behavior of those most disabled by alcohol and drugs—those who have developed dependence.

Public education campaigns have had more success when they have focused on the consequences of alcohol misuse, specifically on drunken driving and the fetal alcohol syndrome. In both instances, public pressure generated by such campaigns has led to changes in public attitudes, corrective legislation, increased funding for research and prevention, and, most importantly, decreases in incidence (Fell 1985; Fell and Klein 1986; Prager et al. 1984).

School-Based Programs. Like public education programs, school-based prevention programs are supposed to increase knowledge about, and change attitudes toward, alcohol and drugs. In addition, in recognition of the presumed malleability of the target population, some of these programs have been designed to teach values and decision-making skills and to help develop social competence.

At least some of these programs have met these ambitious goals (Braucht and Braucht 1984; Rootman 1985). Some observers complain, however, that methodological problems prevent an unequivocal interpretation of these favorable outcomes (Flay 1985), while others have suggested that attitude-clarification and decision-making programs actually undermine the knowledge/attitudes curriculum (Schlegal, Manske, and Page 1984). Most troubling is that documented changes in drinking behavior following full implementation of these programs have been very rare, as have changes in the incidence of drinking and driving or changes in the risk of development of alcoholism later in life.

I suspect that, in many instances, the students who are most responsive to school-based programs are those for whom they are least important. Unhappily, these programs may not be reaching the children who are at greatest risk to develop alcohol and drug problems—those with a family history of abuse, those with a developmental history of antisocial behavior, and those from ethnic and racial minority groups, for example—because many of these children may remain physically or psychologically beyond the reach of traditional school-based prevention programs.

Much the same can be said of college campus–based prevention programs, which have developed in increasing numbers in recent years. These programs have produced clear evidence of changes in the bases of knowledge about alcohol and drugs, as well as in attitudes toward alcohol and drugs (Goodstadt and Caleekal-John 1984; Kraft 1984). Researchers have not, however, been able to document changes in drinking behavior of persons at the greatest risk of misusing alcohol and drugs (Moskowitz 1986).

Control of Availability. In contrast to the diverse educational programs, laws and regulations designed to control the availability of alcohol, by making its acquisition more expensive or by raising the minimum age of purchase, have had a demonstrable impact on both use and misuse.

Even relatively small increases in the price of distilled spirits (due largely to increases in state taxes) have been reported to reduce both consumption and deaths from cirrhosis and automobile crashes (Cook 1981; Cook and Tauchen 1982). In addition, data from a related series of studies suggest that higher prices for beer, the alcoholic beverage of choice among youths, reduce the number of young people who drink and the incidence of both heavy and frequent drinking (Grossman, Coate, and Arluck 1988; Coate and Grossman 1986).

In a complementary group of studies, Saffer and Grossman (1985) investigated relationships between state excise taxes on beer and motor vehicle accident mortality rates for young people during the years 1975 to 1981. They found that states with relatively high excise taxes on beer had lower death rates from motor vehicle accidents for youths between ages fifteen and twenty-four than states with lower excise taxes. Extrapolating from these findings, these investigators estimated that if the federal excise tax on beer had risen with the rate of inflation since 1951 (which it did not), the lives of 1,022 youths would have been saved.

In a discussion of the impact of price changes on demand for beer, wine, and spirits in various countries, Ornstein and Levy (1983) concluded that, in the United States, beer is relatively price inelastic, distilled spirits are price elastic, and the price elasticity of wine remains uncertain. That is, changes in the price of beer are more likely to affect consumption than are changes in the price of spirits or wine.

These findings, taken together, encourage the view that restricting the availability of alcoholic beverages by making them more expensive does affect both alcohol consumption and the consequences of alcohol misuse. In the United States, this impact appears to be the greatest for young people, for whom price is often an important issue.

These findings do not respond directly to the question of whether price is as important a determinant of consumption for those who habitually and regularly abuse alcohol as it is for those who misuse it in the bloom of impoverished youth and the absence of alcohol dependence. In this regard, most informed observers doubt that price alone substantially affects the rates of alcoholism in most Western countries, since the continued availability of alcohol to those dependent on it is more important than its modest cost.

Increasing the minimum age of purchase appears to have affected rates of alcohol misuse. For example, Wagenaar (1986), reported reductions of 16 percent in single vehicle nighttime crash involvement and 19 percent in police-reported alcohol-involved injury after legislation raising the minimum drinking age to twenty-one in Michigan was passed. Similarly, a study of the effects of the nationwide drive to raise the minimum age of purchase by the National Highway Traffic Safety Administration found a net effect of 13 percent fewer fatal crash involvements per year per affected driver in thirteen states in which the minimum age of purchase had been raised.

There is a major difficulty in interpreting these data on the impact of changes in minimum drinking age. At about the same time that the Reagan administration began its campaign to raise the minimum age of purchase, state and local authorities and voluntary groups nationwide launched strong efforts to reduce the incidence of drunk driving by other means. These means included markedly increased enforcement efforts, a dramatic stiffening in the legal and financial consequences of drunken driving, more public attention and effort by citizens' groups such as Mothers Against Drunk Driving (MADD) and Students Against Drunk Driving (SADD), and a quantum jump in public education activities. The net effect, a significant reduction in the involvement of youths in alcohol-related crashes during most of the past several years, has likely been a function of all these factors, both those affecting availability and those focused directly on drunk driving.

In other words, while there has been a reduction in alcohol-related crashes, it is not clear how this came about. That makes it more difficult to plan for similar beneficial changes elsewhere.

Summary. This selective survey of current approaches to prevention suggests that meaningful changes in consumption, especially by alcohol-dependent persons, as a direct result of alcohol education programs are exceedingly difficult to document. In contrast, restrictions on the availability of alcohol, by raising both taxes and the minimum age of purchase, have yielded real changes in both the consumption by youths and the consequences of consumption. Unhappily, we still do not know whether control of availability affects the heaviest drinking 20 percent of the population—those who consume 80 percent of the beverage alcohol. That issue continues to be hotly debated by preventionists who both support and oppose control of availability prevention methods. In the absence of research on the issue, my guess is

Early Intervention

While treatment for clients who have developed long-term alcohol dependence does appear to yield modest positive benefits, predictors of these positive outcomes relate more to the personal resources clients bring to treatment than to variations in the treatments themselves. Moreover, practitioners are better able to prevent some of the consequences of alcohol misuse, including drunk driving and the fetal alcohol syndrome, than long-term alcohol abuse itself.

Given the validity of these conclusions, it seems that even greater efforts to intervene in developing patterns of alcohol misuse make sense. Three promising efforts of this kind come to mind:

1. Early intervention programs for alcohol misusers who have not yet developed the physical and behavioral stigmata of chronic alcoholism
2. Relapse-prevention programs, which recognize the difficulty of maintaining long-term abstinence and are different from programs for achieving abstinence in the first place
3. Rational means to heighten the motivation of alcohol misusers and abusers to make meaningful changes in their drinking behavior

Early Intervention with Young Adult Alcohol Misusers. A number of investigators (including Annis 1986; Miller 1978; Miller, Gribskov, and Mortell 1981; Miller, Pechacek, and Hamburg 1981; Miller, Taylor, and West 1980; Sanchez-Craig et al. 1984; Sanchez-Craig and Wilkinson 1987) have reported promising results from trials of treatment with a special group of clients. Typically recruited through newspaper advertisements, these persons meet selection criteria establishing that they are in good physical health, do not have a history of psychiatric treatment, have maintained good social stability and social support, have been problem drinkers for a relatively short period of time, do not see themselves as alcoholic, reject abstinence as a long-term treatment goal, and wish to receive brief treatment for their drinking problems that will be minimally disruptive of their daily routines. While these clients are variously labeled, they are perhaps best considered young adult alcohol misusers. Few would meet DSM III-R criteria for moderate or severe alcohol dependence (American Psychiatric Association Staff, 1987).

Typically, these clients are seen for several months in outpatient settings. In virtually every instance, the goal of their brief treatment is to enable them to stabilize and ultimately moderate their drinking so that it does not reach alcoholic levels. A variety of behavioral techniques are used to teach clients self-control skills, which are expected to help them make more appropriate choices about when, where, and how much they drink.

The overall result of these attempts to induce young adult problem drinkers to modify a risky pattern of drinking have been promising. Reductions in rates of drinking of 30 percent and more have typically been reported, although follow-up periods have rarely extended beyond a year. Nonetheless, these brief interventions, which are intended specifically for persons who have just begun to misuse alcohol and are designed to prevent the development of alcoholism in the future as much as to treat current misuse, hold considerable promise. Additional research on outcomes is needed. Confirmation of the durability of the treatment effects, determination of the identity of the clients for whom this kind of intervention is most appropriate, and investigation of the extent to which these interventions inhibit the progression of drinking to alcoholic proportions are called for.

It is worth noting that the developers of broad-based employee assistance programs and wellness programs in industry have begun to target the same client population and to entertain similar goals for their ministrations. One of their aims is to attract to treatment not only persons whose alcohol and drug problems are of long duration and great severity, but also those who may have been arrested for the first time for drunk driving, have started to experience problems on the job or at home because of alcohol or drugs, or have begun to ask themselves whether they are beginning to develop a problem. The less insistent interventions associated with wellness programs, which generally focus on other health risks, may work especially well for these individuals (Feldman 1984; Naditch 1984). While data on the degree to which these programs succeed in inducing early alcohol and drug misusers to commit themselves to a program designed to modify their drinking patterns are hard to find, they will no doubt be forthcoming (Nathan 1984a; Nathan 1984b).

Cognitive Mediation of Relapse-Related Phenomena

Marlatt and his coworkers (Marlatt and Gordon 1985; Marlatt and Rohsenow 1980) have identified the importance of controlling cognitively mediated relapse-related phenomena during the alcoholism recovery and maintenance period. Directing their attention to the posttreatment cognitions of recovering alcoholics, Marlatt and his colleagues emphasize the importance of what they have termed the *abstinence violation effect,* the familiar scenario in which a single "slip" by the recovering alcoholic inexorably leads him or her to conclude that recovery is impossible and a quick return to alcoholic drinking is inevitable.

Marlatt and his colleagues propose a series of cognitively based interventions to alter this conviction. In so doing, they offer hope—and a set of intervention approaches—to those who share the belief that treatment does not end when the patient leaves the hospital and that intervention during the maintenance phase of treatment is a long-term enterprise that requires as much attention from both client and clinician as does the inpatient treatment that precedes it.

More recently, Marlatt (personal communication) has applied cognitive therapy methods derived from his relapse-prevention model to the heavy drinking of University of Washington fraternity members. Recognizing the justified association between alcohol misuse and fraternity drinking practices, Marlatt has developed an association with a fraternity at the university that permits him to test a series of intervention strategies designed to help the members of this fraternity moderate their drinking behavior.

Treatment Motivation and Treatment Outcomes

Miller (1985) and Miller and Sanchez (1988) have attempted to gain a more in-depth understanding of the factors that influence motivation for treatment in order to develop procedures to heighten motivation. This research is based on the assumption that increasing treatment motivation will increase the likelihood that alcohol-abusing clients will be able to benefit from treatment.

Miller (1985) concluded from an extensive review of the literature that feedback to the abusive drinker from a trusted friend or counselor on the likelihood that the drinker will develop serious alcohol-related problems is central to most effective motivational programs. His conviction derives in part from a series of studies in both the United States and Europe to the effect that relatively brief interventions, if done right, can have a lasting effect on problem drinking, an effect comparable in magnitude to much more extensive, costly, and prolonged interventions (see, for example, Heather, Whitton, and Robertson 1986; Kristensen 1983; Ritson 1986). Miller and others are impressed by Edwards's classic demonstration (Edwards et al. 1977) that brief advice about the seriousness of a drinking problem can lead to changes in the drinking behavior of alcohol-dependent persons as pronounced as those induced by far more extensive treatment.

At the core of Miller's effort to heighten motivation is the drinker's checkup, a three-hour assessment procedure ostensibly designed to detect both risk factors and the harmful consequences of overdrinking on neuropsychological, physical, social, and psychological behavior (Miller, Sovereign, and Krege in press). Implicit in the assessment is Miller's conviction that informing the early-stage problem drinker of the details of alcohol's harmful effects on him or her may lead the person to do something about the drinking that he or she might not have done in the absence of this information.

Initial research on the drinker's check-up indicates that the results of this assessment have greater short- and long-term effects on drinking when the feedback is presented in such a way as to elicit and reflect the drinker's reactions to it rather than in a confrontational manner. Miller explains these findings by pointing to the importance of getting alcohol misusers to take personal responsibility for a change in their drinking behavior. The drinker's check-up, and the manner in which its results are presented to the drinker, represent a promising vehicle for getting drinkers to take responsibility for their own behavior and benefit from the brief but accurate advice the counselor is able to give.

References

Annis, H.M. 1986. "Is Inpatient Rehabilitation of the Alcoholic Cost Effective? Con Position." *Advances in Alcohol and Substance Abuse* 5:179–85.

APA (American Psychiatric Association) Committee on Drug Abuse. 1987. "Position Statement on Psychoactive Substance Use and Dependence: Update on Marijuana and Cocaine." *American Journal of Psychiatry* 144:698–701.

APA (American Psychiatric Association) Staff. 1987. *Diagnostic and Statistical Manual of Mental Disorders, DSM-III-R*. 3rd, rev. ed. Washington, D.C.: American Psychiatric Press.

Arnold, R.D. 1985. "Effective Raising the Legal Drinking Age on Driver Involvement in Fatal Crashes: The Experience of 13 States." *National Highway Traffic Safety Administration Technical Report*, Department of Transportation HS 806902, Washington, D.C.: GPO.

Braucht, G.N., and B. Braucht. 1984. "Prevention of Problem Drinking among Youth: Evaluation of Educational Strategies." In *Prevention of Alcohol Abuse*, edited by P.M. Miller and T.D. Nirenberg, 253–79. New York: Plenum Press.

Coate, D., and M. Grossman. 1986. "Effects of Alcoholic Beverage Prices and Legal Drinking Ages on Youth Alcohol Use: Results from the Second National Health and Nutrition Examination Survey." Unpublished manuscript, National Bureau of Economic Research, New York.

Cook, P. 1981. "The Effect of Liquor Taxes on Drinking, Cirrhosis and Auto Accidents." In *Alcohol and Public Policy: Beyond the Shadow of Prohibition*, edited by M. Moore and D. Gerstein, 255–85. Washington, D.C.: National Academy Press.

Cook, P., and G. Tauchen. 1982. "The Effect of Liquor Taxes on Heavy Drinking." *Bell Journal of Economics* 13:379–90.

Edwards, G., J. Orford, S. Egert, S. Guthrie, A. Hawker, C. Hensman, M. Mitcheson, E. Oppenheimer, and C. Taylor. 1977. "Alcoholism: A Controlled Trial of 'Treatment' and 'Advice.'" *Journal of Studies on Alcohol* 38:1004–31.

Emrick, C.D. 1974. "A Review of Psychologically Oriented Treatment for Alcoholism. Part 1: The Use and Interrelationships of Outcome Criteria and Drinking Behavior Following Treatment." *Journal of Studies on Alcohol* 35:534–49.

———. 1975. "A Review of Psychologically Oriented Treatment of Alcoholism. Part 2: The Relative Effectiveness of Different Treatment Approaches and the Effectiveness of Treatment versus No-Treatment." *Journal of Studies on Alcohol* 36:88–108.

Feldman, R.H.L. 1984. "Evaluating Health Promotion in the Workplace." In *Behavioral Health*, edited by J.D. Matarazzo, S.M. Weiss, J.A. Herd, N.E. Miller, and S.M. Weiss, 1087–93. New York: Wiley-Interscience.

Fell, J.C. 1985. "Alcohol in Fatally Injured Drivers—1984." *National Highway Traffic Safety Administration Research Notes*, Washington, D.C.: GPO.

Fell, J.C., and T. Klein. 1986. "The Nature of the Reduction in Alcohol in U.S. Fatal Crashes." SAE Technical Paper Series, no. 860038. Society of Automotive Engineers, Warrendale, Pa.

Flay, B. 1985. "What We Know about the Social Influences Approach to Smoking Prevention: Review and Recommendations." In *Prevention Research: Deterring Drug Abuse among Children and Adolescents*, edited by C. Bell and R. Battjes, 67–112. NIDA Research Monograph Series, no. 63. Washington, D.C.: GPO.

Goldstein, P.J. 1985. "The Drugs/Violence Nexus: A Tripartite Conceptual Framework." *Journal of Drug Issues* 15:493–506.

Goodstadt, M., and A. Caleekal-John. 1984. "Alcohol Education Programs for University Students: A Review of Their Effectiveness." *International Journal of the Addictions* 19:721–41.

Grossman, M., D. Coate, and G.M. Arluck. 1988. "Price Sensitivity of Alcoholic Beverages: Youth Alcohol Use and Motor Vehicle Accident Mortality." In *Control Issues in Alcohol Abuse Prevention: Strategies for States and Communities*, edited by H.D. Holder, Greenwich, Conn. JAI Press.

Harwood, H.J. 1984. *Economic Cost to Society of Alcohol and Drug Abuse and Mental Illness: 1980*. Washington, D.C.: Alcohol, Drug Abuse, and Mental Health Administration.

Heather, N., B. Whitton, and I. Robertson. 1986. "Evaluation of a Self-Help Manual for Media-Recruited Problem Drinkers: Six Month Follow-up Results." *British Journal of Clinical Psychology* 25:19–34.

Kraft, D. 1984. "A Comprehensive Prevention Program for College Students." In *Prevention of Alcohol Abuse*, edited by P.M. Miller and T. Nirenberg, 327–69. New York: Plenum Press.

Kristensen, H. 1983. *Studies on Alcohol Related Disabilities in a Medical Intervention*. 2d ed. Malmo, Sweden: University of Lund.

Levy, D., and N. Sheflin. 1983. "New Evidence on Controlling Alcohol Use through Price." *Journal of Studies on Alcohol* 44:929–37.

———. 1985. "The Demand for Alcoholic Beverages: An Aggregate Time Series Analysis." *Journal of Public Policy Marketing* 4:47–54.

Marlatt, G.A., and J. Gordon. 1985. *Relapse Prevention*. New York: Guilford Press.

Marlatt, G.A., and D.J. Rohsenow. 1980. "Cognitive Processes in Alcohol Use: Expectancy and the Balanced Placebo Design." In *Advances in Substance Abuse: Behavioral and Biological Research*, edited by N.K. Mello, Greenwich, Conn.: JAI Press.

Miller, W.R. 1978. "Behavioral Treatment of Problem Drinkers: A Comparative Outcome Study of Three Controlled Drinking Therapies." *Journal of Consulting and Clinical Psychology* 46:74–86.

---. 1985. "Motivation for Treatment: A Review with Special Emphasis on Alcoholism." *Psychological Bulletin* 98:84–107.
---. C.J. Gribskov, and R.L. Mortell. 1981. "Effectiveness of a Self-Control Manual for Problem Drinkers with and without Therapist Contact." *International Journal of the Addictions* 16:1247–54.
Miller, W.R., and R.K. Hester. 1986a. "Inpatient Alcoholism Treatment: Who Benefits?" *American Psychologist* 41:794–805.
---. 1986b. "The Effectiveness of Alcoholism Treatment: What Research Reveals." In *Treating Addictive Behaviors: Processes of Change*, edited by W.R. Miller and N. Heather, 121–74. New York: Plenum Press.
Miller, W.R., T.F. Pechacek, and S. Hamburg. 1981. "Group Behavior Therapy for Problem Drinkers." *International Journal of the Addictions* 16:829–39.
Miller, W.R., and V.C. Sanchez. 1988. "Motivating Young Adults for Treatment and Lifestyle Change." Paper presented at the conference Issues in Alcohol Use and Misuse by Young Adults, University of Notre Dame, April.
Miller, W.R., R.G., Sovereign, and B. Krege. "Motivational Interviewing with Problem Drinkers. Part 2: The Drinker's Check-up as a Preventive Intervention." *Behavioral Psychotherapy*.
Miller, W.R., C.A. Taylor, and J. West. 1980. "Focused versus Broad-Spectrum Behavior Therapy for Problem Drinkers." *Journal of Consulting and Clinical Psychology* 48:590–601.
Moskowitz, J. 1986. *The Primary Prevention of Alcohol Problems*. Berkeley, Calif: Prevention Research Center.
Naditch, M.P. 1984. "The Staywell Program." In *Behavioral Health*, edited by J.D. Matarazzo, S.M. Weiss, J.A. Herd, N.E. Miller, and S.M. Weiss, 1071–78. New York: Wiley-Interscience.
Nathan, P.E. 1984a. "Johnson & Johnson's Live for Life: A Comprehensive Positive Lifestyle Change Program." In *Behavioral Health*, edited by J.D. Matarazzo, S.M. Weiss, J.A. Herd, N.E. Miller, and S.M. Weiss, 1064–70. New York: Wiley-Interscience.
---. 1984b. "Alcohol Prevention in the Workplace." In *Prevention of Alcohol Abuse*, edited by P.M. Miller and T.D. Nirenberg, 387–406. New York: Plenum Press.
Nathan, P.E., and A-H. Skinstad. 1987. "Outcomes of Treatment for Alcohol Problems: Current Methods, Problems, and Results." *Journal of Consulting and Clinical Psychology* 55:332–40.
NIAAA. 1985. *Fifth Special Report to Congress on Alcohol and Health*. Washington, D.C.: National Institute on Alcohol Abuse and Alcoholism.
---. 1987. *Sixth Special Report to Congress on Alcohol and Health*. Washington, D.C.: National Institute on Alcohol Abuse and Alcoholism.
Ornstein, S., and D. Levy. 1983. "Price and Income Elasticities of Demand for Alcoholic Beverages." In *Recent Developments in Alcoholism*, edited by M. Galantov. vol. 1, 303–45. New York: Plenum Press.
Polich, J.M., D.J. Armor, and H.B. Braiker. 1981. *The Course of Alcoholism: Four Years after Treatment*. New York: Wiley Interscience.
Prager, K., H. Malin, D. Spiegler, P. Van Natta, and P.J. Placek. 1984. "Smoking and Drinking Behavior before and during Pregnancy of Married Mothers of Live Born Infants and Stillborn Infants." *Public Health Reports* 99:117–27.

Ravenholt, R.T. 1984. "Addiction Mortality in the United States, 1980: Tobacco, Alcohol, and Other Substances." *Population and Development Review* 10:697–724.

Ritson, B. 1986. "The Merits of Simple Intervention." In *Treating Addictive Behaviors: Processes on Change*, edited by W.R. Miller and N. Heather, 375–87. New York: Plenum Press.

Rootman, I. 1985. "Preventing Alcohol Problems: A Challenge for Health Promotion." *Health Education* 24:2–7.

Saffer, H., and M. Grossman. 1985. "Effects of Beer Prices and Legal Drinking Ages on Youth Motor Vehicle Fatalities." Unpublished manuscript, National Bureau of Economic Research, New York.

Sanchez-Craig, M., H.M. Annis, A.R. Bornet, and K.R. MacDonald. 1984. "Random Assignment to Abstinence and Controlled Drinking: Evaluation of a Cognitive-Behavioural Program for Problem Drinkers." *Journal of Consulting and Clinical Psychology* 52:390–403.

Sanchez-Craig, M., and D.A. Wilkinson. 1987. "Brief Treatments for Alcohol and Drug Problems: Practical and Methodological Issues." Paper presented at the Fourth International Conference on Treatment of Addictive Behaviors, Bergen, Norway, August.

Schlegal, R., S. Manske, and A. Page. 1984. "A Guided Decision-Making Program for Elementary School Students." In *Prevention of Alcohol Abuse*, edited by P.M. Miller and T.D. Nirenberg, 407–39. New York: Plenum Press.

Vaillant, G.E. 1983. *The Natural History of Alcoholism*. Cambridge, Mass.: Harvard University Press.

Wagenaar, A.C. 1986. "Preventing Highway Crashes by Raising the Legal Minimum Age for Drinking: The Michigan Experience Six Years Later." *Journal of Safety Research* 17:101–9.

6
The Assessment and Treatment of Alcohol- and Drug-Related Traffic Offenders

David S. Timken

In 1979, the Colorado state legislature passed legislation that continued and expanded an innovative program to deal with offenders convicted of alcohol- and drug-related traffic offenses. Since that time, the legislation has established itself as a unique, state-of-the-art program in the areas of screening, referral, treatment, and monitoring of offenders, and it has gained acceptance around the country as a model.

The Legislation

The legislation established an Alcohol Drug Driving Safety (ADDS) program in each of the state's twenty-two judicial districts. The ADDS programs are managed by the Alcohol and Drug Abuse Division (ADAD) of the Colorado Department of Health. ADAD then contracts for the services of alcohol and drug evaluation specialists (ADES), who are employed by the probation departments within each judicial district. ADAD is responsible for the training and certification of the ADES. The ADES enters the process after an offender has been convicted, pled guilty, or received a deferred prosecution of sentence to an alcohol- or drug-related offense. The diagnostic classification and referral recommendation made by the ADES is taken into consideration by the judge during sentencing, and the law allows the recommended treatment and/or education to take the place of a significant portion of the jail sentence. The ADES are responsible for monitoring the offender's fulfillment of the education and/or treatment process.

The Law

The law in Colorado that determines at what point a person can be convicted of driving under the influence of alcohol or drugs is similar to other laws throughout the United States. When a law enforcement officer suspects a motorist of an alcohol- or drug-related traffic offense, the officer administers a roadside sobriety test. This test may include the Rhomberg balance, reciting the alphabet, walking a straight line, touching a finger to the nose and earlobe, and the officer's observation of the suspect performing these maneuvers (Ackerman and Lawson 1984). Failure to perform these maneuvers adequately usually results in the driver being charged with driving under the influence (DUI). At this point, the accused is given the choice of a blood or breath test to determine the precise amount of alcohol present in his or her blood. The accused can refuse to submit to either test but will then lose his or her driver's license for three months under the expressed consent law. In the state of Colorado, application for a driver's license automatically signals consent to a blood alcohol concentration (BAC) test if the driver is ever accused of an alcohol- or drug-related offense.

A BAC of 0.05 to 0.099 results in a charge of driving while ability impaired (DWAI). If the BAC is above 0.10, the charge is DUI. Under special circumstances, the charge can be DUI per se, which includes an automatic ninety-day license revocation. The conviction rate in Colorado for alcohol- and drug-related traffic offenses is now more than 85 percent (Akerman and Lawson 1984).

All alcohol- or drug-related traffic offenses carry a mandatory jail term in the state of Colorado. The minimum is two days for a first offense DWAI, escalating to ninety days for a second offense DUI. For a first offense of either DWAI or DUI, the entire mandatory jail term can be suspended. For a second offense, a large part of the jail term may be suspended—up to eighty-three of the ninety days for a DUI. This system of suspending jail time for successfully completing education and/or treatment gives the state of Colorado the opportunity to try to change the drinking and driving behavior of many offenders.

The Evaluation Process

Alcohol and Drug Evaluation Specialists

To be eligible for training as an ADES, a person must have graduated from a four-year college or university with a degree in social sciences, psychology, sociology, substance abuse, or a related field; have experience or training in alcohol or drug evaluation or counseling; or have experience in correctional or probation programs. Prospective ADES are required to complete a forty-hour training program conducted by ADAD. The training program is multifaceted and includes the following subjects: alcohol and drug evaluation techniques, drinker classification, diagnostic referral, client supervision and monitoring, data reporting and program evaluation, highway safety issues, criminal and administrative statutes related to DUI and DWAI, criminal justice system and probation procedures, and treatment modalities.

After completing the ADAD training, prospective ADES become eligible for state certification, which is issued for one year. For the certification to be renewed, ADES must prove that they have taken sixteen hours of approved training in substance abuse, probation-related topics, or management, with at least eight of those hours in substance abuse training, in addition to having performed their job in a manner satisfactory to ADAD.

This system of training and certification has created a highly professional corps of ADES within the state. Having their training and certification done by ADAD while having them employed by the probation departments within the judicial districts rather than by the treatment agencies avoids any possibility of a conflict of interest.

Evaluation Procedures

The ADES uses a variety of procedures to get an accurate picture of the offender's substance misuse and driving behavior. These include the arrest report, the official driving record, the court files, including the BAC and the offender's statement, and records of prior education or treatment if the offender has been previously convicted of an alcohol- or drug-related traffic offense. The ADES also administers the Drinking/Drug History Questionnaire (DDHQ) (Wanberg et al. 1974) and the Court Procedures for Identifying Problem Drinkers, commonly known as the Mortimer-Filkins test (NHTSA 1968). The final tool in the assessment procedure is a structured interview with the offender. All these together provide a reasonably clear picture of the offender's drinking behavior so that accurate classification and appropriate referral can be made.

Background Information. The ADES can learn a significant amount about a client's drinking behavior from the basic information he or she receives. The most useful pieces of information are those about prior arrests and convictions, prior diagnoses of drug and alcohol problems, the BAC at the time of the arrest, the client's employment history, and any complications related to alcohol or drug abuse. A prior arrest for alcohol- or drug-related offenses is the single best indicator of a problem with alcohol or drugs (Timken 1985). The odds are very much against a person being caught while driving under the influence, and a previous arrest is usually an indication of a dangerous pattern of drinking and driving. The ADES closely examines any arrests for hit and run, reckless driving, or careless driving. Many of these may actually have been alcohol- or drug-related traffic offenses that for some reason were not charged as such.

When a client comes to an ADES with a prior diagnosis of alcohol- or drug-related problems, that diagnosis is carefully considered. The ADES looks at where the diagnosis was done, when it was done, and what criteria and tests were used. A prior diagnosis can never be accepted at face value, but if it holds up under thorough examination, the client must be classified as a problem drinker or drug user.

The BAC at the time of the arrest reveals considerable information to the skilled eye. A BAC of 0.25, for example, indicates that the client has developed a tolerance for alcohol that is consistent with problem drinking. A nondrinker would pass out or get sick long before reaching that level.

A client's employment history also may show signs of a problem with alcohol or drugs. The ADES looks for things such as being fired for alcohol or drug use, drinking or drug use on the job, and arriving for work late or hung over. All of these may be indications of a serious drug or alcohol problem.

Certain medical conditions that show up on a physician's report may indicate that there is a serious problem with alcohol. Things such as alcoholic liver disease (fatty liver, alcoholic hepatitis, or cirrhosis), alcoholic pancreatitis, or alcoholic cardiomyopathy lead the ADES to assume a long-term pattern of alcohol abuse.

Drinking/Drug History Questionnaire. The original DDHQ was developed in 1972 by the Alcohol-Driving Countermeasures staff in the state of Colorado. The DDHQ used today is a synthesis of the Minnesota Multiphasic Personality Inventory (MMPI), the Michigan Alcohol Screening Test (MAST), and other drinking history questionnaires used in alcohol treatment programs and diagnostic clinics throughout the country. After analysis of the various testing instruments, only those questions that reliably separate subjects into three broad categories were retained. The categories—problem drinker or drug user, incipient problem drinker or drug user, and social drinker or drug user—are discussed later in this chapter.

The DDHQ was validated on 150 subjects against the following criteria: drinker type diagnosis based on prior drinking record, drinker type diagnosis based on recidivism subsequent to DDHQ diagnosis, and drinker type diagnosis based on the Fort Logan Drinking History Scale (Wanberg 1968), which has been validated on more than four thousand persons (Wanberg et al. 1974). Correlations on these three measures were 0.89, 0.86, and 0.98.

Mortimer-Filkins Test. The Mortimer-Filkins test was developed by Rudolf G. Mortimer and Lyle D. Filkins (NHTSA 1968) of the Highway Safety Research Institute of the University of Michigan and recommended by the U.S. Department of Transportation (Nichols 1987). It was designed to test for alcoholism in drivers charged with DWAI and DUI.

Mortimer and Filkins began development of their test by surveying the professional literature related to drinking and driving and studying the needs of court personnel. Their research determined that good diagnostic procedures should take into account the previous traffic and criminal records of alcohol-related offenders; be structured in a manner that would encourage rapport; be subtle enough to discourage faking; be inexpensive, quick, and easy to use in a variety of settings for people with minimal training; be objective, standardized, valid, and reliable; be easy to understand, score, and interpret; be unambiguous; and cover a variety of signs and symptoms relevant to detection of alcoholism in its early stages. The authors began with more than 450 questions and reduced those to 58 using item analysis and testing against a control group of known alcoholics. The final version of the test has been subjected to diligent testing and has been shown to have a high degree of reliability and validity.

The 58-question test can be administered individually or in groups and takes no more than fifteen minutes. It is followed by an interview that takes approximately thirty minutes. The person conducting the test needs no special qualifications, and the scoring of the test is relatively objective and results in a numerical score that is helpful in explaining the results of the test.

The Mortimer-Filkins test divides the subjects into the categories of problem drinker, incipient problem drinker, and social drinker. The test authors took the philosophical position that it was important to minimize the number of social drinkers who might be misclassified as problem drinkers. In practice, the test underdiagnoses about 17 percent of the time under the assumption that it is better to underdiagnose some problem drinkers than to label some social drinkers as problem drinkers.

The Interview. The interview is the final step in the evaluation process. It should be remembered that this is a diagnostic rather than a therapeutic interview. The purpose is to gather information that will be helpful in making recommendations to the court. The interview is divided into three sections and the interviewer has specific goals for each section.

The opening section of the interview is important because it sets the tone for the entire interview. The interviewer helps the client to feel at ease and to say whatever is important or necessary. The interviewer talks about the law under which the client has been charged and thoroughly explains the testing involved in the evaluation process. The better the client understands what will happen and the more cooperative the client becomes, the easier it is for the interviewer to get the information needed to make the appropriate classification and referral.

The middle part of the interview is where the majority of the information is collected. The ADES are trained to gather as much information as possible in a short period of time. This part of the interview always includes a discussion of the incident that caused the arrest. Hearing what led up to the incident, what happened, what followed, and how the client feels about it gives the interviewer a better understanding of the client as well as the facts of the case. The interviewer then moves into a more general discussion of the client's lifestyle and how alcohol and drugs play a role in that lifestyle.

The closing section of the interview is where the client is told what sort of classification referral is going to be made. Again, the interviewer explains all the information that went into making the decision and goes into as much detail as the client needs to fully understand the result. It is imperative that the client knows exactly what sort of classification and referral recommendation is going to be made so that the judge's ruling does not come as a surprise. The goal at the end of the interview is to leave the client with the feeling that the ADES has been open, honest, and helpful and that he or she had the client's best interests in mind. Clients who leave with these feelings and more likely to be cooperative about receiving help, even if accepting the facts is difficult.

Classification and Referral

When the ADES reaches the point of making a classification, he or she applies a firm set of criteria developed by ADAD (see the chapter appendix). These criteria, based on the factors discussed in the previous section, result in a classification of problem drinker or drug user, incipient problem drinker or drug user, or social drinker or drug user that is objective and leaves no room for charges of personal bias. Of the 300,000 cases handled by ADES since the inception of the program, the offenders were classified as follows: 52 percent problem drinkers or drug users, 30 percent incipient problem drinkers or drug users, and 18 percent social drinkers or drug users (ADAD 1986). Once the classification has been made, the ADES can make the appropriate referral.

When the ADES reaches the point of making a referral, he or she has two different types of decisions to make. The first is whether to refer the client to a Level I education program, a Level II education program, or a combination Level II education and therapy program. These programs are discussed in the following sections. Level I education is reserved solely for those clients who have been classified as social drinkers or drug users. All incipient problem drinkers or drug users are referred to at least a Level II education program. If the offender had a BAC of more than 0.20 at the time of the arrest, had prior alcohol or drug offenses, or requests therapy, he or she is referred to both level II education and therapy. Most clients who are classified as problem drinkers or drug users are referred to both Level II education and Level II therapy. Level II therapy alone is chosen only for those problem drinkers or drug users who have psychiatric or other conditions that would make education ineffectual.

The second decision the ADES has to make is which specific education or treatment program to recommend. Because of the vastly heterogeneous nature of the offender population, there is a wide range of treatment programs and strategies to consider. Every effort is made to match the offender to the most appropriate form of treatment. The client's age, race, sex, sexual orientation, alcohol or drug abuse history, ability to pay, and attitude toward treatment are all considered in the choice of treatment program. There are 221 Level I and II treatment programs licensed by ADAD in both the public and private sector. These offer a variety of services, including group and individual therapy, disulfiram (Antabuse) therapy, and outpatient and inpatient treatment.

Education and Therapy Programs

Level I

Level I programs are short-term didactic alcohol and drug-driving education programs. They are intended to be educational rather than therapeutic and provide information about the effects of alcohol and drugs on driving so that the offenders can learn the facts and decide whether they need to make changes in their behavior.

Any agency or individual may operate a Level I program after being certified by ADAD. To receive certification, a program must provide ADAD with a copy of its curriculum; proof that its instructors have the proper education, experience, or training in social science, psychology, counseling, alcohol or drug rehabilitation, education, traffic safety, or law; its fee schedule; and a detailed written description of the program. After reviewing the written application, ADAD conducts a site visit of the program before issuing certification.

Level I education programs are limited to twenty-five members per class and are required to range between four and eight sessions. Each session must be at least two hours long, for a total of eight to sixteen hours. There is a great deal of flexibility within these requirements. Most programs are conducted once a week for six to eight weeks, but it is acceptable for a program to have a one-day marathon session as long as there are at least four two-hour sessions and all the required topics are covered.

Level I education programs are required to cover the following topics: the history, use, and definition of alcohol; legal and illegal drugs and their effects on driving; the psychological and sociological consequences of the use and abuse of alcohol and drugs; BAC and its effects on driving performance;

court penalties; a review of treatment approaches and programs; and alternatives to drinking and driving. The programs are required to have clients take a pretest and a posttest so that ADAD can judge the effectiveness of the program.

Level I programs also are required to maintain an individual record on each client. These records must include court records; results of the pretest and posttest; attendance records; generalized group notes about the topics and contents of each session; signed releases for the exchange of information with the referring court, the ADES, and the Revenue Department Hearing Section (RDHS); copies of all written reports and correspondence submitted to the court, ADES, and RDHS; and notes on all telephone contact and information exchanged orally with the courts, ADES, and RDHS concerning client cooperation, attendance, treatment progress, modalities, and fee payment.

Level II

The optimal and usual referral is for a combination of both Level II education and Level II therapy. Level II education and therapy programs may be run by any agency that is fully licensed by the Colorado Department of Health as an alcohol or drug rehabilitation program. The counselors must be certified by ADAD at advanced levels or supervised by a certified counselor. Level II programs must have a standardized client intake procedure that includes the ADAD client management methodology and a differential diagnostic procedure.

Education. Level II education is designed to be both educational and therapeutic. This is done by combining the informational approach of Level I education with the therapeutic group process.

Level II education programs are required to meet for eight to twelve sessions, for a total of twenty to thirty hours. These programs are not as flexible as Level I programs. No more than one three-hour session can be held in a twenty-four-hour period, and no more than two sessions can be conducted in any one week. The groups are limited to twelve members rather than twenty-five. Level II education programs have the same content requirements as Level I education programs, along with the added component of the structured group process.

Level II education programs are responsible for keeping the same records as Level I programs, as well as a written service plan specifying general problems, educational interventions planned, and goals to be achieved. The educational sessions are charted similarly to group counseling sessions, with an analysis of group dynamics that focuses on the educational topics covered and the individual clients grasp of the content.

Therapy. Level II therapy is directed toward helping clients overcome their problems with alcohol or drugs. Clients who are classified as incipient problem drinkers or drug users and are referred to therapy are required to complete a minimum of twenty-six hours of group and/or individual therapy conducted over a period of not less than sixteen weeks. Clients classified as problem drinkers or drug users must complete a minimum of forty hours of therapy conducted over a period of not less than twenty weeks. Group therapy sessions are not to be less than ninety minutes in length, and no part of Level II education can count toward the required hours of therapy.

If a Level II program determines that a client needs specialized services or therapies—such as primary drug therapy, mental health counseling, or services for special handicaps—the client is referred to the appropriate service agency for that therapy. If the client is ordered by the court to take disulfiram, the Level II program must make that available under the following guidelines: It must always be used conjointly with the counseling described in the treatment plan, the program must have written policies and procedures for the use of disulfiram that follow ADAD guidelines, and the drug must be ingested in the presence of a staff member.

Level II therapy programs are responsible for keeping the same records as the other programs, along with a progress note in the client's file for each counseling session. This may be in the form of an individual progress note for that client or a combined note for the group sessions that describes the group interaction and adds a brief note regarding the client's participation. These notes also describe the problems dealt with, the progress toward treatment goals, and the length of the session. Under extreme circumstances, the ADES may make a referral to an inpatient Level II therapy program.

Monitoring Clients

The ADES are responsible for monitoring the clients' fulfillment of their sentence requirements. This is done through the reports received from the education or treatment agencies concerning each client's enrollment, participation, attendance, payment, and completion of the required program. If the client fails to meet any of the requirements of the court-ordered program, the ADES tries to contact the offender. If he or she is unable to do so, the ADES asks the court that a bench warrant be issued for the client. When the client is rearrested and returned to court for resentencing, the ADES makes a new recommendation. This new recommendation may be to resentence the client to the original program, to resentence the client to a different program, or, if the ADES determines that the client would not benefit from education or therapy programs, to recommend that they serve the original jail sentence.

Program Evaluation

The 1986 Study

The real test of a drinking and driving intervention program is its effectiveness. In 1986, an extensive study of the ADDS program was done by Robert Booth of ADAD (Booth 1986). The study examined many aspects of the program, including the recidivism rate among various demographic groups, and compared the recidivism rate of those offenders who were referred to and enrolled in treatment with the rate of those who were referred but failed to enroll.

The study group consisted off 3,498 randomly selected subjects chosen from the original evaluation reports of ADES made between July 1981 and December 1982. Of those 3,498, data were obtained from the Division of Motor Vehicles for 2,705 of the subjects, who constituted the sample analyzed in the study. The ADES were then sent questionnaires concerning each offender's participation and termination status and the nature of the intervention required.

The study found the highest rate of recidivism (18 percent) among offenders who were required to enroll for education or therapy and failed to do so. The recidivism rates for those who enrolled ranged from 5.6 percent for Level I education to 13.5 percent for Level II therapy. Among those who enrolled in the required therapy or education, the most meaningful predictor of recidivism was failure to complete the education or therapy.

The 1988 Study

Mendelson (1988) did another study of the ADDS program in 1988 that compared the recidivism rate for offenders who had completed education or therapy with the rate for offenders who had enrolled in treatment and failed to complete it.

The study consisted of 28,898 individuals who were convicted of DUI or DWAI between 1981 and 1986. All of the study subjects were evaluated by ADES between May 1984 and June 1985. ADAD was able to get the necessary data from the Division of Motor Vehicles for 27,593 of the subjects. Of those, 25,369 had treatment records. The 2,224 who did not report for treatment were not included in the study.

Among those who successfully completed Level I education, the recidivism rate was 4.5 percent, compared with 7.2 percent for those who did not complete the program. For those who successfully completed Level II education, the recidivism rate was 6.1 percent, compared with 13.1 percent for those who failed to complete the program. For those who successfully completed both Level II education and therapy, the recidivism rate was 10.4 percent, compared with 14.4 percent for those who failed to complete both programs. For those sent to Level II therapy only, the recidivism rate for those who successfully completed the program was 12.4 percent, compared with 17.1 percent for those who did not complete it. For the study group as a whole, the recidivism rate was 7.1 percent for those who completed their program and 14 percent for those who did not. The results must be interpreted with caution, however, because of the lack of a formally developed control group in which the subjects were not sentenced to education or treatment.

Conclusion

The studies show that the ADDS program has clearly had a positive effect on the behavior of those convicted of alcohol- and drug-related traffic offenses. At the same time, the program has room for expansion. There is a need for refinement in the assessment procedure for those who are convicted of driving under the influence of drugs other than alcohol, and there needs to be more program development in the area of repeat offenders.

The ADDS program has broken new ground in its response to alcohol- and drug-related traffic offenses. Its approach to the screening, referral, treatment, and monitoring of offenders has made it something of a flagship program for the country as a whole.

References

Ackerman, H.R., and H.O. Lawson. 1984. *Driving under the Influence in Colorado: Key Steps in the Process.* Denver: Colorado Division of Highway Safety.

ADAD. 1986. *Standards and Regulations for Alcoholism and Intoxication Treatment and Rehabilitation Programs.* Denver: Colorado Department of Health, Alcohol and Drug Abuse Division.

Booth, R. 1986. *Education/Treatment Intervention among Drinking Drivers and Recidivism.* Denver: Colorado Department of Health, Alcohol and Drug Abuse Division.

Mendelson, B. 1988. *The Effectiveness of Education and Treatment in Reducing Recidivism among Drinking Drivers.* Denver: Colorado Department of Health, Alcohol and Drug Abuse Division.

NHTSA (National Highway Traffic Safety Administration). 1968. *Court Procedures for Identifying Problem Drinkers.* Washington, D.C.: GPO.

Timken, D.S. 1985. *Screening and Referral Manual for Alcohol/Drug Related Traffic Offenders.* Denver: Colorado Department of Health, Alcohol and Drug Abuse Division.

Wanberg, K. 1968. "Fort Logan Drinking History Scale." Unpublished research findings, Denver, Col.

Wanberg, K, R. Daetwiler, J. Vogt, and D. Timken. 1974. *Drinking/Drug Use History Questionnaire*. Denver: Colorado Department of Health, Alcohol and Drug Abuse Division.

Appendix 6–A: Classification Criteria

I. Problem drinker or drug user
   A. A client who exhibits any one of the following indicators:
      1. Two or more previous alcohol- or drug-related arrests or convictions
      2. A BAC ⩾0.25
      3. Loss of control of alcohol or drug use
      4. Self-admission of problem drinking or drug use
      5. A prior diagnosis of problem drinking or drug use
      6. An organic brain disease associated with alcohol or drug use
   B. A client who exhibits two or more of the following indicators:
      1. One prior alcohol- or drug-related arrest or conviction
      2. A Mortimer-Filkins score of ⩾12
      3. A BAC of ⩾0.15
      4. Employment problems due to alcohol or drug use
      5. Previous contact with social or medical facilities for problems associated with alcohol or drug use
      6. Blackouts associated with alcohol or drug use
      7. Passing out associated with alcohol or drug use
      8. Withdrawal symptoms
         a. Tremulousness
         b. Alcoholic hallucinations
         c. Auditory hallucinations
         d. Convulsive seizures
         e. Delirium tremens
      9. Medically diagnosed physical complications
         a. Alcoholic liver disease
            (1) Fatty liver
            (2) Hepatitis
            (3) Cirrhosis
         b. Alcoholic pancreatitis
         c. Alcoholic cardiomyopathy

10. Psychological dependence on alcohol or drugs
11. Personality changes associated with alcohol or drugs
12. Family or social problems associated with alcohol or drug use

II. Incipient program drinker or drug user: A client who exhibits just one of the indicators listed in Section IB
III. Nonproblem social drinker or drug user: A client who exhibits none of the indicators listed in Section I

7
Prevention and Intervention in Schools

Mary VanderWall

Two legislative actions occurred in the second half of the 1980s to promote drug and alcohol education in the schools of Colorado. The first, a revised Colorado law signed by Governor Lamm in 1985, states that educators in Colorado schools must teach the physiological, sociological, and psychological aspects of drug and alcohol use, speak to the illegalities of use, and promote a nonuse focus through curricular materials and classroom activities. Much turmoil surrounded this law, as there were few curricular materials appropriate to meet the law and no money was appropriated to help districts tend to this issue. Through this confusion, much needed attention was brought to drug and alcohol education issues in Colorado.

The second law was signed by President Reagan in 1986. The Drug Free Schools and Communities Act (DFSCA) provides money to the Colorado Department of Education (CDE) and the governor's office for prevention and intervention activities. Ninety percent of the money that is received by CDE flows out to the school districts. In 1987, school districts received approximately $2.15 per student based on the 1980 census. In 1988, districts received approximately $2.65 per student based on the 1987 school district enrollment figures. The broad federal guidelines (see appendix 7–A) have allowed school districts to implement various prevention and intervention programs. They also have resulted in the tremendous task of educating school district personnel and school board members. Colorado is a local district control state. There is no mandated curriculum or program. Each district board of education decides what is appropriate for that district.

Although much prevention research is available today, it has been only during the past fifteen years that this topic has been looked at in a thorough manner. Before that, there was little national effort to promote research in this field. In the 1930s, the government thought that scare tactics would work. Films such as *Reefer Madness* (which is now located in the comedy section of most movie rental stores) were thought to deter drug use. Because of the increase of drug use by youths in the 1960s, renewed attention was given to the problem, but there was no research base on which to work. Scare tactics were tried again, as were straight informational approaches. The thought was that if students knew the harmful effects of alcohol and other drugs, they would not try these substances. These approaches were found to be ineffective (Shaps 1981). In the 1960s, drug use escalated. Educational programs were not showing positive results. Interest in promoting research increased, as did funding to do so.

Behavioral scientists became the leaders in the field of prevention research. Two central themes have surfaced through their work. First, drug and alcohol use and abuse are complex issues that have multiple causative factors (Polich Ellickson and L'ahan, 1984; Murray and Perry 1985; Bernard, Fefoglia, and Perrone 1987). Because there are multiple causes, there must be multiple approaches to prevention. Second, schools cannot tackle this problem by themselves (Buscemi 1985; Bernard, Fefoglia and Perrone 1987; Bray 1987; National Association of State Alcohol and Drug Abuse Directors 1987; Fox and Forbing 1988; Horten 1988). Legislators, every sector of the community, parents, and all school district personnel must understand that this is a long-term, multidimensional issue and work together to achieve results.

Once these generalities were established, more information was documented to build specific programs. Risk factors related to adolescent substance abuse were identified, and programs can now be constructed around each factor to lower the risk in a systematic manner (Hawkins, Lishner, and Catalano 1985). Tobler (1986) analyzed 143 adolescent drug prevention programs to establish the importance of peer programs and social skills building for adolescents. Through this study, the importance of alternative activities for high-risk students was confirmed. Bray promoted the importance of the community and school working closely together (Bray 1987). Her research supports basing such programs within the school as a valid approach to community prevention. Societal change is the issue. Schools cannot and should not attempt to solve this problem alone. Everyone must be involved.

Educational and health education research also have progressed. The School Health Education Evaluation (SHEE) documented many findings regarding the importance of comprehensive and sequential health education for students (Pigg 1985). This study showed that health education works when offered in a planned and sequential manner in kindergarten through twelfth grade (K–12). The fact that it takes more classroom hours to influence attitudes and behaviors than it does simply to gain knowledge was established. The importance of teacher training was verified. And we learned that health education works best when there is a foundation of basic health knowledge rather than starting with categorical health problems.

Results of a recent Harris poll sponsored by the Metropolitan Life Foundation supports the view that comprehensive school health education directly

Health Education Experience

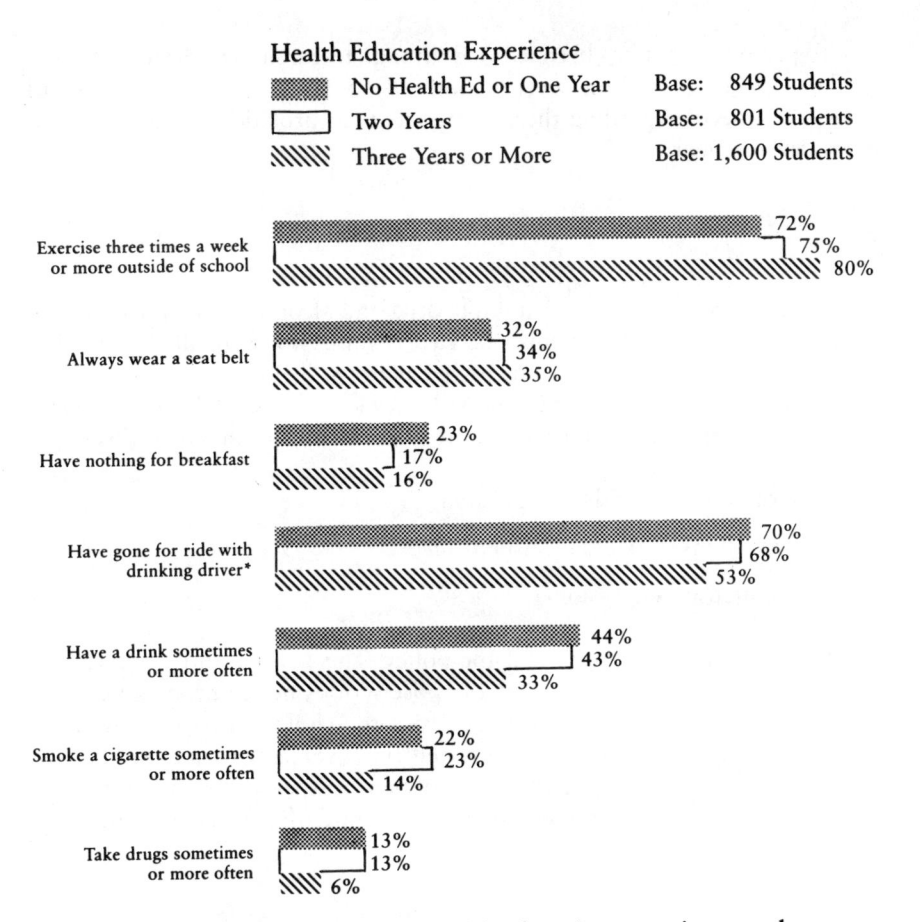

▓▓▓ No Health Ed or One Year   Base: 849 Students
☐ Two Years   Base: 801 Students
▨▨▨ Three Years or More   Base: 1,600 Students

Exercise three times a week or more outside of school
- 72%
- 75%
- 80%

Always wear a seat belt
- 32%
- 34%
- 35%

Have nothing for breakfast
- 23%
- 17%
- 16%

Have gone for ride with drinking driver*
- 70%
- 68%
- 53%

Have a drink sometimes or more often
- 44%
- 43%
- 33%

Smoke a cigarette sometimes or more often
- 22%
- 23%
- 14%

Take drugs sometimes or more often
- 13%
- 13%
- 6%

Figure 7–1. Relationship between health education experience and health-related behavior.

Source: Metropolitan Life Foundation. Reproduced with permission of Louis Harris Assoc.
*Based on seventh to twelfth grades.

affects students' lifestyle choices (McGavin 1988). According to the study, the more health education a student receives, the less likely he or she is to drink, smoke, use drugs, or make other unhealthy choices (Figure 7–1).

Other educational research provided information on effective schools and teaching techniques. The importance of affective learning was established. Also, the fact that students have different learning styles confirmed that teachers must have various teaching styles in a classroom setting if all students are expected to learn. It is important that we draw from all fields of research when forming prevention and intervention programs for our students in the school setting.

To promote what has been learned through research, schools in Colorado are being asked to address several components. Districts are encouraged to assess their needs regarding these components to provide direction for program development.

Policy

Schools must have a fair and equitable drug and alcohol policy for both students and staff members. It must be clearly understood by all that alcohol and other drug sales, possession, or behaviors will not be tolerated in the school setting. The consequences must be severe enough to deter the behaviors. Many districts have adopted a three-offense policy similar to this:

First offense—three-day suspension

Second offense—five-day suspension

Third offense—expulsion

Intervention can be a part of the policy. This action sends the message that alcohol and other drug behaviors pose serious health problems as well as being illegal. The student may be given the choice to participate in an educational program (usually with parent involvement) or referred for assessment and possible treatment instead of being suspended from school. This occurs on the first and/or second offense. The third offense remains the same.

Curriculum

Health educators at CDE encourage a comprehensive, sequential K–12 health education curriculum. This includes all the basic health areas as well as health promotion. It sets the broad health foundation spoken to in the SHEE study (Pigg 1985) and the Harris poll sponsored by the Metropolitan Life Foundation (McGavin 1988). Drug and alcohol use, accidents, suicides, and sexual activity are all major problems of youths today. If educators are to be effective, they must stop treating these issues categorically and help students to be positive about general health practices. Perry and Jessor of the Institute of Behavioral Sciences, University of Colorado, Boulder, found a strong link between common positive health practices and less alcohol and other drug use (Perry and Jessor 1985). They encourage health promotion to change behavior. Health promotion encourages personal responsibility for health, which is a must when dealing with any of the major problems of youths.

The curriculum should contain an adequate piece on social skills building. Social skills promote coping effectively with interpersonal relationships (Goldstein et al. 1980). Assertiveness and decision making also are outcomes of social skills application. To promote social skills education in Colorado, CDE offers training for teachers in a program titled Refusal Skills. This program is a copyright of Roberts, Fitzmahan, and Associates, a company that markets skill-based alcohol and other drug curricula. This particular technique was developed by Elliott Herman, who works with juvenile offenders in a residential setting. Herman based his work primarily on the book *Skill Streaming the Adolescent*, which describes the skill-building process (Goldstein et al. 1980). This program provides a specific method to help students learn how to deal with peer pressure. The student can use the skills anytime he or she must make a decision. CDE offers the two-day teacher training free of charge to school districts and boards of cooperative educational services (BOCES) that choose to participate. Schools can readily integrate this skill-building process into their existing K–12 programs.

Many alcohol and other drug curricula are available. School districts are encouraged to establish frameworks with comprehensive health education, then look at specific alcohol and other drug curricula that may enhance their programs. Some Colorado districts have become involved with curricula promoted by the Juvenile Justice and Delinquency Council in the Colorado Division of Criminal Justice. Two levels of curricula are available at present in Colorado. The Drug/Alcohol Resistance Education (DARE) program is available for grades 4 through 6. Law Related Education (LRE) is appropriate for middle or junior high school. Both involve a uniformed officer and a teacher presenting information as a team. Training is offered by the Colorado Social Science Education Consortium. Evaluation of LRE shows that students in classes where LRE was properly implemented were less likely to be involved in delinquent acts and were better able to make responsible choices about personal acts (Johnson and Hunter 1987).

Staff Development

If we expect schools to take a leadership role in the prevention and intervention arena, teachers and other school district personnel must be trained. The first reason is obvious. Most teachers and other staff members did not receive this training in their preservice education. The second reason promotes a broader perspective. School district staff must begin to understand the societal issues, as well as their own issues, regarding drugs and alcohol.

Molnar (1988) notes that not only are there very complicated political and social issues surrounding drugs and alcohol, but there are also many unhealthy issues surrounding drugs and alcohol, but there are also unhealthy societal behaviors that have similar roots. Molnar states, "Just as with drugs, our various, social addictions have their pushers, and they aren't shadowy foreigners. They attend Rotary meetings, sit on school boards, and help formulate social policy about drugs at every level of government. They are 'good citizens.'"

Health promotion for staff is an important segment of the staff development issue. School personnel should be encouraged to form healthy attitudes if they are going to be effective with children. Well-trained school district staff and good role models are essential to prevention efforts.

Alternatives for Students

Students need alternatives to alcohol and drug use (Bennett 1987; Bray 1987; Tobler 1986). Two major efforts have proven successful in Colorado. First, parents and community members have cooperated with the schools to promote alcohol- and drug-free activities for students. One popular activity has been the after-prom party. This is held at the school and lasts through the night. Not only prom attendees are invited, but other junior and senior students who did not attend the dance also may attend. Activities such as watching videos, dancing, hot-tubbing, and playing video games are offered. Generally, parents and students are the organizers, with financial support from the school, parents, and community.

Second, student groups such as Students Taking a New Direction (STAND), formerly Students Against Drunk Driving (SADD), and ALL-STARS give young people an opportunity to develop their own programs. The need to belong and feel powerful is met through these groups, which allow young people to decide how best to approach drug and alcohol problems with their peers. The Prevention Center in Boulder, Colorado, has taken a lead in training teams of young people throughout the state so that they are knowledgeable about prevention and intervention as well as planning techniques. These students create and implement actions plans regarding alcohol and other drug use for their own peer groups. These programs have been credited in part for the drop in drug- and alcohol-related automobile fatalities among the adolescent population in Colorado between 1986 and 1988.

The "natural high" concept as an alternative to alcohol and other drug use is gaining momentum in Colorado. This method promotes learning control over internal states, thereby reducing the demand for external props. The goal is that of preparing youths to experience moments of joy and pleasure through the development of life-enhancing skills compatible with the values of clear thinking, sound personal health, and community spirit. In the book *Craving for Ecstasy: The Consciousness and Chemistry of Escape* (Milkman and Sunderwirth 1987), the following explanation is offered: "People do not become addicted to drugs or mood-altering behaviors as such, but rather to the sensations of pleasure that can be achieved through types of experience to achieve feelings of well being: relaxation, excitement, and fantasy; these are the underpinnings of human compulsion." These feelings of well-being can be found naturally. Training in this area encourages feeling great without the use of alcohol and other drugs.

Parent and Community Involvement

Parents and community members have a right and a responsibility to be educated regarding alcohol and other drugs. Also, they have a right and a responsibility to know what is being taught in the schools. Of equal importance is the fact that the schools need these people to help plan effective programs.

CDE promotes a four-day seminar called School Team Approach Training Effort (STATE). The five- to seven-member teams are represented by one or more administrators, teachers, counselors, school nurses, parents, and/or other community members. The governor's office offers similar training for community members that include school district representation on their teams. These teams are exposed to the latest information regarding drug and alcohol use and state-of-the-art prevention techniques. They learn how to identify the major problems related to alcohol and other drug use in their school and community and how to work together through a common action plan to address the issues. This has been an excellent method for tapping parent and community expertise and promoting a feeling of everyone working toward a common goal.

Intervention

Historically, intervention has been the most difficult area for schools to approach. How do school staff know if a student is using? How much is he or she using? Do school staff have the right to intervene when the student is using outside of the school setting? What legalities are involved? These questions and others have kept intervention from becoming a reality in many schools. Colorado schools are beginning to tackle this issue based on three factors:

1. The body of the literature is increasing.
2. The Colorado drug and alcohol law speaks to nonuse by students.
3. There is a federal law with money attached to address the issue.

Intervention can be reflected in the school policy. A policy that allows for intervention gives the message that alcohol and other drug use is a health problem and not just the breaking of a rule. Beyond policy, there are different approaches. Following are some examples of how different school districts are approaching intervention.

Adams 12 and Adams-Arapahoe 28J School Districts

Both of the districts have intervention teams and use the IMPACT training program promoted by CARE of Colorado, a private drug and alcohol treatment center. Teams attend a four-day training session during which they learn how to identify, assess, refer, and follow up high-risk behaviors of students. They learn about chemical dependence and explore their personal feelings toward this issue. These teams are the experts in their schools. They deliver regular staff inservices and act as resources when other staff members have a concern about a student. Once a student is identified, the team is responsible for meeting with the parents. This program is intended to build rapport with parents and to obtain appropriate care for the student. It is not intended to confront parents or run family interventions. See appendix 7–B for Adams County School District 12's three-year DFSCA action plan.

These programs function primarily at the high-school level, with some attention given to junior high as more teams are trained. Support groups for children of alcoholics and aftercare are addressed through intervention teams.

St. Vrain School District

This district in Longmont has taken a different approach. It is working closely with the Boulder County Health Department to provide intervention services in the school setting. Through a joint financial effort, part-time intervention specialists from the health department have been placed in the high schools. These specialists, whose offices are in the counseling department, make assessments, contact parents, and refer students to outside agencies. The program has been publicized throughout the community. Referrals come from other school counselors, parents, and the students themselves. Although the program has focused on the high schools, the specialists are also beginning to work with junior high schools.

Boulder Valley Schools

This district intends to begin a similar program. It already has a student assistance program (SAP), which is similar to the previously mentioned intervention teams, and employee assistance programs (EAPs). Teams are trained and have similar responsibilities as IMPACT-trained teams. Originally, the

Boulder teams focused on alcohol and other drug problems, but they are now in the process of organizing this program to assist all at-risk students.

Jefferson County Schools

These schools are working with the Jefferson County Health Department in a unique manner. The health department assists with the training of intervention teams. Once a student is identified, the health department assists with parent contact, assessment, and referral. This program is offered to all schools in the district. To date, the elementary schools have shown the most interest.

El Paso 49 School District

This district is located thirty miles east of Colorado Springs. It has developed an extensive prevention and intervention program that features dramatic presentations to the elementary population. For this, the Children's Awareness Theater (CHAT) is used in the elementary schools. This is a Colorado Springs community theatrical group trained in destructive family issues such as alcohol and other drug use, child abuse, and suicide. One presentation that CHAT delivers emphasizes living in an alcoholic family. Children who identify themselves as living with an alcoholic parent are provided follow-up counseling. See appendix 7–C for the El Paso 49 three-year DFSCA action plan.

Grand County Schools

This district, which includes two rural mountain communities, works closely with the county drug and alcohol task force to promote prevention and intervention activities. Although specific intervention is not part of the current program, the schools do send teams of students to the Colorado Teen Institute (CTI). This training, provided through the Mile High Council on Alcohol and Drug Abuse in a retreat setting, offers students a chance to learn about factors that contribute to alcohol and other drug use, as well as to deal with their own feelings regarding use. They also are taught how to work with their peers. Although intended to promote prevention, this program, which originated in the treatment field, tends to encourage informal intervention.

These intervention strategies should provide a sense of the diversity of programs and people in Colorado. Although the majority of school districts are actively involved in prevention activities, most do not have intervention programs in place. The districts mentioned here are the forerunners. Their leadership will provide direction to other districts throughout the state. (See appendix 7–D for contact personnel in each of these districts.)

Evaluation

A few leading school districts in Colorado have traditionally been involved with evaluation efforts. Unfortunately, effective evaluation has not been a part of most district plans. Although primarily a time and money issue, different philosophies regarding what to measure come into play. The fact that behavior is the issue makes evaluation complicated. Testing to measure content gain by students means little in the effort to affect behavior. Alcohol and other drug use surveys are becoming more popular and far less threatening to schools. The American Drug and Alcohol Survey developed by Fred Beauvais is a comprehensive tool designed to empirically measure the exact nature and extent of drug use among teens. Many Colorado districts are now using this survey. Evaluation is a component of the Drug Free Schools and Communities Act, so evaluation will occur during the time this law is in effect.

Conclusion

Research regarding prevention and intervention is in its infancy compared with other fields of study. Some success is being realized with programs based on current empirical evidence, but more research is needed, especially concerning minorities and other high-risk populations. Research from the fields of the behavioral sciences, education, and health education must be acknowledged if effective programs are to be used in schools. However, literature by itself will not ensure program implementation. Legislation is necessary to bring drug and alcohol education into focus. Money also must continue to be available if schools are expected to continue their response. With all elements in place—research, legislation, and funds—Colorado schools can proceed in a positive direction.

References

Bennett, W.J. 1987. *What Works—Schools without Drugs*. Washington D.C.: U.S. Department of Education.
Bray, B. 1987. "A Fall Review of Four Exemplary Prevention Models." *Prevention Forum* 8 (1): 3–10.
Buscemi, M. 1985. "What Schools Are Doing to Prevent Alcohol and Drug Abuse." *School Administrator* 42 (9): 11–14.

Fox, C, and S. Forbing. 1988. *Fighting Substance Abuse in Our Schools.* Glenview, Ill.: Scott Foresman.

Goldstein, A., R. Sprafkin, N. Gershaw, and P. Klein. 1980. *Skill Streaming the Adolescent.* Champaign; Ill.: Research Press.

Hawkins, J., D. Lishner, and R. Catalano. 1985. "Childhood Predictors and the Prevention of Adolescent Substance Abuse." In *Etiology of Drug Abuse—Implications for Prevention,* edited by C. La Rue Jones, and R.J. Battjes. NIDA Research Monograph Series, no. 56. Washington D.C.: GPO.

Horten, L. 1988. "The Education of Most Worth: Preventing Drug and Alcohol Abuse." *Educational Leadership* 45 (6): 5–8.

Johnson, G., and R. Hunter. 1987. "Using School-Based Programs to Improve Students' Citizenship in Colorado." A report from the Colorado Juvenile Justice and Delinquency Prevention Council, Denver, Col., October.

McGavin, J. 1988. *Education Daily,* October 21.

Milkman, H., and S. Sunderwirth. 1987. *Craving for Ecstasy: The Consciousness and Chemistry of Escape.*Lexington, Mass.: Lexington Books.

Molnar, A. 1988. "Schooling in an Addicted Society." *Educational Leadership* 45 (6): 36.

Murray, D., and C. Perry. 1985. "The Prevention of Adolescent Drug Abuse: Implications of Etiological Development. Behavioral and Environmental Models." In *Etiology of Drug Abuse—Implications for Prevention,* edited by C. La Rue Jones and R.J. Battjes. NIDA Research Monograph Series, no. 56. Washington, D.C.: GPO.

National Association of State Alcohol and Drug Abuse Directors and National Prevention Network. 1987. "Twenty Project Summaries." Alcohol, Drug Abuse, and Mental Health Administration, Office for Substance Abuse Prevention, Washington, D.C.: October.

Perry, C., and R. Jessor. 1985. "The Concept of Health Promotion and the Prevention of Adolescent Drug Abuse." *Health Education Quarterly* 12 (Summer): 169–84.

Polich, J., P. Ellickson, and J. Kahan. 1984. *Strategies for Controlling Adolescent Drug Use.* Santa Monica, Cal.: Rand.

Shaps, E. 1981. "Evaluation of an Innovative Drug Education Program: First Year Results." *NAPA: Pacific Institute for Research and Evaluation.*

Tobler, N. 1986. "Meta-Analysis of 143 Adolescent Drug Prevention Programs: Quantitive Outcome Results of Program Participants Compared to a Control or Comparison Group." *Journal of Drug Issues* 16(4): 537–67.

Appendix 7–A: Hawkins-Stafford School Improvement Act PL 100-297 Title V—Drug Free Schools and Communities Act

DFSCA FEDERAL GUIDELINES

Funding from DFSCA will be used to support the following type(s) of activities:

1. The development, acquisition, and implementation of elementary and secondary school drug abuse education and prevention curricula which clearly and consistently teach that illicit drug use is wrong and harmful
2. School-based programs of drug abuse prevention and early intervention (other than treatment)
3. Family drug abuse prevention programs, including education for parents to increase awareness about the symptoms and effects of drug use through the development and dissemination of appropriate educational materials
4. Drug abuse prevention counseling programs (which counsel that illicit drug use is wrong and harmful) for students and parents, including professional and peer counselors and involving the participation (where appropriate) of parent or other adult counselors and reformed abusers
5. Programs of drug abuse treatment and rehabilitation referral
6. Programs of in-service and preservice training in drug and alcohol abuse prevention for teachers, counselors, other educational personnel, athletic directors, public service personnel, law enforcement officials, judicial officials, and community leaders
7. Programs in primary prevention and early intervention, such as the interdisciplinary school-team approach
8. Community education programs and other activities to involve parents and communities in the fight against drug and alcohol abuse
9. Public education programs on drug and alcohol abuse, including programs utilizing professionals and former drug and alcohol abusers

10. On-site efforts in schools to enhance identification and discipline of drug and alcohol abusers, and to enable law enforcement officials to take necessary action in cases of drug possession and supplying of drugs and alcohol to the student population
11. Special programs and activities to prevent drug and alcohol abuse among student athletes, involving their parents and family in such drug and alcohol abuse prevention efforts and using athletic programs and personnel in preventing drug and alcohol abuse among all students
12. Other programs consistent with the act (specify):

Appendix 7–B: Sample DFSCA Three-Year Action Plan

Adams County School District 12, 1987–1990

Objective	Federal Guideline Activity (Appendix A)	Local Activities Required to Accomplish Objective
Objective 1—to select and implement drug education classroom instructional materials for students (i.e., Here's Looking at You 2,000, Quest, Growing Healthy, THTM, Talking with Your Students about Alcohol, etc.)	1	1. Preview and select curricula to meet building needs 2. Provide teacher training in the selected curricula/instructional materials
Objective 2—to design and implement student-based prevention activities/programs (i.e., ALLSTARS, SADD, "Just Say No" clubs, etc.)	2	1. Identify building-level activity sponsor 2. Select activities 3. Select student participants 4. Conduct trainings 5. Implement program activities
Objective 3—to implement an intervention program (secondary level) with four components: 1. Identification 2. Assessment 3. Intervention 4. Follow-up/support groups	2	1. Identify building-level sponsor 2. Identify faculty team 3. Provide necessary training 4. Deliver services
Objective 4—to provide ongoing in-service opportunities for school and community people in substance abuse prevention, education, and intervention strategies	6	1. Survey building needs 2. Select appropriate in-service topics 3. Provide in-district or outside in-service opportunities
Objective 5—to train student athletes to deliver a drug prevention program to other athletes and students in the district	11	1. Identify sponsor 2. Select students 3. Provide training 4. Implement program

Appendix 7–C: Sample DFSCA Three-Year Action Plan

El Paso School District 49, 1987–88

Objective	Federal Guideline Activity (Appendix A)	Local Activities Required to Accomplish Objective
Objective 1—to adopt K–12 drug curriculum	1, 6, 7	Present to the board of education
Objective 2—to implement K–12 drug curriculum	1, 6, 7	Staff training and in-service TYSAA (Talking to your Students about Alcohol) TYKAA (Talking to your Kids about Alcohol)
Objective 3—to provide alternatives for abusers and nonabusers	10, 11	CARE coalition groups
Objective 4—to adopt and implement a drug use policy districtwide	5, 10	Write the policy and adopt; communicate the policy to all district patrons through newsletters, staff meetings, student assemblies, etc.
Objective 5—to develop intervention programs for students K–12	2, 4, 7, 9	Just Say No club All Star club Alcoholics Anonymous Narcotics Anonymous
Objective 6—to enhance parent awareness of drug use, to inform parents of district programs, and to involve parents	3, 8, 11	Disseminate literature and other forms of communication by district/school newsletters and pamphlets; offer classes to parents by the school

El Paso School District 49, 1988–1990

Objective	Federal Guideline Activity (Appendix A)	Local Activities Required to Accomplish Objective
1988–89		
Objective 1—to evaluate K–12 drug curriculum	1, 6, 7	To develop a criteria reference form; to develop a questionnaire for students, parents, and teachers
Objective 2—to provide training for new staff members	1, 6, 7	Staff training and in-service
Objective 3—to evaluate intervention, policy, alternative, and parent awareness	3, 5, 8, 10, 11	To develop a questionnaire for students, parents, and teachers
1989–90		
Objective 1—to revise the curriculum as needed	1, 6, 7	To continue training and in-service to the staff; to bring in outside guest speakers and help
Objective 2—to update the intervention policy alternative and parent awareness	3, 5, 8, 10, 11	To continue monitoring and upgrading the effective programs through local, state, and federal programs available to the schools

Appendix 7–D: School District Contacts

School District	Number of Students	Contact Person	Address	Telephone
Adams County 12	20,602	Nicky Wolman	11285 Highline Drive, Northglenn, CO 80233	(303) 451-1173
Adams-Arapahoe 28J	25,951	Donna Stefonic	1085 Peoria Street, Aurora, CO 80011	(303) 344-8060
Boulder RE1J	15,081	Elaine Fritz	395 S. Pratt Parkway, Longmont, CO 80501	(303) 776-6200
Boulder Valley RE2J	20,835	Peter Allen	P.O. Box 9011, Boulder, CO 80302	(303) 499-4624
El Paso County 49	2,448	Bill Noxon	10850 Woodman Road, Falcon, CO 80831	(719) 495-3661
Grand County 2	1,045	Patty Laflin	P.O. Box 125, Granby, CO 80446	(303) 887-2581
Jefferson County R1	75,337	Jerry Terrill	1829 Denver West Drive, Golden, CO 80401	(303) 273-6500

8
Employee Assistance Programs as an Early Intervention Strategy for Substance Abuse

Carol L. Hacker

Substance abuse and chemical dependence among employees is of great concern to business and industry today. A 1987 survey reported in *Fortune* magazine listed it as the second most urgent issue of employers. The federal deficit was first. According to estimates by the National Institute on Drug Abuse, as many as 23 percent of all workers use drugs on the job, with 5 percent having serious addiction problems (Backer and O'Hara 1988). Current cost estimates of employee substance abuse to American industry vary, but most put them in the area of $50 billion to $60 billion (Backer 1987; Lewis and Lewis 1986; Mastrich and Beidel 1987; Montgomery 1987).

The direct medical costs to business and industry for treating alcoholism and other substance abuse are only a portion of the problem for an employer. Absenteeism, loss of productivity, on-the-job accidents, tardiness, high turnover, poor quality of work, and secondary health problems also must be included in the financial losses incurred by business and industry. Problems such as poor judgment, deteriorating and poor interpersonal relations with coworkers, family problems, and declining commitment to good job performance are harder to measure in dollars but do affect the cost of substance abuse to employers and society (Lewis and Lewis 1986).

Employers have come to recognize the significant impact that substance abuse and chemical dependence can have on production, the professional and personal relationships of employees, medical care claims, and the organization's morale and quality of work life. A survey of five hundred companies in 1969 showed that 97 percent of the executives would fire an employee using drugs. In 1974, only 10 percent said they would fire a substance-abusing employee (McClellan 1982). Today employers realize that substance abuse is a treatable problem. If the employees get quality treatment for their chemical dependence or substance abuse, they can be productive workers and healthy individuals. Many employers are now offering this help through employee assistance programs (EAPs).

Employee Assistance Programs

History

EAPs are help services provided by an employer for employees who have problems. Personal problems, including chemical dependence and substance abuse, can affect job performance. If employees get effective help for their problems, their job performance should improve if it has gone down, or stay at an acceptable level if help is received in time. By offering employees help through an EAP, an employer can increase the probability that its employees will perform well on the job (Roman and Blum 1985; Roman and Blum 1988).

EAPs began in the 1940s as employers realized the impact that alcohol abuse and alcoholism can have on job performance. They trained supervisors to identify the symptoms of alcohol abuse, such as red eyes, tardiness, absenteeism on Mondays and Fridays, and long lunch breaks. However, supervisors found that these symptoms also could be caused by other problems. The supervisors were then told to focus on job performance as a signal of alcohol problems. They were trained to document poor performance and confront the employee. They eventually realized that work performance would be affected by factors other than alcohol (Dunkin 1982; Forrest 1983; Roman 1981c; Trice and Schonbrunn 1981).

As supervisors and employers realized that employees need help with all kinds of problems, EAPs evolved from employee alcoholism programs to employee assistance programs. These "broad-brush" programs help troubled employees with problems such as marital conflicts, family issues, financial or legal needs, child care, elderly parents, and medical needs.

Having employees able to use the EAP for any problem has helped remove the stigma previously attached to getting help. Employees may be more willing to use a broad-brush EAP for a substance abuse problem than if it is a program only for alcoholics (Foote and Erfurt 1981). There is some concern that trying to help with all types of problems may cause the EAP's resources to become unfocused as it tries to be all things to all people. However, Foote and Erfurt (1981) state that comprehensive EAPs are "generally no less effective than alcohol focused programs at reaching alcoholic employees" (p. 231). Their research shows that if at least one-third of a broad-brush program's clients were alcoholic, they worked with as many alcoholics as an alcohol-only EAP (in similar organizations, i.e., size and purpose). Employed alcohol abusers have shown a higher rate of success than unemployed problem drinkers, both during and after treatment, in several studies reported by Iutcovich and Calderone (1984). Absenteeism, job performance, and EAP assessment were considered.

Models

There are two major models for EAPs—the internal or in-house model and the external or contract service model (Phillips and Older 1981). In the internal model, EAP personnel are hired by the employer organization to provide EAP services. These usually include assessment of troubled employees' problems and referral to appropriate treatment. Depending on its own resources, the internal EAP may provide some therapy, but it will usually refer employees to private therapists, community resources and agencies, substance abuse treatment programs, or resources within the organization. Employees are usually responsible for any costs of treatment beyond what the company's health insurance covers.

The external model is when the employer contracts with an EAP service outside the organization to assess troubled employees' problems and referral for treatment. The external EAP may provide some free treatment as part of the EAP contract. The employer organization can decide what services it wants from the external EAP and is charged accordingly. Most organizations have someone within the organization who monitors the external EAP contract.

Both internal and external EAPs provide training to teach supervisors how to refer their employees to the EAP, marketing of the EAP services to employees, appropriate data on the use of the program, and evaluation. There are benefits and liabilities to each model, and the employer organization must decide which one best provides the services it needs.

Straussner (1988) surveyed fifteen internal and eight external EAPs in metropolitan New York in order to compare the two types of programs. The findings were stratified by program model (internal or external); type of industry (finance and insurance, manufacturing, or service); and size of organization (small—fewer than 10,000 employees; medium—10,000–30,000; large—more than 30,000). Straussner looked at the programs from three different viewpoints: top management, employees, and EAP staff. The study compared a variety of advantages and disadvantages of each model, including costs, confidentiality issues, use, follow-up, and legal liability.

With regard to alcohol abuse, Straussner's study found that internal EAPs dealt with a higher percentage of employees with alcohol problems—31 percent of all employees, compared with 12 percent for external EAPs. Supervisors and medical personnel also made more referrals to internal EAPs, which is probably related to the greater percentage of employees referred to in-house EAPs.

A study by Blum and Roman (1987) also found that internal programs had a higher caseload of employee alcohol cases (37 percent versus 24 percent). These authors also found that internal programs get 39 percent of their employee alcohol cases from self-referrals, while external programs get 51 percent from self-referrals. Supervisory referrals for alcohol were 48 percent in internal and 37 percent in external programs. Assuming that self-referrals occur more often in the early stages of chemical dependence, one should not assume that internal EAPs offer better identification of and help for substance abuse. The perception that the external EAP is less vulnerable to breaches of confidentiality may help explain the higher number of self-referrals, especially when the problem is substance abuse (Lewis and Lewis 1986).

There are several variations on these two models. One is where an internal EAP contracts with an external EAP to provide some services, usually counseling for personal problems. In union-based programs, a union provides EAP services for its members (McClellan 1982). There are also peer referral models, especially for professionals who do not work within organizations, such as doctors or lawyers. Peer referral models also may be used by universities for professors or hospitals for doctors (McClellan 1982; Roman 1981b).

One other model is available to small organizations that have similar interests or needs. They can come together and form an EAP consortium in which they set up the EAP, write a policy statement, and hire the EAP personnel. These consortia can work well for groups such as city and county governments, school districts, and other government agencies. (McClellan 1982).

Confidentiality

All EAPs must have a strong policy statement ensuring that they will keep the names of employees who receive their services confidential. Unless employees are sure that their names and problems will be kept confidential, they will not use the EAP services. There are some legal restrictions on confidentiality, such as child abuse or potential murder or suicide. However, the EAP must be careful about having the employees' permission to share anything about their problems with anyone in the organization.

The policy statement should be agreed on by top management, the EAP staff, and any unions recognized by management. It should include assurances that using EAP services will not affect promotions, continued employment, job evaluations, or job assignments. If the employee is a self-referral, all information must be kept strictly confidential. If it is a supervisory referral, the EAP usually can let the supervisor know that the employee did or did not talk with the EAP. Other information can be disclosed only with the employee's permission.

This emphasis on confidentiality can be a problem when the EAP is working with substance abusers. Company policies concerning drug use on the job, safety issues, federal and state guidelines and mandates on illegal drug use, and company attitudes about chemical dependence can complicate the work of the EAP. Many employers may want to dismiss substance abusers and not offer help (McClellan 1982). Thus, a policy stating that alcoholism is a treatable illness and will not be a cause for dismissal is a must for an effective EAP. This statement should be extended to cover other drugs so that employees will seek help for their chemical dependences. Otherwise, they will continue to use, which can lead them to have an accident, make poor decisions, exhibit deteriorating job performance, or be a safety problem.

In 1983, the Association for Labor-Management Administrators and Consultants on Alcoholism (ALMACA), the National Council on Alcoholism (NCA), the National Institute on Alcohol Abuse and Alcoholism (NIAAA), and other organizations concerned with substance abuse developed a national set of standards for EAPs. (ALMACA 1982; Lewis and Lewis 1986). The standards are voluntary, but they provide guidelines for an EAP policy statement, as well as a basis for developing and implementing an EAP.

Effectiveness

The effectiveness of EAPs in helping chemically dependent or substance-abusing employees is well documented, although much of the quality of the research is questionable (Erfurt and Foote, 1977; Lewis and Lewis 1986; Mastrich & Beidel 1987; McClellan 1982; Roman 1981a; Trice 1980). Most of this documentation focuses on cost savings, which are difficult to assess. However, human resource savings should not be overlooked. A survey of 2,238 EAPs reported that "the two most common reasons for their organization having an EAP are returning employees to productive work and providing an employee benefit" (Backer and O'Hara 1988).

Many of these drug-dependent employees have lost their spouses and families, homes, cars, and material possessions—everything but their jobs. When their substance abuse affects their jobs and they are confronted and offered treatment, many accept it and become sober and straight. The threat of losing their jobs can be the turning point.

EAPs have a unique position in the substance abuse treatment field, as well as in the mental health field, because they work with employees around their jobs. Their strength lies in their ability to intervene and help employees with problems that can affect job performance. They also can do effective follow-up at the work site to see that employees continue to do well.

The contributions of EAPs to the treatment of substance abuse and chemical dependence are affirmed by the increase in the number of employer organizations offering EAPs to their employees. In 1972, 25 percent of the Fortune 500 companies had EAPs; in 1979, 57 percent had them. By 1985, there were more than eight thousand EAPs in the United States (Chiabotta 1985; McClellan 1982).

Prevention, Intervention, and Treatment

There are three levels at which we can work with substance abuse and chemical dependence (Forrest 1983; Longpré 1984; Roman and Blum 1985; Roman and Blum 1988). *Primary prevention,* which is based on giving information about the dangers and effects of drug use and abuse. By educating the at-risk population, it is hoped they will not develop the problem. *Secondary prevention* targets individuals who are in the early stages of having a problem with alcohol or other drugs. Confrontation, crisis intervention, and early identification are the methods used to reduce the duration or prevalence of the problem. *Tertiary prevention* is treatment and rehabilitation of individuals who have developed a problem with substance abuse or chemical dependence. It may have affected their jobs, or they may be afraid that it will.

Traditionally, EAPs have worked mainly on the secondary level of intervention and confrontation. Because they have the lever of job performance, they can give factual documentation when they confront an employee about possible substance abuse, not just suppositions or feelings. They can make it clear to the employee that he or she could lose his or her job if the documented behaviors continue. This has made them very effective in convincing employees to get help with substance abuse problems (Roman and Blum 1985; Roman and Blum 1988).

Currently, some EAPs are doing more with prevention by setting up and/or offering workshops and classes for employees on alcoholism, addictions, substance use and abuse, and other related topics. Offering programs on a healthy lifestyle, nutrition, exercise, blood pressure screening, and other wellness-type activities also may help employees look at their substance use or abuse behaviors. Although these are not traditional EAP activities, they are good marketing strategies that can help employees feel more comfortable about using an EAP's services.

Some EAPs do offer treatment for substance abuse and chemical dependence, but most refer these problems to professional treatment programs. The EAP may sponsor aftercare groups or support groups for all employees who have been through treatment programs. Although EAPs may offer counseling or therapy for most personal problems, they usually do not have the resources and personnel to provide treatment for substance abuse or chemical dependence except on a referral basis.

Referrals

Supervisory. One key to EAPs being effective as an early intervention strategy in substance abuse is the threat of job loss or disciplinary measures for poor job performance. The key to an EAP being able to use these threats effectively is having supervisors who are trained to evaluate job performance, document poor job performance, use constructive confrontation appropriately, and refer employees to the EAP. The EAP can be a consultant to the supervisor on the documentation and confrontation process or be directly involved with the confrontation. Constructive confrontation is when the supervisor (and/or the EAP) discusses the documented poor job performance but adds verbal support for the emotional and personal well-being of the employee, offers EAP assistance, and assures the employee that confidentiality will be maintained (Roman and Blum 1985; Roman and Blum 1988; Trice and Beyer 1984).

Problems can arise when the supervisor is not trained to identify and document poor job performance. The EAP may have to coach the supervisor in this process and provide support for the necessity of documentation. The EAP may need to do the constructive confrontation based on the supervisor's documentation and observations if the supervisor does not feel capable. In these situations, EAPs must be careful not to appear to be disciplinarians. Their purpose is to get the employee to treatment based on the behaviors seen on the job. The EAP is there to help not punish.

Often the organization will not have job descriptions that describe objective work performance criteria. This is especially true of technical and professional jobs. Therefore, it may be difficult for supervisors to document work performance problems objectively when they know of or suspect substance abuse. By the time work performance problems can be documented, the employee may be far into the progression of the disease, where denial is very strong. It may be difficult to convince the employee that he or she needs help and at the same time keep the employee from being dismissed for poor job performance (McClellan 1982).

There also can be problems if the supervisor sees alcoholism or other drug use and abuse as a moral issue or a weakness of character that should be punished. The EAP may need to educate the supervisor on alcoholism as a disease, suggesting that the problem may be beyond the conscious control of the employee and not simply a matter of willpower. The supervisor should not diagnose the problem or accuse the employee of being an alcoholic or a substance abuser. The supervisor should just document job performance and let the facts speak for themselves.

A supervisor also may have substance use or abuse problems of his or her own or in his or her family and therefore may be hesitant to say anything, much less document or confront an employee with similar problems. The EAP must be sensitive to this possibility and provide support and information to any supervisors who appear to be resistant to intervening with chemically dependent employees.

A supervisor may be hesitant to refer an employee to the EAP because he or she does not want the work group to look bad. The EAP must be careful not to provide management with data that imply a certain department or supervisor has more problems than others. Confidentiality is a must for a successful EAP so that employees, including supervisors, can be sure that their problems will not become public knowledge.

Another problem can arise if the substance-abusing employee is performing well on the job despite chemical dependence. The employee's supervisor and coworkers may know about the problem, but the only performance problem might be absences, especially on Mondays. In this situation, the supervisor may be hesitant to do anything, even though the employee needs someone to intervene and help him or her get appropriate treatment. Waiting until there are job performance problems could take a long time and even be hazardous, depending on the employee's job and health. For instance, waiting until a drinking bus driver or cocaine-using airplane pilot exhibits a job performance problem could be dangerous.

In this case, the EAP can be a consultant to the supervisor on how to handle the situation. Discussing what the supervisor knows from personal observation and from coworkers may give enough evidence that intervention is called for. By educating the substance-abusing employee about what he or she is doing to himself or herself and what the potential consequences might be, both professionally and personally, the supervisor and the EAP may be able to get the employee to treatment before he or she slides too far into impairment.

Self-Referrals. Most EAPs have more self-referrals than supervisory referrals, with as many as 85 percent being self-referrals (Bernstein and Dolan 1988; Roman 1981c). This shows good employee acceptance of EAP services. Usually the main presenting problems are personal, such as marital or family, financial, or legal. Very few alcoholics or drug abusers who self-refer to EAPs state their chemical dependence as the presenting problem (Presnall 1981).

The EAP must be adept at knowing and seeing the symptoms of substance abuse when assessing the presenting problem of the self-referred employee. If the EAP offers three to seven free therapy sessions, the substance abuse problem may surface. If the EAP sees the employee only once or twice to assess the situation and then refers to other providers, the EAP must be confident that these counselors or therapists are able to diagnose substance abuse and refer the employee back to the EAP or to appropriate treatment if the provider is not skilled in that area. EAPs must be able to assess the skills of all the therapists they use and make their expectations concerning chemically dependent employees clear.

Coworkers and family members may approach the EAP about an alcoholic or drug-abusing employee. They often hope that the EAP will intervene and get the employee to treatment without their being involved. The EAP should never confront an employee based on hearsay. It is best to have the coworkers or family members involved in the confrontation after they have been trained by the EAP on what to say. Their caring and concern should be supported and encouraged by the EAP, but they must give factual behaviors as evidence of the problem.

The EAP is the appropriate vehicle for intervening with substance-abusing and chemically dependent employees. However, the EAP must rely on the documented behaviors and observations of supervisors, coworkers, and family members to identify and confront these employees unless the employees self-refer for appropriate treatment.

Treatment Information

The EAP can be the best source of information on the most effective treatment for alcoholism, drug abuse, and other addictions. It must be up-to-date on the various treatment programs and options, their costs, their requirements, and the available insurance coverage (Bernstein and Dolan 1988; McClellan 1982). The alcoholic or substance-abusing employee does have a job and is functioning in society. No longer do alcoholics have to hit rock bottom before they are willing to get help. Many younger employees may be polyaddicted and become worried about their addictions because of the costs, the threat to their health, some impairment of their memory, or interpersonal problems. They may self-refer before anyone else realizes they have a chemical dependence.

Outpatient programs may be the most appropriate and cost-effective treatment for many workers (Borenstein 1988; McClellan 1982). If they are highly motivated and not too impaired, going to group and individual counseling, as well as to Alcoholics Anonymous (AA), four to seven times a week may be very effective. This allows them to continue working, which saves money for both the workers and the employer. They do not use sick leave, need a substitute, need coworkers to cover for them, or use as much insurance coverage. They also continue in their own environment and learn to cope with their daily problems without chemicals.

Some employees do need inpatient treatment because they are so heavily addicted that they need a total change of environment and lifestyle. They may need medical treatment, good nutrition, and an opportunity to focus on themselves and their current dysfunction. Many treatment programs now offer a variable length of stay, which can be less than the traditional twenty-eight days. Employees may then enter an intensive day or evening treatment program or a less intensive program.

Each type of treatment can include family members or friends. They attend groups specifically designed for them and then get special counseling with the substance abuser. The EAP can help employees and their families select the best program for them. If the substance abuser is a relative of the employee, the EAP can help in intervention and confrontation and refer the family member to treatment.

Aftercare

A treatment program is only the beginning of sobriety. Aftercare is very important, and the EAP can be helpful in supporting and facilitating this process. The purpose of aftercare is to assist the recovering employee in remaining free of alcohol and other drugs. He or she needs to establish a strong foundation on which to base the rest of his or her life. The EAP can encourage the employee to attend AA, take Antabuse, get more therapy, and find a temporary AA sponsor. Some EAPs require Antabuse, urine or blood testing, or other help depending on company policy.

The help and support that a recovering employee gets after treatment for substance abuse is the key to preventing a relapse (Abrams 1987; Miller 1986). During the first three months after treatment, the person is especially susceptible to relapse. After that, the probability of staying sober or abstinent for one year increases. If the recovering person participates in good aftercare, his or her chances of staying sober or abstinent increase (Miller 1986). Aftercare can include self-help groups such as AA, outpatient programs, individual or group therapy, and support and follow-up from the EAP.

An important part of aftercare is the supervisor (Singer 1986). If the employee has been off the job for treatment, the EAP might conduct a back-to-work conference several days before the employee goes back to the job. The EAP, the recovering employee, selected supervisors, and the treatment counselor attend the conference. The employee can tell the supervisors what he or she did and learned in treatment and even show the supervisors the program if the conference is held at the treatment center. The supervisors state what is expected of the employee on the job, such as attendance and performance requirements. The employee discusses what he or she needs from the employer, the EAP, and the supervisors to remain sober, such as positive support or time to attend AA. Any job-related problems that occurred before treatment should be discussed, and everyone must be clear on any disciplinary measures. If Antabuse or drug testing is recommended or required, the process can be set up at this conference.

With the permission of the recovering employee, the EAP can educate his or her coworkers on the employee's addiction, treatment, and recovery. This gives the EAP an opportunity to answer coworkers' questions, especially those concerning how they should treat the recovering employee when he or she comes back to work. This makes the transition easier and should help everyone feel more confident about the situation.

Drug Screening

The issue of drug screening has entered the EAP arena. Many companies now do preemployment drug testing or testing for cause. Some do random testing of all or certain groups of employees. This is a very controversial issue (Bickerton 1986; Masi and Burns 1986). The purpose is usually to identify substance abusers before hiring them, to have cause to fire or discipline them, or to try to rehabilitate them. In some organizations, the EAP monitors the entire drug-screening process. In others, the EAP assesses and refers to treatment any employee who tests positive. The EAP must be careful not to become part of any disciplinary measures or to tell management who tests positive. There can be a conflict of interest if the EAP must report positive drug tests to management when company policy says that users of certain drugs will be dismissed (Darling 1986; Evans 1986).

The EAP as an Information Resource

Substance Abuse Policies

If an organization decides to institute a drug use/substance abuse policy, the EAP can be an excellent source of information. The EAP can stress the positive aspects of rehabilitation and treatment for both the employee and the employer. There are federal guidelines and laws for certain organizations concerning confidentiality guarantees for employees who admit they are alcoholic and want treatment. They cannot be dismissed for drinking, but they can be fired for poor job performance that is well documented. The EAP should provide the employer with information about such laws, as well as about other companies' policies and court cases. This information can help the employer avoid making mistakes in writing a policy statement. The EAP also can educate management about the advantages of rehabilitation over punishment and help build in a process that will facilitate treatment for employees.

Acquired Immunodeficiency Syndrome

The concerns of employers about acquired immunodeficiency syndrome (AIDS) in the workplace is another issue where the EAP can help both the employer and the employee. Some employees may get AIDS from intravenous drug use. The EAP can be a resource for management and supervisors so they can formulate policy and recommendations on AIDS. The EAP can help the ill employee get treatment for AIDS and for the drug abuse and give support as needed (Bunker, Eriksen, and Kinsey 1987; Stotz and Steiner 1988).

Union Support

One very important aspect of an EAP is having the strong support of any unions or collective bargaining units to which employees belong (McClellan 1982). Without that support, employees will not use EAP services and may see the program as an arm of or a spy for management. The issues surrounding substance abuse should be discussed thoroughly with union leaders. They will want to be sure that union members' rights will not be violated and that the EAP will help employees get effective treatment. Some unions have their own EAPs, which usually work only with alcohol problems. Union leaders also should be consulted if a drug policy is written and implemented.

Health Benefits

The EAP can be a source of information for the benefits department of the organization concerning health insurance coverage for chemical dependence treatment. Educating the decision makers on all the treatment options and costs can help the organization save money and the employee get effective treatment. The EAP also can recommend treatment programs as preferred providers if appropriate.

The rise in health care costs has forced employers to find ways to control or reduce this benefit to employees. The May 1988 issue of *The ALMACAN* focuses on managed health care and the EAP's role in this cost-containment effort. Yandrick and Rothermel (1988) report that health insurance claims and costs rose alarmingly during the late 1980s. For instance, they note that "expenditures for the worst case substance abuse problems have increased about 70% since 1984, and the work place has borne 54% of the total cost for [chemical dependency/mental health] problems" (p. 17). Employers are trying to find ways to curb their costs without affecting the quality of care. Lightman and Wagman (1988) suggest how EAPs can help control health care use, quality, and claims in a cost-effective way while not sacrificing quality or access. They offer two proposals concerning what EAPs can do as well as what a health insurance plan should offer for chemical dependence.

Some professionals in the substance abuse treatment field state that a lack of insurance coverage is a significant barrier to employees who need treatment. This may be true in some cases, but a study by Tramm and Herman (1988) found that even when good insurance coverage for substance abuse is available, it is underused by substance-abusing employees who do not have contact with an EAP. In this study, these employees' use of medical claims was seven times greater than that of a control group comprising non–substance abusers and two times greater than that of substance-abusing employees who used an EAP. Treatment costs of EAP users were 53 percent of non–EAP users.

Codependency

Codependency and the problems of adult children of alcoholics are other areas in which EAPs can educate and facilitate appropriate help. Employees in these categories may not realize that some of their personal and job-related problems stem from having an alcoholic or other drug-abusing relative. An EAP should be able to recognize when this is a possibility and help such employees start on a path to health and recovery through appropriate treatment.

Other Addictions

The roots of EAPs are in alcohol identification and treatment. The issue of cross-addiction or polyaddiction has made the EAPs' work more difficult. Younger employees grew up in an atmosphere where use of illegal drugs was an accepted practice. Most users of alcohol who are under age thirty-five also use other drugs such as marijuana and cocaine (McClellan 1982). The use of legal drugs such as nicotine, amphetamines, and barbiturates also can affect job performance. Since each of these drugs has a different detoxification period and different symptoms, EAPs must be able to identify cross-addiction and drug use symptoms in order to refer addicted employees to appropriate treatment.

The Future

Although EAPs have a long and positive history in helping alcoholics, the needs of employers and employees are much more demanding today than in the past. Among the reasons for this are the following:

- More employees are addicted to more than one drug.
- The variety of treatment options can be overwhelming.
- The cost of treatment can be very high.
- Employees are requesting help at a younger age.
- The awareness of the substance abuse problem in society has increased.
- Employers are being held liable for the emotional well-being of employers.
- Work stress is now considered an occupational disease by the courts.
- Health insurance claims have increased beyond all projections.
- Employers are concerned with conserving human resources as well as with financial costs and profits.

EAPs have a proven track record as effective resources for getting impaired employees to treatment. Now they must be resources on the above issues, as well as consultants to supervisors and referral sources for treatment of substance-abusing and chemically dependent employees. EAPs are effective because they can work with employees who have jobs but need help with chemical dependence. The fear of losing their jobs will get many employees to treatment and push them to work hard both in treatment and after treatment. EAPs can monitor their work performance before and after treatment to see if and when they need help. The support and caring of an EAP can make employees feel that it is all right to get help with their chemical dependence and to return to the EAP for help if their sobriety is threatened.

An EAP functions in the real world of the workplace and, as such, is one of the best resources for help not only with substance abuse and chemical dependence, but also with codependency, AIDS, managed health care, and other related issues. Today EAPs are available to help troubled employees with many problems. However, as Roman and Blum (1988) state, "The continued focus of EAPs on alcohol and drug abuse problems ... remains a vibrant, indispensable part of employee assistance programming" (p. 22).

References

Abrams, L. 1987. "An Employer's Role in Relapse Prevention." *ALMACAN* 17 (7): 20–22.
ALMACA. 1982. "Standards for Employee Alcohol/Assistance Programs." *Resource Information on Employee Alcoholism/Assistance Programs.* Arlington, Va.: ALMACA.
Backer, T.E. 1987. *Strategic Planning for Workplace Drug Abuse Programs.* Rockville, Md.: National Institute on Drug Abuse.
Backer T.E., and K. O'Hara. 1988. "A National Study on Drug Abuse Services and EAPs." *ALMACAN* 18 (8): 24–26.
Bernstein, M., and J.J. Dolan. 1988. "Internal and External EAPs in the MMHC Environment." *ALMACAN* 18 (5).
Bickerton, R.L. 1986. "Urinalysis: Dilemma of the '80s." *EAP Digest* 6 (6).
Blum, T.C., and P.M. Roman. 1987. "Internal vs. External EAPs." In *Employee Assistance Programs: Benefits, Problems, and Prospects,* 95–104. Washington, D.C.: Bureau of National Affairs.
Borenstein, B. 1988. "Multi-Company EAP Case Tracking." *ALMACAN* 18 (6):
Bunker, J.F., M.P. Eriksen, and J. Kinsey 1987. "AIDS in the Workplace: The Role of EAPs." *ALMACAN* 17 (9).
Chiabotta, B. 1985. "Evaluating EAP Vendors." *Personnel Administrator* 30 (8): 39–43.
Darling, E. 1986. "Dose Drug Testing Undermine the EAP's Occupational Role?" *ALMACAN* 16 (12).
Dunkin, W.S. 1982. "A Brief History of Employee Assistance/Alcoholism Programs." *Labor Management Alcoholism' Journal* 11: 165–68.
Erfurt, J.C., and A. Foote. 1977. *Occupational EAPs for Substance Abuse and Mental Health Problems.* Institute of Labor and Industrial Relations.

Evans, D.G. 1986. "Drug Testing, Work Performance, and EAPs: Recent Legal Guidelines." *ALMACAN* 16 (12).
Foote, A., and J.C. Erfurt. 1981. "Effectiveness of Comprehensive EAPs at Reaching Alcoholics." *Journal of Drug Issues* 2:217–32.
Forrest D.V. 1983. "EAPs in the 1980's: Expanding Career Options for Counselors." *Personnel and Guidance Journal* 62:105–7.
Iutcovich J., and J. Calderone. 1984. "Evaluation of the Treatment Process for Employee Alcohol Abusers: Structure and Strategies for Successful Programming." In *EAP Research*, edited by C.H. Grimes, 48–61. Troy, Mich.: Performance Press.
Lewis, J.A., and M.D. Lewis 1986. *Counseling Programs for Employees in the Workplace*. Monterey, Calif.: Brooks/Cole.
Lightman, R., and J.B. Wagman. 1988. "A Working Proposal for the EAP Role in a Managed Care System." *ALMACAN* 18 (5).
Longpré, J.G. 1984. "Scope of an EAP." *ALMACAN* 14 (1): 5.
Masi, D.A., and L.E. Burns. "Urinalysis Testing and EAPs." *EAP Digest* 6 (6).
Mastrich, J., and B. Beidel. 1987. "Employee Assistance Programs Cost-Impact." *ALMACAN* 17 (6): 34–36.
McClellan, K. 1982. "An Overview of Occupational Alcoholism Issues for the 80's." *Journal of Drug Education* 12 (1): 1–27.
Miller, R. 1986. "Job Reintegration and Aftercare of the Recovering Worker." *ALMACAN* 16 (8): 12–16.
Montgomery, R.H. 1987. "Alcoholism Treatment Benefits: Cost or Savings?" *ALMACAN* 17 (5): 22–25.
Phillips, D.A., and H.J. Older. 1981. "Models of Service Delivery." *EAP Digest* 4 (4): 12–15.
Presnall, L.F. 1981. *Occupational Counseling and Referral Systems*. Salt Lake City: Alcoholism Foundation.
Roman, P. 1981a. "Corporate Pacesetters Making EAP Progress." *Alcoholism* 1 (4): 37–41.
———. 1981b. "Dealing with Alcohol Problems among the Faculty of Colleges and Universities." In *Alcohol Problems and the Campus Community*, edited by J.C. Deans and W.A. Bryan, 10–20. Washington, D.C.: American Personnel and Guidance Association.
———. 1981c. "Employee Alcoholism to Employee Assistance: De-emphasis on Prevention and on Alcohol Problems in Work-Based Programs." *Journal of Studies on Alcohol* 42:244–72.
Roman, P.M., and T.C. Blum. 1985. "The Core Technology of Employee Assistance Programs." *ALMACAN* 15 (3): 8–9, 16–19.
Roman, P.M., and T.C. Blum. 1988. "The Core Technology of Employee Assistance Programs: A Reaffirmation." *ALMACAN* 18 (8): 17–22.
Singer, G. 1986. "Return to Work Conference Eases the Way." *EAP Digest* 6 (3): 45–49.
Stotz, E.S., and J.R. Steiner. 1988. "AIDS and the Emerging Role of the EAP Professional." *EAP Digest* 8 (4): 33–39.
Straussner, S.L.A. 1988. *Comparison of In-House and Contracted-Out Employee Assistance Programs*. Boston: National Association of Social Workers.
Tramm, M.L., and R. Herman 1988. "Insurance Coverage for Chemical Dependency:

How Well Does It Work?" In *EAP Research*, edited by C.H. Grimes, 99–107. Troy, Mich.: Performance Press.

Trice, H.M. 1980. "Applied Research Studies: Job Based Alcoholism and Employee Assistance Programs." *Alcohol Health Research World* 4 (3): 4–16.

Trice, H.M., and J. Beyer 1984. "Work Related Outcomes of the Constructive-Confrontation Strategy in a Job Based Alcoholism Program." *Journal of Studies on Alcohol* 45 (5): 393–404.

Trice, H.M., and M. Schonbrunn. 1981. "A History of Job-Based Alcoholism Programs: 1900–55." *Journal of Drug Issues* 2:171–98.

Yandrick, R., and S. Rothermel. 1988. "For 30 Years, Health Care, Costs Have Been on a Collision Course." *ALMACAN* 18 (5).

Part III
Multiproblem Patients

Prologue

William A. Frosch

The great fourteenth-century English Franciscan monk and scholar William of Occam taught that we should believe what we see and that we should then explain it as simply as possible: "As between two hypotheses, both of which will account for a given fact, prefer the simpler" and "What can be explained on fewer principles is explained needlessly by more" (Jones 1952). (This principle became known as Occam's razor.) Certainly, those of us old enough to have lived with DSM II have lived within these rules. If patients had auditory hallucinations, they had schizophrenia; if they abused alcohol, they were alcoholics; if they abused drugs, they were addicts. Sometimes the world is more complex, and too simple an explanation leaves out too much of what we have observed. One of the important contributions of DSM III has been the introduction of a number of axes, forcing us to think of personality as well as disease, of physical illness as well as mental illness, of external stressors and functional abilities. DSM III-R (American Psychiatric Association Staff 1987) has further multiplied our diagnostic possibilities by discarding many of the hierarchic exclusions. We have entered the era of comorbidity, of multiple diagnoses.

These three chapters focus on this increasing complexity. We have moved from the shunned world of drunks and drug fiends to the complicated but real problems of patients with multiple problems and to the imperative to provide help.

Sederer deals with the important issue of patients with more than one psychiatric diagnosis. As diagnoses are descriptive and not explanatory, they do not provide causal relationships. (Even the commonly used primary/secondary distinction refers, properly, to temporal sequence and does not imply causality.) Sederer presents many possible model relationships between diagnoses, such as accidental concurrence, causality, change in risk exposure, and modifier. As he makes clear, both the fact of multiple diagnoses and our understanding of the relationship between the diagnoses in an individual patient are important for what they tell about who should treat the patient, with what techniques, in which sequence, and with what hope of success.

Sheila Blume shifts the focus to distorting prejudices and stereotypes, to the peculiar ways in which we imagine people behave, and to the ways in which social expectation pushes individuals into defined, but not necessarily natural, roles. Her example, perhaps the most important one in this context, deals with alcohol and drug problems in women. Parallel chapters could have been written about Native Americans, blacks, Irish, or Jews. Biased expectations change both our perceptions and, to some extent, the way people really behave. Blume reminds us that while biology is important, it is not fully determinative. Alternatively, we must remember that there are known brain differences between men and women and that these and other differences may be responsible for perceived differences, both real and imagined, in incidence, severity, symptom profile, and so on. Similar factors need to be considered in other intergroup comparisons. Removing bias may not do away with difference. Social controls, however imposed, may in some instances merely modify genetic determinants.

While we may think of Sederer's paper as discussing illness issues, perhaps biological in nature, and Blume's as applied sociology, we should also examine the role of psychology—the meaning of the act and of the impact of the act—in the world of personality (and personality disorder). Although these issues are traditionally in the psychoanalyst's realm, DSM III's multiple axes and increasing interest in cognitive psychology and child development have moved these issues toward the center of consciousness of those who try to care for patients with problems such as substance abuse. While meanings are not necessarily causal, they typically complicate treatment. Vaillant's chapter on the elements of recovery leads us behind the addict's self-assessed reasons for relapse. Too often we remain unaware of the forces that drive people (to either health or illness, abstinence or relapse) and offer "explanations" that do not explain and that, therefore, do not help us to plan appropriate interventions. Vaillant's suggestion that a good outcome for substance abusers is affected by compulsory supervision, new relationships, inspirational group membership, and substitute dependence leads us to an understanding of how to help, what can go wrong, and how to correct it.

In summary, these three chapters provide an appropriately complicated view of substance abuse. They remind us that we must maintain multiple models, which help us think of our patients as individuals and not as types and plan our treatments accordingly for their unique combination of character, social context, and illness. These chapters also remind us of how much we have yet to learn.

References

American Psychiatric Association Staff. 1987. *Diagnostic and Statistical Manual of Mental Disorders, DSM-III-R.* 3rd, rev. ed. Washington, D.C.: American Psychiatric Press.

Jones, W.T. 1952. *History of Western Philosophy.* Harcourt, Brace and Company: New York.

9
Mental Disorders and Substance Abuse

Lloyd I. Sederer

Multiproblem patients are those people who present for treatment with more than one psychiatric disorder. They are men and women who suffer simultaneously with, for example, an anxiety disorder *and* alcoholism or mania *and* cocaine abuse. Multiproblem patients are different from those patients with only a single disorder, even if that disorder subjects them to more than one clinical problem or symptom (for example, the depressed patient who suffers from sleep, appetite, and mood disturbances). They are different because their multiple disorders create diagnostic confusion. They also are different because their treatment must be specifically fashioned to encompass their multiple disorders if they are to have a reasonable chance of recovery. They also may have quite a different course and prognosis because of the interaction between their illnesses.

This chapter focuses on those patients who suffer simultaneously with a mental disorder and a substance abuse disorder. Of course, some patients have more than one mental disorder or more than one substance abuse disorder. And some patients have a medical illness (such as heart disease or diabetes) as well as a psychiatric disorder. This chapter, however, deals only with patients who have a DSM-III-R Axis I or Axis II mental disorder as well as a substance abuse disorder (American Psychiatric Association Staff 1987).

Multiproblem patients may represent a sizable proportion of a clinician's practice if he or she treats a generally more ill population and if he or she is able to recognize multiple disorders when they do exist. Regrettably, there has been a tendency for multiproblem (or dual-diagnosis) patients to be treated either by the mental health professional community or by the substance abuse professional community. When this has occurred, both patients and professionals have suffered.

This chapter first presents a variety of models for understanding multiproblem or dual-diagnosis patients. It then reviews concurrent Axis I and substance abuse disorders and concurrent Axis II and substance abuse disorders. To the extent possible, differentiations are made among the different substances of abuse as they interact with psychiatric illnesses and personality disorders. Throughout, the clinical implications of dual diagnosis are emphasized. My aim is to depart from any ideological differences that may have existed in the fields of psychiatry and substance abuse. I hope to replace such differences with clinical realities so that the needs of the patient become the clinician's only guide.

Models of Dual Diagnosis

A variety of conceptual models have been offered to aid in understanding those illnesses that exist concurrently (Sederer 1985; Nace 1987; Donovan 1986; Meyer 1986). The terms that have denoted concurrent disorders include *dual diagnosis, comorbidity,* and *multiproblem patients.* In this section, I examine five ways of understanding patients who have comorbid conditions (table 9–1).

The first model, *parallel disorders,* is the simplest, which may not be a conceptual or a clinical virtue. In this model a mental disorder and a substance abuse disorder coexist but are fully independent of each other. They happen to occur simultaneously but share no etiologic relationship and do not significantly influence each other. This model has limited use because it does not allow disorders to share common causes. This model also is blind to the interactive effects of concurrent disorders (Sederer 1988).

The second model is *causation.* This is a model of primary and secondary disorders. For example, a patient who has chronic alcoholism may develop, as a direct consequence of his or her alcoholism, a secondary major depres-

Table 9–1
Models of Dual Diagnosis

Parallel
Independent disorders present concurrently.

Causation
Primary substance abuse *causes* secondary psychiatric disorder.
Primary psychiatric disorder *causes* secondary substance abuse.

Risk
Primary psychiatric disorder *increases risk* of substance abuse.
Primary substance abuse *increases risk* of psychiatric disorder.

Modifier
Primary psychiatric disorder *modifies* course of substance abuse disorder.
Primary substance abuse disorder *modifies* course of psychiatric disorder.

Berkson's law
Unrelated disorders appear together because those with more than one problem are more likely to seek professional help.

sion or secondary maladaptive personality traits such as antisocial behavior or impulsivity. According to this model, the secondary disorder would not have occurred had there been no primary disorder. Vaillant (1983a) exemplifies this model when he argues that the personality disturbances seen in chronic alcoholics are the product of the drinking and did not exist prior to the substance abuse. Bean-Bayog (1988) also offers a primary/secondary disease model in her hypothesis that alcoholism is a traumatic experience that causes psychopathology. Khantzian (1985, 1978) illustrates how a primary psychiatric disorder can cause secondary substance abuse. Khantzian also views certain substance abusers as having sought out and repetitively used (then abused) psychoactive drugs in order to self-medicate a primary mood disorder or a primary attention deficit disorder (ADD).

The third model emphasizes *risk*. In this model the presence of a primary psychiatric disorder increases the risk of developing a substance abuse disorder. Examples include certain anxiety disorders in which alcohol and other drugs may be used to control panic, childhood ADD, and antisocial personality. Conversely, the presence of a primary substance abuse disorder may increase the risk of developing a psychiatric disorder. Alcohol and cocaine abusers whose addictions leave them at increased biochemical and ego vulnerability to develop depressive illnesses illustrate this latter relationship.

The fourth model highlights how a preexisting disorder may modify a comorbid condition. This *modifier* model hypothesizes, for example, that a primary psychiatric disorder will modify the course of a substance abuse disorder or, conversely, that a primary substance abuse disorder will modify the course of a concurrent psychiatric disorder. This model is illustrated by those alcoholic patients who also have an affective disorder that renders them more vulnerable to relapse into drinking if they become depressed when in the abstinent state. This model also may be seen in patients with severe character pathology (with generalized ego weakness and impulsivity) who abuse drugs. Their addictive illness tends to show an earlier onset, a more rapid progression, and a generally poorer response to treatment.

The final model is a statistical phenomenon called *Berkson's law*. According to this law, two unrelated disorders may appear together because there is a greater likelihood that people who suffer with more than one disorder are more likely to seek professional help. The disorders are unrelated, except through the help-seeking behavior of subjects with multiple illnesses.

These five models, though presented separately, are not necessarily exclusive of each other. I have presented them in this manner for conceptual clarity. It is possible that risk and modifier dimensions can coexist, as it is possible (perhaps probable) that parallel disorders can modify each other. Further conceptual and empirical work is needed before an integrated model for clinical practice is available.

Concurrent Axis I and Substance Abuse Disorders

Axis I of the DSM III-R refers to the clinical syndromes that exist within the domain of psychiatric practice. Axis I is differentiated from Axis II (which encompasses personality traits or disorders) and from Axis III (which catalogs all medical illnesses, including neurological diseases). To be sure, these axes were distinguished from one another by some measure of reason, by some measure of appreciation of how these disorders are generally understood, and by which specialty generally treats the illness. In all, the groupings created by the multiple axes represent, for better or worse, the conceptual and nosological conventions of our time.

The principal Axis I disorders that tend to coexist with substance abuse disorders are identified in table 9–2. This section discusses substance abuse–induced organic mental disorders; the major mental illnesses that psychiatrists treat (with an emphasis on schizophrenia, affective disorders, and anxiety disorders); and adult, or residual, ADD.

Substance-Induced Organic Mental Disorders

Psychoactive drugs of abuse alter the brain, which is why they are used. In doing so, they can induce a variety of abnormal mental states, both desired and undesired, transient and permanent. Table 9–3 outlines these abnormal states or disorders, using alcohol as the offending agent. Clearly, other substances can induce a similar range of untoward effects, as can the use of multiple chemicals simultaneously.

The limits of this chapter do not allow for an elaboration on these varied and important disorders. The clinician must be familiar with all of them and be able to identify each and distinguish how each is different according to its relation to states of intoxication, withdrawal, and as persistent sequelae to drug abuse.

Table 9–2
DSM III-R Axis I Disorders: Clinical Syndromes

Organic Mental Disorders
Substance induced

Major mental illnesses
1. Schizophrenia
2. Affective disorders: major depression, dysthymic disorder, bipolar affective disorder
3. Anxiety disorders: Panic disorder, generalized anxiety, simple and social phobias, obsessive-compulsive disorders, post-traumatic stress disorders
4. Bulimia nervosa, anorexia nervosa

Attention deficit disorder: adult

Table 9–3
Psychoactive Substance-Induced Organic Mental Disorder: Alcohol

Transient
1. Alcohol intoxication
2. Alcohol idiosyncratic intoxication; pathological intoxication
3. Uncomplicated alcohol withdrawal
4. Alcohol withdrawal delirium
5. Alcoholic hallucinosis

Severe
1. Alcohol amnestic disorder; Wernicke's encephalopathy; Korsakoff's syndrome
2. Dementia

The Major Mental Illnesses

Psychiatry has as its major illnesses (in addition to psychoactive substance dependence) the disorders of schizophrenia, the affective (mood) disorders, and the anxiety disorders. Other major clinical syndromes exist, but these illnesses represent the vast proportion of prevalent psychiatric disorders. For this reason (as well as the fact that the most is known about dual diagnosis in these patient populations), I focus entirely on these three categories of illness.

Schizophrenia. Schizophrenia is a chronic mental illness characterized by psychotic symptoms during the active phase of the illness, functioning below a level previously achieved, and a duration of at least six months. Schizophrenia must be differentially diagnosed from alcoholic hallucinosis, a generally self-limited, principally auditory hallucinatory psychotic state that develops in some later stage alcoholics at a time when they have reduced their alcohol consumption. Schizophrenia must be distinguished from psychoactive-induced psychotic states as seen with cocaine and PCP toxicity. The latter occur during intoxication and are self-limited, whereas schizophrenia shows a markedly different onset and course.

In a study by Gottheil and Waxman (1982), approximately 10 to 15 percent of hospitalized schizophrenics had what they reported to be a serious drinking problem. Interestingly, in this population, 10 to 15 percent of outpatient and hospitalized alcoholics were considered to have a schizophrenic illness. These latter data are of remarkably high prevalence, for the lifetime prevalence of schizophrenia in the general population is only 1 percent.

Estimates of the prevalence of substance abuse among the young adult, chronically mentally ill population (most of whom are schizophrenic) have ranged from 15 to 60 percent. In a study of hospitalized young, chronic patients admitted to a private mental hospital outside of New York City, about 50 percent of the subjects diagnosed as schizophrenic were substance abusers, either of a single drug or multiple drugs (Gralnick et al. 1988). In this population, the drug abuse followed the onset of the psychotic illness. These young, severely mentally ill patients reported that they used psychoactive chemicals to relieve and to medicate themselves for the negative symptoms of schizophrenia (such as apathy, withdrawal, and anhedonia) (Sederer 1986).

In a study of community-based, state hospital aftercare schizophrenics in the Boston area, approximately 45 percent of the sample evidenced alcohol use (Drake, Osher, and Wallach 1988). A substantial proportion of the alcohol users also used street drugs. Of crucial importance clinically were the findings that those patients who used alcohol had more difficulty maintaining housing, obtaining food, and managing their finances. In addition, suicidal behavior was significantly greater in the population that used alcohol. Furthermore, there was a significantly greater rate of rehospitalization in the alcohol-using group. The triple scourges of the chronic population appear to be correlated: suicide, homelessness, and substance abuse. Finally, the authors of this study discovered essentially no difference between those patients who used minimal amounts of alcohol and those who used more substantial quantities. In this population, even mild use was destabilizing. Any use of alcohol was associated with a poorer course and prognosis. Why this was so was not clear but might relate to alcohol as a gateway to other drug use.

Affective Disorders. The principal affective disorders that I review here are major depression, dysthymic disorder, and bipolar disorder. Major depression and dysthymic disorder are generally considered together as possibly major and minor variants, whereas bipolar disorder must be considered separately.

The coexistence of alcoholism and depression has been well established (Weissman, Meyer, and Keener 1980; Hesselbrock, Meyer, and Keener 1985; Dackis et al. 1986; Mirin 1984; Schuckit 1986). Patients who present for treatment of alcoholism frequently report a depressed mood and the vegetative (sleep and appetite) and cognitive disturbances typical of depressive states. Depending on the population and setting studied and the manner in which the data were collected, the prevalence of depressive symptoms in the alcoholic population ranged from 20 to 90 percent. Because of the central nervous system (CNS) effects of alcohol abuse, many of these patients must be diagnosed as having an organic affective disorder that will remit with abstinence. Indeed, this is the case, for a significant proportion will have a remission of their depressive symptoms within several weeks of detoxification (Schuckit 1983; Overall et al. 1985). The implication of this clinical course is that many depressed alcoholics do not require specific antidepressant medication once they have achieved sobriety. However, the subgroup of patients who remain depressed when sober does have a concurrent major depression or dysthymic disorder, tends to have a family history of affective disorder, and is at greater risk to relapse into drinking if their depressive illness is not treated effectively.

Patients with a primary diagnosis of depression (that is, a history of depression prior to developing an alcohol disorder) do not appear to be at greater risk for developing alcohol dependence than the general population. The view that primary depressives will abuse alcohol as a consequence of their dysphoria does not seem to hold up to research scrutiny (Woodruff et al. 1985; Merikanges et al. 1985). Although the alcoholic patient is at high risk to develop depressive symptoms (and in some cases a depressive disorder), the primary depressive patient does not appear to carry a vulnerability that exceeds the risk rate in society.

Opiate addicts tend to show very high lifetime prevalence rates for depression—as high as 50 to 74 percent (Rounsaville et al. 1982; O'Brien, Woody, and McLellan 1984). In more than 90 percent of the cases, however, the first depressive episode occurred after the onset of significant opiate abuse. These data do not support a view that opiates are used to self-medicate an affective disorder, but rather that the affective disorder in this population may be a secondary organic affective syndrome. Methadone maintenance patients also show high rates of depression, supporting this hypothesis. As with alcoholics, a persistent depressive disorder in this population requires treatment (with tricyclic antidepressants) to enhance relapse prevention.

In a study of hospitalized chronic cocaine abusers, more than 50 percent of the sample showed evidence of an affective illness (Weiss et al. 1986). The prevalence was significantly higher than in the control sample of opiate and depressant drug (for example, alcohol, tranquilizers, and hypnotics) abusers. Furthermore, the first-degree relatives of the cocaine abusers had significantly greater rates of affective disorder than the relatives of the controls. Those patients with depressive disorders appeared to use cocaine to self-medicate dysphoria, whereas those with bipolar disorders used the drug to enhance euphoria. Specific treatment of the depression is crucial in this population because of the presence of both organic and major depressive disorders and because of the high rates of relapse when not treated.

Bipolar (manic-depressive) patients frequently abuse alcohol as a complication of their illness. Bipolars typically abuse alcohol when in the manic phase of their illness. Those manic patients who drink show a more problematic course and prognosis than do those who do not (Morrison 1974; Dunner, Hensel, and Fieve 1979; Reich, Davies, and Himmelhoch 1974). Both sedative and euphoric effects appear to be sought from the ethanol. Careful differential diagnosis is needed to distinguish the mood lability of alcoholism from a true bipolar disorder. Bipolar patients do better when treated with lithium, which stabilizes the affective disorder and may diminish the craving for alcohol (Fawcett et al. 1987). As noted earlier, bipolars may abuse cocaine as a means for enhancing or prolonging periods of euphoria. Opiate abusers are not well represented in the bipolar population.

Anxiety Disorders. Because anxiety is characteristic of alcohol and depressant drug withdrawal and characteristic of stimulant intoxication, care must be taken to recognize anxiety as a component symptom of active drug abuse, when that is its basis. Anxiety disorders include generalized anxiety, simple phobias, panic disorders with and without agoraphobia, posttraumatic stress disorder, and obsessive-compulsive disorder. Samples of alcoholics demonstrate rates of anxiety disorders of 20 to 40 percent (Bowen et al. 1984; Weiss and Rosenberg 1985). The treatment of anxiety with benzodiazepines must be assiduously avoided in this dual-diagnosis group. Behavioral techniques in combination with psychotherapy and specific anxiolytic drugs (such as imipramine, phenelzine, and buspirone) can be very effective in this population.

Attention Deficit Disorder: Residual Type

Attention deficit disorder (ADD), formerly known as hyperactivity, can persist into adulthood, where it is known as adult or residual-type ADD. Symptoms of this disorder in adults include impulsivity, irritability, impaired concentration, and explosive personality traits. Alcohol use and abuse can be of early onset and considerable severity in this population, where prevalence rates have been reported at 27 percent (Tartar et al. 1977; Wood et al. 1976). Cocaine use (and even extreme cocaine dependence) has been reported in adult ADD patients, with a prevalence of about 5 percent (Khantzian 1983). There is evidence that substance abusers who are residual ADD patients may benefit from treatment with psychostimulants. These medications allow ADD patients to "feel normal" and not to experience the powerful craving to medicinally use alcohol and cocaine (Khantzian 1983; Turnquist et al. 1983; Weiss, R.D., Pope and Mirin 1985).

Concurrent Axis II and Substance Abuse Disorders

Axis II of the DSM III-R portrays qualities of human character as they manifest themselves as traits or disorders. Although traits are relatively immutable, they do not have the maladaptive consequences that are characteristic of the personality disorders (table 9–4). DSM III-R also clusters these traits and disorders as being odd or eccentric; dramatic, emotional, or erratic; and anxious or fearful (table 9–5).

As with concurrent Axis I disorders and substance abuse, the Axis II problem must not be confused with the intoxication and withdrawal symptomatology of substance abuse. Drug abusers who are actively using chemi-

Table 9-4
DSM III-R Axis II Disorders

Personality traits
Enduring patterns of perceiving, relating to, or thinking about the environment and oneself. They are exhibited in a wide range of social and personal contexts.

Personality disorders
Conditions manifested by *inflexible, maladaptive traits* that cause *social or occupational consequences and/or personal discomfort*. Although the individual may not consider the trait(s) undesirable, others may.

Table 9-5
DSM III-R Axis II Disorders: Personality Traits and Disorders

Odd or eccentric behavior
1. Paranoid
2. Schizoid
3. Schizotypal

Dramatic, emotional, or erratic behavior
1. Borderline
2. Narcissistic
3. Antisocial
4. Histrionic

Anxious or fearful behavior
1. Avoidant
2. Dependent
3. Obsessive compulsive
4. Passive dependent

cals can show many symptoms (during toxic states, withdrawal, and early abstinence) that resemble personality traits and disorders. Careful diagnostic assessment includes attempting to define personality functioning prior to drug abuse (including collaborative information from family) and observing these patients once stable in the abstinent state. Because a personality diagnosis generally cannot be made until recovery has begun, the patient's apparent dual-diagnostic disorder treatment cannot be started by treating the underlying character disorder. Drugs of abuse may serve as coping mechanisms to support ego defenses and aid in aspects of regulation of the self. The patient's ego functions may undergo a type of "disuse atrophy," thereby making accurate personality assessment impossible until recovery is well established (Milkman and Frosch 1973; Khantzian 1986; Mirin 1988).

The three personality profiles or disorders that dominate the findings in dual-diagnosis studies of substance abuse and Axis II are borderline disorder, narcissistic personality, and antisocial personality. I address each of these separately, although there may be some overlap in their clinical presentation.

Borderline Personality Disorder

Borderline patients are characteristically impulsive, unpredictable, and affectively unstable; feel empty and bored; are plagued by identity confusion; show addictive trends; and are self-destructive. The symptom cluster described is reminiscent of drug abuse, and there may be nosological problems in their similarity. It is no surprise, therefore, that borderline disorders are reported to coexist with substance abuse at a rate of 43 percent (Koenigsberg et al. 1985). Primary borderline disordered patients appear to be at significant risk to develop substance dependence. Substance abusers can be confused with borderline characters because of the behavioral and mood instability seen with chemical dependence.

In a study of borderline patients with alcoholism, Nace and colleagues (1986) reported that 13 to 18 percent of a sample of women and men had concurrent disorders. In a Norwegian study, 66 percent of the female alcoholics met criteria for borderline personality disorder (Vaglum and Vaglum 1985). Mirin (1988) reported that borderline patients tend to prefer depressant drugs such as alcohol, tranquilizers, and sedatives. Borderline patients may select these agents to quite excessive affective states. Opiate use among borderline patients also has been identified. Approximately 12 percent of opiate abusers have met criteria for borderline pathology. This group also tends to show depression, which tends to remit with treatment of the addictive disorder (Kosten et al. 1982). Cocaine abuse is seen in borderline patients, but this does not appear to be their drug of choice (Weiss et al. 1986; Mirin 1988).

Narcissistic Personality Disorder

Narcissistically disordered patients display a pervasive sense of grandiosity (imagined or behavioral), a hypersensitivity to the opinions of others, and a limited capacity for empathy. Their self-esteem is extremely fragile, and their interpersonal relationships are impaired because of entitlement and self-centeredness.

In private hospital samples of personality-disordered patients with concurrent addictive disease, the subgroups of narcissistic patients tended to prefer to use cocaine (Weiss et al. 1986; Mirin 1988). Narcissistic patients appear to seek the excitement and stimulation that the drug offers. In addition, cocaine can offer a temporary boost to the flagging self-esteem to which these people are so vulnerable. In these same studies, the Axis II disturbances to which substance abusers were subject demonstrated sex differences. Male abusers tended to show narcissistic and antisocial disorders, whereas female abusers tended to be borderline personalities. Narcissistic disorders do not appear to be prevalent among the opiate-abusing population, although narcissistic trends are likely in this group during active drug taking and as an element of the antisocial personality disturbances to which they are prone.

Narcissistic disturbances, not narcissistic pathology (defined previously), probably characterize the alcoholic population. Alcoholics appear to suffer from vulnerabilities in self-regard (that is, narcissistic disturbances) that may be best understood and treated from a self-psychology or narcissistic theoretical framework. As a consequence, there will be some concurrence of alcoholism and narcissistic behaviors. This concurrence is, of course, enhanced by the debilitating effects of chronic alcoholism on narcissistic personality structures (Khantzian and Mack 1987).

Antisocial Personality

Irresponsible and antisocial behavior beginning in childhood or early adolescence typifies this disorder. Childhood behaviors often include stealing, truancy, lying, running away, vandalism, and cruelty. As adults, these people disregard social norms and expectations and regularly violate the law. Violence, reckless behavior, promiscuity, and addictions are common in this population. Remorse appears to elude these character disorders. Male sociopaths are at least three times more common than female sociopaths.

Antisocial personality is the Axis II disorder most frequently associated with alcoholism. Schuckit (1973) reported that 20 percent of male alcoholics and 5 percent of female alcoholics in public and private facilities met the criteria for primary antisocial personality with secondary alcoholism. Another study, using an inpatient population, found that 49 percent of men and 20 percent of women alcoholics met DSM III criteria for antisocial personality (Hesselbrock, Meyer, and Keener 1985). This latter group evidenced the personality disturbance prior to the alcoholism in more than 90 percent of cases. These studies illustrate primary antisocial personality with secondary alcoholism. Primary alcoholism with secondary antisocial trends or symptoms was reported by Vaillant (1983b). In these patients, the chronic substance abuse–induced personality disturbances were consistent with the antisocial disorder. In most cases, well-established abstinence presumably would allow for the sociopathy to remit. For sure, alcoholics as a group cannot be considered to be sociopaths. However, sociopaths do show a remarkable tendency to develop alcoholism.

Opiate use is well recognized in this population (O'Brien, Woody, and McLellan 1984). Opiates appear to have antiaggressive properties and can calm excessive states of anger and rage. Perhaps these qualities make opiates the drug of choice among the antisocial population, which is known to suffer from these dysphoric states. Although cocaine abuse was not associated with antisocial personality in populations seen in private mental hospitals, we can suspect that this drug is highly popular among sociopaths at large, as well as among those in public treatment settings and in correctional facilities.

Discussion

Substance abuse is widespread in American society. Among psychiatrically disordered populations, the use and abuse of psychoactive chemicals is alarmingly high, as is the dependence on them. Mental health professionals must face and begin to master the clinical problems and challenges presented by these dual-diagnosis patients.

The importance of identifying concurrent substance disorders in the Axis I and II psychiatric populations is outlined in table 9–6. Comorbid psychiatric and substance abuse disorders affect differential diagnosis (the capacity to differentiate disorders from one another), the course and prognosis of psychiatric illness, the potential efficacy of treatment efforts, the qualifications of the staff needed for treatment, and the staging of treatments provided to the dually diagnosed.

Examples of how active chemical abuse can mimic a variety of psychiatric illnesses appear throughout the previous discussions of Axis I and Axis II disorders. The capacity to make an accurate psychiatric diagnosis is complicated by the presence of substance abuse. Figure 9–1 illustrates how substance abuse creates symptom disorders that can mask psychopathology. This figure also suggests a time frame for the differential diagnosis of comorbid conditions.

When patients are actively abusing drugs, their symptom picture is apt to be that of intoxication or toxicity. These substance-induced organic mental disorders are outlined for alcohol in table 9–3. Alcohol intoxication can occur, and severe intoxication can lead to stupor and even coma. With cocaine intoxication, a range of mental states can occur, from euphoria and hyperactivity to paranoia. As blood levels of the abused drug drop, withdrawal symptoms begin to dominate the clinical presentation. With alcohol, these are minor or major (for instance, delirium tremens) withdrawal syndromes. There are similar problems with benzodiazepines and barbiturates. With co-

Table 9–6
Importance of Identifying Dual-Diagnosis Patients

1. Diagnostic clarity
2. Course
3. Prognosis
4. Therapeutic efficacy
5. Need for professional treatment
6. Treatment staging

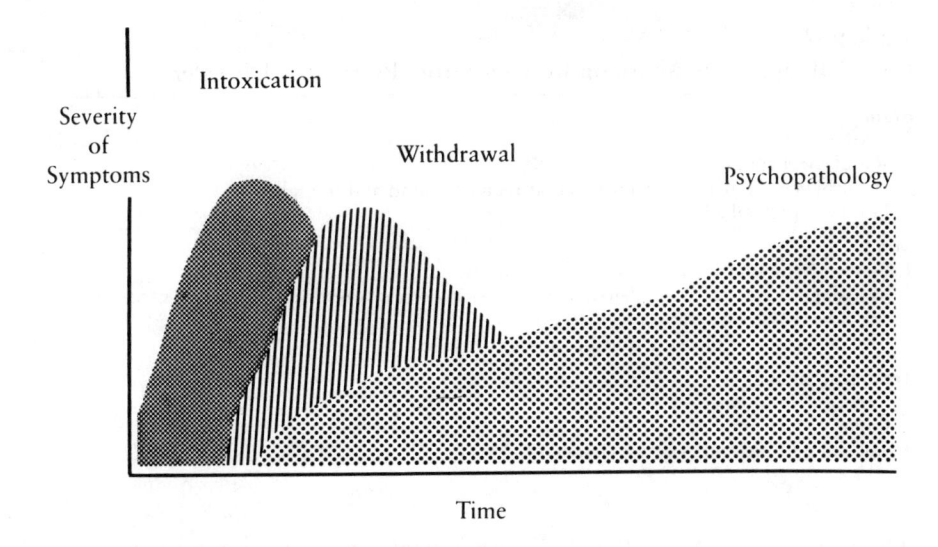

Figure 9–1. Differential diagnosis.

caine, a crash and craving ensue. Acute withdrawal from chemicals of abuse can extend from days to weeks, depending on the agent(s) used. Severe and chronic abuse of potent psychoactive agents such as alcohol and cocaine may produce more subtle withdrawal problems that last for several months. As recovery proceeds, and as toxic and withdrawal states abate, underlying Axis I and II disorders become more evident. This is illustrated in figure 9–1, as psychopathology emerges over time in the abstinent state. Examples of this process include a manic illness that emerges as drug abuse symptomatology wanes and a panic disorder that expresses itself after all depressant drug abuse has ceased.

The course and prognosis of psychiatric disorders, as well as the efficacy of treatments, are influenced greatly by concurrent substance abuse. We saw the highly destabilizing effects of concurrent drug abuse on the schizophrenic population's course and prognosis. A similar phenomenon occurs with bipolar patients. In sober alcoholics, the presence of an inorganic affective illness places them at greater risk for relapse into active drinking (and then prone to a poorer course and prognosis for the affective disorder) if the mood disorder is not treated effectively. Similarly, depression in cocaine and opiate addicts requires active treatment of the mood disorder. Table 9–7 outlines the many ways in which substance abuse can impede recovery from psychiatric illness.

Psychoactive drugs of abuse can adversely influence the psychiatric patient in three principal ways: by influencing the brain, by impairing the mind,

Table 9–7
Effects of Substance Abuse on Recovery from Psychiatric Disorder

Brain
1. Intoxication
2. Withdrawal states
3. Disturbances on neurotransmitters that regulate mood and thought
4. Effects of prescribed medications

Mind
1. Ego weakening: affective flooding, impulsivity
2. Maladaptive ego defenses: denial, externalization, repression
3. Selective recall: how substance felt, not actual behavior evoked
4. Craving: wish for pleasure, idealization of the high

Treatment alliance
1. Capacity for alliance
2. Capacity for compliance
3. Collusion in life-endangering behavior

and by damaging the treatment alliance (see table 9–7). In all these ways, the course of the illness, its prognosis, and the efficacy of treatment are crucially affected.

Substance abuse affects the brain during intoxication and withdrawal by creating secondary substance-induced mental disorders that mask other disorders and that further impair and debilitate the CNS. Furthermore, the principal psychoactive drugs of abuse (alcohol, stimulants, tranquilizers, hypnotics, opiates, marijuana, and hallucinogens) have direct and deleterious effects on neurotransmitters, which are instrumental in the regulation of mood and in the maintenance of normal cognitive processes. These adverse effects occur during states of both intoxication and withdrawal. Finally, the use of nonprescription drugs of abuse can markedly impair the prescribed psychopharmocologic treatment of Axis I and II disorders. Many drugs of abuse enhance liver activity, thereby causing excessive metabolism (and lower serum levels) of potentially beneficial medications. Toxic states (which are sometimes life-threatening) can occur if nonprescription substances are ingested when a patient is receiving drugs such as lithium, tricyclics, and monoamine oxidase inhibitors. The brain is a delicately balanced organ that demands respect if recovery is to occur.

The effects of chemicals on the mind is in no way less marked (see table 9–7). Substance abuse and dependence have at least two major effects on ego functioning. First, the ego is weakened in its control capacities, and second, a regression in ego functioning is fostered. Evidence for ego weakening is seen in the inability of patients to contain or otherwise control powerful feeling states, affects, and drives. The result is the experience of being flooded (or overwhelmed) by feelings, the breakthrough of destructive impulses, or both. Evidence of ego regression is seen in the emergence of more primitive and maladaptive ego defenses. The defenses of denial, externalization, and repression are typical of ego regression in substance abusers. The patient with a weakened and regressed ego cannot effectively engage in self-care and cannot adequately participate in a treatment aimed at ego development and regulation of behavior and mood. Furthermore, a mind that is chronically intoxicated is given to selective recall. Rather than recalling actual behaviors, the substance abuser is apt to recall how he or she felt. Sometimes this can be confused with denial, but it may be a separate and coexisting problem. If recall is selective and reality compromised as a consequence, it becomes impossible to develop a treatment based on the remediation of unacceptable behaviors and the unwanted consequences of drug abuse. Finally, if substance abuse is sustained, the mind is at risk of pursuing one of its favorite activities—the pursuit of pleasure. The wish to be high, the idealization of the high, and the pleasure principle (even if a self-deception) are extremely compelling human mental processes. Craving can eclipse the recovery process and cause the patient's and the clinician's treatment efforts to founder.

Substance abuse also can impede recovery through its impact on the treatment or therapeutic alliance. A treatment alliance is a partnership between patient and clinician in the process of rehabilitation, recovery, or cure. The alliance is based on the patient's capacity to observe and feel the adverse consequences of his or her pathology and the ability, however rudimentary, to have a modicum of trust that the therapist can be of some help to him or her. When engaged in active drug taking, a patient has a severely hindered ability to develop and sustain a therapeutic alliance. The limitations derive from all the adverse effects on the brain and the mind outlined above. As a consequence of the limitations of alliance, there are commensurate limitations in the patient's ability to comply with the treatment plan. Unless someone appreciates why he or she is seeking help, why he or she needs help, and how the clinician can be of help (all realizations that are impossible without an alliance), the person cannot be expected to comply with the treatment plan, regardless of how seemingly well crafted it may be. Finally, for a clinician to condone through silence a patient's continuing abuse of drugs is to collude with the patient in the perpetuation of self-destructiveness. Such collusion also is seen in cases where other self-destructive behaviors are not confronted and an effort is not made to work through them (for example, repetitive slashing and cutting or compulsive binges or starvation). In all these instances, if the clinician fails to address fully the negative effects of the self-destructive behavior, he or she is colluding in a variety of self-induced mutilations and making a mockery of the therapeutic alliance.

The importance of identifying dual-diagnosis patients (table 9–6) extends to decisions about who will best be able to treat the patient. Substance abusers without an Axis I or II diagnosis can do quite well with peer counseling and self-help through Alcoholics Anonymous. However, if a concurrent psychiatric diagnosis exists, these nonprofessional providers will be without the professional tools and technologies (medications, hospital, specific forms of psychotherapy, and so on) that these patients require (O'Brien 1988). The more severe the Axis I and II disorders, the greater is the need for professional training and resources. This point is best illustrated by the acute cocaine-abusing manic or the chronic alcoholic schizophrenic, although its importance in the care of other concurrent disorders should not be underestimated.

Finally, the importance of dual diagnosis is seen in what has been called treatment staging (Abroms 1981). Treatment staging refers to the sequence of interventions—that is, what must be done first, second, and so on. If a patient is not identified as having a concurrent substance abuse and psychiatric disorder, the clinician cannot attend first to detoxification and second to the psychiatric disorder. As another example, treatment of a depression cannot proceed safely or effectively while drug use continues. (Some inpatient units have begun routine blood and urine screening for substances in order to ferret out a dual diagnosis in light of the profound denial of many patients.) Still another example is that of embarking on a long-term, intensive exploratory psychotherapy in a drug-abusing borderline patient. The treatment may be the definitive psychodynamic road to altering underlying character pathology, but it will not serve that aim unless the patient has achieved a considerable amount of sobriety and affective and behavioral stability.

As we have seen, psychiatric disorders and substance abuse disorders are frequently concurrent (Regier et al. 1981; Helzer and Pryzbeck 1988). Not to recognize their coexistence is to be mystified clinically and defeated in our efforts to heal. This patient population can be helped. To do so, providers must bridge the gap between the substance abuse and psychiatric professional communities. The reward will be the experience of seeing our patients improve.

References

Abroms, E.M. 1981. "Psychiatric Serialism." *Comprehensive Psychiatry* 22:372–78.
APA (American Psychiatric Association) Staff. 1987. *Diagnostic and Statistical Manual of Mental Disorders DSM-III-R.* 3rd, rev. ed. Washington, D.C.: American Psychiatric Press.
Bean-Bayog, M. 1988. "Alcoholism as a Cause of Psychopathology." *Hospital and Community Psychiatry* 39:352–54.
Bowen, R.C., D. Cipywnyk, C. D'Arcy, D. Keegan. 1984. "Alcoholism, Anxiety and Agoraphobia." *Alcoholism: Clinical and Experimental Research* 8:48–50.
Dackis, C.A., M.S. Gold, A.L.C. Pottash, D.R. Sweeney. 1986. "Evaluating Depression in Alcoholics." *Psychiatry Research* 17:105–9.
Donovan, J.M. 1986. "An Etiologic Model of Alcoholism." *American Journal of Psychiatry* 143:1–11.

Drake, R.E., F.C. Osher, and M.A. Wallach. 1988. "Substance Abuse among Community Schizophrenics." Paper presented at the annual meeting of American Psychiatric Association, Montreal, May 10.

Dunner, D.L., B.M. Hensel, and R.R. Fieve. 1979. "Bipolar Illness: Factors in Drinking Behavior." *American Journal of Psychiatry* 136:583–85.

Fawcett, J., D.C. Clark, C.A. Agensen, V.D. Pasini. 1987. "A Double Blind, Placebo-Controlled Trial of Lithium Carbonate Therapy for Alcoholism." *Archives of General Psychiatry* 44:248–56.

Gottheil, E., and H.M. Waxman. 1982. "Alcoholism and Schizophrenia." In *Encyclopedic Handbook of Alcoholism*, edited by E. Pattison and E. Kaufman, 636–46. New York: Gardner Press.

Gralnick, A., C.L. Caton, S. Bender, J Gantz. 1988. "Young Adult Chronic Patients." Paper presented at the annual meeting of the American Psychiatric Association, Montreal, May 10.

Helzer, J.E., and T.R. Pryzbeck. 1988. "The Co-occurence of Alcoholism with Other Psychiatric Disorders in the General Population and Its Impact on Treatment." *Journal of Studies on Alcohol* 49:219–24.

Hesselbrock, M.N., R.E. Meyer, and J.J. Keener. 1985. "Psychopathology in Hospitalized Alcoholics." *Archives of General Psychiatry* 42:1050–55.

Khantzian, E.J. 1978. "The Ego, the Self and Opiate Addiction." *International Journal of Psychoanalysis* 5:189–98.

———. 1983. "An Extreme Case of Cocaine Dependence and Marked Improvement with Methylphenidate Treatment." *American Journal of Psychiatry* 140:784–85.

———. 1985. "The Self-Medication Hypothesis of Addictive Disorders." *American Journal of Psychiatry* 142:1259–64.

———. 1986. "Alcoholism: The Challenge of Conceptualization and Consensus." *Journal of Substance Abuse Treatment* 3:251–54.

Khantzian, E.J., and J.E. Mack. 1987. "A.A. and Contemporary Psychodynamic Theory." In *Recent Developments in Alcoholism*, edited by M. Galanter. New York: Plenum Press.

Koenigsberg, H.W., R.D. Kaplan, M.M. Gilmore, et al. 1985. "The Relationship between Syndrome and Personality Disorder in DSM III." *American Journal of Psychiatry* 142:207–12.

Kosten, T.R., B.J. Rounsaville, et al. 1982. "DSM III Personality Disorders in Opiate Addicts." *Comprehensive Psychiatry* 23:572–81.

Merikangas, K.R., J.F. Leckman, B.A. Prusoff, et al. 1985. "Family Transmission of Depression and Alcoholism." *Archives of General Psychiatry* 42:367–72.

Meyer, R.E. 1986. "How to Understand the Relationship between Psychopathology and the Addictive Disorders." In *Psychopathology and Addictive Disease*, edited by R.E. Meyer. New York: Guilford Press.

Milkman, H.B., and W.A. Frosch. 1973. "On the Preferential Use of Heroin and Amphetamine." *Journal of Nervous and Mental Disease* 154:242–48.

Mirin, S.M. 1984. *Substance Abuse and Psychopathology.* Washinton, D.C.: American Psychiatric Press.

———. 1988. "Character Pathology in Substance Abusers." Paper presented at the annual meeting of the American Psychiatric Association, Montreal, May 9.

Morrison, J.R. 1974. "Bipolar Affective Disorder and Alcoholism." *American Journal of Psychiatry* 131:1130–33.

Nace, E.P. 1987. *The Treatment of Alcoholism.* New York: Brunner/Mazel.
Nace, E.P., J.J. Saxon, et al. 1986. "Borderline Personality Disorder and Alcoholism Treatment." *Journal of Studies on Alcoholism* 47:196–200.
O'Brien, C.O. 1988. "Impact of Dual Diagnosis on Treatment." Paper presented at the 141st annual meeting of the American Psychiatric Association, Montreal, May 8.
O'Brien, C.P., G.E. Woody and A.T. McLellan. 1984. "Psychiatric Disorders in Opioid Dependent Patients." *Journal of Clinical Psychiatry* 45:9–13.
Overall, J.E., E.L. Reilly, J.T. Kelley, et al. 1985. "Persistence of Depression in Detoxified Alcoholics." *Alcoholism: Clinical and Experimental Research* 9:331–33.
Regier, D.A., J.K. Myers, M. Kramer, et al. 1981. "The NIMH Epidemiologic Catchment Area Program." *Archives of General Psychiatry* 412:934–41.
Reich, L.H., R.K. Davies, and J.M. Himmelhoch. 1974. "Excessive Alcohol Use in Manic-Depressive Illness." *American Journal of Psychiatry* 131:83–86.
Rounsaville, B.J., M.M. Weissman, J. Crits-Christoph, et al. 1982. "Diagnosis and Symptoms of Depression in Opiate Addicts." *Archives of General Psychiatry* 39:151–56.
Schuckit, M.A. 1973. "Alcoholism and Sociopathy." *Journal of Studies on Alcohol* 34:157–64.
———. 1983. "Alcoholic Patients with Secondary Depression." *American Journal of Psychiatry* 140:711–14.
———. 1986. "Genetic and Clinical Implications of Alcoholism and Affective Disorder." *American Journal of Psychiatry* 143:140–147.
Sederer, L.I. 1985. "Diagnosis, Conceptual Models and the Nature of This Book." In *The Addictions,* edited by H. Milkman and H. Shaffer, Lexington, Mass.: Lexington Books.
———. 1986. "Schizophrenia." In *Inpatient Psychiatry: Diagnosis and Treatment,* 2d ed., edited by L.I. Sederer, 53–80. Baltimore: Williams & Wilkins.
———. 1988. "An Organizing Model for Those Entering the Field of Psychiatry." *Journal of Psychiatric Education* 12(2).
Tartar, R.E., H. McBride, N. Buonpane, et al. 1977. "Differentiation of Alcoholics." *Archives of General Psychiatry* 34:761–68.
Turnquist, K., R. Frances, W. Rosenfeld, et al. 1983. "Pemoline in Attention Deficit Disorder and Alcoholism." *American Journal of Psychiatry* 140:622–24.
Vaglum, S., and P. Vaglum. 1985. "Borderline and Other Mental Disorders in Alcoholic Female Psychiatric Patients." *Psychopathology* 18:50–60.
Vaillant, G.E. 1983a. *The Natural History of Alcoholism.* Cambridge, Mass.: Harvard University Press.
Vaillant, G.E. 1983b. "Natural History of Male Alcoholism: Is Alcoholism the Cart or the Horse to Sociopathy?" *British Journal of Addiction* 78:317–26.
Weiss, R.D., S.M. Mirin, J.L. Michael, et al. 1986. "Psychopathology in Chronic Cocaine Abusers." *American Journal of Drug and Alcohol Abuse* 12:17–29.
Weiss, R.D., J.G. Pope, and S.M. Mirin. 1985. "Treatment of Chronic Cocaine Abuse and ADD, Residual Type, with Magnesium Pemoline." *Drug and Alcohol Dependence* 15:69–72.
Weiss, K.J., and D.J. Rosenberg. 1985. "Prevalence of Anxiety Disorder among Alcoholics." *Journal of Clinical Psychiatry* 46:3–5.

Weissman, M.M., R.E. Meyer, and J.J. Keener. 1980. "Clinical Depression in Alcoholism." *American Journal of Psychiatry* 137:372–73.

Wood, D.R., F.W. Reimher, P.H. Wender, et al. 1976. "Diagnosis and Treatment of Minimal Brain Dysfunction in Adults." *Archives of Genral Psychiatry* 33:1453–60.

Woodruff, R.A., S.B. Guze, P.J. Clayton, et al. 1985. "Alcoholism and Depression." *Archives of General Psychiatry* 28:97–100.

10
Alcohol and Drug Problems in Women: Old Attitudes, New Knowledge

Sheila B. Blume

Persian mythology has given us one of the many legends about women and alcohol. It seems that Jamshid, a mythical emperor circa 2000 B.C., had a passion for grapes. He collected grapes from all over the known world and stored them in a great warehouse, carefully arranging them by region and type. Jamshid found, however, that once in a while some of the grapes would spoil, and a peculiar liquid would collect in the bottom of the vats. He thought it was a poison, and being a frugal emperor, he had this liquid collected and put into crocks labeled "poison." The crocks were put on a shelf in the storehouse, just in case they should be needed.

In Jamshid's court lived a woman whose name we do not know. This woman suffered from what we would today call migraine headaches. After a life of pain, she decided to kill herself. She stole into the emperor's storehouse and drank from the jar marked "poison." To her amazement, however, she did not die. Instead, she fell into a deep sleep and awoke feeling much better.

The legend of the first alcoholic woman continues. Day after day, the woman stole into the warehouse and drank from the jars until they were all empty. It was then that she found herself at that point familiar to so many alcoholic women (and men). She could not go forward, and she could not go backward.

She threw herself on the mercy of the court. After hearing her story, Jamshid decreed that this wonderful liquid should be fermented for all. Hence, in the story of the discovery of alcohol in Persian mythology, the first word for alcohol translates as "a delightful poison" (Youcha 1986).

This is just one of the many legends linking women and alcohol, illustrating an intense social interest, past and present, in this relationship. Unfortunately, most of this interest has been negative.

Nearly every society in which alcohol is used has separate norms for the way men and women are permitted to drink. Sometimes those norms are very different. In the early days of ancient Rome, for example, any drinking of alcoholic beverages by women was prohibited. Records from that society confirm that some women were put to death for drinking wine. According to

McKinlay (1959), the Law of Romulus included the death penalty for women's drinking in the same sentence as the penalty for adultery by women. The Romans explained that the reason women were prohibited from drinking was that alcohol predisposed women to debauchery. This pattern of thinking has persisted into contemporary society, as will be discussed below.

In 1798, the German philosopher Immanuel Kant wrote about women and alcohol. He speculated on a possible explanation for the lower incidence of alcoholism among both women and Jews than among Christian males. He attributed this difference to a "higher standard of conduct" to which women and Jews adhered, at least in theory. Because these two groups owed their special place in society to this higher standard of conduct, they could not risk the scandal of intoxication (Jellinek 1941).

The negative interest in the relationship between women and alcohol continues today. Alcoholic and drug-dependent women are, at present, subject to a triple stigma. First, they are victims of the same stigma attached to all alcoholics. Pollsters have found that although the vast majority of Americans will agree with the statement "alcoholism is a disease," these same people also believe that alcoholics are weak willed and immoral. The acceptance of the disease concept of alcoholism remains only skin-deep in American society.

Second, women's place in society, for whatever reasons, is often on a pedestal. Consequently, when women fall, they fall much farther than do men. Conduct that is acceptable for men, as Kant pointed out, may be considered scandalous for women. Consider the expression "drunk as a lord." Now consider its female counterpart, "drunk as a lady."

Third, and most injurious, is the pernicious sexual stigma attached to women who drink or use drugs. In American society, these women are automatically considered promiscuous and fair game for sexual aggression. The 1983 New Bedford, Massachusetts, case in which an intoxicated twenty-two-year-old woman who was gang-raped on a pool table in a bar vividly illustrates society's perception. Many blamed the victim for her rape. During the trial of her attackers, demonstrators outside the courthouse carried signs protesting that she got what she deserved. The victim, an alcoholic woman, died three years later, in 1986, as a result of her disease (Rovner 1988). The Neil Simon film *Only When I Laugh* contains a similar stereotype of the female alcoholic. It includes a scene in which the heroine, an alcoholic woman who has relapsed, is followed and beaten in an attempted rape by a man who had sat next to her in a bar. Later on, when asked what happened, she expresses the thought "You get what you ask for." With such blatant stigmatization of alcoholic women, it is understandable that female alcoholics find it particularly difficult to accept the nature of their problems and to reach out for help. Furthermore, it is not surprising that many alcoholic women who do manage to enter treatment have histories of being the victims of rape and other abuse.

Clinical experience with women in treatment for other drug dependence has been similar.

The intense social stigma thus acts as a major barrier to the identification and treatment of women who desperately need help. Since the alcoholic woman grows up in the same society as the rest of the population, she applies these stereotypes to herself and keeps her problem hidden because of guilt and shame. She tends to drink alone, often in her kitchen or bedroom. The nature and extent of her drinking or other drug use is often not appreciated by her family and friends until she has reached an advanced state of her disease. In addiction, although she may seek medical help repeatedly because of her failing health, nervousness, and insomnia, the stereotype of the alcohol- or drug-addicted female as the "fallen woman" makes health professionals unlikely to suspect these diagnoses in their well-dressed, socially competent female patients. The chemically dependent woman seldom recognizes the basic nature of her own problem, since, viewed from within, these substances are her attempt at solving the many other problems she perceives as her "real trouble." She thus brings many complaints to her medical visit, but seldom do these complaints include her dependence on alcohol or other drugs. More often than not, she leaves the doctor's office with a prescription for additional sedative drugs rather than a referral for addiction treatment.

William George and his colleagues have studied the attitudes of college students toward men and women who drink, using videotapes and written descriptions of young adult dating scenes (George, Skinner, and Marlatt 1986; George, Gournic, and McAfee 1988). Videotapes or written scenarios of nearly identical scenes, which varied only in small details, were presented to the students. Both male and female students rated the woman in the dating scene more sexually available and more likely to have intercourse if the scene showed her ordering an alcoholic beverage rather than a soft drink. Furthermore, they rated her even more likely to be sexually available if the male paid for the drinks than if they split the cost.

The Drinking or Drug-Taking Woman as Victim

Research by Klassen and Wilsnack (1986) indicates that women who drink are not made promiscuous by alcohol. In an extensive survey of more than one thousand women who used alcohol to some extent, only 8 percent said they had become less particular in their choice of sexual partner when they had been drinking. However, 60 percent of the women surveyed said that someone else who was drinking had become sexually aggressive toward them. This percentage was constant for light drinkers, moderate drinkers, and heavy drinkers. Thus, society appears to sanction aggression, including sexual aggression, toward women who drink. This concept is further supported by the work of Fillmore (1985) in her studies of social victimization caused by another person's drinking. She found that women who drink in bars (that is, those who are exposed to others while drinking) were far more likely to be victimized, even if they were not themselves heavy or problem drinkers. Problem drinkers or those who often drank heavily were most victimized among both men and women.

Miller and her colleagues have studied the experiences of women as victims, both in childhood and adulthood (Miller and Downs 1986; Miller et al. 1987; Miller, Downs, and Gondoli 1987). Their studies compared forty-five alcoholic women recruited from Alcoholics Anonymous and a treatment program with forty matched controls from a community sample. Sixty-seven percent of the alcoholic women reported that they had been the victims of sexual abuse by an older person during childhood. Only 28 percent of the matched control group reported this, a significant difference. The alcoholic women were not only more likely to have one such experience, but also reported more frequent experiences over longer periods of time, especially if they were daughters of alcoholic parents. In these families, the father was not usually the aggressor. Rather, there was a lack of protection for the child who was abused by others (Miller et al. 1987). In adulthood, 38 percent of the alcoholic women reported that they had been victims of violent crime, as opposed to only 18 percent of the controls. Sixteen percent of the alcoholic women had been raped, as opposed to none of the controls (Miller and Downs 1986). These women were victimized not only by outsiders, but also by their own spouses. The alcoholic women had significantly more experience with spousal violence at every level, from verbal abuse (insults and swearing) to serious assaults with fists or weapons (Miller, Downs, and Gondoli, 1987).

Implications for Prevention

Although the entrenchment of this stigma in society today derives from persistent cultural stereotypes and the differences between cultural expectations for men and women, cultural sex differences also may have positive protective effects. The fact that there are twice as many male as female alcoholics is not simply a matter of heredity but is largely due to extrafamilial environmental factors (Cloninger et al. 1978). In nearly every society, women are expected to drink less than men, and this difference may serve to protect women. Women are generally lighter in weight than men. Even in a man and woman of equal weight, the same amount of alcohol will create higher blood alcohol levels in the woman, due to her lower body water content. Therefore, a woman who matches drink for drink with a man will be far more impaired.

Any society that expects such behavior as the norm will be likely to have more alcohol problems in women than in men.

The custom of men drinking in all-male groups or in mixed-sex groups and women drinking chiefly in mixed groups is another sociocultural factor that protects women. Unfortunately, these norms are changing in contemporary American society. The advertising and marketing of alcoholic beverages, a $2-billion-a-year effort that inundates society daily, sends messages that can change cultural norms. Advertisers of these beverages see women as a growth market. Because market research indicates that women make a significant proportion of the purchases of beverage alcohol, women are being increasingly targeted by alcoholic beverage advertising (Jacobson, Hacker, and Atkins 1983). Beverage manufacturers and retailers who used to cater to a male market with advertisements emphasizing the masculinity of drinking are now portraying the genteel refinement of women drinking and are increasingly showing them drinking with other women. In a further attempt to change the cultural norms, advertisers are trying to identify more times and places in which it can become appropriate to use alcohol. Thus, cultural norms that have served to protect women may be vanishing.

To counteract this movement, a multimodal prevention program called Woman to Woman has been established by the Association of Junior Leagues (660 First Avenue, New York, NY 10016) in major cities across the United States. Its purpose is to educate women about alcohol through community and campus activities, radio and television messages, and other initiatives. Woman to Woman and other prevention programs may be able to help maintain or reinstate some protection for women through education. However, the immense resources of the alcoholic beverage advertising budget can hardly be matched by any current prevention program.

Barriers to Chemical Dependence Treatment

Case Finding

Current surveys show that women are underrepresented in chemical dependence treatment. Data from the National Institute on Alcohol Abuse and Alcoholism (NIAAA) indicate that the ratio of male to female problem drinkers is 4 to 1 in treatment, while it is approximately 2 to 1 in the community (USDHHS 1987). Thus, women are appropriately called the hidden alcoholics. Research supports the theory that women are more likely to drink alone and that their problems are more likely to be denied by their families than is the case with their male counterparts. This too is not astonishing, given the long history of stigma attached to women who drink.

These are not the only reasons for the underrepresentation of women in treatment. One clue to this lies in their expressed motivation for seeking help and the systems for early intervention. Studies indicate that when treatment populations are asked "How did you get here?" men's most frequent responses are "problems on the job" and "problems with the law." Women's responses are more likely to be "problems with health" or "problems with family" (see, for example, Sclare 1970).

The most common systematic case-finding methods in use today, including EAPs, public inebriate programs, and especially drinking driver programs, are strongly male oriented. A common male-to-female ratio in programs for persons convicted of drinking while intoxicated or for public inebriates is 9 to 1. Since these programs are major case finders, it is not surprising that women are underrepresented in treatment. EAPs have historically found it easier to identify alcohol and drug problems in men than in women (Trice and Beyer 1979). It is possible to improve this situation, however, and increased attention has recently been paid to devising more effective strategies to reach female employees (Cahill, Volicer, and Neuberger 1982; Trice and Beyer 1979).

Sensitivity to women's responses regarding their reasons for seeking alcohol treatment also can lead to the development of new and improved case-finding systems for women. Both alcoholic and drug-dependent women may be reached through systematic screening in doctors' offices, hospitals, and medical clinics.

Two recent studies provide excellent examples of such case finding. Halliday and her colleagues (1986) studied two private gynecological practices, one in Boston and one in a Boston suburb. They used the simple four-question CAGE test as an initial screening tool, followed by an interview employing the alcohol section of the Diagnostic Interview Schedule (DIS). They found that of 147 women visiting these offices for routine care, 12 percent satisfied the DSM III diagnosis for alcohol abuse or dependence—more than twice the community rate. Of ninety-five women who had come for treatment of premenstrual syndrome (PMS), 21 percent satisfied the diagnosis of alcohol abuse or dependence.

Subsequently, Cyr and Wartman (1988) studied men and women coming to an ambulatory medical primary care unit in an urban teaching hospital for their first visit. This study used the Michigan Alcohol Screening Test (MAST), a twenty-five item questionnaire that focuses on drinking problems. Of the 147 women in the study, with an average age of thirty-seven, 17 percent were alcoholic. Twenty-six percent of the eighty-five male patients screened were in the alcoholic range, a male-to-female ratio of 1.5 to 1. This ratio demonstrates the value of medical facilities as fertile ground for the identification of alcoholic women.

Women's special problems with alcohol (including effects on pregnancy and the rapid progression of the late-stage physical complications of alcoholism in women), coupled with women's strong representation in medical facilities, reinforce the need for effective systematic screening, diagnosis, and referral of women with alcohol and drug problems in the health care system (Blume 1986a). Such case-finding systems will not only prevent fetal alcohol syndrome and other fetal alcohol effects, but they also have the potential to relieve much individual and family suffering.

There are a number of effective screening tools for alcoholism, both written and oral. The CAGE and MAST tests are good examples of screening tools. Another screening instrument has been designed specifically for women. Dr. Marcia Russell at the New York State Research Institute on Alcoholism developed the questionnaire as part of a statewide fetal alcohol syndrome prevention campaign. This questionnaire appears in Blume (1981) and was later adapted to include other drugs of abuse (Blume 1988). This later questionnaire appears here as a chapter appendix.

Laboratory testing also can be helpful in screening. Hollstedt and Dahlgren (1987) analyzed the records of one hundred women undergoing their first episode of alcoholism treatment in the city of Stockholm. They found that increased mean corpuscular volume of the red blood cells (MCV) was present in 48 percent of these women and an increase in the enzyme gamma-glutamyl transferase (GGT) in 42 percent of them. If *either* an elevated MCV *or* an elevated GGT were considered the screening criterion, 67 percent of the alcoholic women would be correctly identified. This rose to 75 percent if abnormal values for serum aspartate aminotransferase (serum albumin) and an abnormal thrombocyte count were added to the screening criteria.

Less research work has been done to investigate methods to identify alcoholic and addicted women in family service agencies, but these are other appropriate sites for systematic case finding. MAST, CAGE, and the screening test for women would all be appropriate to use in a family service setting. Because family problems, separation, and divorce are so common among women with alcohol and drug problems, lawyers specializing in divorce, custody, and family law also would make excellent case finders.

Other Barriers

Case finding is but one aspect of access to treatment. Unfortunately, women in need of treatment for chemical dependence are often faced with additional barriers. In a multi-city survey of services for alcoholic women conducted by the Woman to Woman program, the most frequently mentioned institutional barrier to treatment was the lack of child care services for women needing residential care. A few model programs in several states have developed such services, but the need is largely unmet. In addition, many women in need of chemical dependence treatment are divorced or separated and unemployed, leaving them without health insurance coverage.

A further deterrent to treatment may be found in legal definitions of child abuse and neglect. In many states, the habitual or addictive use of alcohol or drugs by a parent makes that parent a child abuser or neglector by definition. This definition becomes a barrier to care, particularly for disadvantaged and single mothers who must rely on public social service agencies for child care in order to enter treatment. Asking for help in such a situation puts them in jeopardy of losing custody of their children. Paradoxically, continuing their chemical dependence without seeking help does not, in general, have this effect. Child abuse laws can be altered not only to remove this barrier but also to provide an inducement for the alcoholic or addicted parent to accept treatment (Blume 1986b). New York revised its definitions so that an addicted parent who is participating in a program of recovery is not presumed to be guilty of abuse or neglect without additional evidence.

Special Problems of Chemically Dependent Women

Dual Diagnosis

Once the alcoholic woman is identified and reaches treatment, a careful clinical assessment is extremely important. One major difference between the clinical presentation of alcoholism in women as compared to men is related to the presence of additional psychiatric diagnoses. Alcoholism may be classified as primary when it develops in an individual with no preexisting psychiatric illness and secondary when another diagnosable illness is present before the alcohol abuse develops (Schuckit et al. 1969). In a typical treatment population, primary alcoholism prevails. However, when alcoholism is secondary, there is a difference between men's and women's primary diagnoses. In men with secondary alcoholism, the most common primary diagnosis is antisocial personality disorder. Women's most prevalent primary diagnosis is major depression.

Helzer and Pryzbeck (1988) have added significantly to our knowledge in this area. Analyzing data from the Epidemiological Catchment Area study of the prevalence of forty-four "core" psychiatric diagnoses in nearly twenty thousand American adults in a general community sample, they found that nearly 13 percent satisfied a lifetime DSM III diagnosis of alcohol abuse or dependence. Of those that satisfied an alcoholism diagnosis, 47 percent also met criteria for a second core psychiatric diagnosis. In contrast, only 32 percent of those who had any core diagnosis had a second psychiatric diagnosis. Thus, alcoholics in the general population were significantly more likely to have a dual diagnosis than persons with other psychiatric disorders.

Their work also revealed significant differences between the types of additional diagnoses found in alcoholic men and women. First, women were more likely than men to have a dual diagnosis. Sixty-five percent of female alcoholics, compared with 44 percent of males, had a second diagnosis. Antisocial personality disorder, present in 15 percent of the alcoholic men and 10 percent of the women, was the only second diagnosis more common in males than in females. A second diagnosis of drug abuse or dependence was found in 31 percent of the women, compared with 19 percent of the men. Major depression was nearly four times as frequent in the women (19 percent) than in the men (5 percent). Phobic disorder was diagnosed in 31 percent of the alcoholic women, compared with 13 percent of the men, and panic disorder was found in 7 percent of the women and only 2 percent of the men. Even a diagnosis such as mania, which was rare, occurred in 4 percent of the alcoholic women but in only 1 percent of the alcoholic men. Some of the sex differences found may relate to the unusually high male-to-female ratio for alcohol abuse and dependence in the Epidemiological Catchment Area study (greater than 5 to 1). This contrasts with previous studies using a variety of survey criteria. It may be that the women who satisfied the DSM III diagnoses in this study were more severely affected than those in other studies. This might be related to the structure of the screening instrument used (the DIS).

The Helzer and Pryzbeck study further clarifies the prevalence of dual diagnosis in female alcoholics by comparing the prevalence of the most frequent core diagnoses in alcoholic women with their prevalence among women in the total population. For example, 5 percent of the general population of women studied satisfied a diagnosis of substance abuse or dependence, compared with 31 percent of the diagnosed alcoholic women. Major depression was diagnosed in 7 percent of the women in the general community sample, but the rate nearly tripled in alcoholic women (19 percent). Similarly, the incidence of phobias in women with alcoholism was 31 percent, almost double the community rate (16 percent). Most telling was the finding that antisocial personality, which existed in only a fraction of a percentage of the women in the community (0.81 percent), was diagnosed in 10 percent of the women alcoholics studied. Thus, the rate was more than twelve times higher in alcoholic women.

In addition, Helzer and Pryzbeck analyzed their data to separate primary from secondary alcoholism in those cases in which alcoholism and major depression were the only diagnoses present. They found that in 78 percent of such men, the alcoholism was primary and the depression secondary (that is, developed after the alcoholism). In contrast, the alcoholism was primary in only 34 percent of the women. Two-thirds of the women had suffered from depression before developing alcoholism.

Treatment populations may be expected to have even higher rates of dual diagnoses than would be found in the general public. Helzer and Pryzbeck reported that the number of additional diagnoses other than substance abuse present along with the diagnosis of alcoholism was a very strong determinant of whether or not the individual sought treatment, regardless of the severity of the alcoholism itself. In their study, alcoholic women were more likely to have had some type of mental health treatment than were alcoholic men, although the nature and appropriateness of the treatment could not be judged by the data. However, the overall findings confirm the common-sense expectation that more complicated dual-diagnosis cases are more likely to reach clinical attention.

In a clinical sample of ninety women alcoholics, Hesselbrock, Meyer, and Keener (1985) found, that 80 percent satisfied one or more additional lifetime psychiatric diagnoses. Another substance abuse was diagnosed in 38 percent of the sample, and 52 percent of the women were diagnosed as having major depression. Phobia was diagnosed in 44 percent, panic disorder in 14 percent, and obsessive-compulsive disorder in 13 percent. Twenty percent of the clinical sample of women satisfied diagnostic criteria for antisocial personality disorder. All other diagnoses were present in less than 10 percent of the women. This profile differed significantly from the patterns shown by the 261 male alcoholics in the study. Among the males, 75 percent had one or more additional diagnoses. This figure was not significantly different from the figure for the female alcoholics. Forty-five percent of the men had substance abuse, 32 percent had major depression, 20 percent had phobia, 8 percent had panic disorder, and 12 percent had obsessive-compulsive disorder. As in the community sample, antisocial personality was the only additional diagnosis in which males greatly outnumbered females. Forty-nine percent of the alcoholic men met these diagnostic criteria, compared with 20 percent of the alcoholic women.

Of particular interest is the fact that both Helzer and Pryzbeck (1988) and Hesselbrock, Meyer, and Keener (1985) identified major depression as the most common primary diagnosis in women with secondary alcoholism. Both studies indicate that depression was primary in approximately two-thirds of the alcoholic women with depression. Depression was found to be primary in 41 percent of the alcoholic men in the treatment sample, compared with 22 percent in the general population sample.

Thus, effective treatment planning must rest on a careful and comprehensive assessment of the multiple problems common to chemically dependent women. Current psychiatric problems must be evaluated, but it is also important that any additional psychiatric illnesses be placed chronologically in the patient's life history in relationship to the development of alcoholism. Primary depression, for example, would be more likely to recur during a period of sobriety than would depression that developed secondary to the patient's alcoholism. Long-term treatment planning should take such factors into account.

Assessment Failures

Referring to patients who relapse as "failures" is unacceptable. More often it is the initial assessment and resulting treatment plan rather than the patient that have failed. Primary or secondary psychiatric diagnoses are often overlooked and untreated. Unrecognized sexual abuse, particularly incest, is another common assessment failure in alcoholic women. Since incest and other equally sensitive aspects of a woman's personal history may not be adequately covered in a routine interview or social history, it is imperative that the time be taken to ask gently about these experiences. History taking concerning these issues should continue throughout treatment. Treatment planning should be adjusted when a history of abuse is discovered to include individual counseling with a therapist trained in this area and in some cases a "survivors" group for patients with this experience.

Codependence Issues

Another important clinical issue receiving increasing attention is broadly described as codependence. Much time and energy has been wasted in arguing over the value and timing of addressing codependence issues in those alcoholic and/or drug-dependent patients who are also codependents—that is, who have grown up with, or currently live with, a chemically dependent person. Perhaps the best definition and formulation of current thinking on codependence are found in Cermak (1986).

Many chemically dependent women may be characterized as codependents in that they are daughters and/or spouses of alcoholics or drug addicts. How and when to encompass these facts of life in a patient's treatment plan depends on the individual case and must be dictated by a good assessment and common sense. For example, if admitting her own alcoholism is unusually traumatic for a patient who hates and does not want to forgive her alcoholic mother, these feelings must be explored initially rather than left for later on, since they are likely to interfere with initial recovery. Likewise, a patient who is living with an active alcoholic or addict can hardly afford postponing attention to the influence of this relationship on her life. There are, however, a number of long-term influences—for example on a person's capacity for intimacy or on a perceived needs to control interpersonal situations—that may result from living in a family system affected by chemical dependence. Such problems may correct themselves to some degree as abstinence is established, especially if the patient has become actively engaged in a twelve-step program. Those problems that persist may be more appropriately addressed later in treatment. Referrals to Alanon, Naranon, or Cocanon (or, for that matter, Gamanon or Oanon)—all self-help programs for families of addicted people—can be made when the need arises. In my experience, however, such referrals are more effective if held until the patient has become engaged with and adjusted to her own primary abstinence self-help group.

Treatment Outcomes

It is important to remember that treatment for chemical dependence is a necessary but not sufficient condition to produce recovery in those abusers who suffer from a multitude of other problems. Alcoholism treatment alone cannot be expected to succeed when needs for health care, housing, employment, job training, and social supports are unmet. However, treatment outcomes for those patients with established support systems in the community are very hopeful.

The Chemical Abuse Addiction Treatment Outcome Registry (CATOR) studies (Harrison and Hoffman 1987; Hoffman and Harrison 1986) tracked both adults and adolescents after inpatient rehabilitative treatment in a number of different facilities. For adolescents, girls had a slightly better recovery rate than boys. Seventy-four percent of the girls, compared with 66 percent of the boys, completed inpatient treatment. Only 5 percent of the girls (versus 13 percent of the boys) were discharged due to behavior problems. Fifty percent of the 313 girls reinterviewed a year after treatment had remained abstinent, compared with 40 percent of the 602 boys. Because of differences between former patients contacted for follow-up and those who could not be located, the overall recovery rate was not known. However, only one-third of the former patients contacted reported prolonged or multiple relapses.

Adult males and females from relatively stable socioeconomic environments had equally high recovery rates. Approximately 53 percent of 1,957 adult patients (55 percent married and 76 percent employed, homemakers, or students) were followed for two years after discharge. Of those interviewed, only 28 percent had relapsed to multiple or extended periods of substance use. Correcting for the influence of patients who were not contacted, the authors felt it was safe to conclude that about half of the men and women treated at the inpatient chemical dependence units studied maintained total abstinence for at least two years.

Rounsaville et al. (1982) found that among opiate addicts, women had a higher treatment retention rate than men. In another follow-up study, Rounsaville et al. (1987) tracked alcoholic men and women for one year after treatment. They found that those with the dual diagnosis of antisocial personality and alcoholism, whether men or women, had poor outcomes. Women with the dual diagnosis of alcoholism and major depression did slightly better than average.

Unfortunately, there has been little research on the effectiveness of treatment programs or modalities designed specifically for chemically dependent women. Most studies of treatment effectiveness, if they include female subjects at all, look at men and women together in the same treatment programs. Whatever differences may exist in the services received by male and female subjects are not described. Vannicelli (1986), reviewing ninety-five treatment outcome studies that included women, concluded that there was too little scientific evidence to support the superiority of any particular type of therapy for alcoholic women. I see little progress in the time since Vannicelli's review.

Mortality rates are high for alcoholic women who do not achieve recovery. Smith, Cloninger, and Bradford (1983) followed 103 women treated for alcoholism at two hospitals in St. Louis. Eleven years after discharge, 31 percent of the women were dead at an average age of 51.5 years. Their mortality rate was 4.5 times the age-corrected general population rate, and they lost an average of 15 years from their expected life span. Those who attained abstinence, however, did not experience a higher mortality rate than the general population.

A recent report from Sweden confirms these findings. Lindberg and Agren (1988) followed nearly four thousand male and nearly one thousand female patients following hospital treatment for alcoholism over a period ranging from two to twenty-two years. The excess mortality rate was higher for the alcoholic women (5.2 times the expected rate) than for the men (3 times the expected rate). Causes of death in excess of the expected rate for women were alcoholism, intoxication, cirrhosis, breast cancer, and a variety of types of violence. For males, the excess rate was attributed to alcoholism, cirrhosis, pancreatitis, tuberculosis, pneumonia, intoxication, suicide, violence, heart disease, and cancer of the upper digestive tract, liver, and lung. The excess mortality rate was highest in the first year following treatment but continued to be elevated throughout the follow-up period. Since the data were obtained from official death records, the alcoholism recovery status of the former patients was not known. It can be inferred from the causes of excess mortality, however, that these deaths occurred predominantly in those who continued to drink.

Summary

New knowledge about alcohol and drug problems in women provides both bad news and good news. Affected women are still subject to the intense stigma fostered by old attitudes. They are often victims of aggression and abuse. They are underrepresented in treatment and face special barriers limiting their access to care, but they do well if they can be reached and receive appropriate services in spite of their high incidence of dual diagnosis. The good news is that we have an opportunity to improve prevention, outreach, assessment, and treatment based on current research. The federal Omnibus Drug Bill of 1988, recognizing the special problems of women, mandated that 10 percent of federal funding granted to the states for alcoholism and drug abuse prevention and treatment be devoted to new and expanded programs for women. This funding will provide an opportunity to develop new case-finding, prevention, and treatment services for chemically dependent women. The responsibility rests with clinicians. The stakes are high for the present generation as well as for generations to come.

References

Blume, S.B. 1981. "Drinking and Pregnancy." *New York State Journal of Medicine* 81:95–98.

———. 1986. "Women and Alcohol: A Review." *Journal of the American Medical Association* 256:1467–70.

———. 1986b. Women and Alcohol: Public Policy Issues. In *Women and Alcohol: Health-Related Issues*, NIAAA Research Monograph, no. 16. DHHS pub. no. (ADM) 86-1139. Washington, D.C.: GPO.

———. 1988. *Alcohol/Drug Dependent Women: New Insights into Their Special Problems, Treatment, Recovery*. Minneapolis: Johnson Institute.

Cahill, M.H., B.J. Volicer, and E. Neuburger. 1982. "Female Referral to Employee Assistance Programs: The Impact of Specialized Intervention." *Drug and Alcohol Dependence* 10:223–33.

Cermak, T.L. 1986. *Diagnosing and Treating Codependence*. Minneapolis: Johnson Institute.

Cloninger, R.C., K.O. Christiansen, T. Reich, and I.I. Gottesman. 1978. "Implications of Sex Differences in the Prevalence of Antisocial Personality, Alcoholism, and Criminality for Familial Transmission." *Archives of General Psychiatry* 35:941–51.

Cyr, M.G., and S.A. Wartman. 1988. "The Effectiveness of Routine Screening Questions in the Detection of Alcoholism." *Journal of the American Medical Association* 259:51–54.

Fillmore, K.M. 1985. "The Social Victims of Drinking." *British Journal of Addiction* 80:307–14.

George, W.H., S.J. Gournic, and M.P. McAfee. 1988. "Perceptions of Postdrinking Female Sexuality: Effects of Gender, Beverage Choice and Drink Payment." *Journal of Applied Social Psychology* 18:1295–1317.

George, W.H., J.B. Skinner, and G.A. Marlatt. 1986. "Male Perceptions of the Drinking Woman: Is Liquor Quicker?" Paper presented at the meeting of the Eastern Psychological Association, New York, April.

Halliday, A., B. Bush, P. Cleary, M. Aronson, and T. Delbanco. 1986. "Alcohol Abuse in Women Seeking Gynecologic Care." *Obstetrics and Gynecology* 68:322–26.

Harrison, P.A., and N.G. Hoffman. 1987. "CATOR Adolescent Residential Treatment, Intake and Follow-up Findings: 1987 Report." Ramsey Clinic, St. Paul.

Helzer, J.F., and T.R. Pryzbeck. 1988. "The Co-Occurrence of Alcoholism with Other Psychiatric Disorders in the General Population and Its Impact on Treatment." *Journal of Studies on Alcohol* 49:219–24.

Hesselbrock, M.N., R.E. Meyer, And J.J. Keener. 1985. "Psychopathology in Hospitalized Alcoholics." *Archives of General Psychiatry* 42:1050–55.

Hoffman, N.G., and P.A. Harrison. 1986. "CATOR 1986 Report: Findings Two Years After Treatment." Ramsey Clinic, St. Paul.

Hollstedt, C., and L. Dahlgren. 1987. "Peripheral Markers in the Female 'Hidden Alcoholic.'" *Acta Psychiatrica Scandinavica* 75:591–96.

Jacobson, M., G. Hacker, and R. Atkins. 1983. *The Booze Merchants*. Washington D.C.: CPSI Books.

Jellinek, E.M. 1941. "Immanuel Kant on Drinking." *Journal of Studies on Alcohol* 1:777–78.

Klassen, A.D., and S.C. Wilsnack. 1986. "Sexual Experiences and Drinking among Women in a U.S. National Survey." *Archives of Sexual Behavior* 15:363–92.

Lindberg, S., and G. Agren. 1988. "Mortality among Male and Female Hospitalized Alcoholics in Stockholm 1962–1983." *British Journal of Addiction* 83:1193–1200.

McKinlay, A.P. 1959. "The Roman Attitude toward Women's Drinking." In *Drinking and Intoxication*, edited by R.G. McCarthy, New Haven, Conn.: College and University Press: New Brunswick, NJ.: Rutgers Center of Alcohol Studies.

Miller, B.A., and W.R. Downs. 1986. "Conflict and Violence among Alcoholic Women as Compared to a Random Household Sample." Paper presented at the 38th Annual Meeting of the American Society of Criminology, Atlanta.

Miller, B.A., W.R. Downs, and D.M. Gondoli. (*in press*) "Spousal Violence among Alcoholic Women as Compared to a Random Household Sample of Women." *Journal of Studies on Alcohol*.

Miller, B.A., W.R. Downs, D.M. Gondoli, and A. Keil. 1987. "The Role of Childhood Sexual Abuse in the Development of Alcoholism in Women." *Violence and Victims* 2:157–72.

Rounsaville, B.J., Z.S. Dolinsky, T.F. Babor, and R.E. Meyer. 1987. "Psychopathology as a Predictor of Treatment Outcome in Alcoholics." *Archives of General Psychiatry* 44:505–13.

Rounsaville, B.J., T. Tierney, K. Crits-Christoph, M.M. Weissman, and H.D. Klelur. 1982. "Predictors of Outcome in Treatment of Opiate Addicts." *Comprehensive Psychiatry* 23:462–78.

Rovner, S. 1988. "Women, Alcohol and Sex: Troubled Trio." *Washington Post*, November 1.

Schuckit, M., F.N. Pitts, T. Reich, L.J. King, and G. Winokur. 1969. "Alcoholism. Part I: Two Types of Alcoholism in Women. Archives of General Psychiatry 20:301–6.

Sclare, A.B. 1970. "The Female Alcoholic." *British Journal of Addiction* 65:99–107.

Smith, E.M., C.R. Cloninger, and S. Bradford. 1983. "Predictors of Mortality in Alcoholic Women: A Prospective Follow-up Study." *Alcoholism: Clinical and Experimental Research* 7:237–43.

Trice, H.M., and J.M. Beyer. 1979. "Women Employees and Job-Based Alcoholism Programs." *Journal of Drug Issues* 9:371–85.

USDHHS (U.S. Department of Human Services). 1987. *Sixth Special Report to the U.S. Congress on Alcohol and Health*. DHHS pub. no. ADM 87-1519. Washington, D.C.: GPO.

Vannicelli, M. 1986. "Treatment Considerations." In *Women and Alcohol: Health-Related Issues*, NIAAA Research Monograph Series no. 16. Washington, D.C.: USGPO.

Youcha, G. 1986. *Women and Alcohol: A Dangerous Pleasure*. New York: Crown Publishers.

Appendix 10–A: DIS Questionnaire

Please check answers below.

1. When you are depressed or nervous, do you find any of the following helpful to feel better or to relax?

	Very Helpful	Not Helpful	Never Tried
a. Smoking cigarettes	____	____	____
b. Working harder than usual at home or job	____	____	____
c. Taking a tranquilizer	____	____	____
d. Taking some other kind of pill or medication	____	____	____
e. Having a drink	____	____	____
f. Talking it over with friends of relatives	____	____	____

2. Think of the times you have been most depressed; at those times did you:

	Yes	No
a. Lose or gain weight	____	____
b. Lose interest in things that usually interest you	____	____
c. Have spells when you couldn't seem to stop crying	____	____
d. Suffer from insomnia	____	____

3. Have you ever gone to a doctor, psychologist, social worker, counselor, or clergyman for help with an emotional problem? ____ ____

4. How many cigarettes a day do you smoke? Check one.

   _____More than 2 packs   _____ 1–2 packs

   _____Less than 1 pack   _____ None

5. How often do you have a drink of wine, beer, or a beverage containing alcohol?

   _____3 or more times a day   _____Once or twice a week

   _____Twice a day   _____Once or twice a month

   _____Almost every day   _____Less than once a month   _____Never

6. a. If you drink wine, beer, or beverages containing alcohol, how often do you have four or more drinks?

   _____Almost always   _____ Frequently   _____ Sometimes   _____ Never

   b. If you drink wine, beer, or beverages containing alcohol, how often do you have one or two?

   _____Almost always   _____ Frequently   _____ Sometimes   _____ Never

7. What prescribed medications do you take? _____
   _____

8. What other drugs or medications do you use? _____
   _____

	Yes	No
9. Does your drinking or taking other drugs sometimes lead to problems between you and your family, that is, wife, husband, children, parent, or close relative?	_____	_____
10. During the past year, have close relatives or friends worried or complained about your drinking or taking other drugs?	_____	_____
11. Has a friend or family member ever told you about things you said or did while you were drinking or using other drugs that you do not remember?	_____	_____
12. Have you, within the past year, started to drink alcohol and found it difficult to stop before becoming intoxicated?	_____	_____
13. Has your father or mother ever had problems with alcohol or other drugs?	_____	_____

9/88

11
Elements of Recovery: A Longitudinal Analysis

George E. Vaillant

Most of the literature on addiction seems to take addicts' reasons for relapse at face value. More interesting and applicable than mere acceptance of "I lost my job" or "My pet dog died," however, is an understanding of how the addict had previously managed *not* to relapse. Longitudinal studies of addicts after treatment that demonstrate a low level of patient relapse have usually been interpreted to mean that the treatment was good and effective. However, when a diabetic looks healthy three years after hospitalization for diabetic acidosis, this is not interpreted to mean that the hospitalization was good and effective; rather, it is assumed that the diabetic has a good outpatient physician, takes insulin regularly, and watches what he or she eats. It is understood that, with diabetes, it is not acute treatment intervention that is important but the restructuring of the diabetic's life. Understanding of relapse prevention for alcoholics and addicts, therefore, depends on insight into the restructuring of the person's life.

While working in a hospital detoxification unit, I have observed that when alcoholics who have been active in Alcoholics Anonymous (AA) sought admission, it was incorrect to accept the alcoholic's reasons for relapse at face value or to assume that relapse was due to AA failure. Careful questioning of the alcoholic would usually reveal that the individual had been taking benzodiazepines while attending AA meetings or had completely stopped going to AA. This pattern can be compared to people with congestive heart failure who have stopped taking their digitalis or to those who have not flossed their teeth for six months yet expect a painless visit at the dentist's office. We cannot assume that dental health will result from the fillings received two years ago. We also cannot assume that prevention of relapse in alcoholics can result from a treatment modality received two years ago. In both instances, a look at the intervening restructuring of the individual's life will provide useful insight.

Relapse prevention is a new area of addiction research. The most reasonable approach might be to assemble all the people in a given cohort who are doing well, examine what they are doing with their lives, and compare those lives with the lives of addicts who are relapsing.

In this chapter, I focus on two groups—one hundred male heroin addicts and one hundred male alcoholics. Each group was studied prospectively for abstinence and relapse incidence (Vaillant 1988). Originally all members of both groups had been hospitalized. The heroin addicts had been addicted for an average of two years prior to hospitalization in 1952, and treatment consisted of detoxification, hospitalization for up to five months, and meeting in weekly groups while hospitalized. Aftercare was limited.

The alcoholics had an average history of ten years of alcohol abuse before hospitalization in 1971, and treatment consisted of a ten-day detoxification, group meetings every day while in treatment, an introduction to and emphasis on AA, and unlimited weekly aftercare at no cost. The average age of the heroin addict was twenty-five years, compared with forty-five years for the alcoholics. A significant modal difference between the alcoholics and the heroin addicts was demonstrated by the fact that 50 percent of the heroin addicts were delinquent prior to using heroin, while only 5 percent of the alcoholics were delinquent prior to using alcohol.

Follow-up for the alcoholic group was every eighteen months for ten to fourteen years. The heroin addicts were seen once a year for at least three years, and most were seen once a year for six years. The heroin addicts were then recontacted at twelve years, and their public records were searched again at eighteen years. With the passage of time, more individuals from both groups became stable in their abstinence, with significant rates of relapse throughout the earlier years. Specifically, 95 percent of the alcoholics relapsed at some point, but 59 percent of them also were abstinent for at least six months at some point. In both groups, a significant number of the subjects died. After ten to fourteen years of tracking the alcoholics, 37 percent of the subjects had died, a number comparable to the death rate for breast cancer. At the most recent follow-up, 38 percent of the alcoholics had been abstinent for a year or more. Only 17 percent of the alcoholics were alcohol dependent twelve years after treatment. After eighteen years, only 25 percent of the heroin addicts were actively using heroin. In both groups, a significant number got better and a significant number got worse (tables 11–1 and 11–2). This is clearly a paradox. An understanding and appreciation of this paradox can be gained by attempting to answer three questions: Why does addiction occur? Why does relapse occur? Why does relapse *not* occur?

Why Does Addiction Occur?

Obviously, there is no one explanation for why people become alcoholics or drug addicts. Multiple risk factors are involved, including genetics, economics, and environment. Consider also that heroin addicts might become addicts because of the introduction of another risk factor. Heroin addicts typically

Table 11–1
Outcome of One Hundred Heroin Addicts at Three Points in Time after Index Hospital Discharge

	Time after First Hospitalization		
	5 Years	10 Years	18 Years
Stable abstinence	10%	23%	35%
Uncertain status	31%	25%	17%
Dead	6%	11%	23%
Active narcotic addiction	53%	41%	25%

Table 11–2
Outcome of One Hundred Alcohol-Dependent Individuals at Three Points in Time after Index Hospital Discharge

	Time after First Hospitalization		
	4 Years	8 Years	About 12 Years
Stable abstinence	24%	32%	25%*
Uncertain status (or institutionalized)	3%	17%	21%
Dead	12%	27%	37%
Alcohol dependence	61%	27%	17%

*Thirty-eight percent were abstinent at time of death or last contact.

have premorbidly unstable lives. Their homes are unstructured; their relationships are unstable; parental discipline is not congruent; object relations are not stable; and the congruence between their environment and that of their parents is unstable. This instability is then carried over into their adolescent and adult lives. They fail to develop what behaviorists have termed "competing sources of gratification." When heroin addicts are compared to an inner-city population, striking similarities between heroin addicts and delinquents emerge (Chein et al. 1964). Further evidence for the instability of early life as a risk factor in heroin addiction can be found in Robins's research on heroin abusers returning home from Vietnam (Robins 1974). Unlike the hospitalized heroin addicts, the Vietnam heroin abusers represented relatively normal males. When these soldiers returned to the United States, they had a 95 percent recovery rate. Instability of their prior life and polydrug abuse, rather than severity of addiction in Vietnam, predicted who would remain addicted.

Alcoholics are different from heroin addicts. Statistically, alcoholism *causes* occupational and relationship instability. Once an individual is an alcoholic, alcohol becomes the dominant form of gratification. Hodgson et al. (1978) used the degree to which alcohol occupies an individual's thoughts and behavior as a measure of physiological dependence in order to define the syndrome of alcoholism. This is in keeping with the familiar Japanese proverb "First the man takes a drink, then the drink takes a drink, then the drink takes the man."

Why Does Relapse Occur?

With this understanding of why addiction occurs, we can attempt to answer the question "Why does relapse occur?" Again, there are multifactorial considerations. Some people do take that relapse drink, cigarette, or shot when the dog dies. Some addicts never intended to stop. They make the decision to relapse consciously and deliberately. The latter group is probably not representative of most addicts.

Consideration of the secondary reinforcers that maintained the addiction in the first place allows for better insight into relapse. Most addicts give proximal reasons for relapse, but the idea of "budding," or building up to that first drink, shot, or cigarette, is not a part of most addicts' self-reports. Essentially, the events associated with taking the drug, rather than the drug itself, reinforce the individual. The use of alcohol, for example, is much more reinforcing once an individual is addicted than it ever was before. Alcohol is a poor tranquilizer, but it does serve to calm the shakes of thousands of alcoholics every morning. The potential for secondary reinforcement and conditioned withdrawal is increased in addicts.

Conditioned withdrawal is illustrated by Dole and Nyswander's (1965) documentation of a heroin addict (whose opiate receptor sites were blocked with methadone) who experienced withdrawal symptoms when faced with an anxiety-provoking incident on the "street." Conditioned withdrawal and secondary reinforcement can be compared to subliminal advertising in movie theaters. Audience members do not know that they have seen an advertisement for soda, but they do know that they are thirsty and suddenly find themselves at the concession stand buying a soda. Therefore, when relapsed addicts give proximal reasons for relapse, they simply do not know that their unstructured lives have been inviting this potential. The more unstructured an addict's life, the more prone he or she is to unconscious relapse due to secondary reinforcers.

Relapse rates seem extremely high to people who work in detoxification units. For example, at first glance, data from one freestanding detox unit looks discouraging (Vaillant 1983). Five thousand patients accounted for nineteen thousand admissions. However, a closer look reveals that twenty-five hundred of those patients were detoxified once and never returned. In other words, half of the patients who did well accounted for only 12 percent of the nineteen thousand admissions. Such a 50 percent recovery rate is actually found in random community samples (Vaillant 1983). It is much more encouraging and hopeful than detox workers tend to expect. This is because an "uncurable" 0.5 percent of the five thousand patients relapsed an average of one hundred times each and also accounted for 12 percent of the admissions. Extraction of information from data about the individuals who do *not* relapse will help answer the remaining question, "Why do people not relapse?"

Why Do People Not Relapse?

The prognosis is clearly better for addicts who are married, have been employed for at least four years, and were raised in their parents' culture (Vaillant 1966a; Vaillant 1966b; Vaillant 1966c). In contrast, criminality and other forms of antisocial behavior were not factors in prognosis, just as length of prior addiction will not predict a patient's future long-term outcome. Motivation is also not a factor in prognosis, simply because all addicts, at some level, are motivated. A common assumption about drug and alcohol treatment centers that cater to wealthy clients is that their data point to high recovery rates because their clients have more to lose. Consider instead that the life to which these addicts will return is highly structured. In fact, innercity males, when compared with male Harvard graduates, had higher eventual recovery rates than their wealthy counterparts (Vaillant 1983). Their more severe alcoholism may have led them eventually to more completely restructure their lives.

Community sampling also points to life structure as a factor in a good prognosis for alcoholics and drug addicts. A longitudinal study by Glueck and Glueck (1950) and by Vaillant (1983) followed 400 nondelinquent inner-city youths from adolescence until age forty-seven. At the onset of the study, the youths were matched with a group of delinquents for ethnicity, IQ, and high-crime neighborhoods. Of the 400 subjects, 110 became alcohol abusers. Of those 110, 49 achieved at least one year of abstinence. Only 30 percent of this abstinent group received any kind of treatment for their alcoholism. However, 32 percent of the abstinent group developed new personal relationships, 49 percent were under compulsory supervision of some sort, 53 percent developed a substitute dependence, and 49 percent attended an inspirational group. The point of the data is this: You do not avoid relapse because you have a spontaneous recovery. Not relapsing is a difficult, full-time job, as the data indicate.

Pathways to Recovery

Further interpretation of the abstinent group's methods of recovery is necessary at this point. Table 11–3 compares the community alcoholics in the preceding paragraph to the two groups of hospitalized addicts in tables 11–1 and 11–2. First, consider the importance of new relationships. By the time most alcoholics and addicts are ready for recovery, they owe a lot of people a lot of different things, from money to apologies to restitution. It is readily understandable, then, that recovery is facilitated by new relationships that are less guilt provoking.

Compulsory supervision adds a dimension of a "keeper," a superego removed from the self to alleviate the need for willpower. This is, of course, in keeping with the first step of AA: "We admitted we were powerless over alcohol." Other "keepers" that helped the abstinent group in recovery included Antabuse or the development of an ulcer that caused pain when the person drank. Some men were on probation. Other men finally realized, "When I drink, I feel awful, not better." These external experiences, with their external superego and potentially negative consequences, are very different from other experiences alcoholics are accustomed to, such as having a wife who constantly threatens to leave but never gets farther than the driveway.

Anyone who has ever been to an AA meeting knows that there are a lot of heavy smokers there; anybody who has quit smoking knows that they might gain weight. Recovery from addiction often includes these substitute dependencies, as the data indicate. Sometimes the substitute is gambling; sometimes it is compulsive trout fishing. Thus, Antabuse is not enough unless the addict has something else to take the place of the alcohol that the Antabuse has removed.

Table 11–3
Factors Associated with Absence of Relapse for a Year or More

	Untreated Abstinent Alcoholics ($n = 49$)	Treated Abstinent Heroin Addicts ($n = 30$)	Treated Abstinent Alcoholics ($n = 29$)
Compulsory supervision	49%	47%	34%
Substitute dependence	53%	60%	55%
New relationships	32%	63%	31%
Inspirational group membership	49%	About 20%*	62%

*During the follow-up period (1952 to 1970), Narcotics Anonymous and self-help groups were not yet well established. Three addicts, however, became involved in fundamentalist religion or self-help groups, and three were employed by agencies helping other addicts.

Lastly, consider those who joined an inspiration group. In this particular sample, most of the men joined AA and some of them joined fundamentalist religious groups. Due to their repeated relapses, alcoholics feel hopeless and desperate, and the belief in a higher power seems to alleviate or diminish that feeling.

These same factors were evident in the recovery (not relapsing) of heroin addicts (Vaillant 1966d). Compulsory supervision was part of the recovery process for 47 percent of the heroin addicts who did not relapse, and 60 percent developed a substitute dependence. Most often the substitute dependence was heavy drinking for about a year after treatment. In most cases, the heavy drinking eventually ceased. Sixty-three percent of the heroin addicts who did not relapse formed new relationships, usually with someone who was dependent on the addict. These kinds of relationships might be compared to the twelve-step process in AA. Parole, with its compulsory supervision and outside superego, added a further dimension of structure to many of the addicts' lives. Not surprisingly, many of the addicts who had never been employed joined the military. Unfortunately for the military, about 50 percent were dishonorably discharged. Fortunately for the addicts, 50 percent were not dishonorably discharged. A community treatment program for heroin addicts would be thrilled with a 50 percent recovery rate. Methadone maintenance is, of course, a substitute dependence, but regular visits to the methadone clinic provide addicts with compulsory supervision as well.

Summary

Four factors for a good prognosis for alcoholics and drug addicts have been identified: compulsory supervision, new relationships, inspirational group membership, and substitute dependence. Obviously, the easiest way for an addict in the community to find all of this is to go to AA. Compulsory supervision (an external conscience) is provided in the stories of other abstinent alcoholics and perhaps in a sponsor. New relationships in which one is not a debtor are provided. The cigarettes, coffee, and friendliness (all part of AA) are a substitute dependence. While this dependence frightens some clinicians and family members, a gentle reminder that diabetics are dependent on insulin might alleviate their fear. Obviously, AA and NA (Narcotics Anonymous) are inspirational groups, but other structured programs also can facilitate recovery. Many recovering addicts join and become active in a church; others join a charismatic treatment team in a drug or alcohol addiction center. What these groups have in common is compulsory supervision, new relationships, inspirational group membership, and a substitute dependence. In order for alcoholics and drug addicts not to relapse, these four variables must be present to some degree.

References

Chein, I., D.L. Gerard, R.S. Lee, and E. Rosenfeld. 1964. *The Road to H.* Narcotics, Delinquency & Social Policy. New York: Basic Books.

Dole, V.P., and M. Nyswander. 1965. "A Medical Treatment for Diacetylmorphine (Heroin) Addiction. *Journal of the American Medical Association* 193:646–50.

Glueck, S., and E. Glueck. 1950. *Unraveling Juvenile Delinquency.* New York: Commonwealth Fund.

Hodgson, R.T., T. Stockwell, H. Rankin, and G. Edwards. 1978. "Alcohol Dependence: The Concept, Its Utility and Measurement. *British Journal of Addiction* 73:339–42.

Robins, L.N. 1974. *"The Vietnam Drug User Returns:" Final Report.* Washington, D.C.: USGPO.

Vaillant, G.E. 1966a. "A 12 Year Follow-up of New York Narcotic Addicts. Part 3: Some Social and Psychiatric Characteristics." *Archives of General Psychiatry.* 15:599–609.

———. 1966b. "A 12 Year Follow-up of New York Narcotic Addicts. Part 4: Some Characteristics and Determinants of Abstinence." *American Journal of Psychiatry* 123:573–84.

———. 1966c. "Parent-Child Cultural Disparity and Drug Addiction." *Journal of Nervous and Mental Disease* 142:534–39.

———. 1983. *Natural History of Alcoholism.* Cambridge, Mass.: Harvard University Press.

———. 1988. "What Can Long-Term Follow-up Teach Us about Relapse and Prevention of Relapse in Addiction? *British Journal of Addiction* 83:1147–57.

Part IV
Treatment and the Law

Prologue

Norman E. Zinberg

The extent of agreement among the authors of this part is impressive. The chapters as a group show a growing consensus; the efforts to implement that consensus take place in settings as diverse as a prosecutor's office, a program for juveniles, and an adult correctional institution. Although the specter of AIDS is not explicitly mentioned, any reading of these chapters highlights the painful paradox that as a result of this plague, there may be more money and political energy behind these programs than there otherwise would have been. In this prologue, I review the five areas of agreement in these chapters and then discuss some of the problems raised by this agreement.

Areas of Agreement

1. All the authors recognize the complex, interactive relationship between intoxicant use and crime. To the public at large, the issue seems straightforward. Figures cited by Hunter and Pudim in Chapter 12 show that as many as 80 percent of those incarcerated for a crime committed the offense under the influence of an intoxicant. Therefore, drugs cause crime. In this view, the reasons can be as direct as committing the crime to get money to buy the intoxicant or as indirect as the intoxicant's reduction of usual inhibitions and moral standards.

Obviously, there is a connection between drug use and crime, but it is nowhere near that simple. The crime seems to come first. According to Hunter and Pudim, 50 percent of those currently convicted with histories of intoxicant use had difficulties with the law *before* they were users. They became intoxicant users *after* they embarked on a deviant or antisocial path. Certainly such use did not reduce their criminal activity, despite the depressing physiological effects of many of the drugs of choice, such as alcohol, opiates, and tranquilizers. In all likelihood, the original social antagonism, further unleashed by the chronic disorientation of heavy intoxicant use, became more fixed and less amenable to a rational relationship with society in general and the criminal justice system in particular.

If one thinks in terms of the potential for long-term treatment of this group's severe psychological difficulties, it is necessary first to address the possible addiction. But if one subscribes to the intoxicant-to-blame theory, cleaning up the addicted individuals might be as far as treatment can go. If one thinks in terms of a vicious-cycle theory, treatment might involve a more expensive and prolonged attempt to achieve social rehabilitation.

2. The authors all report a well-documented position that harsh punishment (in fact, punishment in general) does not serve as a deterrent to crime. I have pointed out elsewhere that "a good law punishes as few as possible and deters as many as possible, while a bad law deters few and punishes many (Zinberg and Robertson 1972). For a law to deter rather than punish, it must be backed by a strong social consensus. The drug laws, in contrast to the laws against assault, for instance, have not had the consensus, although there is an emerging social thrust related to issues such as driving while intoxicated. Yet even in this regard, in Chapter 14 Sidoff, Christianson, Merrefield, and Brown reiterate the belief that increasing the length of sentencing seems to do little to change the behavior of this group of perpetrators.

This is a vital point. As long as lawmakers believe that they can manage or reduce the problem by upping the ante of punishment, they will be unwilling to invest the resources necessary for treatment. In fact, imposing harsh penalties is not even cheap, as the Bar of the City of New York pointed out in its report on the disastrous failure of the so-called Rockefeller Drug Law of 1973 (Association of the Bar of the City of New York 1976).

3. The need for reeducation and treatment other than incarceration or punishment alone is inescapable. All of the writers report practical and clinical experience that supports the logic of such a step, and they take this reasoning a crucial step further from the vantage point of quite different institutional structures. They all insist that part of the treatment is planning and preparation for the transition back into the community.

Taking this step, which on the surface seems so obvious, requires a considerable acceptance of the role of social setting in managing intoxicant use. Even since the drug revolution began in 1962, it has been true that if you want to know if so-and-so uses, see if his or her friends do. Yet developing a comprehensive theory that realistically includes social-setting planning along with the personality, history, and intoxicant use of the individual is complicated. Remember that treatment always follows theory. This does not mean trying to put square pegs in round holes, but it does mean that without the underlying theoretical hypotheses that point the way, changes in treatment planning cannot occur. First, the social setting must be included in treatment planning. Then, if it is recognized that the social setting itself cannot be changed (which is often the case), continuous efforts must be directed at changing the individual's relationship to that setting—in other words, at community transition.

4. The authors recognize the need for innovative approaches to treatment. While everyone supports fresh approaches, actually implementing a new program means that something can go wrong and the innovator is open to criticism. Yet these authors are recommending treatment possibilities such as taking youngsters into the wilderness to learn to live on their own, using the prosecutor's office to force admission to treatment programs [as suggested by George Vaillant years ago (Vaillant 1977)], and establishing the sort of administrative/therapist split in criminal justice programs advocated so strongly by Alfred Stanton and Morris Schwartz in *The Mental Hospital* (Stanton and Schwartz 1954).

5. Without taking these sorts of chances, treatment will not improve and attempts at social rehabilitation will continue to fail. For any lasting good to come from these efforts, the programs must be rigorously evaluated, as Stein, Garrett, and Christiansen so carefully demonstrated in chapter 13. Only by specifying what a program does and then following the participants to determine the effects of the interventions can an objective observer evaluate the program's success. Well-meaning people can easily get caught up in what they do and see success because they want it so badly. Programs such as those described here are hard to evaluate because so many human interactions are involved. These variables are virtually impossible to quantify. Determining what actually were the effective interventions means attempting to consider subjective factors as part of the evaluation process. Including such variables can be more rigorous and demanding than attempts to express these evaluative results in numbers. In fact, qualitative variables must be included if there is to be any hope of replication and improved program effectiveness, for it will be the evaluation of these subjective interactions that may prove crucial.

Problems

In these chapters, treatment and the law are considered without too much concern for exactly what treatment means and by whom it will be performed. To call a treatment "cognitive-behavioral" says little about the experience, background, or exact theoretical orientation of the therapist and supervisors. Also, questions concerning choices between individual and group approaches, both formal and informal, will occupy other writers.

Similar issues exist in the area of education. There is an enormous difference between emphasis on acquiring facts and efforts to consider the emotional inhibitions that have made it hard for people to learn when data have been available to them. Even more difficult is assessing the availability and use of social learning. What does it mean to think about "teaching" what we decide is responsibility?

Next, for people to work effectively with this difficult population, intensive and ongoing training is essential. There are surprisingly few senior teachers and few, if any, established training centers that can provide the clinical and theoretical expertise to train the people necessary to staff, supervise, and evaluate these programs. This is an extremely serious problem. Without appropriate training, individuals attracted to this field by interest and goodwill must fly by the seat of their pants. They have to either reinvent the wheel, which is enormously time-consuming and wasteful; try to get along by using their personalities, a process that can easily become self-indulgent or dependence producing; or rely on gimmicks such as family recreation or role modeling, which hardly address the issues that impeded effective functioning in the first place.

The advantages of using the law as coercion in the treatment of 1989 intoxicant use have been addressed elsewhere (Zinberg and Trainor 1989). It suffices to say that coercion can help the client to accept treatment and maintain a sense of self-esteem (even if based on a so-called negative identity) and can set the boundaries appropriate to social rehabilitation.

How far can this reliance on coercion go? The authors of these chapters agree that there are probably at least two rough groupings of clients. The larger one is more or less amenable to rehabilitation; if reasonable procedures and programming were in place, the success rate, in the sense of reducing intoxicant use and criminal activity, would be high. The other group is hardcore and difficult to reach. This group may be as small as 2 percent of the population at large, but it apparently does 40 percent of the damage. How do we improve our ability to identify this group early? And how far can we go toward coercing individuals into prolonged treatment situations without violating their civil rights? Attempting to use the criminal justice system to promote treatment demands a complex balancing and a careful concern about abuse of that power. Extending that power by isolating a particular group as potentially destructive in advance of any offenses touches a sore spot in our political system. It is ironic that improving and implementing treatment programs within the criminal justice system may lead more directly to considering this painful question than our current haphazard treatment efforts.

Finally, if we are to address the relationship between treatment and intoxicant use, some attention must be given to the complicated question of controlled versus compulsive use. It is far easier (particularly with this group) not to bother with that distinction. Certainly with adolescents or younger children, and even with adults, the general public simply wishes that they "just wouldn't do it." That is hardly realistic in this society or any society.

Perhaps we need programs based on *how*, as opposed to *whether*, these individuals use intoxicants.

Again, there are likely to be at least two groups. One, probably much the larger, can acquire rules for use and can understand that it is the *controlled* quality of use that is crucial. The other group, whose tendency to use compulsively may be so ingrained as to make the effort to develop rules for controlled use irrelevant, would require a different approach. So far, little careful thought has gone into separating these groups and planning how to deal with them. In part this is because of the quandary caused by our social policies toward licit and illicit drugs. Would one want to convert controlled marijuana users to alcohol? Today therapists or educators could hardly consider working with these clients to assure them of remaining controlled users of marijuana. Many such problems remain, but the following chapters get us off to a good start in examining them.

References

Association of the Bar of the City of New York. 1976. *The Effect of the 1973 Drug Laws on the New York State Courts*. New York: Association of the Bar of the City of New York.

Stanton, A.H., and M.S. Schwartz. 1954. *The Mental Hospital*. New York: Basic Books.

Vaillant, G.E. 1977. *Adaptation of Life*. Boston: Little, Brown.

Zinberg, N.E., and J.A. Robertson. 1972. *Drugs and the Public*. New York: Simon & Schuster.

Zinberg, N.E., and K.B. Trainor. 1989. Treatment of Users of Different Intoxicants. Unpublished manuscript. Boston, Mass.

12
The Prosecutor's Goals Beyond Conviction

Alexander M. Hunter
Robert A. Pudim

A job description for prosecuting attorneys usually does not include guidelines about goals beyond conviction. A prosecuting or district attorney's job is to use his or her skills and resources in representing the people of the community and to argue persuasively before judge and jury so the offender will be found guilty. After conviction, what happens to the lawbreaker is someone else's problem—the legislature's, judge's, penal authority's, or probation officer's.

Unfortunately, it is not that simple. For example, prosecutors are continually confronted with the decision whether to release or detain defendants prior to trial. Release, in some cases, means more crimes will be committed, particularly if the offender has an alcohol or some other substance abuse problem. Given crowded court schedules and jails at or above inmate capacity, the decision whether to accept a plea to a lesser charge and some form of probation becomes an even greater concern for prosecutors. Quite often the problem is further complicated by offenders who abuse or are addicted to substances.

Data for offenders convicted of drug offenses in 1986 (U.S. Bureau of Justice Assistance 1988) show that only 20 percent were sentenced to prison. Almost one-third of the drug offenders were sentenced to a local jail, making this the most common sentencing alternative for drug users. More than one-fourth were sentenced to probation, perhaps including some form of court-ordered counseling. These are the figures for *confirmed* users. The data on non–drug-related crimes show that most offenders are sentenced to probation or released on parole.

The statistics for non–drug-related crimes show an obvious relationship between drugs and crime, however. Drugs alter behavior and consciousness. The use of drugs affects moods and emotions, chemically changes the brain, and leads to loss of control, paranoia, lower inhibition, and greater expression of frustration and anger. The cost of drugs, both financial and psychological, leads to an unwillingness or inability to hold a regular job. Thus, drugs are a major cause of robbery, burglary, assault, and other "non–drug-related" crimes.

Several studies show that two-thirds to three-fourths of all people arrested for other than drug charges tested positive for some drug at the time of arrest. During one test in New York City, 92 percent of those arrested for robbery and 80 percent of the burglars apprehended tested positive for drugs. The U.S. Bureau of Justice Statistics (1988) reported that 35 percent of all state prison inmates were under the influence of an illegal drug at the time they committed the crime for which they were imprisoned. Half of those serving sentences for robbery, burglary, and theft were daily users of some illegal drug. The 1986 survey found that 43 percent of all inmates were daily users of some illegal drug in the month before they committed the crime for which they were convicted. When legal drugs such as alcohol are added, the figures almost double.

Clearly, prosecutors must look beyond conviction when dealing with offenders. Merely convicting lawbreakers so they may be punished is not good enough. This survey found that many inmates began to use drugs only *after* their criminal careers started. Half the inmates who had ever used a major drug such as heroin, cocaine, methadone, PCP, or LSD did not do so until after their first arrest. About 60 percent of regular drug users did not become such until after their first arrest. In addition, only about one-seventh of the inmates fit the pattern of drug addicts who committed crimes to support their habits. According to this report, the greater the use of major drugs by the offender, the more prior convictions he or she had for all types of crimes. Fewer than 13 percent of those who had never used a drug had six or more convictions. This compares to more than twice as many convictions for daily users of major drugs.

Conviction and Punishment

It might be instructive to look at what conviction means. Simply stated, conviction of a crime triggers punishment for committing that crime. Criminal law is justified by what it supposedly does. If the law is to be respected for what it does, it must be applied in such a manner as to achieve a specific end. Conviction and punishment in our society serve a changing mixture of objectives. Generally, there are five major ends, some of which are in conflict with others. They involve attempts to reform, restrain, and deter the offender and others; to achieve justice; and to indicate what is or is not acceptable behavior.

Conviction and subsequent punishment are basically moral issues, although they are often obscured by pragmatic considerations such as crowded court schedules and jails. Conviction and punishment are related to society's notion of balance and the desire that an individual should be held accountable for misconduct. Society requires that people be held accountable for what they have chosen to do. Criminal law adds one additional requirement—that they intended to do what they have done. Hidden in this notion is one other requirement—that the offender have the capacity to choose. Generally, American society does not hold people responsible for acts over which they have no control; thus, the question of drugs and compulsive/addictive behavior is a lively issue in the field of criminal behavior.

Reasons for Punishment

Punishment is used to enforce morality. Society uses punishment to achieve one or more secondary goals. Some of these goals are in conflict with others or are more appropriate for some kinds of crime than for others.

All societies, ancient or modern, technologically advanced or primitive, punish errant members. In most places today, incarceration or death are the preferred forms of punishment. This is a relatively modern development. Before imprisonment and capital punishment were instituted, offenders faced exile, repayment, or ordeal for their unacceptable behavior. Exile might be permanent or for a specified period of time. (In some areas of the world, exile amounted to a death penalty.) Repayment might involve replacing property, paying a fine or a specified amount of money to victims, or actually replacing a dead person with the offender's own self for a specified period of time. Ordeals, seldom heard of today, might involve memorizing and participating in elaborate rituals or undergoing a demanding physical test.

One reason for punishment is to maintain a balance. Evil should not go unpunished, and the wrong a person does should be returned to him or her in equal degree, if not in kind. This notion is part of a gut-level sense of rightness and appropriateness. Justice is most satisfying when it is carried out along these lines. Despite this, it is unpopular to defend retribution as a punishment goal. Even though retribution is a feature of the oldest legal codes known, it runs counter to some aspects of the underlying Judeo-Christian principles of American society. It is seen as cruel, primitive, and unenlightened, lacking in compassion and forgiveness. It also can be argued that retribution is impractical or even illegal in some cases. As someone once said, "Revenge costs everyone too much."

In spite of its unpopularity as a goal of punishment, there is a strong impulse to connect an eye-for-an-eye solution with the concept of justice. One development in the criminal justice system has been a steady and gradual expansion of restitution and repayment sentences to offenders. Sometimes this is linked to a short term of imprisonment, but more often it is used in combination with the threat of a deferred sentence to pay back victims for losses or expenses.

For substance abuse–related crimes, restitution can lead to selling drugs in order to meet the court's requirements or provide yet another reason to abuse substances. Retribution resolves the victim's complaints with his or her sense of justice but does little for the offender and his or her unacceptable behavior.

A second reason for punishment, often found in state legislatures and used to justify increased penalties for crimes, is deterrence. Lawmakers believe that punishment deters others from committing the same crime. They assume that if penalties are increased, people in general will heed the lesson being given and refrain from such behavior. There is evidence that these lessons are taken to heart in direct proportion to how much individuals identify themselves with the offender. The more a person resembles the individual punished, the more strongly the penalty deters. It is said that if we have felt the same urges of the punished person and have come close to doing the same thing, the punishment is a positive deterrent. The flip side of the argument, however, suggests that alcoholics or other substance abusers who have strong denial defenses do not identify themselves with substance-abusing offenders. Like healthy, nonaddicted people who observe addicts being punished, substance abusers are not deterred from taking drugs themselves because they perceive the offender as different from themselves.

For criminal activity in general, increasing penalties does not seem to result in reducing crime (Jokach 1988). Most offenders believe they will not be caught breaking the law. The penalty, no matter what it is, is not a consideration. It becomes something to worry about only after arrest.

The question of mental capacity also enters into using deterrence as a reason for punishment. Morally, we find it cruel and unjust to punish a person who is "not responsible for his or her actions," regardless of the societal ends punishment serves. Whether a person under the influence of drugs is responsible is an interesting legal problem. From this viewpoint, increasing penalties for such crimes would be an immoral act of law.

A third reason for punishment is symbolic. Punishment is the way society states what is acceptable behavior and what is not. The severity of the punishment is a measure of how strongly the community feels about a specific type of misbehavior compared with other antisocial acts. Like deterrence, the symbolic reason for punishment is aimed at the normal mind, not the defective one. It is aimed at people who can understand that there are consequences for intentional acts, some more severe than others. As with deterrence, legislatures make laws and assign penalties to them for largely symbolic reasons. Unfortunately, prosecutors, judges, and prison authorities must deal with these laws as realities, not symbols.

A fourth reason for punishment is rehabilitation. American society would like to use punishment to correct an offender so he or she will not continue to commit crimes. The unstated assumption is that punishment will improve an offender's conduct and, further, that the offender is capable of rehabilitation. From this perspective, the death penalty is an admission that the criminal's conduct will not improve and that his or her rehabilitation is deemed impossible. Rehabilitation requires that the offender have a mind that is able to guide his or her behavior and is willing to be educated or changed. Theoretically, mentally deficient offenders who are unable to help themselves would not be candidates for such punishment.

If rehabilitation is the reason for punishment, states such as Colorado would have to create a prison system geared toward education, retraining, and gentle brainwashing. Offenders theoretically would not be released until they had undergone a change in attitude and thinking. The strange thing is that some aspects of the Chinese prison system do this very thing.

Rehabilitation is a particularly attractive approach to punishment if the society subscribes to a disease model for substance abuse. The punishment period would allow an addict to become drug free. This would be followed by an extensive education program that would deal with drug use, misuse, and abuse. This could, in turn, be buttressed by teaching coping techniques, stress-reduction methods, and self-discipline. From a budgeting point of view, it would be expensive.

A fifth reason for punishment is that it should be used to prevent a person from repeating an offense or from hurting others. In terms of this goal, there is no need to correct the criminal. An offender who is a danger to other inmates would suffer capital punishment. Others would be restrained until they were too old or feeble to repeat their offenses. This goal requires that the prison system's attention be directed at controlling the offender. Most U.S. prison systems operate under the restraint goal of punishment. In regard to substance abusers, the restraint system of punishment keeps them relatively drug free while incarcerated but does little for them when they ultimately return to their communities and may very well increase drug abuse (U.S. Bureau of Justice Statistics 1988).

The restraint approach to punishment has an interesting consequence in how the legal system should go about restraining an offender. It is a practice of the criminal justice system to restrain sane offenders in prison and insane ones in mental hospitals. Most prison systems attempt to handle this by having hospital incarceration facilities or prison psychotherapeutic facilities. Hospitals and prisons by nature are incompatible institutions. Another question to be asked is how incarceration in a prison is compared with equivalent incarceration in a hospital, since treatment sentences last much longer than straight prison time with good days off (Cousineau and Veevers 1972).

The criticism of restraint as a reason for punishment is that all it does is warehouse people. The restraining facilities vary from tightly controlled institutions for the most dangerous to "country club" holding pens for the least dangerous. When offenders are released from such a prison system, they often commit more crimes and return. It is argued that the revolving-door phenomenon is a result of a lack of rehabilitative facilities. In the long run, it costs more to restrain people than to rehabilitate them. For substance abusers, restraint merely keeps them relatively drug free in prison. It does nothing to protect the community from the consequences of renewed drug abuse after they are released.

Some states estimate that 70 to 80 percent of all offenders on probation or parole have substance abuse problems. Of the offenders who are released, few receive treatment for substance abuse because it is not included as a condition of parole or probation. In some cases, such treatment is not required because the crime was not related to drugs. In other cases, there is a lack of treatment services in the community or the offender is unable to pay for available services.

According to the U.S. Department of Justice, in 1986 the number of people on probation (2,094,405) or parole (326,752) represented 1.36 percent of all adults in the United States (U.S. Department of Justice 1987). The total number of adults in the United States under some form of correctional supervision amounted to one in every fifty-five adults. These numbers have been increasing steadily. In the same period, time served in prison has been decreasing. The median time served in confinement in 1984 was seventeen months, or 45.4 percent of an offender's original court-ordered sentence (Minor-Harper and Innes 1987). Those released for violent offenses served a median time of twenty-eight months, but twice as long as either property or drug offenders.

It is obvious that more and more offenders are being released earlier than ever before and that many can associate their involvement with the justice system to drug misuse or abuse. Prosecutors and judges must not only improve their ability to identify offenders with drug problems, but they must refer more of them to treatment if anything is going to be done to reduce the crime rate. Decisions related to pretrial and postimprisonment release must include an assessment of the risk an offender runs of resuming his or her substance abuse career. Finally, more must be done to monitor an offender's compliance with drug treatment conditions of release and treatment progress. The statistics quoted earlier show that treatment can be a basic crime-prevention tool.

Prosecutors must have goals beyond conviction. Sentencing means that in about a year and a half, the offender will be back on the streets. One way of mitigating the impact of released offenders on the community is to see that they receive treatment for drug use.

This is not to say treatment is a panacea in crime prevention. With certain kinds of offenders, treatment will not work. A study of Chaiken and Johnson (1988) suggests that there are two kinds of drug-involved offenders who should be kept off the streets. One is a serious adolescent dealer who uses multiple substances and commits property and violent crimes at high rates. This profile represents only 2 percent of all adolescents, but such youths account for 40 percent of total robberies and assaults by adolescents and are responsible for 60 percent of all teenage felony thefts and drug sales. Unless they are diverted into special programs tailored to give them the context and skills for a more constructive lifestyle, they are likely to continue committing crimes as adults. These youngsters are high-rate dealers linked with the adult world of drug distribution. They do not meet the stereotype of "strung-out junkies," although many are daily users of drugs.

The other type of drug-involved offender who should be kept off the streets is the adult who is involved in moderate to heavy use of multiple drugs, usually including cocaine and heroin. These offenders commit many crimes while under the influence. Their major source of income comes from criminal activity, and they usually play mid-level roles in drug distribution to both adolescents and adults.

To help prosecutors get these serious offenders off the streets, improved methods of identifying them must be found. Criteria dealing with prior convictions for robbery, burglary, arson, forcible rape, sex crimes involving a child, or kidnapping should be developed. Histories of completion of previous sentences and probation and parole conformance must be evaluated, and the offender's pretrial release status when arrested for a new crime must be included. Information not currently available, such as juvenile convictions for robbery and indications of persistent or frequent drug use before arrest, also must be included. One way of determining drug use would be to conduct a urinalysis of all those arrested to test for specific drugs.

One goal of prosecutors must be to reduce the frequency of use and the amount of drugs consumed by offenders. Criminal activity and behavior stops or lessens during periods of abstinence or greatly reduced consumption.

Outcome studies of a small number of programs, many taking place in prisons and continuing with care after release, report that these programs appear to reduce participants' involvement with drugs and crime (Wexler, Lipton, and Johnson 1985). By working with treatment services in the community, jails and prisons can increase the chance that offenders will not return. Judges and parole or probation officers can reduce the number of recidivists, who commit many crimes before they are tried or rearrested, by cooperating with police and treatment providers.

A prosecutor's goals after conviction must include treatment requirements as part of a pretrial release and as a condition of probation and parole, not only in drug-related crimes but in crimes such as burglary, theft, and assault, where drugs and alcohol were a peripheral, but important, element of the offense.

References

Chaiken, M.R., and B.D. Johnson. 1988. *Characteristics of Different Types of Drug-Involved Offenders.* Washington, D.C.: National Institute of Justice.

Cousineau, and Veevers. 1972. "The Concept of General Deterrence.", University of Alberta.

Jokach, H.C. 1988. *The Impact of Severe Penalties on Drinking and Driving.* Washington, D.C.: AAA Foundation for Traffic Safety.

Minor-Harper, S., and C. Innes. 1987. *Time Served in Prison and Parole, 1984.* Washington, D.C.: Bureau of Justice Statistics.

U.S. Bureau of Justice Statistics. 1988. *Profile of State Prison Inmates, 1986.* Washington, D.C.: U.S. Bureau of Justice Statistics.

———. 1988. *Report on Drug Control.* Washington, D.C.: U.S. Bureau of Justice Statistics.

U.S. Department of Justice. 1987. "Probation and Parole, 1986." *Bureau of Justice Statistics Bulletin,* December 1987.

Wexler, H., D. Lipton, and Johnson. 1985. *Prison Drug Treatment: The Critical 90 Days of Re-entry.* San Diego: American Society of Criminology.

13
Treatment Strategies for Juvenile Delinquents to Decrease Substance Abuse and Prevent Adult Drug and Alcohol Dependence

Susan L. Stein
Carol J. Garrett
Dave Christiansen

Those in the human services field are called upon to serve two very difficult populations—youths involved in the use and abuse of drugs and/or alcohol and those exhibiting sustained patterns of delinquent behavior. The Colorado Alcohol and Drug Abuse Division (ADAD), in collaboration with the Colorado Division of Youth Services (DYS) has been funded by the Office of Substance Abuse Prevention (OSAP) to develop and implement an exciting new concept in the treatment of juvenile delinquency and substance abuse. Known as the Colorado OSAP Project, this program is designed to serve youths with extensive problems in both areas who are at high risk for continuing these maladaptive behaviors.

Attempts to develop and implement programs for these high-risk youths are not new, but the effectiveness of previous programs, particularly in the area of delinquency, has been questioned (Martinson 1974). Among the reasons given for the frequent failure of treatment groups to outperform comparison groups in statistical analyses is the failure to anchor the program in a theoretical base. Further, research and evaluation in the human services area has frequently been woefully inadequate to detect a significant difference when one exists (Sechrest, White, and Brown 1979).

Two prime concerns in developing the Colorado OSAP Project were to tie program elements to current research and theory on the causes and correlates of delinquency and drug use and to incorporate a thorough formative process and outcome evaluation. This chapter discusses the theoretical basis of the program, the program itself as currently implemented, the characteristics of the youths to be served, and the evaluation plan.

Theoretical Model

Evidence indicates that the etiology of delinquency and drug use may be very similar. Hawkins et al. (1986) summarized the following factors consistently identified in the research as correlates of both delinquency and drug use.

1. Early antisocial behaviors
2. Parent and sibling drug use and criminal behavior
3. Poor, inconsistent parenting
4. Family conflict
5. Family social deprivation
6. School failure
7. Low commitment to education and attachment to school
8. Peer factors
9. Attitudes and beliefs (bonding) toward conventional institutions, persons, and so on
10. Neighborhood attachment/community disorganization
11. Mobility
12. Constitutional and personality factors

These risk factors, in combination with research on successful programs, provide a guide to program development and subsequent evaluation. The addition of an integrated theory of the causal chain linking these risk factors to subsequent deviant behavior strengthens both program and evaluation design and contributes to theory building.

The Integrated Social Psychological Model (Elliott, Ageton, and Canter 1979) provides the theoretical basis for the Colorado OSAP Project. The model integrates elements of strain theory (Cloward and Ohlin 1960), social control theory (Hirschi 1969), and social learning theory (Bandura 1977; Bandura and Walters 1963). While each of these individual theories explains a portion of the variance in delinquency or drug use, the explained variance is relatively small and does not account for those cases that do not conform to predictions based on the theory.

An empirical examination of the Integrated Social Psychological Model (Elliott and Huizinga 1984) revealed weak direct links between blocked or limited opportunity (strain) and delinquent behavior or drug use. Similarly, these researchers found a weak direct link between bonding to conventional institutions and these outcome behaviors. The direct link between bonding with delinquent peers and subsequent delinquency and drug use was very strong, however, as was the link between prior delinquent behavior and subsequent behavior. The Elliott causal model indicates that strain and conventional bonding act through bonding with delinquent peers to effect both delinquency and drug use.

The Colorado OSAP Project is designed to intervene in the causal chain to reduce the incidence of both behaviors. The project uses skill-based education and vocational training to increase the probability that youths will be able to reach conventional goals. It provides opportunities to become involved with conventional institutions, persons, and activities through school, work, recreation, and cultural outlets. Through modeling and reinforcement in these normative contexts, youths can develop some commitment to and belief in these normative institutions.

A major criticism of treatment programs for delinquent youths has been that positive changes are relatively sure to occur in an institutional setting but that these changes do not generalize to the community once a youth is released. In the past, little emphasis has been placed on reintegrating the youth back into the community to which he or she will return (Coates et al. 1978; Coates 1981). Furthermore, evidence from Massachusetts (Coates, et al. 1978) indicates that the more normalized the treatment setting, the more likely the youth is to avoid subsequent illegal behavior. The project was, therefore, designed to be located in the community as an alternative to secure institutionalization.

Treatment Components

The activities of the project are carried out through four phases: assessment, wilderness experience, alternative lifestyle, and community transition.

The *assessment process* occurs after the juvenile is committed to DYS. Juveniles eligible for the project are sixteen- to eighteen-year-old males from Colorado. In the assessment process, the juveniles are tested for levels of functioning and maladaptive behaviors. Juveniles who are determined to be eligible for the project are asked to sign a voluntary agreement. The Community Review Board approves the placement of the juvenile in the project, and the continuity of care plan is developed.

The *wilderness experience* is provided by Adventures in Change, a program of Porter Memorial Hospital. The experience involves a small group of juveniles who are led on a fifteen-day venture into the wilderness for the purpose of promoting prosocial bonding, team building, self-esteem, leadership, and group cohesiveness in a drug-free environment. Fifteen juveniles have attended the wilderness experience in three cohorts. This has been effective in reducing the runaway rate that is common in community-based residential programs for delinquents.

The *alternative lifestyle* component is provided by Adventures in Change.

This residential program provides a healthful community environment with a substance abuse prevention and intervention curriculum. A heavy emphasis is placed on two areas: (1) the development of an adult sense of responsibility, and (2) appropriate education and vocational training for youths. The Challenge Program at the Community College of Denver is working with Adventures in Change to implement these objectives.

The *community transition* component attempts to reinforce the skills obtained in the alternative lifestyle by providing support after the juveniles are removed from the residence. This is accomplished through the involvement of many service providers. Adventures in Change and the Challenge Program assist youths in the identification of community resources and job placement. Denver Partners matches juveniles with a "significant other" who facilitates the transition. The DYS parole officer oversees the progress of the juvenile in maintaining prosocial behaviors.

The involvement of multiple public and private agencies in the provision of services is a goal of the Colorado OSAP Project. A management team of administrators from the program oversees the project and administers grants. The history and development of the system linkages, as well as the degree of collaboration, are being investigated in the evaluation.

Project Clients

In the fall of 1985, DYS, with funding provided through a contract with ADAD, began the development of a comprehensive assessment instrument designed to measure delinquent youths' self-reported involvement with drugs, alcohol, and delinquent behavior. The resulting instrument, the drug and alcohol assessment, has been administered to committed delinquents during the assessment process immediately following commitment. A report on the instrument appears in Tjaden et al. (1986).

The clients in the Colorado OSAP Project are selected from the population of committed juveniles. A profile of substance use obtained from the drug and alcohol assessments of juveniles committed in 1986 provides insights into the characterstics of the project clients. A comparison of the profiles of project clients and the total population is planned as the number of project clients increases.

Table 13–1 presents the percentage of youths acknowledging ever having used (prevalence rate) one of thirty-one drugs. Virtually all the youths have tried beer, wine, hard liquor, tobacco, and marijuana. The prevalence rates for all drugs are higher than those of the probability sample of youths in the 1982 National Institute on Drug Abuse (NIDA) survey (Miller et al. 1983).

Characteristics of the use of various drugs are presented in table 13–2. Use of alcohol and marijuana started almost two years prior to all other drugs

Table 13–1
Prevalence of Drug Use among 1986 Committed Juveniles
(percent who ever used)

Alcohol	
Beer	98.4
Wine	77.1
Hard liquor	88.9
Tobacco	85.9
Marijuana	94.1
Cocaine	39.9
Amphetamines	46.7
Hallucinogens	
Acid	52.3
Peyote	5.2
Mushrooms	35.6
Mescaline	3.6
PCP	11.1
Inhalants	
Gasoline	18.0
Paint	14.4
Rush	34.0
Lighter fluid	3.9
Glue	12.4
Heroin	7.5
Pain killers	
Opium	9.2
Codeine	9.5
Morphine	3.3
Dilaudid	0.7
Percodan	5.6
Others	2.6
Barbiturates	8.2
Quaaludes	12.1
Librium	10.5
Ritalin	3.9
Tranquilizers	2.9
Nitrous oxide	5.9
Other	7.6

with the exception of inhalants. The youths reported starting to use alcohol at 12.1 years on the average and marijuana at 12.5 years. Cocaine use did not begin until 14.8 years. Alcohol and marijuana were the drugs most likely to be used several times a day and were the ones with which youths were most likely to perceive having a problem [although, on a scale of 1 (not a problem) to 5 (a very bad problem), these respondents did not perceive having even a moderate problem with any drug].

Table 13–2
Characteristics of Drug Use

	Average Age at First Use	Average Perceived Problem*	% Using Several Times Per Day
Alcohol (n = 304)	12.1	1.7	58
Marijuana (n = 289)	12.5	2.0	82
Cocaine (n = 122)	14.8	1.6	34
Amphetamines (n = 144)	14.2	1.2	34
Hallucinogens (n = 171)	14.7	1.7	43
Inhalants (n = 139)	13.7	1.4	31
Heroin (n = 22)	14.6	1.5	—
Pain killers (n = 47)	14.4	1.2	—
Sedatives (n = 47)	14.0	1.2	—
Tranquilizers (n = 32)	14.7	1.2	—

*5 = very bad; 1 = no problem.

The relationship between delinquency and drug use is explored in the assessment. The youths' delinquent history was typically extensive. Thirty-six percent had two or more prior adjudications, with their offenses ranging from serious offenses against persons (25 percent) to those against property (75 percent). Drugs appeared most likely to be involved in the offense when property offenses were committed.

These data do not imply a cause and effect relationship between delinquency and drug use, although Elliott, Huizinga, and Ageton (1985) attempted to explore the causal chain. One might speculate that social norms are more likely to be violated under the influence of drugs and that some proportion of delinquent activity would be eliminated if drug and alcohol problems could be moderated.

The results of the 1986 drug and alcohol assessments of committed juveniles support the conclusion that the population from which project clients are selected are heavily involved in the use of drugs and alcohol as well as in delinquent activity. A link between the two is strongly suggested, although the exact nature of that link has not been explored. The results continue to support the need to address drug and alcohol problems in youths in the Colorado OSAP Project.

Evaluation Plan

The evaluation of the Colorado OSAP Project was planned to provide a thorough ongoing understanding of the Colorado OSAP Project and its impact.

To accomplish this end, the evaluation was designed to provide useful, complete, and valid evaluation as proposed by Patton (1978). Success in the implementation of the planned evaluation depends on flexibility and innovation.

The evaluation plan for the Colorado OSAP Project involves the documentation of the *development* of project components, the recording of the *implementation* of project components, and the assessment of the *effectiveness* of project components. Within each of these phases, the evaluation involves three methodologies for assessment. *Measures* are used to record stages of project development, activities implemented, and pre-post instrumentation. *Observation* is used to interview participants and record insights. *Videotaping* is conducted during all stages of the project, and participating juveniles are videotaped at selected times throughout their project involvement. The *Evaluation Review Board* comprises four professionals who provide direction and feedback for the research.

The evaluation objective is to study the effectiveness of the project in bringing about short-term and long-term changes in the juvenile's attitudes and behaviors. All newly committed youths are screened for eligibility. When there is an opening in the project, an eligible juvenile is placed in the project group. A juvenile may be removed from the project group if the Community Review Board finds the juvenile inappropriate or the juvenile elects not to participate. If no opening is available at the time of commitment, the juvenile is placed in the comparison group. Over a three-year period, 75 juveniles will participate in the project group and 165 in the comparison group.

The project group and the comparison group are given a battery of tests at intake, at release, three months after release, twelve months after release, and two years after release. The tests are designed to measure relevant constructs. These constructs are listed in table 13–3 along with the selected measurement instruments.

In addition, the evaluation records participation in activities, attitude and behavior changes, and relevant skill attainment for the project group. The project group and the comparison group are assessed on the following outcome measures:

1. Reduction of alcohol and drug involvement
2. Reduction of delinquency
3. Increased vocational and educational skills for enhanced employability
4. Reintegration into the community

The evaluation of the Colorado OSAP Project is being carried out by OMNI Research and Training. A three-person team has the responsibility and opportunity to explore an exciting treatment program guided by a comprehensive theoretical framework. It is the hope and anticipation that the evaluation will provide information necessary for the improvement and the eventual replication of the Colorado OSAP Project.

Table 13-3
Delinquency Factor Assessment

Constructs	Measurement Instrument
Neighborhood factors Social bonding Moral disengagement Labeling by parents Perceived sanctions Normative orientation of peer group	Elliott National Youth Survey (Elliott, Huizinga, and Ageton 1985)
Personality styles Expressed concerns Behavioral correlates	Million Adolescent Personality Inventory (Million, Green, and Maegher 1982)
Locus of control	Nowicki-Strickland Locus of Control (Nowicki and Strickland 1973)
Self-esteem	Rosenberg Self-Esteem Scale (Rosenberg 1965)
Work attitudes Work competence	Crites Career Maturity Inventory (Crites 1978)

References

Bandura, A. 1977. *Social Learning Theory.* Englewood Cliffs, N.J.: Prentice-Hall.
Bandura, A., and R.H. Walters. 1963. *Social Learning and Personality Development.* New York: Holt, Rinehart & Winston.
Cloward, R., and L.E. Ohlin. 1960. *Delinquency and Opportunity: A Theory of Delinquent Gangs.* Glencoe, Ill.: Free Press.
Coates, R.B. 1981. "Deinstitutionalization and the Serious Juvenile Offender: Some Policy Considerations." *Crime and Delinquency* 27:477-86.
Coates, R.B., D.M. Alden, and L.E. Ohlin. 1978. *Diversity in a Youth Correctional System: Handling Delinquents in Massachusetts.* Cambridge, Mass.: Ballinger.
Crites, J. 1978. *The Career Maturity Inventory.* Beverly Hills, Calif.: Sage Publishing.
Elliott, D.S., S.S. Ageton, and R.J. Canter. 1979. "An Integrated Theoretical Perspective on Delinquent Behavior." *Journal of Research in Crime and Delinquency* 16:3-27.
Elliott, D.S., and D. Huizinga. 1984. *The Relationship between Delinquent Behavior and ADM Problems.* Boulder, Colo.: Behavioral Research Institute.
Elliott, D., D. Huizinga, and S. Ageton. 1985. *Explaining Delinquency and Drug Use.* Beverly Hills, Calif.: Sage Publishing.
Hawkins, J.D., D.M. Lishner, J.M. Jenson, and R.F. Catalano. 1986. "Delinquents and Drugs: What the Evidence Suggests about Prevention and Treatment Pro-

gramming." Paper presented at the NIDA-Technical Review on Special Youth Populations, Rockville, Md., July.

Hirschi, T. 1969. *Causes of Delinquency.* Berkeley: University of California Press.

Martinson, R. 1974. "What Works?—Questions and Answers about Prison Reform." *Public Interest* 35:22–54.

Miller, J., I. Cisin, H. Gardner-Keaton, A. Harrel, P. Wirtz, H. Abelson, and P. Fishburne. 1983. *National Survey on Drug Abuse: Main Findings—1982.* Rockville, Md.: National Institute on Drug Abuse.

Millon, T., C.J. Green, and R.B. Maegher. 1982. *Million Adolescent Personality Inventory.* Minneapolis: National Computer Systems.

Nowicki, S., and B.R. Strickland. 1973. "A Locus of Control Scale for Children." *Journal of Consulting and Clinical Psychology* 40:148–54.

Patton, M.Q. 1978. *Utilization-Focused Evaluation.* Beverly Hills, Calif.: Sage Publishing.

Rosenberg, M. 1965. *Society and the Adolescent Self-Image.* Princeton, N.J.: Princeton University Press.

Sechrest, L., S.O. White, and E. Brown. 1979. *The Rehabilitation of Criminal Offenders: Problems and Prospects.* Washington, D.C.: National Academy of Sciences.

Tjaden, C.D., K.W. Wanberg, C.J. Garrett, and J. Embree. 1986. *The Relationship between Drug Use, Delinquency and Behavioral Adjustment Problems among Committed Juvenile Offenders.* Denver: Colorado Division of Youth Services.

14
Rehabilitation of Multiple DUI Offenders: An Innovative Model

Phillip G. Sidoff
Carole Christianson
Steven P. Merrefield
Judy Brown

This chapter has four major goals:

1. To provide an overview of an innovative program being pilot tested in Colorado and aimed at intensive rehabilitation of multiple driving under the influence (DUI) offenders.
2. To review the pertinent literature that provided the context for the development of this model
3. To offer demographic and psychosocial characterization of the clients treated in the Colorado model
4. To offer suggestions for replication and extension of the model in other locations and settings

Background

Driving while under the influence of alcohol or other drugs has become a major public health and safety issue. Since 1980, attitudes among the general public with respect to drunk driving have become increasingly polarized with the emergence of Mothers Against Drunk Driving (MADD), Remove Intox-

---

The authors wish to thank the following contributors for their assistance with this project:
  Michael W. Kirby, Jr., Ph.D., executive director; Darrell Rishel, C.A.C. III, director of treatment services; Sharon Doyle, M.A., C.A.C. II; Linda Hauck, intern, Metropolitan State College; Beverly Koenigsberg, B.A., C.A.C. II, all associated with Arapahoe House Comprehensive Substance Abuse Treatment Center
  Sandra Schroth, B.A., Ann Allen and Associates; Diane Schultz and Frank Minkner, 18th Judicial Probation Department; Lieutenant Robert H. Sprecher and Sheriff Patrick J. Sullivan, Jr., Arapahoe County Sheriff's Department; David Timken, Ph.D., clinical services consultant, Colorado Department of Health, Alcohol and Drug Division; the ACRC staff, including Thomas E. Everett, director, and Paul Michael Daniel, case manager.

icated Drivers (RID), and other similar organizations, which have been highly successful in forcing legislation in the area of drinking and driving (Voas 1986). According to a report by the National Highway Traffic and Safety Administration (NHTSA), during the five legislative sessions from 1981 through 1985, states enacted 478 new alcohol safety laws (NHTSA 1985). A U.S. Bureau of Justice Statistics study indicated that arrests for DUIs increased nearly 223 percent between 1970 and 1986, while the number of licensed drivers for that same period increased only 42 percent (U.S. Bureau of Justice Statistics 1988).

This nationwide concern over drinking and driving has led to the development of a number of treatment strategies to address this difficult offender population. According to Jones and Joscelyn (1978), prior to 1970, fines, license restraints, and jail sentences were the only legal sanctions typically used by the judiciary for alcohol-involved traffic offenders. Since 1971, however, both alcohol education and treatment programs have proliferated.

In a two-part review of the literature in this area, Siegal has described the evolution of rehabilitation efforts (Siegal 1985). Siegal characterizes these efforts as first-, second-, and third-generational models.

The first generation in DWI (driving while intoxicated) or DUI treatment tended to be exclusively educational. This approach, while appealing because of its ease of implementation and relatively low cost, generally proved to be ineffective in terms of actual reduction in DUI offenses.

The second generation of programs targeted at the drunk driver derived directly from the theoretical work of McClelland (1977), which represented an effort to identify causes of drinking and driving behavior. McClelland hypothesized that problem drinkers drink because it helps them feel more powerful and in control of themselves and their surroundings. Accordingly, power motivational training (PMT) was created as a method of teaching problem drinkers coping strategies for situations in which they feel powerless. In addition, PMT offered training in relaxation techniques and social skills. As was found for the first-generation models, PMT did educate and lead to some attitude change, but DUI recidivism was not affected by the PMT model (Swenson et al. 1981).

The third generation of drunk driver rehabilitation programs as described by Siegal is exemplified by the Weekend Intervention Program, which combines the results of work with the first- and second-generation approaches, as well as concepts adapted from the employee assistance and crisis intervention areas. The Weekend Intervention Program was initiated by Siegal and colleagues. During these treatment weekends, each client receives group counseling, alcohol education, and an extensive assessment and diagnosis. These results and recommendations often become a condition for probation (Siegal 1985).

The Existing System in Colorado

Since 1979, any driver in Colorado convicted of, pleading guilty or no contest to, or receiving deferred prosecution for an alcohol-related traffic offense must undergo an evaluation to determine the extent of substance abuse. This evaluation is conducted by individuals trained and certified by the Colorado Alcohol and Drug Abuse Division (ADAD), and it must be completed prior to sentencing.

This evaluation serves as the basis for the alcohol evaluator to make a determination as to the course of education and/or treatment. This evaluation encompasses a number of indicators, including the following:

- Number of prior substance abuse–related arrests
- Blood alcohol level (BAL)
- Mortimer-Filkens score
- Prior treatment for substance abuse
- Self-reported problems because of substance abuse

Based on this evaluation, the defendant is categorized into one of three classes:

1. Social drinker or drug user
2. Incipient problem drinker or drug user
3. Problem drinker or drug user

Depending on the classification, the defendant can be sentenced to Level I education, Level II therapeutic education, or Level II treatment. Level I education consists of didactic lessons emphasizing traffic safety. Only social drinkers and drug users are referred to Level I education. Four to eight sessions of two hours each are the typical length of this program.

Level II therapeutic education combines education and group therapy. This modality is most appropriate for incipient and problem drinkers and drug users. Program length is eight to twelve sessions of two to three hours each. Group size is limited to twelve.

Level II treatment, also designed for incipient and problem drinkers and drug users, consists of individual and group therapy on either an inpatient or outpatient basis. The therapy occurs over a minimum period of four months, for twenty-six or forty hours, depending on whether the client is classified as an incipient or a problem drinker or drug user.

In 1986, ADAD undertook a study to assess the outcomes of this system across the state (Booth 1986). A total of 3,498 defendants were subjects, having been randomly selected from the state's twenty-two judicial districts. Sampling occurred from 2 to 3.5 years following arrest. The districts supplied information regarding evaluation and treatment participation, and the Colorado Division of Motor Vehicles provided driving data from before and after the arrest.

In this study, 19.6 percent of the offenders were sentenced to Level I education; 25.7 percent to Level II therapeutic education; 12.4 percent to Level II treatment; and 35.7 percent to Level II treatment and therapeutic education. An additional 6.6 percent were not sentenced to any of these modalities.

In summary, the principal findings revealed that there was a significant relationship between the intensity of the education and/or treatment and recidivism. More specifically, the highest recidivism occurred for defendants who were referred to education and/or treatment but did not enroll. The more intense the intervention, to which more severe clients were sentenced, the higher the recidivism. Participants in Level I education showed a 6 percent recidivism rate, followed by participants in Level II therapeutic education at 7 percent. Defendants referred to Level II treatment and combined treatment and education had recidivism rates of 13.5 percent and 12.8 percent, respectively.

Based on the results of this research, Booth made a number of recommendations, including the following:

> All convicted DUI clients should be referred to an education/treatment intervention unless they have been through this system several times and are unlikely to benefit from it. In these instances clients should be sentenced to jail and/or an intensive outpatient (if employed) or inpatient (if unemployed) modality. (Booth 1986, 75)

This study points to a substantial deficit in the Colorado system. Despite the fact that this system works effectively for the vast majority of defendants, those defendants who cycle through several times do not appear to benefit. The Colorado model for rehabilitation of the multiple DUI offender was developed to address this specific systems deficit, which is widely recognized among judges, evaluators, and treatment providers.

The Melding of Treatment and Corrections

Another approach to treatment of multiple DWI offenders has been jail sentencing. Voas (1986) indicates that jail sentences have been available as a penalty for drunk driving in the United States for more than 70 years. The State of New York enacted DWI law in 1910 and as early as 1924, Connecticut jailed 254 drivers for driving under the influence of alcohol. Whereas most state laws make provisions for jail terms of up to one year for drunk driving, the imposition of a jail penalty, particularly for first offenders, was rare until the last decade. (Voas 1986, 47)

Voas also notes that legislators found that "increasing the length of the jail term for drunk driving was a very easy and inexpensive approach to toughening drunk driving laws. This was easy because incarceration was a local civic responsibility only, and, therefore, did not have an impact on state budgets" (Voas 1986, 48).

The Prince George, Aspen, and Longwood treatment programs, as well as the Colorado model, represent a fourth generation of treatment approaches used in dealing with the chronic DUI recidivist.

Prince George is a minimum security dormitory-style facility located in Prince Georges County, Maryland. This program is operated by the Maryland Department of Corrections (DOC) and can accommodate fifty men and ten women. Work release is available for those who have a present job, and work assignments are provided for those who do not (Goldhamer 1987).

"The primary treatment program at the Prince George County Facility is known as the 'intervention approach.' It emphasizes the use of a crisis period (incarceration in the case of DWIs) to focus on assessment, diagnosis, denial and motivation for recovery" (Goldhamer 1987, 8). The elements of this program design also include heavy reliance on community resource organizations such as AA and MAD, among others. These community support groups are brought into the ongoing operations of the facility.

Goldhamer goes on to say, "Treatment is accomplished through small peer group sessions combined with individual counseling" (p. 9). During the evening and on weekends, residents are involved in group counseling and individual sessions. They also are shown films and engage in discussion sessions. In addition, "a primary goal of developing a year-long aftercare plan is implemented during the year of probation.... Failure to comply with treatment while on probation is a probation violation and can result in additional detention in a traditional jail facility" (p. 9).

Profiles of residents at the Prince George facility in 1985 indicated the following statistics (Goldhamer 1987):

Stage of Alcoholism	*% of Residents*
Early	30.0
Middle	48.3
Late	20.0
Social drinkers	1.7

Goldhamer describes a second program that combines incarceration and treatment at the Arizona State Prison. Aspen is a state DOC facility. When the 200-bed institution opened in 1983, it was "the first prison in the United States to house only DWI offenders" (Goldhamer 1987, 17). The Aspen program consists of a work program where "DWI offenders are expected to work 40 hours a week without compensation" (p. 18).

The Phoenix South Community Mental Health Agency provides treatment services. This program uses a variety of intervention methods. These interventions focus on alcohol education, promoting self-esteem, increasing self-awareness, breaking through denial systems, and beginning the recovery process.

AA groups are held six nights a week, and a separate Spanish-speaking AA meeting is conducted weekly. Arizona DOC policy holds that inmate program involvement is voluntary, but in reality it is "a term and condition of probation" (pp. 19–20).

The third program, the Longwood Treatment Center in urban Boston, Massachusetts, began in 1985. This is the state's first minimum security prison designed exclusively to detain and provide alcoholism education and treatment to the multiple DUI offender.

Treatment services in the 125-bed facility are provided to both men and women. Under Massachusetts's drunk driving law, second-time offenders have the option of a jail sentence or participation in one of the three 14-day residential treatment programs run by the state Department of Health. For those who have received a third DUI, sentences are between two months and two years and this time can be served in a county prison facility or at Longwood if the offender is accepted into treatment. Those excluded from treatment are offenders with prior histories of violent crimes. "The advantages of Longwood over prison include its treatment program and an environment conducive to treatment. All residents are subject to reduction in sentence time and release date depending on their involvement in treatment" (Goldhamer 1987, 12).

The Longwood treatment program uses the services of a private treatment provider and the DOC staff. Its therapeutic approach is that of reality therapy.

Treatment consists of three phases, each lasting approximately four to six weeks. The client must satisfy a review board that he or she has accomplished phase 1 goals before moving on to the next phase. These goals consist of an understanding of the disease process of chemical dependence and insight into the cause and effect relationship between chemical dependence and life manageability. Phase 2 goals include the ability to identify and share unmanageable life situations with others, use of AA, and understanding the process of relapse. Upon completion of this phase, the offender moves into phase 3, which involves community service, work release for those eligible, and aftercare planning (Goldhamer 1987).

Outcome findings indicate that from 1985 to 1987, approximately five hundred sentenced offenders completed treatment. Of that group, only 6 percent had returned to prison, as opposed to a Massachusetts DOC recidivism rate of 25 percent (LeClair, Felici, and Klotzbin 1987).

The Colorado Model for Rehabilitation of Multiple DUI Offenders

The DUI Task Force

The impetus for the development of a program designed specifically to address the multiple DUI offender program in Colorado derived from a task force created by ADAD in 1985. In April 1986, Arapahoe House presented a concept paper to this task force proposing two models of varying intensity for the multiple DUI offender. Based on a review of the literature available at that time, the paper identified six key elements that must be incorporated in any program concentrating on multiple DUI offenders:

1. The program must be highly intensive.
2. Although educational material should be included, the major emphasis should be on a confrontational therapeutic approach.
3. The criteria for noncompliance with the program need to be clearly defined and understood, and when these criteria are met, the legal alternative to treatment must be immediate, unequivocal, and severe in consequences.
4. Because one ultimate objective is to help these clients become more productive citizens, the program should be designed to interfere minimally with their employment or ability to pursue gainful employment.
5. The program should occur over a minimum period of twelve months and be structured to ensure continuous sobriety throughout this period.
6. The proposed model must be economically feasible, offering a cost/benefit ratio that will afford implementation in a number of locations throughout the state via a combination of client fees, fines, and reasonable state reimbursement rates.

The model that was implemented represented an integrated combination of a correctional setting and an established substance abuse treatment provider. Some background about these two key entities is necessary.

Arapahoe House is a not-for-profit comprehensive alcohol and drug abuse treatment center established in 1976. The major modalities of treatment are nonmedical detoxification, short-term intensive residential treatment, intermediate residential treatment, a transitional living and vocational program, adolescent and family services, and five outpatient clinics.

The Arapahoe County Residential Center (ACRC) is a private corrections program operated by Community Corrections, Inc. (CCI). CCI contracts with public correctional agencies. Many of the offenders residing at the community corrections facility have been placed there by the Arapahoe County courts through the Arapahoe County Sheriff's Department. The principal focus of ACRC is on resident accountability and public protection rather than on constituting a therapeutic milieu per se.

Thus, in the model, the correctional facility provides the residential setting, monitoring, and security for clients. The substance abuse treatment provider is responsible for the structure of the educational and therapeutic programming for clients. Obviously, it is essential that the correctional setting and the treatment program operate in a coordinated and consistent manner.

Phases 1, 2, and 3

The residential portion of the Colorado model consists of three discrete phases occurring over a period of twenty weeks:

1. Phase 1 is six weeks in duration, encompassing five 2-hour therapy groups per week and three special activity groups.
2. Phase 2 also extends for six weeks, with a configuration of therapy and special activity groups identical to that of the first phase.
3. Phase 3 lasts eight weeks, during which clients are employed during the day and participate in three 2-hour evening therapy groups each week.

Twice-weekly AA meetings that began in phase 1 are continued throughout the second and third phases. Following the residential segment, clients participate in twenty-six weeks of aftercare, which is an outpatient program offered at any of five Arapahoe House outpatient clinics. Additionally, clients remain under legal electronic monitoring supervision for the balance of their sentence. Electronic monitoring permits the clients to live at home yet serve their jail sentence. This form of supervision permits a graduated reduction of structure and a reminder of the fact that the client remains under sentence. For some, it provides a needed external influence to structure their lives and help them avoid acting on impulse.

Phase 1 is oriented toward a comprehensive assessment of each client, including extensive face-to-face interviewing conducted by two therapists. This assessment incorporates administration of several standardized instruments, including the Addiction Severity Index (NIDA 1988), the Millon Clinical Multi-Axis Inventory (Millon 1987), and a psychosocial history.

No unsupervised activities are permitted during phase 1. In phase 2, a limited number of unsupervised activities are allowed. Clients can begin to fulfill their community service obligations and may use assigned segments of time for productive activities, such as reading, exercise, or vocational and academic studies.

Phase 1 and 2 clients all participate in the special activity groups, which are considered a companion piece to the therapy component and continually integrate new material into the two-hour daily therapy format. Topics covered include medical aspects of alcoholism and drug dependence, the phases of alcohol and drug addiction, relapse dynamics, and structured stress and anger management classes. Additionally, all clients are required to keep a daily feelings journal; to write an autobiography that focuses on behavior patterns, family structure, and alcohol and drug abuse history; and to share their story with the group.

A key component of the special activity groups is a series of lectures and experiential exercises used to accelerate the facilitation of group bonding. In addition, clients can practice self-disclosing and learn how to both give and accept feedback in a nonthreatening context.

Phase 3 concentrates on reintegration into the community and development of an aftercare plan. In addition, a three-part family education series is offered, as is couples counseling. Admission criteria for the Colorado multiple DUI offender program are shown in table 14–1.

Table 14–1
Admission Criteria for Colorado Multiple DUI Offender Program

1. Minimum sentence to serve of 12 months
2. Screening for the multiple DUI offender, which is done cooperatively by personnel from Arapahoe House and Arapahoe County Residential Center
3. Client must have two or more previous substance abuse–related driving arrests
4. Client must have a previous history of court-ordered referral to an alcohol education program and/or therapeutic substance abuse treatment program
5. Candidate must be eighteen years or older
6. Absence of substance withdrawal syndrome
7. Absence of medical or psychiatric condition that would result in danger to self or others
8. Client must agree to follow through with basic procedures, including abstinence, treatment participation, and adherence to all rules and regulations of the community correctional facility
9. Client must be capable of caring for self, capable of performing daily activities, and physically eligible for job placement
10. Client must have mental capacity to comprehend group process and daily assignments
11. Client's criminal behavior must be capable of being directly reduced by substance abuse intervention

Preliminary Results

Complicating the alcohol and/or drug dependence problems with the repeat offender are secondary pathologic characteristics that may include antisocial personality patterns, often manifest in defiance toward authority, as well as risk-taking behaviors. Although no one personality pattern has emerged, the clients in this program appear to be low in self-esteem and to exhibit self-defeating behavior. Feeling powerless to control their substance abuse and their world, these clients sometimes attempt to recapture power via rule breaking and manipulation. Feelings of helplessness and victimization at the hands of an unfair legal system, reinforced by residential confinement, are recurrent treatment issues often encountered during the first several weeks of group therapy.

Failure/Success of Groups

The first group, consisting of ten participants, commenced in March 1988. Two of the ten terminated prior to completion of the residential portion of the program. One of these participants chose to return to jail, stating that the program was too intense. The second participant was discharged because of a positive urinalysis for alcohol. Five of the remaining eight participants completed the residential portion of the program. Two of the three who did not complete terminated because of sentence expiration; the third participant terminated in phase 3 by obtaining a reconsideration of his sentence.

The second group began treatment in November 1988 and completed the first two phases of the residential portion in January 1989. This group consisted of nine participants, all of whom successfully completed the first two phases and were enrolled in the third phase when this book went to press.

The most important indicator of success for a program of this nature is recidivism. These data will be collected for all participants at annual intervals.

Clinical and Programmatic Observations

The basic model described in this chapter has six essential elements:

1. It is highly intensive, both in terms of the weekly schedule and the length of the program.
2. It combines the correctional residential setting, which is requisite to adequate monitoring and supervision of these clients, with focused and time-tested substance abuse treatment methods.
3. It emphasizes group therapy and development of a group process.

4. The program and its rules must be strictly adhered to, and failure to comply carries clear, swift, and unambiguous consequences.
5. Cofacilitators, one male and one female, are present for most group activities, which simultaneously enhances their ability to observe and interact with group members and their ability to provide support to one another.
6. Therapy focuses on the here and now, using reality therapy, confrontation, and feedback as salient techniques.

Summary and Future Applications

The multiple DUI offender program targets the treatment of drunk drivers who have had repeated contact with the law. These offenders have failed to respond to traditional treatment and education programs. Likewise, periods of incarceration have failed to produce lifestyle changes.

Typically, few sentencing choices have been available to the courts. Therefore, the usual sentence involves recycling the offender through treatment programs previously offered or mandating a long jail sentence without treatment. The multiple DUI offender program presents another option by permitting a relatively long jail sentence but providing an intensive opportunity to changing behavior. The unusual blend of correctional and service agencies involved emphasizes the fulfillment of elements of punishment, restructuring, and caring.

No conclusions can be formed from the small sample group, but data are being generated early in an effort to evaluate program results and to begin guiding agencies in identifying offenders' profiles, which will improve the selection of participants. For example, this program is inappropriate for offenders who can respond to less intensive programs or for hard-core offenders who are treatment resistant.

There is no doubt that the number of legally supervised persons is growing at an alarming rate. The findings of a U.S. Bureau of Justice Statistics survey conducted in 1983 indicate that about 7 percent of all persons confined in local jails on June 30, 1983, were either charged with or convicted of DUI and nearly 13 percent of these inmates had a current charge or prior conviction for DUI (U.S. Bureau of Justice Statistics 1988).

The Colorado Community Corrections Program supervises offenders in community-based residential programs. Offenders are placed either by the courts as a "diversion" from prison or by the DOC as a transition from prison back to the community. It is at the community residential program level that a program model based on the multiple DUI offender program presents a unique opportunity for a pilot program application.

References

Booth, R. 1986. *Education/Treatment Intervention among Drinking Drivers and Recidivism.* Denver: Colorado Department of Health, Alcohol and Drug Abuse Division.

Bureau of Justice Statistics. 1988. *Drunk Driving.* Rockville, Md.: U.S. Department of Justice.

Goldhamer, A. 1987. *Drunk Driver Treatment: An Overview of Three Model Centers.* National Association of State Alcohol and Drug Abuse Directors.

Jones, R.K., and K.B. Joscelyn. 1978. *Alcohol and Highway Safety, 1978: A Review of the State of Knowledge Summary.* Ann Arbor: University of Michigan, Highway Safety Research Institute.

LeClair, D., L. Felici, and E. Klotzbin. 1987. *The Use of Prison Confinement for the Treatment of Multi-User Driver Offenders: An Evaluation of Longwood Treatment Center.* Boston: Massachusetts Department of Corrections.

McClelland, D. 1977. "The Impact of Power Motivation Training on Alcoholics." *Journal of Studies on Alcohol* 38 (1): 142–44.

Millon, T. 1987. *Manual for the MCMI-II.* (2d ed.) Minneapolis: National Computer Systems.

NHTSA. 1985. *National Commission against Drunk Driving: A Progress Report on the Implementation of Recommendations by the Presidential Commission on Drunk Driving.* DOT pub. no. AS 806-885. Washington, D.C.: GPO.

NIDA. 1988. *Guide to the Addiction Severity Index: Background, Administration and Field Testing Results.* DHHS pub. no. ADM 88-1419. Washington, D.C.: GPO.

Siegal, H.A. 1985. "The Intervention Approach to Drunk Driver Rehabilitation. Parts 1 & 2." *International Journal of the Addictions* 20 (5): 661–89.

Swenson, P.R., D.L. Struckman-Johnson, V.S. Ellingstag, T.R. Clay, and J.L. Nichols. 1981. "Results of a Longitudinal Evaluation of Court-Mandated DWI Treatment Programs in Phoenix, Arizona." *Journal of Studies on Alcohol* 42 (7): 642–52.

Voas, R. 1986. "Evaluation of Jail as a Penalty for Drunk Driving." *Alcohol, Drugs and Driving* 2: 47–70.

Part V
Treatment Alternatives

Prologue

Howard J. Shaffer

> Observer: Danny can get him sober. He's done it before.
> Danny: ... I need two aspirin, some tomato juice and some Worcestershire sauce.
> Observer: Two aspirin, and some tomato juice?
> Danny: Right, and some goat cheese and some chicken fat.
> Second Observer: That should do it. That's the Danny Rose formula. I still can't figure out how it works.
> Danny: I promise you're going to be OK tonight. My hand to God.
> —Woody Allen, Broadway Danny Rose

Mark Twain said, "When your only tool is a hammer, then every problem is a nail." In substance abuse treatment, as with other fields of health care, practice follows theory. Theories or models of substance abuse determine how, when, and where clinicians intervene. These conceptual systems guide treatment. They determine the nature of chemical dependence problems.

Chapter 16 describes, for example, how the conceptual system of cognitive-behavioral theory differs from that of the traditional disease model and how cognitive-behavioral theory generates specific assessment and treatment activities on the part of the therapist.

Theory also determines whether a substance-abusing person will accept help. Because these theoretical models identify the nature of potential solutions, treatment alternatives are either accepted or rejected by prospective patients and their lay explanation of addiction.

In the United States, for example, 85 to 90 percent of the population believes that alcoholism is a disease (Caetano 1987; Shaffer 1987). Yet, in the first part of this century, only 20 to 25 percent of the population held this belief (Room 1983). This change in perception is the result of a social learning process. Other cultures do not perceive substance abuse as do Americans. Because of the enormous growth of interest in the field of substance abuse and addictive behavior, as well as the popularity of the disease model, this is a time for special contemplation and consideration.

For example, Orford (1985) notes with concern that the popularity of the disease model has led to the application of psychosurgery for addictive behavior patterns. Clinicians have used psychosurgery—electroconvulsive shock treatment, or lobotomy—as a treatment for heroin, alcohol, cocaine, and gambling addictions. In spite of this excessive and inappropriate use of treatment choices, most drug treatment programs apply treatment uniformly. Drug treatment services, particularly inpatient units, employ a uniformity of treatments that ignore the individual. There is little prescriptive treatment planning. I would encourage clinicians, for example, to read a patient's treatment plan to the rest of the staff working on an inpatient drug treatment service. Can the staff identify the patient from their treatment plan? In the majority of drug treatment settings, the staff cannot. Health care providers can readily identify patients from treatment plans on intensive care, neurology, surgery, and other medical care units.

As chapter 15 demonstrates, research findings do not support the efficacy of the most popular substance abuse treatment interventions. Treatment must be prescriptive if clinical efforts are to be more successful. Prescriptive treatment for substance-abusing patients requires that we "make contact" (Havens 1986). Clinicians need to obtain a better understanding of the experience of being a substance abuser (Kleinman 1988). Drug treatment specialists need to discover what drug abuse and addiction mean to their patients. This process permits clinicians to develop treatment interventions individually and prescriptively.

In chapter 15, Miller briefly identifies a major shortcoming of contemporary substance abuse treatment: "denial busting." It is quite common to hear clinicians talk about addiction as a "disease of denial." This view implies the necessity to break through the denial. Without understanding exactly what drug abuse means to an individual, however, confronting and destroying denial can be therapeutically destructive. Patients can experience this confrontation as psychotherapeutic persecution.

In fact, treatment may not be the reason patients remain sober. It is more likely that their posttreatment life maintains their abstinence and minimizes their risk of relapse (Marlatt and Gordon 1985; Shaffer and Jones 1989). Treatment may provide a "safe place" (Havens in press) where patients gather their resources to change the structure of their lives. From this perspective, we can expect that natural recovery (that is, recovery without formal treatment interventions) is not only possible but is the predominant mode of behavior change. Conversely, there are many substance abusers who need help to change their excessive patterns of behavior. In chapter 18, Harris examines treatment models that emphasize the need to change the structure of family relationships. These changes are essential to the process of recovery, regardless of the recovery change methods. Chapter 19 demonstrates the critical need for ongoing family involvement in successful intervention for adolescents with substance abuse problems.

There are many entrances to substance abuse, but most people think that there are only two exits from addiction: treatment and death. There is a third option: natural recovery. Do you know someone who stopped smoking cigarettes? How did he or she do it? Almost everyone knows someone who stopped a cigarette habit on his or her own, without any treatment. The process of natural recovery occurs with illicit as well as licit drugs (Stall and Biernacki 1986). Shaffer and Jones (1989) found that this phenomenon also occurs with compulsive cocaine addicts.

Researchers estimate that as many as 90 percent of ex-smokers stop without any assistance. If, as the Surgeon General reports, tobacco produces physical dependence equal to dependence on heroin, then it should not surprise you to learn that other drug addicts also stop without treatment. Researchers estimate that addicts recover from illegal drug addiction between about 10 and 60 percent of the time.

Many people avoid treatment because they feel guilty about having the problem. They assume that they are capable of overcoming it on their own. Some people simply do not like or trust treatment professionals. They want to escape the stigma of labeling. They do not want someone to call them an alcoholic or addict. Research demonstrates that these patient concerns are correct (Rohman et al. 1987). At times, treatment providers do hold moral objections against these patients. Sometimes their clinical treatment offerings are very difficult to distinguish from retribution. Treatment providers should be aware of this concern and recognize that they do not have the *only* answer.

Chapter 17 reminds us that there are important affective and regulatory approaches that reside with the patient. Recovering people can learn to alter their consciousness naturally so that exogenous chemicals become less meaningful. Chapter 16 likewise addresses how change in the patient's cognitive processes can facilitate recovery from substance abuse. Similarly, chapter 20 demonstrates that behavioral contingencies, not insight, may be among the more important substance abuse treatment options.

Vaillant has demonstrated the need for an understanding of the natural history of substance abuse problems. In his classic work on the natural history of alcoholism, Vaillant (1983) notes the importance of natural healing processes. Shaffer and Jones (1989) suggest that natural cocaine quitters (that is, expert recoverers) have much to teach professional treatment providers. According to this view, addiction treatment specialists should think about how to facilitate natural paths to recovery.

Treatment providers must be ever vigilant to ensure that their attempts to treat do not make their patients worse. There are few situations so bad that we cannot make them worse. Prescriptive treatment helps prevent unnecessary and irrelevant interventions. When clinical interventions result from careful assessment, clinicians can determine which treatment approach, for which patient, at which phase of recovery will work best for which therapist (Marlatt 1988). Treatment evaluation and quality assurance also are essential. These evaluative techniques provide the instruments necessary to document recovery from addictive disorders by directed as well as natural processes.

References

Caetano, R. 1987. "Public Opinions about Alcoholism and Its Treatment." *Journal of Studies on Alcohol* 47:153–60.

Havens, L. 1986. *Making Contact*. Cambridge, Mass.: Harvard University Press.

———. In press. *Safe Places*. Cambridge, Mass.: Harvard University Press.

Kleinman, A. 1988. *The Illness Narratives: Suffering, Healing and the Human Condition*. New York: Basic Books.

Marlatt, G.A. 1988. "Matching Clients to Treatment: Treatment Models and Stages of Change." In *Assessment of Addictive Behaviors*, edited by D.M. Donovan and G.A. Marlatt, 474–83. New York: Guilford Press.

Marlatt, G.A., and J. Gordon, eds. 1985. *Relapse Prevention: Maintenance Strategies in the Treatment of Addictive Behaviors*. New York: Guilford Press.

Orford, J. 1985. *Excessive Appetites: A Psychological View of Addictions*. New York: John Wiley & Sons.

Rohman, M.E., P.D. Cleary, M. Warburg, T.L. Delbanco, M.D. Aronson. 1987. "The Response of Primary Care Physicians to Problem Drinkers." *American Journal of Drug and Alcohol Abuse* 13: 199–209.

Room, R. 1983. "Sociological Aspects of the Disease Concept of Alcoholism." In *Research Advances in Alcohol and Drug Problems*, Vol. 7, edited by R. G. Smart, F.B. Glasev, Y. Israel, H. Kalant, R.E. Popham, and W. Schmidt. 47–91. New York: Plenum Press.

Shaffer, H.J. 1987. "The Epistemology of "Addictive Disease": The Lincoln-Douglas Debate." *Journal of Substance Abuse Treatment* 4:103–13.

Shaffer, H.J., S.B. Jones. 1989. *Quitting Cocaine: The Struggle against Impulse*. Lexington, Mass.: Lexington Books.

Stall, R., P. Biernacki. 1986. "Spontaneous Remission from the Problematic Use of Substances: An Inductive Model Derived from a Comparative Analysis of the Alcohol, Opiate, Tobacco and Food/Obesity Literatures." *International Journal of the Addictions* 21:1–23.

Vaillant, G. 1983. *The Natural History of Alcoholism*. Cambridge, Mass.: Harvard University Press.

15
Alcohol Treatment Alternatives: What Works?

William R. Miller

What works in the treatment of alcohol problems? The question is highly charged and hotly contested. It is a political question, with multibillion-dollar implications for an ever-growing alcohol treatment industry. Most professionals in the field have strong opinions about how to treat alcohol problems properly and effectively.

It is also an empirical question that can be answered by adherence to the canons of scientific method. Within a broadly scientific view, treatment interventions can be seen as independent variables with a hypothesized impact on certain dependent variables (outcomes). The effectiveness of a particular treatment, then, is subject to experimental verification. A well-designed experiment will examine the impact of treatment on outcome while controlling for the influence of other variables. The usual procedure to accomplish this in treatment outcome research is the randomized clinical trial in which individuals are assigned at random to alternative treatment conditions. With a sufficient sample size, randomization effectively equates groups on pretreatment characteristics. Thus, differences observed between groups can more confidently be attributed to the impact of treatment.

With the help of my colleague Reid Hester, I have spent part of the past ten years reviewing research on the effectiveness of different approaches to the treatment of alcohol problems. The literature is enormous, now comprising more than six hundred studies, of which about two hundred are controlled clinical trials. In the course of reading this literature, it became evident to us that the results of properly controlled studies are much more consistent than are those reported from uncontrolled research. Uncontrolled reports often vary widely in their rates of successful outcome, which can be affected by differences in many factors other than the treatment itself (such as population characteristics, variations in treatment procedures, and criteria for success ratings). In contrast, treatment methods found to have a specific effect on alcohol problems in one well-designed study often show a similar effect in other studies. Other treatments that have appeared to be successful in uncontrolled reports are consistently found to be ineffective when proper controls are employed. This has renewed our confidence in the controlled trial as a reliable indicator of treatment effectiveness.

In this chapter, it is not possible to provide a comprehensive review of treatment research. Documentation for the points to be discussed here can be found in other detailed reviews (Miller and Hester 1980; Miller and Hester 1986a; Miller and Hester 1986b; Miller and Hester 1986c). Here I attempt to provide some "bottom line" conclusions that have immediate and practical implications for the treatment of alcohol problems. In drawing these conclusions, I have relied most heavily (for reasons just discussed) on the findings of randomized clinical trials and other studies that have controls for the influence of confounding variables.

Five Myths of Treatment

In my reviews with Hester, I have been impressed by the fact that the conclusions one would draw from the available controlled studies of treatment are greatly at variance with current common beliefs about how alcohol problems should be treated. Treatment programs in the United States have been guided by a largely unproven philosophy of the nature of alcohol problems and their remission.

There are at least five common beliefs about the treatment of alcohol problems that are not substantiated by current evidence. These beliefs are not necessarily consistent with one another, and all five are not likely to be held by the same individual. Each one, however, represents a view that is seemingly frequent among professionals and/or the general public.

1. No one recovers without treatment. One common myth, now particularly promoted by advertisements for treatment programs, is the view that no one recovers from alcohol problems without receiving treatment. To the contrary, longitudinal studies of untreated individuals show that alcohol problems remit in the natural environment over time (Donovan, Jessor, and Jessor 1983; Fillmore and Midanik 1984; Ösejö 1981). In a forty-year longitudinal study, Vaillant (1983) reported that the rate of recovery among untreated individuals was similar to that of persons who received treatment for alcohol problems. Similar evidence has emerged from controlled trials that have observed significant improvement, sometimes comparable to that of treated groups, among individuals receiving only brief interventions (Chick et al. 1988; Edwards et al. 1977; Kristenson et al. 1983).

Such change is not properly described as spontaneous. Remission without treatment often occurs in response to specific life experiences and discrete events in the natural environment (Tuchfeld 1981). This is consistent with the finding that outcomes after treatment are much less influenced by treatment events than by experiences and conditions in the individual's life following treatment (Finney, Moos, and Mewborn 1980).

2. Nothing works. A second myth is that alcoholism cannot be treated effectively, that nothing really works. This is clearly refuted by evidence from controlled treatment trials, about 40 percent of which have reported significant benefits from specific treatments. Even brief interventions have been shown to yield significantly more improvement than no treatment at all (Elvy, Wells, and Baird 1988; Heather, Whitton and Robertson 1986; Kristenson et al. 1983).

3. Everything works about equally well. A third myth is that all forms of treatment for alcohol problems work about equally well. It follows from this that the specific content of a treatment program is not a matter of great consequence. This reduces to a cynicism not unlike the second myth—that nothing works. In fact, there appear to be substantial differences in the effectiveness of available treatment alternatives. Some treatment modalities have received strong support from research to date, whereas others are rather consistently found to be of little benefit (Miller and Hester 1986a). There is no ground for deeming *all* forms of treatment effective. Well-designed comparative studies have reported substantial differences in effectiveness among alternative treatments (see, for example, Azrin et al. 1982).

4. There is one superior treatment. A fourth myth is that there is a single treatment of choice for alcohol problems. The assertion is that although there are different treatments, one approach stands head and shoulders above the rest in its effectiveness. Others are a second choice if, for some reason, the best treatment does not work. The fact is that no single treatment approach can legitimately claim superiority to all others. No one treatment has been shown to work for all, or even most people who receive it. Rather than one treatment of choice, we have at our disposal a range of promising alternatives to try.

5. Hospital treatment is most effective. Finally, contemporary advertising creates the impression that treatment in a specialized hospital is the only (or at least the most) effective way to address alcohol problems. There is no reasonable support to be found for this belief among the controlled studies on treatment outcome. Randomized comparative trials have found no overall advantage for residential, intensive, or longer treatment over less expensive alternatives. Inpatient and outpatient programs have been found to yield comparable rates of successful outcomes, and increasing the length of residential stay does not result in superior long-term improvement (Miller and Hester 1986b).

In fact, several randomized trials have found that well-planned, brief interventions consisting of assessment plus one session of counseling yield outcomes similar to those following more intensive treatment (Chapman and Huygens 1988; Chick et al. 1988; Edwards et al. 1977; Miller, Taylor, and West 1980; Zweben in press).

Specific Treatment Modalities

More than thirty specific treatment methods have been evaluated for their impact on alcohol problems (Miller and Hester 1980). For most of these, initial uncontrolled evaluations have reported positive outcomes. When subjected to the more stringent test of properly controlled trials, however, many have failed to show a significant beneficial impact—often contrary to the expectations of the investigators.

Alcohol-Suppressing Strategies

What methods have been found to be effective? Based on a review of the controlled studies (Miller and Hester 1986a), empirically supported strategies seem to fall into one of two categories. The first of these consists of strategies that have a direct suppressing effect on alcohol consumption itself. Three strategies of this kind appear particularly promising.

Aversion therapies are designed to help the individual lose his or her desire for alcohol and to develop a distaste for drinking. Different approaches have been tried. Electric shock aversion (pairing drinking with shocks) produced inconsistent results and has largely been abandoned. Nausea-producing drugs such as emetine and ipecac also have been used for half a century in alcohol aversion therapy. After administration of the drug, the person is exposed to his or her favorite alcoholic beverages while becoming nauseous and eventually vomiting. This approach can produce a strong aversion to alcohol (Cannon and Baker 1981; Cannon et al. 1986), but no well-controlled evaluations have been reported. Positive results also have been reported using covert sensitization, a form of aversion therapy conducted totally through imagery (Elkins 1980; Rimmele 1988). When conducted on an individual basis in a manner that produces conditioning, covert sensitization appears to suppress alcohol consumption after treatment.

Behavioral self-control training involves teaching a variety of self-regulation strategies designed to help clients modify their own drinking (Miller and Muñoz 1982). It can be conducted with either an abstinence or a moderation goal (Sanchez-Craig 1984). Research has shown self-control training to be superior to no intervention, alcohol education, and briefer or alternative treatments (Miller and Hester 1986a).

Disulfiram is a medication that, taken daily, causes a person to become ill if he or she consumes alcohol. Several recent and well-designed studies have found no benefit from prescription of disulfiram, although clients who take the medication faithfully do show more improvement. This suggests that disulfiram should be accompanied by a compliance program designed to ensure that the medication is taken. In a well-designed study, Azrin et al. (1982) demonstrated that a simple compliance program (involving the spouse or significant other as a monitor) markedly increased the success of treatment with disulfiram. For married clients, the disulfiram compliance procedures proved as effective as a more intensive treatment approach and substantially better than traditional outpatient treatment.

Broad Spectrum Strategies

The second category of empirically supported strategies might be termed *broad spectrum*. These strategies focus on life problems other than drinking that may be functionally related to alcohol problems. The strategy is to prevent relapse by helping the individual cope successfully with problems that might otherwise encourage resumption of drinking. This again is consistent with the finding that outcome is influenced by post-treatment life experiences (Finny, Moos and Mewborn 1980).

Social skills training has received consistently positive support in a series of controlled trials. The typical study has compared outcomes following a multiple-component alcoholism treatment program with or without the addition of social skills training. Clients receiving social skills training (randomly assigned) have been found in several studies to fare better during follow-up than those receiving the same treatment without social skills training. The training has typically focused on effective communication skills, assertion, and resistance to peer pressure.

Behavioral marital therapy also has been shown to improve marital functioning of alcoholics and to decrease post-treatment drinking and problems. This form of therapy commonly focuses on improving communication patterns and increasing positive shared experiences of the couple.

Stress management strategies, designed to decrease posttreatment tension and anxiety, have been found to be of benefit when added to treatment. Relaxation training alone has yielded mixed results, but positive findings have been reported with systematic desensitization, aerobic exercise, biofeedback, and stress management training.

Substantial treatment effects have been reported in evaluations of the *community reinforcement approach* (Azrin 1976; Azrin et al. 1982). This approach combines a variety of broad spectrum strategies, including job-finding training, behavioral marital therapy, monitored disulfiram, and problem-solving training. In comparison with traditional treatment strategies, the community reinforcement approach has yielded some of the largest effects in the alcohol treatment literature (Miller and Hester 1986a).

On the whole, positive studies to date indicate that successful treatment consists of strategies to help clients suppress their drinking (and, perhaps, their urges to drink) and interventions to alter other life problems that could lead to relapse. Programs that have combined both types of strategies (see, for example, Azrin et al. 1982) have yielded strong treatment effects.

Traditional Strategies

The strategies typically used in U.S. treatment programs overlap little, if at all, with the foregoing list of methods found to be effective interventions. Although there is substantial variance in the content of programs, several common elements emerge as components of traditional treatment.

Alcoholics Anonymous (AA) is by far the most common element of U.S. programs. Treatment is often guided by an AA philosophy, and clients are often urged or required to attend AA meetings. By its very nature, AA is difficult to evaluate. Reported correlations between AA attendance and abstinence are common, but causal interpretation is difficult: Does AA cause abstinence, or do people drop out of AA as they resume drinking? Only four controlled trials of AA strategies, each with methodological problems, have been reported to date (Brandsma, Maultsby, and Welsh 1980; Ditman et al. 1967; Powell et al. 1985; Stimmel et al. 1983). None of these has found a beneficial treatment effect.

Some form of *counseling* or *psychotherapy* is commonly offered, often with a confrontational focus. Many controlled trials, however, have failed to show any beneficial treatment effect from generic alcoholism counseling or insight-oriented psychotherapy. The confrontational style typical of alcoholism counseling has been found to be associated with poorer outcomes. Positive treatment effects are rather consistently linked with the therapeutic style described by Carl Rogers as "empathy" (Miller 1985; Miller, Taylor, and West 1980; Valle 1981). Confrontational counseling may be particularly detrimental with low self-esteem clients (Annis and Chan, 1983). *Group psychotherapy* likewise has consistently been found to be of no therapeutic value in controlled evaluations of its efficacy.

Educational films and lectures are traditional components of alcoholism treatment but have never been shown to yield a beneficial impact on drinking outcomes. Informational strategies have been more thoroughly evaluated within prevention programs, where they have typically been found to have no positive impact on alcohol and drug use.

Medications, particularly disulfiram, are frequently prescribed for alcoholics. Disulfiram has been found to be no more effective than a placebo in its impact on post-treatment drinking, except where specific compliance-ensuring strategies have been included (Azrin et al. 1982). Compliance assurance has not typically been used by programs prescribing disulfiram. No other medication has been shown to produce a beneficial effect on alcohol abuse (Miller and Hester 1986a).

In short, the components of a typical U.S. alcoholism treatment program have never been shown to be effective. The combination of such strategies into an intensive or hospital-based program appears to yield no better outcomes than more minimal alternatives (Miller and Hester 1986b). Although favorable improvement rates have been reported in uncontrolled studies of such programs (see, for example, Alford 1980), causal inferences cannot be made based on such studies, and successes may be attributable to uncontrolled factors such as the pretreatment characteristics or post-treatment experiences of those treated. Treatment strategies that have been supported by methodologically sound studies remain largely unused in current U.S. programs.

Client-Treatment Matching

Because treatment approaches are diverse, the question "Does treatment work?" cannot be answered simply. Equally diverse are the clients who present themselves for treatment. New research increasingly confronts us with the heterogeneity of individuals with alcohol problems. Rather than a single, unitary disorder, alcohol problems appear to be multifaceted and highly variable among individuals.

In this context, it is likewise unrealistic to ask "Which treatment is best?" No treatment is optimal for all individuals. For each specific treatment, however, it may be possible to identify characteristics of individuals who respond well. It appears that these "responder" profiles are not consistent across treatments. That is, the predictors of favorable outcome are not the same for all treatments but vary substantially. In fact, client characteristics that predict failure with one treatment may predict success with another (Miller and Hester 1986c). Given two different treatments, precisely opposite types of individuals may be optimal candidates.

This has several important implications. First, it is inappropriate to offer the same treatment program or components to all clients. What benefits one may be detrimental to another (see, for example, Annis and Chan 1983). Second, treatment plans should be tailored to the needs and characteristics of the individual. Treatment goals, settings, and strategies should be matched to the client. Third, this means that a comprehensive treatment system needs to include a range of effective alternatives to which clients may be matched. There is wisdom, too, in building in a feedback system to detect matching errors: Which clients were inappropriately assigned to each treatment?

The literature on matching is relatively recent (Miller and Hester 1986c). It appears that severity of alcohol problems or dependence may be an important differential predictor. Those with more severe alcohol problems seem to fare better with an abstinence goal and may benefit differentially from more intensive treatment. In contrast, less severe problem drinkers may have a better prognosis with briefer interventions and a moderation goal. Residential treatment may be optimal for socially unstable (homeless or indigent) individuals with more severe alcohol dependence (Miller and Hester 1986b). Client preferences, cognitive style, and personality characteristics may affect the probability of success with specific treatment approaches (Miller and Hester 1986c).

Conclusions

What works? The question is, in many ways, too simplistic to answer. Based on currently available research, however, six conclusions seem justifiable.

1. Alcoholism treatment can be quite effective. Positive clinical trials demonstrating significant treatment effects are encouragingly evident in the literature. This is not to be taken as an unqualified endorsement of *all* alcoholism treatment approaches or efforts but rather as a reason for optimism about the effectiveness of *some* approaches.

2. There is no one superior approach. No single treatment method has been shown convincingly to be more effective than all others. A good analogy here is a deck of playing cards. In the alcoholism field, we do not have a single ace, or even a pair or trio of aces, but rather a larger deck of alternatives. If you are using only one approach in your own treatment efforts, you are not playing with a full deck.

3. Not all treatment approaches are equal in effectiveness. Pursuing the previous analogy, not all cards in the deck are equally powerful. Controlled clinical trials provide support for a finite number of strategies, including aversion therapies, behavioral self-control training, monitored disulfiram, social skills training, behavioral marital therapy, stress management, and community reinforcement. What these strategies have in common, aside from their support in the scientific literature, is the fact that they are rarely used in current U.S. treatment practice. In contrast, the typical components of current treatment programs have in common a lack of empirical evidence for effectiveness. Those in alcoholism treatment seem to have been relying on a limited range of "playing cards" with relatively low numbers while leaving unused some "face cards" with apparently greater impact. It follows that the efficacy of alcoholism treatment could be substantially improved by incorporating those strategies that have been supported as having a specific impact on alcohol problems.

4. *Optimal treatment varies with client characteristics.* In the card game of bridge, which card will win a hand depends on the suit that is led. An ace of clubs is useless when hearts have been led. People with alcohol problems are not a homogeneous population and do not respond uniformly to treatment programs. Alcohol problems are not unitary in nature. The outcomes of treatments apparently differ substantially according to the characteristics of individuals. Further, current data suggest that treatment should be addressed not only to alcohol and other drug use but also to the person's broader spectrum of life problems. Finding the best treatment is not a matter of settling on any single formula or program. If we follow the witness of the hundreds of studies now available, we will expand the range of options employed in treatment. Perhaps more importantly, we will fashion treatment programs to fit the characteristics of individual clients rather than pressing clients to fit the characteristics of the programs.

5. *Length, intensity, and setting of treatment do not appear to be powerful determinants of overall effectiveness.* The outcome of a card game is not much affected by where it is played. Hospital and outpatient settings seem to yield comparable success rates in alcoholism treatment. The outcome of treatment may be more affected by what is done than by where it is done. Even rather brief but well-planned outpatient interventions have been found to have a significant beneficial effect for alcohol abusers and in some cases to be comparable in impact to more extensive and expensive treatment.

6. *Therapist characteristics seem to have an important influence on treatment impact.* Client motivation, dropout, and outcome all have been shown to be affected by the therapist's style and personal characteristics. The typical alcoholism treatment in the United States is relatively odd in many ways. Based on a model that posits built-in denial and resistance as part of the disease, it has featured aggressive confrontation designed to tear down defenses, with the primary treatment agents often being people who are themselves recovering from the same disease. Outside the United States, such an approach to treatment is rare. Even within the United States, very few other conditions are treated in this way. We rarely use such tactics in the treatment of anxiety, depression, psychosis, diabetes, or hypertension. Instead, the modal therapeutic style is more empathic and supportive. The "denial-busting" style has been reserved mostly for alcoholics, drug addicts, and criminals. At least in the area of alcoholism, however, current research clearly points to an empathic and supportive style as more effective. Perhaps the same principles of

healing and recovery should be applied to alcohol problems as to other human frailties.

A serious reader of the available scientific literature on alcoholism treatment would be led to approaches that differ radically from present standard and state-of-the-art programs. Treatment methods currently in use have been shaped more by historic accident and economic considerations than by systematic research. There is every reason to believe that if treatment practices were changed to conform more closely to the available evidence, we could be much more effective in reducing the incidence and effects of alcoholism.

References

Alford, G. 1980. "Alcoholics Anonymous: An Empirical Outcome Study." *Addictive Behaviors* 8:53–58.

Annis, H.M., and D. Chan. 1983. "The Differential Treatment Model: Empirical Evidence from a Personality Typology of Adult Offenders." *Criminal Justice and Behavior* 10:159–73.

Azrin, N.H. 1976. Improvements in the Community-Reinforcement Approach to Alcoholism." *Behaviour Research and Therapy* 14:339–48.

Azrin, N.H., R.W. Sisson, R. Meyers, and M. Godley. 1982. "Alcoholism Treatment by Disulfiram and Community Reinforcement Therapy." *Journal of Behavior Therapy and Experimental Psychiatry* 13:105–12.

Brandsma, J.M., M.C. Maultsby, and R.J. Welsh. 1980. *The Outpatient Treatment of Alcoholism: A Review and Comparative Study.* Baltimore: University Park Press.

Cannon, D.S. and T.B. Baker. 1981. "Emetic and Electric Shock Alcohol Aversion Therapy: Assessment of Conditioning." *Journal of Consulting and Clinical Psychology* 49:20–33.

Cannon, D.S., T.B. Baker, A. Gino, and P.E. Nathan. 1986. "Alcohol-Aversion Therapy: Relation between Strength of Aversion and Abstinence." *Journal of Consulting and Clinical Psychology* 54:825–30.

Chapman, P.L.H. and I. Huygens. 1988. "An Evaluation of Three Treatment Programmes for Alcoholism: An Experimental Study with 6- and 18-Month Follow-ups." *British Journal of Addiction* 83:67–81.

Chick, J., B. Ritson, J. Connaughton, A. Stewart and J. Chick. 1988. "Advice versus Extended Treatment for Alcoholism: A Controlled Study." *British Journal of Addiction* 83:159–70.

Ditman, K.S., G.G. Crawford, E.W. Forgy, H. Moskowitz, and C. MacAndrew. 1967. "A Controlled Experiment on the Use of Court Probation for Drunk Arrests." *American Journal of Psychiatry* 124:160–63.

Donovan, J.E., R. Jessor, and L. Jessor. 1983. "Problem Drinking in Adolescence and Young Adulthood: A Follow-up Study." *Journal of Studies on Alcohol* 44:109–37.

Edwards, G., J. Orford, S. Egert, S. Guthrie, A. Hawker, C. Hensman, M. Mitcheson,

E. Oppenheimer, and C. Taylor. 1977. "Alcoholism: A Controlled Trial of 'Treatment' and 'Advice.'" *Journal of Studies on Alcohol* 38:1004–31.

Elkins, R.L. 1980. "Covert Sensitization Treatment of Alcoholism: Contributions of Successful Conditioning to Subsequent Abstinence Maintenance." *Addictive Behaviors* 5:67–89.

Elvy, G.A., J.E. Wells and K.A. Baird. 1988. "Attempted Referral as Intervention for Problem Drinking in the General Hospital." *British Journal of Addiction* 83:83–89.

Fillmore, K.M. and L. Midanik. 1984. "Chronicity of Drinking Problems among Men: A Longitudinal Study." *Journal of Studies on Alcohol* 45:228–36.

Finney, J.W., R.H. Moos, and C.R. Mewborn. 1980. "Post-treatment Experiences and Treatment Outcome of Alcoholic Patients Six Months and Two Years After Hospitalization." *Journal of Consulting and Clinical Psychology* 48:17–29.

Heather, N., B. Whitton, and I. Robertson. 1986. "Evaluation of a Self-Help Manual for Media-Recruited Problem Drinkers: Six Month Follow-up Results." *British Journal of Clinical Psychology* 25:19–34.

Kristenson, H., H. Ohlin, M-B. Hulten-Nosslin, E. Trell, and B. Hood. 1983. "Identification and Intervention of Heavy Drinking in Middle-Aged Men: Results and Follow-up of 24–60 Months of Long-Term Study with Randomized Controls." *Alcoholism: Clinical and Experimental Research* 7:203–9.

Miller, W.R. 1985. "Motivation for Treatment: A Review with Special Emphasis on Alcoholism." *Psychological Bulletin* 98:84–107.

Miller, W.R., and R.K. Hester. 1980. "Treating the Problem Drinker: Modern Approaches." In *The Addictive Behaviors: Treatment of Alcoholism, Drug Abuse, Smoking, and Obesity*, edited by W.R. Miller, 11–141. Oxford: Pergamon Press.

———. 1986a. "Inpatient Alcoholism Treatment: Who Benefits?" *American Psychologist* 41:794–805.

———. 1986b. "The Effectiveness of Alcoholism Treatment: What Research Reveals." In *The Addictive Behaviors: Processes of Change*, edited by W.R. Miller and N. Heather, 121–74. New York: Plenum Press.

———. 1986c. "Matching Problem Drinkers with Optimal Treatments." In *The Addictive Behaviors: Processes of Change*, edited by W.R. Miller and N. Heather, 175–203. New York: Press.

Miller, W.R. and R.F. Muñoz. 1982. *How to Control Your Drinking*. Rev. ed. Albuquerque: University of New Mexico Press.

Miller, W.R., C.A. Taylor, and J.C. West. 1980. "Focused versus Broad-Spectrum Behavior Therapy for Problem Drinkers." *Journal of Consulting and Clinical Psychology* 48:590–601.

Ösejö, L. 1981. "Long-Term Outcome in Alcohol Abuse and Alcoholism among Males in the Lundby General Population, Sweden." *British Journal of Addiction* 76:391–400.

Powell, B.J., E.C. Penick, M.R. Read, and A.M. Ludwig. 1985. "Comparison of Three Outpatient Treatment Interventions: A Twelve-Month Follow-up of Men Alcoholics." *Journal of Studies on Alcohol* 46:309–12.

Rimmele, C., W.R. Miller, and M. Dougher. 1988. "Aversion Therapies." in *Handbook of Alcoholism Treatment Approaches: Effective Alternatives*, edited by R.K. Hester and W.R. Miller. New York: Pergamon Press.

Sanchez-Craig, M. 1984. *Therapist's Manual for Secondary Prevention of Alcohol Problems: Procedures for Teaching Moderate Drinking and Abstinence.* Toronto: Addiction Research Foundation.

Stimmel, B., M. Cohen, V. Sturiano, R. Hanbury, D. Korts, and G. Jackson. 1983. "Is Treatment of Alcoholism Effective in Persons on Methadone Maintenance?" *American Journal of Psychiatry* 140:862–66.

Tuchfeld, B.S. 1981. "Spontaneous Remission in Alcoholics: Empirical Observations and Theoretical Implications." *Journal of Studies of Alcohol* 42:626–41.

Vaillant, G.M. 1983. *The Natural History of Alcoholism: Causes, Patterns, and Paths to Recovery.* Cambridge, Mass.: Harvard University Press.

Valle, S.K. 1981. "Interpersonal Functioning of Alcoholism Counselors and Treatment Outcome." *Journal of Studies on Alcohol* 42:783–90.

Zweben, A., S. Pearlman, and S. Li. in press. "A Comparison of Brief Advice and Conjoint Therapy in the Treatment of Alcohol Abuse: The Results of the Marital Systems Study." *British Journal of Addiction* 83:899–916.

16
Cognitive-Behavioral Treatment of Problem Drinking

Chad D. Emrick
Gregory A. Aarons

A number of alternative theories have been proposed to account for the etiology and maintenance of alcohol disorders. Among them are classic psychoanalytic, psychoanalytic structural, ego psychoanalytic, pharmacodynamic, pharmacologic, bioamine, systems, genetic, classic disease, behavioral, cognitive, and social learning theories (Pattison 1984; Saxe et al. 1983; Wilson 1987). Each theory has its adherents, and each, no doubt, describes some part of the complex process that is typically referred to as "alcoholism." We are in agreement with Pattison's view that "each [theory] describes only one type of alcoholic or accounts for only one aspect of behavior associated with alcoholism" (Pattison 1984, 92).

The purpose of this chapter is to elucidate one theory that has gained adherents largely in the social science field—cognitive-behavioral theory. Our intent is to summarize some of the contributions that this theory and associated research have made to understanding the development, maintenance, and treatment of alcohol problems.

Although endorsed by a growing number of social scientists, the cognitive-behavioral approach to the problem of alcohol abuse has not received broad endorsement from the alcoholism treatment community, at least in the United States. Instead, the alcohol treatment field has been dominated by the "'classic disease concept of alcoholism'" (Fingarette 1988). The disease concept or model has changed little since its roots were planted in the 1930s, despite a wealth of scientific evidence calling for radical modifications in the model (Fingarette 1988; Nathan and Skinstad 1987; Peele 1986; Room 1980; Vaillant 1983). Although the cognitive-behavioral approach is not a

---

The authors are grateful for the significant contributions made by Jeanne C. Maytag, Ph.D., in the development of the ideas presented in this chapter. Significant portions of this chapter also appear in C.D. Emrick, J. Hansen, and J.C. Maytag, "Cognitive-Behavioral Treatment of Problem Drinking," in *The Addictions: Multidisciplinary Perspectives and Treatments*, edited by H.B. Milkman and H.J. Shaffer (Lexington, Mass.: Lexington Books, 1985), 161–73.

particularly popular one in the alcohol treatment establishment, we believe that it merits attention inasmuch as it suggests potentially efficacious clinical assessment and treatment approaches that may help reduce the considerable amount of harm caused by abusive drinking.

One aspect concerning the significance of cognitive-behavioral therapy in the treatment of alcohol problems should be emphasized before embarking on a discussion of cognitive-behavioral theory. Cognitive-behavioral therapists hold a view regarding themselves and their clients that is fundamentally different from that held by most clinicians in the alcohol treatment community. Most traditional therapists view the patient as suffering from a disease and in need of externally imposed discipline in order to deal with his or her disease. The therapist's role centers on helping the client accept the "fact" that he or she has a disease that can be arrested only through surrender of personal power to a "higher power" or other external source of control.

In contrast, the cognitive-behavioral therapist considers the patient to be suffering from "maladaptive cognitive processes and environmental contingencies" (Brickman et al. 1982, 380), which can be corrected through behavioral skills training and through education that is directed toward developing effective cognitive strategies for coping with life's challenges. The role of the therapist is primarily that of an educator who expects clients to "set their own standards, monitor their own performance, and reward or reinforce themselves appropriately" (Brickman et al. 1982, 380). In this respect, the therapist strives to help the client become his or her own therapist. This strategy contrasts with that of traditional behavioral therapy, which relies more on externally applied techniques (such as aversive conditioning and contingency management) to alter the client's behavior.

With such divergency in conceptualization between cognitive-behavioral, traditional behavioral, and disease-oriented therapists, clients are likely to have remarkably different experiences depending on which type of therapist provides treatment.

Theory

Behavioral Factors

The cognitive-behavioral approach to problem drinking rests, in part, on the premise that an individual's choices regarding alcohol use are determined by his or her behavioral repertoire. For example, does the person possess effective social skills? Does he have the capacity to regulate his feelings through the identification, experience, and expression of affect? Is she able to anticipate danger to herself and take appropriate action to protect herself? Is he able to act assertively when faced with interpersonal conflict or the need to resist social pressure to engage in self-destructive or other types of destructive behavior? Does she have the ability to participate in a personally satisfying way with conventional institutions such as school, work, family, church, or synagogue? Does he possess the skills necessary for managing the stress of daily living? Does she have the ability to bring gratification to herself through healthy habits such as jogging, aerobic exercise, and swimming? Is he able to generate fun and stimulation through activities such as reading, playing card (or other) games, hunting, fishing, gardening, knitting, and pursuing a host of other hobbies (see Ludwig 1988)? The presence or absence of such behavioral skills may in and of itself affect the probability that an individual will choose to drink at all, as well as when, where, with whom, what, and how much he or she will drink. Such behavioral abilities, or the lack thereof, also will interact with cognitive, biological, and social processes to yield a greater or lesser likelihood that drinking will occur and what the characteristics of such drinking will be.

Social Factors

Social/environmental factors also contribute to the development and maintenance of drinking patterns. Different cultures have widely varying rates of alcohol-related problems. For example, Irish Catholics are known to have a high rate of alcohol-related social problems, whereas traditional Jews have a low rate (Cahalan 1970). Differences in age, sex, ethnic/religious background, and socioeconomic status are consistently found in large epidemiological studies of alcohol use and related problems. Although such variability could possibly be due to physiological differences between groups, physiological factors do not by themselves appear to be sufficiently explanatory. In contrast, the differences appear to be more "consistently explained in sociocultural terms—in terms of group norms, group cohesiveness, social supports, social controls, etc." (Braucht 1983, 85).

Laboratory studies of how factors such as group norms influence drinking behavior have shown that modeling is a powerful variable. In an especially interesting study, Hendricks, Sobell, and Cooper (1978) attempted to separate the modeling effects of imitation and coaction on drinking behavior. Imitation refers to the passive observation of another's behavior and repeating that behavior at a later time. Coaction requires the simultaneous and interactive performance of a behavior. These researchers found that a confederate's amount of drinking affected the subject's drinking only in a coaction task, where both the subject and the confederate "tasted" wine at the same time. When the subject saw the confederate "taste" the wine before he did (the imitative condition), drinking was unaffected.[1]

George and Marlatt (1983) see these and similar findings as suggesting that for adult drinkers, "coaction rather than imitation best describes the modeling effects" (p. 125). During childhood and early adolescence, however, imitative modeling effects may be more potent.

Perhaps the strongest outcome of modeling is the development of alcohol-related cognitions concerning what effects alcohol can be expected to produce, how people are likely to function when drinking, and what factors cause people to drink.

Cognitive Factors

Cognitive-behavioral theorists and therapists believe that the choice of if, when, what, and how much to drink is strongly influenced by a person's interpretation of a given situational complex. The potential drinker's choices regarding drinking will be shaped by his or her deliberate or automatic thoughts, beliefs, assumptions, or predictions concerning questions such as these: Will I be able to cope effectively with this situation without alcohol? If I drink a small amount of alcohol, what effect will this have on my feelings, perceptions, and actions? If I drink a large amount of alcohol, what effects do I anticipate? How will my drinking or not drinking affect those around me? Answers to these and other questions are often formed during childhood and adolescence, with some answers being arrived at before any drinking is done (see Goldman, Brown, and Christiansen 1987). With subsequent drinking experiences, new cognitions are acquired and old ones are altered to fit the particular cognitive, behavioral, affective, and environmental complex of the individual drinker. One type of cognition that is particularly salient in understanding the development of alcohol use patterns is that of expectancies.

Expectancies. While traditional behaviorism suggests that the actual outcome of a behavior is what determines the probability of an action being taken, cognitive-behavioral theory suggests that the *expected* outcome of a behavior also is a potent determinant. People act in accordance with an expected outcome, although the actual outcome may influence a person's continued acceptance of a particular expectancy (Beck 1976). Besides the feedback given by the actual outcome of an act, expectancies are influenced by the folklore and logic of one's culture through the process of socialization. Once these expectancies are acquired, individuals test their hypotheses for validity. Those that are judged to be valid (whether or not they conform to objective reality) become guideposts for making decisions and undertaking specific courses of action.

Expectancies can be positive or negative in nature. Those that have positive value motivate the individual toward certain behaviors because the behaviors are predicted to lead to desired outcomes. For example, if a person is anxious, he may crave a drink if he expects alcohol to relax him. Negative expectancies lead to avoidance behaviors, inasmuch as undesired outcomes are anticipated. If a person expects to be arrested for driving while intoxicated, for instance, she is likely to refrain from drinking altogether or at least she will be less likely to consume large amounts of alcohol at a party when she plans to drive home at the end of the evening.

Sources of Alcohol Outcome Expectancies. Marlatt (1985a) has identified several factors that are involved in the development and maintenance of outcome expectancies regarding alcohol use. First, stimuli that have been associated with the effects of drinking may, through classical conditioning, become cues for seeking out anticipated rewards from alcohol or for avoiding the negative consequences of drinking. As an example, if a person has frequently experienced pleasure (for example, from physiological arousal and enhanced social contact) while drinking beer in a bar setting, he may be prompted to have a beer from seeing beer advertised on television, from smelling beer when someone next to him at a ball game is drinking, or from merely walking into a bar with its familiar sights, sounds, and smells.

Second, physiological withdrawal symptoms may, with repeated episodes of heavy drinking, become cues for the belief that more drinking will lead to a temporary reduction in aversive physical symptoms. Thus, an alcohol-dependent individual may desire a drink upon awakening after a night of heavy drinking because she expects that alcohol will "treat" the physical discomfort involved in alcohol withdrawal.

A third influence in developing outcome expectancies regarding alcohol consists of physical and social environmental factors (Marlatt 1985a). For instance, an individual may develop alcohol outcome expectations that are specific to a particular setting. He may expect alcohol to sedate him if he drinks alone in his bed at night. He may expect the same amount of alcohol to arouse him if he is drinking in the presence of attractive others in a party setting. Pertinent to this hypothesis, Pliner and Cappell (1974) found that alcohol affected physical symptoms (ratings of dizziness and clear thinking) more when subjects drank alone but that it affected psychological and interpersonal symptoms (such as ratings of friendliness, boredom, euphoria, and unhappiness) more when subjects drank in groups. Obviously, differences in the perceived effects of drinking will result in alcohol outcome expectancies that vary with the setting in which drinking occurs.

A fourth source of alcohol outcome expectancies consists of the beliefs an individual holds about the effects of alcohol. A considerable amount of research has been done to explore this factor (see, for example, Brown, Christiansen, and Goldman 1987; Brown et al. 1980; George and Dermen 1988; Goldman, Brown, and Christiansen 1987; Leigh 1987; Wilson 1987).

Evidence for Alcohol Outcome Expectancies—Indirect. Indirect evidence for the existence of alcohol outcome expectancies was initially obtained from a body of research that used the balanced placebo design. In this research, some subjects were led to believe that they were getting alcohol when in fact they were not, others were told that they were not receiving alcohol when in fact they were, and still others actually received the beverage (either alcohol in tonic water or tonic water alone) that they had been led to believe they were getting. Thus, a subject's belief about whether or not he or she was drinking an alcoholic beverage was manipulated, and the subject's responses were then observed. This research generated some fascinating findings regarding the effects of merely believing that alcohol is being consumed.

For example, alcohol-dependent individuals have reported more craving for alcohol and have consumed larger amounts of a beverage when they believed they were receiving alcohol (Goldman, Brown, and Christiansen 1987; Marlatt, Demming, and Reid 1973). Men and women have reported experiencing an increase in sexual arousal if they believed they were consuming alcohol (see Goldman, Brown, and Christiansen 1987). In some research, the belief that alcohol has been consumed has been found to result in increased aggression (see, for example, Lang et al. 1975), but such has not always been observed (Rohsenow and Bachorowski 1984). For males, simply believing that alcohol has been consumed has been found to decrease anxiety in an interpersonally stressful situation, but for females a similarly stressful interpersonal situation experienced in an expect-alcohol condition has been observed to lead to an increase in anxiety measures (Goldman, Brown, and Christiansen 1987). Variable findings have been obtained concerning the impact on cognitive and motor functioning of believing alcohol is or is not being consumed (Goldman, Brown, and Christiansen 1987). The effects of such beliefs generally appear to be minimal or nonexistent with respect to these areas of functioning (Marlatt 1985a). Commonly, alcohol has been observed to have an impairing effect on cognitive and motor functioning regardless of whether or not the drinker has been led to believe that he or she is drinking alcohol (Marlatt 1985a).

One possible mediator of the findings from balanced-placebo design research is the expectancy a subject holds concerning alcohol's effects. For example, if a male subject expects alcohol to make him more relaxed in a social setting, he is likely to show a relaxation effect in response to instructions leading him to believe that he is drinking alcohol. However, the relaxation response could be mediated by other factors. For example, through the process of classical conditioning, the subject might experience relaxation when presented with stimuli associated with an alcoholic drink (for example, sight, smell, and taste), even though there may be no alcohol in the drink. A conditioned response, rather than the effects of expectancy, may thereby underpin the relaxation effect.

Inasmuch as balanced-placebo research does not assess in a straightfoward fashion the expectancies people have about alcohol's effects, other research has been needed to explore the expectancy variable more directly.

Evidence for Alcohol Outcome Expectancies—Direct. Of particular importance in understanding the development and maintenance of alcohol problems has been research showing that heavy drinkers or alcohol-dependent individuals have expectations regarding the effects of alcohol that are different from those of nondrinkers or from light or nonproblem drinkers. For example, heavier drinkers have been found to have relatively strong expectations regarding alcohol's enhancement of sexual and aggressive behavior (Brown et al. 1980). Adolescent problem drinkers have been observed to have relatively strong expectations regarding improvement in cognitive and motor functioning and enhancement of social functioning (Christiansen and Goldman 1983; Canter 1985). Among college students, problem drinkers have been identified as focusing on alcohol as a tension reducer (Brown 1985a). For college students in general, relatively heavy drinking has been observed to be mediated by the expectations that alcohol will produce social and physical pleasure as well as social assertion (Mooney et al. 1987). Heavier drinkers, compared to lighter drinkers, have been found to expect more stimilation and "pleasurable disinhibition" and to perceive themselves as more dominant when they become moderately intoxicated (Southwick et al. 1981).

Consistent with these findings is the finding that alcohol-dependent patients are at greater risk for having a drinking relapse during or after alcohol treatment if they have positive alcohol-outcome expectancies (Brown 1985b; Eastman and Norris 1982). In the study by Brown (1985b), the expectancy of relaxation and tension reduction was a particularly strong predictor of relapse.[2]

Not only do heavier drinkers have stronger specific expectations regarding the effects of alcohol (expectations that are both positive and negative in nature), but there is also some evidence that they *evaluate* such effects differently than lighter drinkers. Specifically, they have a more favorable evaluation of the positive effects of alcohol, and they evaluate at least some of the negative effects less unfavorably than do lighter drinkers (see, for example, Leigh 1987; McCarty, Morrison, and Mills 1983).

Of course, heavier drinkers may, for a variety of psychological, social, and biological reasons, be affected differently by alcohol than are lighter drinkers. Differences in response are not always or simply mediated by expectancy factors. For example, alcohol-dependent individuals have been observed to experience a greater reduction in pain sensation with increasing doses of alcohol, whereas non–alcohol-dependent persons have reported feeling no decrease or have experienced an increase in pain sensation with higher doses of alcohol (Goldman, Brown, and Christiansen 1987). Whatever processes contribute to these differences in response to alcohol, drinkers who experience pain reduction with alcohol are certainly at greater risk for developing excessive drinking habits than are those who feel pain more strongly as the amount of drinking increases.

This qualifier notwithstanding, research on the beliefs drinkers have about the effects of alcohol (plus the evaluation of such effects) has added significantly to our ability to understand how drinking patterns are developed and maintained. Of course, drinking behavior is shaped by other expectancies in addition to those that deal with the effects of alcohol per se.

Self-Efficacy Expectancies. Closely related to but distinct from alcohol-outcome expectancies are the beliefs one has about the role of alcohol in facilitating or enhancing competent performance (that is, alcohol-efficacy expectancies). Such beliefs are developed within the context of a person's more global assessment of his or her skills in dealing with various aspects of life (that is, self-efficacy expectations) (Bandura 1977). Before undertaking a consideration of alcohol-efficacy expectations, let us look briefly at this broader area of self-efficacy expectations.

A sense of self-efficacy is a function of the beliefs one has regarding his or her repertoire of coping skills for meeting the demands of the environment. For example, a woman may believe she is skilled at aerobic exercise. She also expects exercising to have a rejuvenating effect after a stressful day at work. She will thereby be likely to do some aerobic exercising after a difficult day not only because she thinks exercising will have a positive outcome (an outcome expectation) but also because she thinks of herself as able to undertake the activity (an efficacy expectation).

On the other hand, this woman may lack a sense of efficacy in particular areas of functioning and thereby not engage in certain behaviors even though she believes that the behaviors will produce a positive outcome. For example, she may believe that talking to attractive people at a party will bring pleasure, but she will not attempt to do so if she believes she lacks the social skills necessary to carry on an effective conversation.

Of course, this woman may actually possess the necessary skills to function competently in a particular area but lack self-efficacy because her coping responses are inhibited by anxiety or negative thoughts. For example, she may in reality possess the skills for carrying on effective conversations, but because of anxiety, she converses poorly with strangers. Being a poor conversationalist under these conditions, she is likely to develop the expectation that she is unable to socialize effectively with people she does not know very well.

Then again, she may actually function relatively poorly in a certain area yet venture forth because she believes (mistakenly) that she is competent. For example, a false belief about her "excellent" singing voice may lead her to subject her friends to a painfully off-key performance.

As these examples show, for a sense of self-efficacy to exist, an individual needs only to possess confidence that is built on the belief that he or she is able to acquire and execute those skills successfully in the face of situational demands. Such confidence may or may not be supported by one's actual skills.

Alcohol-Efficacy Expectancies. With respect to the relationship between self-efficacy expectations and alcohol use, cognitive-behavior theory suggests that people are more likely to abuse alcohol if they lack a sense of self-efficacy in a situation where they expect alcohol to enable them to achieve the desired outcome. For example, our socially anxious female may be at increased risk for abusing alcohol in a social setting if she comes to expect that alcohol use will result in effective socializing. According to George and Marlatt (1983) such "alcohol-efficacy expectations" derive from several sources:

1. Experiences in which performance was effective while drinking (the woman makes a new friend when under the influence of alcohol at a party)
2. Observations of others behaving effectively while drinking (the woman sees her friends carrying on enjoyable conversations with unfamiliar people when they are drinking)
3. Encouragement and reinforcement from others for drinking (the woman's friends tell her she is more fun to be around when she is drinking)
4. Reduction of anxiety by alcohol, with a resultant expression of coping skills (the woman successfully approaches an attractive person at a party after experiencing an alcohol-induced reduction in anxiety)

Case studies that further exemplify the role of alcohol-efficacy expectancies in the development and maintenance of alcohol problems are presented later in this chapter.

An intriguing aspect involved in the development of alcohol-efficacy expectations is the possibility that alcohol will reduce one's awareness of functioning poorly when under the influence of alcohol. Consistent with this possibility, Yankofsky et al. (1986) found that alcohol intoxication resulted in interference with the awareness of negative feedback regarding social performance, with the result that drinkers erroneously believed that they had performed well. To the extent that alcohol reduces such awareness (see Hull and Young 1983), some alcohol-efficacy expectations may be based on distortions rather than on alcohol's actual performance-enhancing effects. Such cognitive distortions deserve further consideration as we seek to understand more about the formation and maintenance of alcohol-efficacy expectations.

Regardless of the degree of perceptual distortion involved, there is some research evidence to the effect that heavy drinking is associated with the pursuit of performance enhancement. For example, laboratory studies of drinking show that interpersonal stress increases the amount of alcohol drunk by problem drinkers but not by social drinkers (see, for example, Allman, Taylor, and Nathan 1972). Apparently, problem drinkers expect alcohol to help them cope with interpersonally stressful situations, whereas social drinkers do not harbor such expectations. Another research group (McClelland et al. 1972) found evidence in support of the hypothesis that men who drink heavily lack a sense of personal power and seek alcohol in order to create a perception of power and control. Their studies demonstrated that, as men consume larger amounts of alcohol, fantasies of personal power and control emerge.

Of course, such research does not directly test the hypothesis that drinking is mediated by deficits in a sense of self-efficacy, but the findings are certainly consistent with the hypothesis. More research is clearly needed to identify the role played by alcohol-efficacy expectations in the use and abuse of alcohol under a variety of conditions.

Attributions. Closely related to expectancies are attributions, which are causal explanations for human behavior (Marlatt 1985a). If an individual drinks, he or she may explain the behavior in a variety of possible ways. For example, the cause of drinking may be attributed to factors that are external (such as receiving social pressure to drink) or internal (such as a lack of commitment to abstinence), uncontrollable (such as alcohol withdrawal symptoms) or controllable (such as not going to an AA meeting), global (such as generalized lack of willpower) or specific (such as a lack of skills in relaxation to reduce job-related stress), and stable (such as an inborn inability to refrain from drinking) or unstable (such as fluctuations in mood). The causal explanations one gives for drinking or not drinking will influence if, when, where, how much, and how often drinking will occur.

Marlatt (1985a) has, for example, used attribution theory to help explain how a lapse into drinking following a period of abstinence can develop into a full-blown relapse. On the one hand, the probability of a lapse evolving into a relapse becomes greater the more an individual attributes his or her lapse to internal, global, stable, and uncontrollable factors—attributions that augment what Marlatt has called the abstinence violation effect (Marlatt and Gordon 1985). On the other hand, causal explanations attributing drinking to external, specific, unstable, and controllable factors should reduce the probability of any drinking progressing into a full-blown relapse.

Because of the powerful influences of social and behavioral factors, expectancies, and attributions on drinking behavior, an understanding of the cognitive and behavioral factors involved in problem drinking is seen as vitally important in the attempt to help problem drinkers. Let us now turn to the application of cognitive-behavioral theory in the assessment and treatment of alcohol problems.

Treatment

Assessment

Cognitive-behavioral theory and research suggest that a thorough analysis of the cognitive, social, and behavioral factors involved in the drinking behavior of an alcohol abuser is essential before effective treatment can be undertaken. For example, examination needs to be made of the individual's cognitions regarding his or her ability to cope effectively with various situations with and without alcohol. Also, assessment needs to explore the drinker's repertoire of intrapersonal and interpersonal resources for coping effectively with stress, including unpleasant feelings (depression, anxiety, loneliness, or anger), biological states (hunger, sexual arousal, excitement, tiredness, physical illness, pain, or hypoglycemia), social encouragement to drink (at parties or on holidays), and interpersonal events (fights with children, spouse, or supervisors; divorce; separation; or death of a loved one). Attention to these aspects of a drinker's life serve to augment the data obtained from a more traditional assessment regarding the type, amount, and frequency of a person's drinking; the actual effects of such drinking on his or her functioning in a variety of life areas; and the degree of physiological dependence that is involved in the disorder.

Alcohol Expectancies. With respect to the assessment of alcohol-efficacy and alcohol-outcome expectancies per se, a variety of strategies can be formulated. For example, a detailed clinical interview can be conducted, with the client being asked specifically about how alcohol affects mood, thinking, working, socializing, physical pain, hunger, sexual arousal, tiredness, marital and other family relationships, and the like.

Several formal assessment instruments that allow for a systematic exploration of the client's alcohol expectancies have been developed. One such instrument in the Alcohol Use Inventory (AUI) (Wanberg, Horn, and Foster 1977). This questionnaire measures the individual's perceptions regarding the effects of alcohol on social, physical, and intellectual functioning; affect regulation; behavioral self-control; and marital interactions.

The Comprehensive Drinker Profile developed by Miller and Marlatt (1984) provides another formal procedure for identifying alcohol expectancies. This profile specifically asks clients to report any positive effects (such as tension reduction, increased positive feelings, increased perception of power and control, or facilitation of interpersonal relationships) they have experienced while drinking. Experiences with negative effects from drinking (such as negative physical symptoms, cognitive impairment, negative feelings, and negative behavior) are explored as well. Examination of these perceived effects generates clues about which alcohol expectancies the drinker may have developed.

The Alcohol Expectancy Questionnaire (AEQ) (Brown, Christiansen, and Goldman 1987) offers another means of systematically assessing alcohol-outcome expectancies. This questionnaire comes in both adult and adolescent versions. The adult form measures expectancies concerning alcohol's effects on global positive changes, sexual enhancement, physical and social pleasure, social assertion, relaxation and tension reduction, and arousal and aggression. For adolescents, the AEQ measures alcohol expectancies concerning global positive changes, changes in social behavior, improved cognitive and motor abilities, sexual enhancement, cognitive and motor impairment, increased arousal, and relaxation and tension reduction.

Still another questionnaire, developed by Southwick et al. (1981), may be used to assess the client's alcohol expectancies. With this questionnaire, clients indicate how they expect alcohol to affect them on the following dimensions: stimulation/perceived dominance, pleasurable disinhibition, and behavioral impairment. Clients are asked to report how both a moderate amount of alcohol and too much alcohol affect these dimensions. As such, this instrument has the advantage of giving a clinician insight into a client's alcohol-outcome expectancies at different levels of intoxication.

The data obtained concerning alcohol expectancies can help the therapist develop an effective treatment plan. The following case illustrates this point.

Case Illustration 1. A male client in his late thirties had a history of "social drinking" that evolved into a brief period of alcohol dependence. Over the years of drinking, he had acquired the expectation that he could function effectively in social situations only as long as he had an alcoholic drink at hand. He even believed that he did not need to consume the drink to experience some reduction in social anxiety. Having a drink in his hand was sufficient to initiate effective social functioning.

Following an aversive alcohol-related event, this client stopped drinking altogether. Because he believed that effective social functioning was possible only with the aid of an alcoholic beverage, he became socially isolated at the time he became abstinent from alcohol. When he sought treatment, he had been abstinent and socially inactive for approximately two years. In his desire to become socially active once again, he wished to resume drinking but to keep the drinking at a moderate level.

Because this client had strong alcohol-efficacy expectancies regarding the enhancement of social functioning with alcohol, treatment focused on reducing social anxiety through in vivo desensitization. With the reduction of anxiety and the consequent carrying out of all social activities he had previously seen as impossible without alcohol, he developed a perception of himself as able to function effectively in social situations while abstinent. Only then was it appropriate to address the issue of whether or not this individual should ever drink again, because he no longer believed that he needed to drink in order to socialize.

Coping Resources. With respect to the examination of a client's coping resources, a clinical interview might include specific questions regarding the management of feelings as well as the client's typical responses to various physical states, social situations, and past and current life crises. Such questioning can lead to a discovery of defects and deficiencies in coping resources that will need attention in treatment. A client might report, for example, that she believes she cannot say no when someone offers her a drink in a social situation. Another may report that she used to meditate to relax but that she stopped this behavior years ago and now drinks to relax. A client may be found to suffer from clinical depression, in response to which he has drunk to anesthetize the dysphoria. Another may experience panic attacks that have been "treated" with alcohol. A client may report that her marriage is highly conflictual and that she drinks in response to her husband's verbal abuse because she sees herself as being unable to respond otherwise. A client may report that he drinks whenever his pain from an old injury becomes unbearable.

Formal assessment instruments can provide information about coping resources that supplements that obtained in the clinical interview. For example, the Situational Competence Test (Chaney, O'Leary, and Marlatt 1978) can be used to evaluate skills for coping with situations that are likely to trigger drinking. Problems with social assertiveness can be identified and specified using one of any number of self-report instruments (see, for example, Rathus 1973). Problems in coping with the challenges of life can be assessed indirectly by identifying the difficulties a patient is having in the areas of affect regulation, interpersonal relationships, and physical health. The Minnesota Multiphasic Personality Inventory (National Computer Systems, Inc.), and the SCL-90 (Derogatis 1977) can be used to identify difficulties in these areas. Specific to the domain of affect regulation, the Beck Depression

Inventory is available for measuring depression (Beck et al. 1961), and the Profile of Mood States (McNair, Lorr, and Droppleman 1971) is designed to measure anxiety and other moods.

While various strategies exist for measuring a client's coping resources, the clinician need only select a few that he or she deems most useful in his or her own practice. The data obtained from these procedures can assist the therapist in developing treatment goals and selecting interventions toward those goals. The following case offers an example:

Case Illustration 2. A male patient in his early forties requested treatment to explore his excessive use of alcohol. The clinical interview revealed that he drank large amounts of alcohol after work, particularly when on assignment out of town. He perceived that alcohol enabled him to shift from placing a considerable amount of stress on himself while on the job to relaxing in the company of others. He believed that alcohol was particularly effective in enabling him to think clearly after a difficult day at work, allowing him to remember experiences that were otherwise unretrievable.

Early in treatment, his expectations that he could neither relax nor think clearly in the evenings without alcohol were challenged, with the result that he was willing to experiment with alternatives to drinking as a means of relaxing (that is, physical exercise and deep muscle relaxation). Once he stopped drinking, he learned that he could relax effectively and have a good memory at his disposal without alcohol. The active ingredient in memory improvement was relaxation, not alcohol. The client was thus freed from an expectation about the impact of alcohol on intellectual functioning through developing alternative skills for managing stress. With these cognitive and behavioral changes, he was able to stop drinking excessively after work.

Interventions

Once the initial assessment has been completed, the clinician needs to select those cognitive-behavioral strategies that best address the identified problems. Training in social skills and affect regulation can be conducted using well-established behavior therapy procedures. For example, in vivo desensitization techniques can be used to help clients overcome their fears regarding seeking employment or speaking in public. Patients can be instructed in the use of effective strategies for problem solving. Clients can be helped to manage emotional arousal through the use of meditation, relaxation, and aerobic exercise (Marlatt 1985b).

Cognitive variables that are found to underlie and maintain abusive drinking can be corrected through the application of a variety of approaches that have been developed by Beck (1976); Ellis et al. (1988); Low (1950); Marlatt and Gordon (1985); Maultsby (1978); and others (for example, Ludwig 1988; Vogler and Bartz 1982). Through such interventions, the client can develop more effective, realistic, and logical responses to internal and external events, with the result that he or she can gain greater control of emotions and interpersonal situations. Alcohol is then less likely to be sought as a means to induce a state of perceived control or as a way to escape stress through its anesthetic properties.

With the achievement of cognitive and behavioral changes, factors that might otherwise contribute to continued drinking are removed, with a consequent increase in the probability that the client will be able to stop abusing alcohol. Weiner and Fox (1982) offer an excellent example of how cognitive-behavioral therapy can be used to treat substance abuse. Two cases (from the clinical practice of the senior author of this chapter) are presented here to exemplify how treatment is approached within the cognitive-behavioral framework.

Case Illustration 3. At the urging of his wife, a married, highly successful businessman in his early forties sought treatment for excessive drinking. At the start of treatment, he was regularly consuming four to sixteen drinks a day, drinking mostly in the presence of others either at home or in a restaurant or bar. His blood alcohol level was estimated to reach 40 to 240 milligrams percent, depending on the amount consumed. When he was experiencing unpleasant emotions, he would drink even more alcohol. Often he would drive home intoxicated and engage in a hostile interchange with his wife. He perceived drinking alcohol as "fun" and viewed the idea of not drinking as "dumb." His drinking activities were often isolated from his family life, with the result that his lifestyle was fragmented. Drinking was undertaken not only to escape or express unpleasant feelings and to produce the pleasure of intoxication, but also to maintain a highly established habit. He drank simply because he "had to do it." One factor involved in maintaining his habit strength was the extremely heavy drinking of a close business associate. Through the power of coactive modeling, he was encouraged to maintain a pattern of heavy, daily drinking.

Over the course of treatment, this client reduced his drinking to a nonproblem level through the use of several behavioral strategies:

- Self-monitoring of drinking behavior
- Substituting alcoholic beverages with nonalcoholic drinks (soda, mineral water, or tap water)

- Developing a new lifestyle with a focus on physical health (through active involvement in physical exercise)
- Increasing skills in the verbal expression of feelings and desires (most notably with his wife and business associates)

Along with these behavioral changes, this individual developed negative expectancies regarding excessive drinking and positive expectancies about nonproblem drinking. For example, he came to view overdrinking as harming his physical health; impairing his ability to be an observant, active parent and husband; endangering both himself and others when he would drive while intoxicated; and increasing the risk of his being hostile with his wife and thereby damaging his marital relationship. Among the self-efficacy expectations that he acquired about nonproblem drinking were the following:

- "I can carry on long social conversations with people who are not drinking."
- "I can express my feelings to my wife effectively when I am not intoxicated."
- "I can have fun exercising and working out."
- "I can spend sober time with my children."
- "I can choose when I drink—it is no longer a daily habit."
- "I can choose how much I drink regardless of how much those around me are drinking."
- "I can enjoy the taste of alcohol and its effects more when I drink in limited amounts."

In summary, through cognitive-behavioral treatment, this client developed a healthy relationship with alcohol. He changed his lifestyle and underwent significant shifts in his expectations concerning both intoxication and sobriety.

Case Illustration 4. A married female executive in her late thirties sought treatment at the urging of her husband because she was habitually drinking excessively at home in the evenings. On the nights of heaviest consumption, she was drinking a mixture of wine and distilled spirits, consuming a total of approximately nine drinks over a three-hour period, leading to an estimated blood alcohol level of 145 milligrams percent.

This client suffered from considerable work-related stress, in part because she was perfectionistic, placed high expectations on others, and experienced evaluation anxiety when interacting with superiors. After work, she would often have physical pain, which she sought to "treat" with alcohol. She also consumed alcohol to relieve work-related anxiety and worry and help her to fall asleep, particularly on Sunday evenings. In addition, she had come to expect alcohol to override her tiredness and thereby give her energy for doing household chores. Besides drinking as a function of alcohol outcome expectancies, her at-home drinking also was determined to be partially the result of a well-established habit pattern.

Assessment revealed that this individual suffered from a significant degree of anxiety in nonwork social settings, particularly when she faced meeting new people. Years of drinking had resulted in her acquiring the expectation that alcohol would lower her social anxiety and enable her to function at least adequately in social situations. Thus, at times she would drink excessively at social events.

At the beginning of treatment, this client reported a great struggle with the urge to drink, indicating that on about half of the days, she would drink despite her conscious intention not to drink. Such drinking led to an abstinence violation effect (Marlatt 1985a) inasmuch as she attributed her drinking to a personal weakness in her ability to control her drinking behavior. Additionally, her husband would express displeasure with her when she drank too much, augmenting her experience of guilt and shame.

Because physical pain, tiredness, frustration, unhappiness, and anxiety were assessed to be major antecedents to drinking, treatment was undertaken to help this client develop effective nondrug ways of managing her cognitions and associated emotions as well as of coping with her physical state. She was given progressive relaxation training to reduce anxiety and pain and to revitalize herself after a day of work-related stress. She was counseled in cognitive strategies for reducing frustration and unhappiness. She also was taught about the importance of using nonalcoholic drink substitutes when faced with the urge to drink alcoholic beverages. Additionally, she was given assertiveness training, particularly in the area of negative assertion (for example, setting limits and disagreeing with others). Social skills training also was undertaken, especially in the area of establishing and maintaining conversation with new people.

Although this client has not yet completed treatment, she has enjoyed a remarkable reduction in the amount and frequency of her drinking. Her anxiety has lessened significantly; her outlook is considerably brighter; and she has had an increase in self-efficacy expectations regarding her skills in refraining from drinking in the evenings, her ability to get to sleep without alcohol, and her capacity to complete household tasks without the energizing and pain-reducing effects of alcohol.

Both of the clients engaged in excessive drinking at some point during the course of treatment, at which time cognitive-behavioral strategies were employed. When "lapses" occur during cognitive-behavioral treatment, the client is helped to moderate the destructive potential of the lapse by learning effective cognitive and behavioral responses to the event. Instead of the drinking event developing into a full-blown relapse, the client is helped to use the lapse to enhance his or her perceptions regarding the negative effects of drinking and to identify areas in which coping skills need to be developed. Marlatt and his colleagues (see, for example, Marlatt and Gordon 1980; Marlatt and Gordon 1985) have been particularly instrumental in developing techniques for teaching clients rational cognitive responses to relapse situations. The techniques that they have developed are a significant component of cognitive-behavioral treatment for alcohol problems and in our estimation contribute greatly to helping alcohol-abusing clients maintain whatever gains they make during treatment. In a field that has been plagued by failures to help clients receive long-term, stable benefits from treatment (see, for example, Polich, Armor, and Braiker 1980), such a contribution is most welcome.

Conclusion

This chapter has explored cognitive-behavioral theory and some of its related research. The theory has been found to be helpful in understanding some aspects of the development and maintenance of drinking problems and in devising assessment and treatment strategies. Yet despite the important contributions of the theory, we realize that many hypotheses that derive from it have not been tested adequately. For example, attributions regarding the locus of causality (that is, internal versus external) have only an apparent relationship with the development and maintenance of problem drinking (Marlatt and Donovan 1982). Also, treatment interventions based on cognitive-behavioral theory have yet to be refined to the point where the most potent aspects of the treatment can be isolated and the relatively inert components can be eliminated. Nonetheless, the theory appears to offer enough promise for improving our understanding and treatment of problem drinking to merit additional development and empirical testing. Research by Marlatt and Gordon (1985) and Ellis et al. (1988) are particularly noteworthy for the contributions they have made in the application of cognitive-behavioral theory and treatment to the field of alcohol abuse. Inasmuch as the generally prevailing treatment methods have very narrow appeal and generally poor long-term effectiveness (Polich, Armor, and Braiker 1980), the investment of financial and human resources in the further development and application of cognitive-behavioral theory seems clearly warranted.

Notes

1. Consistent with the findings from Hendricks, Sobell, and Cooper (1978), Caudill and Marlatt (1975) demonstrated strong coactive modeling effects on drinking behavior, at least with male heavy social drinkers in an experimental setting.

2. Relapse into the abuse of alcohol also has been found to be associated with another form of alcohol-related expectancy—the belief that if a person drinks alcohol, he or she will be unable to control his or her intake. Heather, Rollnick, and Winton (1983) found a statistically significant relationship between the abuse of alcohol (if any drinking was done after discharge from an inpatient treatment program) and the patient's belief that he or she could not control the intake of alcohol should any drinking be done.

References

Allman, L.R., H.A. Taylor, and P.E. Nathan. 1972. "Group Drinking During Stress: Effects on Drinking Behavior, Affect, and Psychopathology." *American Journal of Psychiatry* 129:669–78.

Bandura, A. 1977. "Self-Efficacy: Toward a Unifying Theory of Behavioral Change." *Psychological Review* 84:191–215.

Beck, A.T. 1976. *Cognitive Therapy and the Emotional Disorders*. New York: International Universities Press.

Beck, A.T., C.H. Ward, M. Mendelson, J. Mock, and J. Erbaugh. 1961. "An Inventory for Measuring Depression." *Archives of General Psychiatry* 4:561–71.

Braucht, G.N. 1983. "How Environments and Persons Combine to Influence Problem Drinking: Current Research Issues." In *Recent Developments in Alcoholism*, vol. 1: *Genetics, Behavioral Treatment, Social Mediators and Prevention, Current Concepts in Diagnosis*, edited by M. Galanter, 79–103. New York: Plenum Press.

Brickman, P., V.C. Rabinowitz, J. Karuza, Jr., D. Coates, E. Cohn, and L. Kidder. 1982. "Models of Helping and Coping." *American Psychologist* 37:368–84.

Brown, S.A. 1985a. "Expectancies versus Background in the Prediction of College Drinking Patterns." *Journal of Consulting and Clinical Psychology* 53:121–30.

———. 1985b. "Reinforcement Expectancies and Alcoholism Treatment Outcome after a One-Year Follow-up." *Journal of Studies on Alcohol* 46:304–8.

Brown, S.A., B.A. Christiansen, and M.S. Goldman. 1987. "The Alcohol Expectancy Questionnaire: An Instrument for the Assessment of Adolescent and Adult Alcohol Expectancies." *Journal of Studies on Alcohol* 48:483–91.

Brown, S.A., M.S. Goldman, A. Inn, and L.R. Anderson. 1980. "Expectations of Reinforcement from Alcohol: Their Domain and Relation to Drinking Patterns." *Journal of Consulting and Clinical Psychology* 48:419–26.

Cahalan, D. 1970. *Problem Drinkers: A National Survey.* San Francisco: Jossey-Bass.
Canter, W.A. 1985. "Adolescent Problem Drinking: An Analysis of a Social Learning Model." *Dissertation Abstracts International* 45:3930B–31B. (Doctoral dissertation, Wayne State University, 1984.)
Caudill, B.D., and G.A. Marlatt. 1975. "Modeling Influences in Social Drinking: An Experimental Analogue." *Journal of Consulting and Clinical Psychology* 43:405–15.
Chaney, E.F., M.R. O'Leary, and G.A. Marlatt. 1978. "Skill Training with Alcoholics." *Journal of Consulting and Clinical Psychology* 46:1092–1104.
Christiansen, B.A., and M.S. Goldman. 1983. "Alcohol-Related Expectancies versus Demographic/Background Variables in the Prediction of Adolescent Drinking." *Journal of Consulting and Clinical Psychology* 51:249–57.
Derogatis, L.R. 1977. *SCL-90-R Manual.* Baltimore, Md.: Clincial Psychometrics Research Unit, Johns Hopkins University School of Medicine.
Eastman, C., and H. Norris. 1982. "Alcohol Dependence, Relapse and Self-Identity." *Journal of Studies on Alcohol* 43:1214–31.
Ellis A., J.F. McInerney, R. DiGiuseppe, and R.J. Yeager. 1988. *Rational-Emotive Therapy with Alcoholics and Substance Abusers.* New York: Pergamon Press.
Fingarette, H. 1988. *Heavy Drinking: The Myth of Alcoholism as a Disease.* Berkeley: University of California Press.
George, W.H., and K.H. Dermen. 1988. "Self-Reported Alcohol Expectancies for Self and Other as a Function of Behavior Type and Dosage Set." *Journal of Substance Abuse* 1:71–78.
George, W.H., and G.A. Marlatt. 1983. "Alcoholism: The Evolution of a Behavioral Perspective." In *Recent Developments in Alcoholism,* vol. 1: *Genetics, Behavioral Treatment, Social Mediators and Prevention, Current Concepts in Diagnosis,* edited by M. Galanter, (105–38). New York: Plenum Press.
Goldman, M.S., S.A. Brown, and B.A. Christiansen. 1987. "Expectancy Theory: Thinking about Drinking." In *Psychological Theories of Drinking and Alcoholism,* edited by H.T. Blane and K.E. Leonard, 181–226. New York: Guilford Press.
Heather, N., S. Rollnick, and M. Winton. 1983. "A Comparison of Objective and Subjective Measures of Alcohol Dependence as Predictors of Relapse Following Treatment." *British Journal of Clinical Psychology* 22:11–17.
Hendricks, R.D., M.B. Sobell, and A.M. Cooper. 1978. "Social Influences on Human Ethanol Consumption in an Analogue Situation." *Addictive Behaviors* 3:253–59.
Hull, J.G., and R.D. Young. 1983. "The Self-Awareness Reducing Effects of Alcohol Consumption: Evidence and Implications." In *Psychological Perspectives on the Self,* vol. 2, edited by J. Suls and A.G. Greenwald, 159–90. Hillsdale, N.J.: Lawrence Erlbaum Associates.
Lang, A.R., D.J. Goeckner, V.J. Adesso, and G.A. Marlatt. 1975. "The Effects of Alcohol on Aggression in Male Social Drinkers." *Journal of Abnormal Psychology* 84:508–18.
Leigh, B.C. 1987. "Evaluations of Alcohol Expectancies: Do They Add to Prediction of Drinking Patterns?" *Psychology of Addictive Behaviors* 1:135–39.
Low, A.A. 1978. *Mental Health through Will-Training: A System of Self-Help in Psy-*

chotherapy as Practiced by Recovery, Incorporated. Boston: Mass. Christopher Publishing House.

Ludwig, A.M. 1988. *Understanding the Alcoholic's Mind: The Nature of Craving and How to Control It.* New York: Oxford University Press.

Marlatt, G.A. 1985a. "Cognitive Factors in the Relapse Process." In *Relapse Prevention: Maintenance Strategies in the Treatment of Addictive Behaviors,* edited by G.A. Marlatt and J.R. Gordon, 128–200. New York: Guilford Press.

———. 1985b. "Coping and Substance Abuse: Implications for Research, Prevention, and Treatment." In *Coping and Substance Abuse,* edited by S. Shiffman and T.A. Wills, 367–86. New York: Academic Press.

Marlatt, G.A., B. Demming, and J.B. Reid. 1973. "Loss of Control Drinking in Alcoholics: An Experimental Analogue." *Journal of Abnormal Psychology* 81:233–41.

Marlatt, G.A., and D.M. Donovan. 1982. "Behavioral Psychology Approaches to Alcoholism." In *Encyclopedic Handbook of Alcoholism,* edited by E.M. Pattison and E. Kaufman, 560–77. New York: Gardner Press.

Marlatt, G.A., and J.R. Gordon. 1980. "Determinants of Relapse: Implications for the Maintenance of Behavior Change." In *Behavioral Medicine: Changing Health Lifestyles,* edited by P.O. Davidson and S.M. Davidson, 410–52. New York: Brunner/Mazel.

———. 1985. *Relapse Prevention: Maintenance Strategies in the Treatment of Addictive Behaviors.* New York: Guilford Press.

Maultsby, M.C., Jr. 1978. *A Million Dollars for Your Hangover: The Illustrated Guide for the New Self-Help Alcoholic Treatment Method.* Lexington Ky.: Rational Self-Help Books.

McCarty, D., S. Morrison, and K.C. Mills. 1983. "Attitudes, Beliefs and Alcohol Use: An Analysis of Relationships." *Journal of Studies on Alcohol* 44:328–41.

McClelland, D.C., W.N. Davis, R. Kalin, and E. Wanner. 1972. *The Drinking Man.* New York: Free Press.

McNair, D.M., M. Lorr, and L.F. Droppleman. 1971. *Profile of Mood States.* San Diego: Educational and Industrial Testing Service.

Miller, W.R., and G.A. Marlatt. 1984. *Manual for the Comprehensive Drinker Profile.* Odessa, Fla.: Psychological Assessment Resources, Inc.

Mooney, D.K., K. Fromme, D.R. Kivlahan, and G.A. Marlatt. 1987. "Correlates of Alcohol Consumption: Sex, Age, and Expectancies Relate Differentially to Quantity and Frequency." *Addictive Behaviors* 12:235–40.

Nathan, P.E., and A.H. Skinstad. 1987. "Outcomes of Treatment for Alcohol Problems: Current Methods, Problems, and Results." *Journal of Consulting and Clincial Psychology* 55:332–40.

National Computer Systems, Inc. *Minnesota Multiphasic Personality Inventory.* Interpretative Scoring Systems, P.O. Box 1416, Minneapolis, MN 55440.

Pattison, E.M. 1984. "Types of Alcoholism Reflective of Character Disorders." In *Character Pathology: Theory and Treatment,* edited by M.R. Zales, New York: Brunner/Mazel.

Peele, S. 1986. "The Implications and Limitations of Genetic Models of Alcoholism and Other Addictions." *Journal of Studies on Alcohol* 47:63–73.

Pliner, P., and H. Cappell. 1974. "Modification of Affective Consequences of Alcohol:

A Comparison of Social and Solitary Drinking." *Journal of Abnormal Psychology* 83:418–25.
Polich, J.M., D.J. Armor, and H.B. Braiker. 1980. *The Course of Alcoholism: Four Years after Treatment*. Report no. R-2433-NIAAA. Santa Monica, Calif.: Rand Corporation.
Rathus, S.A. 1973. "A 30-Item Schedule for Assessing Assertive Behavior." *Behavior Therapy* 4:398–406.
Rohsenow, D.J., and J.A. Bachorowski. 1984. "Effects of Alcohol and Expectancies on Verbal Aggression in Men and Women." *Journal of Abnormal Psychology* 93:418–32.
Room, R. 1980. "Treatment-Seeking Populations and Larger Realities." In *Alcoholism Treatment in Transition*, edited by G. Edwards and M. Grant, 205–24. Baltimore: University Park Press.
Saxe, L., D. Dougherty, K. Esty, and M. Fine. 1983. *Health Technology Case Study 22: The Effectiveness and Costs of Alcoholism Treatment*. Washington D.C.: GPO.
Southwick, L., C. Steele, A. Marlatt, and M. Lindell. 1981. "Alcohol-Related Expectancies: Defined by Phase of Intoxication and Drinking Experience." *Journal of Consulting and Clinical Psychology* 49:713–21.
Vaillant, G.E. 1983. *The Natural History of Alcoholism*. Cambridge, Mass.: Harvard University Press.
Vogler, R.E., and W.R. Bartz. 1982. *The Better Way to Drink*. New York: Simon & Schuster.
Wanberg, K.W., J.L. Horn and F.M. Foster. 1977. "A Differential Assessment Model for Alcoholism: The Scales of the Alcohol Use Inventory." *Journal of Studies on Alcohol* 38:512–43.
Weiner, H., and S. Fox. 1982. "Cognitive-Behavioral Therapy with Substance Abusers." *Social Casework: The Journal of Contemporary Social Work* 63:564–67.
Wilson, G.T. 1987. "Cognitive Studies in Alcoholism." *Journal of Consulting and Clincial Psychology* 55:325–31.
Yankofsky, L., G.T. Wilson, J.L. Adler, W.H. Hay, and S. Vrana. 1986. "The Effect of Alcohol on Self-Evaluation and Perception of Negative Interpersonal Feedback." *Journal of Studies on Alcohol* 47:26–33.

17
Affective Modes in Multimodality Addiction Treatment

Robert Vaughn Frye

People take psychoactive drugs to vary their conscious experience. There are other ways of altering consciousness, including "listening to music, making music, dancing, falling in love, hiking in the wilderness ... visiting a city ... having sex, daydreaming, watching fireworks, going to a movie or play, jumping into cold water after taking a hot sauna, [and] participating in religious rituals" (Weil and Rosen 1983, 14). Weil and Rosen conclude that changing consciousness is something people like to do. Frye (in press) writes, "It appears that consciousness includes an awareness of the environment and an awareness of that awareness. Within that conscious awareness appear vicissitudes prompted by environmental cues; which modulate affect, that conscious subjective aspect of an emotion; and produce feelings, moods and temperament."

Using a theoretical position from evolutionary biology, Frye (1980a; 1980b; 1981a; 1986b) hypothesized that humankind's inclination for psychotropic drug use may be based on genetically carried behavior that once contributed to human survival and that drugs of abuse appear to mimic substances in the body that mediate crucial human functions. These crucial human functions include the ability to withhold unpleasant sensations from oneself, thereby allowing one to take steps to overcome unpleasant stress-producing stimuli. Conversely, these endogenous substances appear to mediate pleasant, or euphoric, feelings. It would appear expeditious (in the treatment of addiction) if recovering individuals could be trained to self-regulate (without chemicals), to some degree, these endogenous systems, thereby giving them some internal control of unpleasant and pleasant feelings.

Treatment Planning

In the late 1960s, multimodality programming for the treatment of addiction was developed as a response to the factionalism that had developed among different methods of treating opiate addiction. This programming consisted of an organized system of clinics with a central intake unit and special support units under one administrative authority. This approach included services such as detoxification, therapeutic communities (TCs), mental health counseling, confrontation therapy, methadone maintenance, group therapy, narcotic antagonists, vocational counseling, social work, and religious counseling (Frye 1986b). With the exception of TCs, most of the services were drawn from professional disciplines: medicine, social work, psychiatry, and theology (the clergy). TCs offered a global view of rehabilitation, using recovering addicts as staff and emphasizing personal responsibility, honesty, self-reliance, drug abstinence, self-disclosure, peer support, and the self-help philosophy of Alcoholics Anonymous (AA) Frye 1980b; Frye 1981b; Frye 1984b; Frye 1986a).

Community hospitals increased their chemical dependence units by 50 percent between 1980 and 1984 (Carper 1986). In addition, corporations have been setting up chains of profitable treatment centers. Most use a variation of the traditional medical model and employ the AA philosophy in their units. With the recent increase in the frequency of cocaine abuse, some proprietary drug treatment programs have devised treatment modalities specifically tailored to cocaine abuse. Such modalities are cocaine recovery support groups, resort retreats, aversive therapy, and short- and long-term residential treatment (Wesson and Smith 1985).

Current treatment philosophies include the biomedical approach, which treats addiction as a physician would treat a disease; the behavioral approach, which assumes that addictive behaviors are mostly acquired through learning; the cognitive approach, which assumes that thoughts and expectations have great influence on human behavior; the psychodynamic approach, which focuses on early childhood experiences; and the humanistic/existential approach, which views humans as having the freedom to make responsible choices and to anticipate the consequences of actions (Milkman and Sunderwirth 1987). Treatment delivery includes group approaches such as TCs; family therapy, in which there is a belief that the addicted individual is usually enmeshed in a network of disturbed family members; and spiritual orientation, in which addiction and craving is thought to reflect a state of spiritual disharmony and control may be achieved by placing one's faith in a higher power (Milkman and Sunderwirth 1987).

A multimodality, or heterodox, approach is eclectic and uses a combination of what I call cognitive, behavioral, and affective modalities (Frye 1985a; Frye 1985b; Frye 1986b). A better understanding of the need for a comprehensive, multimodality program has evolved in recent years. Since addictions may permit individuals to cope, or appear to cope, by altering stressful environment assessments and perceptions (impediments) that may affect survival, *successful treatment leading to cessation of that addictive behavior must consist of training in other, less destructive ways of coping.* Drawing on modalities or submodalities from cognitive, behavioral, and affective modes, treatment for addictive behavior, including psychotropic substance abuse, may need to consist of a heterodox approach aimed at the following (Frye 1986b):

1. Using cognitive and behavioral modes (such as rational emotive therapy and contingency contracting) to achieve abstinence from the behavior or modification of that behavior
2. Using affective modes (such as charismatic group therapy and stress management training) to help substitute other behaviors to fill the void created by abstinence
3. Using cognitive, behavioral, and affective modes to provide skill training in altering consciousness to overcome perceived environmental impediments on a long-term basis

Such an approach may succeed in promoting change and recovery.

Change and Recovery

Recovery and change is a process, not an event. This implies that recovery and change are related, if not synonymous. Recovery *is* change, and without change there could be no recovery. To achieve recovery and continued abstinence from psychoactive substances, the individual must progress through three crucial and effective steps (Steinbroner 1985): detoxification, support system building, and, perhaps most important, learning and participating in activities that bring satisfaction and pleasure, giving the *natural high* that individuals seek through psychotropic chemicals.

To change is to become different, to replace one behavior with another. It may be an alteration, a substitution, a variation, a shift, a conversion, a reversal, a turn, a metamorphosis, an adjustment, or a transformation. Changes may involve how one relates to people; how one communicates; how one expresses true feelings; how one modifies habits, values, or lifestyle; and how one recasts or remolds one's life free from psychotropic chemicals. Change may be painful, may deny pleasure, may force the giving up of harmful but emotionally satisfying relationships, may make one do what one does not wish to do, and may cause strong emotional stress (Frye 1976). The objectives of most therapies in substance dependence treatment programs is to promote change in the client—the change to abstinence from nonabstinence; the change from alienation to support system; and the change from drug-induced pleasure or relief to transcendence and natural pleasure states.

Affective Modes

Affective modes or modalities are biopsychological and stimulate a state of altered awareness of consciousness. Such modes alter the brain's biological state. Verbal patterns and visual images may be changed (Mandell 1985). Such altered awareness is thought to result from changes in neural/neurochemical mechanisms in the brain, brought about by increasing or decreasing neurotransmission. Endogenous chemicals called neurotransmitters appear to control neurotransmission, and addictions appear to alter consciousness or awareness by changing levels of neurotransmission. Environmental factors (that totality of physical and social phenomena that surround or affect an individual) also may affect neurotransmission. The ability to alter consciousness and neurotransmission may be a defense mechanism used by vertebrates (including humans) to augment their evolutionary chances of survival under circumstances in which a cold and correct environmental assessment might be sufficiently demoralizing to result in the difference between life and death (Frye 1980a; Frye 1980b; Frye 1986a).

Achieving an affective experience is the goal of affective modes or modalities. Clients may be trained in achieving an affective experience that may alter consciousness and awareness and produce feelings, emotions, moods, and temperament. If such feelings, emotions, moods, and temperament are pleasant or exhilarating, such a state may be called a *natural high*. Natural highs may help fill the void caused by abstinence from psychotropic substances and may be an important adjunct on the road to individual recovery from the use and abuse of psychotropic chemicals. Weil and Rosen (1983) note that getting high without drugs often takes longer than doing so with psychotropic chemicals and often is not as powerful, but

> the goal should be to learn how to get high in ways that do not hurt yourself or others, and that do not necessarily require huge expenditures of time or money for special materials and equipment. Furthermore, you should be able to get high in enough different ways so that you can have the experience wherever you are, even if your external resources are minimal. You should also be willing to experiment with new methods of getting high as you mature and change. People who use drugs regularly may have to work especially hard to get high in other ways, because they often grow accustomed to the physical sensations of their drugs and consider them necessary components of the experience. (p. 172)

Smith (1982) reports on evidence showing that "being high" is an altered state of consciousness, and alcoholics, if not most substance abusers, do not understand that the brain has an ability to get high naturally, without psychotropic substances. Smith lists several factors that will increase the likelihood of attaining peaks of altered consciousness:

- Knowing about altered states
- Giving oneself permission to "let go"
- Selecting a conducive environment
- Relaxing
- Concentrating
- Adopting a noncritical stance
- Using breathing exercises and rhythms (music, dance, and so on)

Often a person is not convinced that he or she can have a sober high until he or she has experienced an altered state without drugs.

The third step in recovery and change identified by Steinbroner (1985) is learning and participating in activities that bring satisfaction and pleasure, giving the natural high that individuals seek through drugs, which may begin in the substance dependence treatment program. In addition to using cognitive and behavioral modalities, the program may emphasize what may be called affective modes, which alter awareness or consciousness and produce feelings, emotions, moods, and temperament. Such modes may include stress management training, meditation, biofeedback, creative therapies, charismatic group therapy, suggestion, and group marathon therapy, among others.

Stress Management Training

Although stress management training may affect behavior and could be called a behavioral mode, reports indicate that stress management training produces affective as well as behavioral and cognitive changes in heavy drug users (Rohsenow, Smith, and Johnson 1985). Frye (1986b) reports that such training may involve the following:

1. Verbal suggestions to achieve deep muscle relaxation
2. Visual imagery to produce cognitive calming
3. Progressive relaxation to achieve a tension-relaxation contrast
4. Autogenic therapy promoting heaviness and warmth in the extremities and calming of the autonomic nervous system
5. Automated systematic desensitization in which the client imagines a hierarchy of anxiety-producing situations under conditions of physical relaxation with the goal of weakening anxiety responses

Basic Relaxation Response Instruction. I have used a basic suggestive protocol developed by Rothschild (1987) with groups of inpatient substance-dependent persons in a hospital setting. This training uses an anchor, such as touching the left shoulder with the right hand. The anchor is used as a signal for the patient to go into the relaxation response so that the individual may use this technique in the future without the need for props or exteroceptive stimulation or suggestion. After individuals assemble in a quiet room where interruption is unlikely, the stress management facilitator will repeat a version of the following instruction:

> Make yourself comfortable. Get yourself in a comfortable position. Close your eyes. Touch your left shoulder; feel the sense of gravity. Pay attention to no sound other than my voice. Let yourself experience gravity—pulling you down—pulling you down. Let yourself give in to gravity. Let your body sag into the chair—sag into the chair. Feel the gravity pulling you down—pulling you down. Feel the gravity pulling you down. Just let go—going deeper and deeper—deeper and deeper—deeper and deeper—getting more and more relaxed—getting more and more relaxed—getting more and more relaxed—more and more relaxed. Feel the gravity pulling you down—pulling you down—going deeper and deeper—deeper and deeper—more and more relaxed—more and more relaxed. Your thoughts will come and go, but nothing will be troublesome—getting more relaxed, serene. Nothing you think will be troublesome. As I talk, you get more relaxed—letting your body sag—letting your body sag—not falling asleep but letting your body sag—deeper and deeper—deeper and deeper.
>
> Now, listening to my voice, imagine that you have a bottle or pitcher filled with water. When I start counting backward from ten, drain the pitcher. See the water coming out of the pitcher or bottle. As you see the water draining out, you will feel the tension draining out of your body, and when it is over, you will be totally relaxed. Ten, nine, eight, seven, six, five, four, three, two, one—very relaxed—very relaxed—physically relaxed—mentally serene—no thoughts or ideas are troublesome. You are physically relaxed—mentally serene—very nice.
>
> Now with your mind's eye, I want you to look at your serene face. Notice how there is no muscle tension, no tightness in your face—relaxed—no tension—no tightness—no anger. Your face is calm; your face is in control.
>
> Now I am going to ask you some questions. Answer them silently. Can you feel gravity on your face, neck, and cheeks? Can you feel gravity pulling down on your shoulders and forearms? Can you feel gravity pulling down on your chest, back, and buttocks? Can you feel gravity pulling down on your legs, feet, and toes? Can you feel gravity pulling you down—down—down—very nice.
>
> In a moment, I will ask you to get back to your ordinary state but hold on to the sense of calm and relaxation for a good number of hours. I will count backward from three. When I say three, get yourself mentally ready. When I say two, open your eyes and move your bodies around—get the blood flowing. When I say one, give each other a smile and get ready to talk. Three—get yourself mentally ready. Two—open your eyes and move your

bodies around; get your blood flowing. Very good. And one—give a smile please.

After clients have been trained in the relaxation response, a continuation of such training should include demonstrating that they can be alert and active while staying in the relaxed mode. Before counting backward from three, continue the instruction as follows:

> Holding on to your state of physical relaxation and mental calm, I will ask you to straighten yourself in your chairs and open your eyes. Please do that now: Straighten up; open your eyes. Thank you. Hold on to the calmness; hold on to the relaxation. Your eyes are open; you are able to talk. How is everyone feeling? Fine—still feeling relaxed—(discussion).
>
> It's very important to understand that you can do a great deal when you are mentally relaxed—physically relaxed. Most of life does not require the tension that you people have been walking around with. You can be relaxed with your eyes open. This is evidence of that. Okay? Ready to go back? Close your eyes; go back into it. Okay—very good.
>
> I'm going to ask you, one at a time, to open your eyes, get up, go outside to the drinking fountain, get a drink, then come back to the room and sit down, closing your eyes again. You will keep yourself mentally and physically relaxed going outside of the room. (Call on each member until all have accomplished this task.)

Rohsenow, Smith, and Johnson (1985) investigated the effectiveness of stress management training as a drinking reduction program for heavy social drinking college students. They found that six hourly sessions, twice a week, achieved modest overall success in modifying the cognitions, daily moods, and alcohol consumption of these students. A control group showed no decrease in drinking.

Covert conditioning or sensitization has gained some acceptance in the treatment of persons addicted to drugs. This technique, which consists of the use of imagined scenes as aversive events and as rewarding events (Frye 1986b), may be added easily to stress management training. For example, at some point in the basic suggestive dialogue, the facilitator may add an imagined scene where the client will learn to experience nausea when he or she approaches the addictive substance.

Meditation

Daniel Goleman (1977) writes that for millennia, meditation has been a path for persons who seek to go beyond the limiting goals of the everyday world. Although meditation apparently may produce altered states of consciousness, such states are rare and never happen to the majority of meditators. What meditation can produce in most meditators is the *relaxation response,* a term for a normal physiological state in which the body is relaxed, restoring itself from stress or exertion. The physiological effects of meditation are opposite those identified by medicine as being characteristic of the effort to meet the demands of stress (Selye 1975). Goleman (1976; 1984) states that the regular routine of meditation or relaxation is an effective way to guard against the mental and physical toll of stress. The routine need be only fifteen to twenty minutes in length. Like drug using, meditation appears to alter the individual's perception of stressful situations and promotes behavior changes toward objects and circumstances perceived to be threatening (Frye 1981a). A simple meditation technique centered on breathing or the breath may involve a mantra or sound pattern as an incantation (Benson 1984).

Meditation invokes the relaxation response, which is characterized by a change in awareness and may produce subjective states that have been described as feeling at ease with the world, a sense of well-being, or peace of mind. Such a response is hypothesized to be a coordinated physiological reaction brought about by the stimulation (change in neurotransmission) of the hypothalamic regions in the brain. The elements needed to provoke the relaxation response are a quiet environment, decreased muscle tone, a passive attitude, and a mental device such as a sound repeated audibly or silently (Benson 1984). Teaching clients in a substance dependence treatment program the self-control techniques of relaxation and stress management to reduce anxiety, nervousness, and dysphoric moods may be teaching them an *alternative* to drug use and may help to increase their psychological and adaptive resources for dealing more effectively with stress without the use of chemicals (Charlesworth and Dempsey 1982).

Verbal Invocation. A facilitator, teaching clients individually or in groups, may use a verbal invocation similar to the following (Goleman 1984; Benson 1984):

> Take this time for yourself to get clear, calm, and deeply relaxed. In meditation, you will focus on breathing—on your breath and its rhythm. Whenever your mind wanders off, gently bring it back to your breath. Your body will shift to a relaxed state. You may say to yourself some word such as one, peace, or love. The word should be comforting. You may use a word silently or just be aware of your breathing.
>
> Stay alert and awake. Sit in a comfortable position with your head up and your body straight. Get comfortable; close your eyes; bring your attention to your breath. Notice the natural, easy passage of your breath in and out of the nose. Don't try to control your breath but be aware of the sensation of breathing; be aware of every breath—the in-breath and the out-breath. If other thoughts pass through your mind, let them go and gently bring your mind back to your breath. If outside noises or inside sensations

distract you, let them go and bring your attention back to your breath. If you need to change your position, do so slowly. Be totally attentive to your breath—the in-breath—the out-breath—breathing in—breathing out. Keep your attention on your breath. If you find your mind wandering, bring your mind back to your breath—each in-breath—each outbreath. Be fully aware; be fully alert; be aware of your breathing—breathing in—breathing out—breathing in—breathing out. Any sounds you hear, let them go. Gently bring your mind back to your breath—breathing in—breathing out—the whole in-breath—the whole out-breath. Do not try to control your breath. Breathe naturally—breathing in—breathing out. (Continue the verbal instructions for about fifteen minutes, with an occasional long pause.)

If you wish to focus your attention more on your breath, you may take a deep inhalation—a deep in-breath—a deep out-breath—breathing in—breathing out—breathing in—breathing out. Before we end, take a few moments to feel your body. Just as you have been watching your breath, scan your body from head to toe—feeling complete and whole—at peace—rested and relaxed and refreshed. When you feel you are ready, gently open your eyes and stretch. Get the blood flowing. Do it easily and slow. Get back to the here and now—back into your day—slowly—gradually—relaxed—refreshed.

Carrington (1978) relates the potential effects of meditation as noted in her patients:

1. A dramatic reduction in overall tension and anxiety
2. An unaccustomed surge of energy and increased physical stamina
3. Improved self-esteem by a marked diminishment of self-recrimination
4. An elevation and stabilization of mood in patients with depressive tendencies
5. An increased availability of affect, with reports of strong feelings previously suppressed
6. Tension-release side effects (temporary psychological and/or physiological symptoms
7. An increased sense of separate identity (a convincing sense of self)
8. An antiaddictive effect (a marked decrease or discontinuance of nonprescription drugs)

Biofeedback

Fehmi (1978) has found many modalities of biofeedback useful with patients, especially for symptoms associated with pain, tension, and stress. Fehmi believes that properly used biofeedback enhances the client's functional capacity and sense of well-being. In biofeedback, changes in the physiological process being monitored are reflected by a change in a sensory signal, such as a tone or light.

Although biofeedback is a purely behavioral means of achieving certain levels of physiological response, it may be able to modulate affect and produce the relaxation response. Clinical research has reported the correlation of alpha brain wave (where alpha was associated with mental relaxation and a noncritical attitude toward the environment) with reports of relaxation, letting go, and pleasant affect. Nonalpha brain wave was associated with alertness or visual attention. Other studies have associated alpha brain wave with well-being, pleasure, tranquility, and relaxation. Interestingly, Shapiro (1977) has suggested that biofeedback techniques may be adapted to induce the psychophysiological patterns known to be associated with particular drugs. Subjects can be asked to self-regulate these same patterns without the aid of drugs.

If a goal of addiction treatment is to teach the client a skill that will partially replace the relief afforded by psychoactive chemicals and produce calming effects, then biofeedback may be useful at an early treatment stage. These skills must be learned well enough to become a dependable and reliable asset. Since alpha biofeedback requires equipment, it may be useful only in early treatment, as later treatment should foster autonomy from existential crutches (Frye 1986b).

Charismatic Group Therapy

Charismatic therapy is often used in drug-free therapeutic communities and in AA, encounter groups, est, Gestalt therapy, and religious groups. It may alter affect. Newcomers in treatment may present as depressed and anxious. Often clients are characterized by feelings of inadequacy, lowered activity, and pessimism about the future. Anxiety may be manifested in feelings of mingled dread and apprehension without a specific cause for the fear. Ideally, these conditions can be mediated in a nonchemical way.

Charismatic therapy may occur in what Galanter (1980; 1982) calls "large groups." These groups may be defined as a large number of persons in a cohesive association who espouse a zealous philosophy with attendant rituals and who often meet in small groups. The group's goals and functions redefine the social roles and behavioral norms of the group members. Symbol identification is important for group cohesion. Galanter's (1978) model for anxiety-relief psychotherapy in charismatic groups specifies that such groups have more than twelve members and be associated with a zealous movement. In addition, such groups must have totemic objects and rituals, such as Synanon "games" or the AA "Big Book." A behavior code, such as the twelve steps of AA or the value concepts of the drug-free therapeutic community, is necessary for the relief effect to take place. Role diffusion is observed, and there is often limited differentiation between the care giver and the recipient (Frye 1984a; Frye 1984b).

In discussing the *relief by affiliation* in members of a religious group, Galanter (1986) writes:

> Behavioral expectations . . . were further adapted to the needs of individual members by central figures, or middle-echelon religious and administrative leaders. These leaders provide advice and support individually or in small exhortative group exchanges, so as to encourage members with problems to adapt to the group. This counseling . . . is not unlike that used by therapeutic mentors in zealous healing groups such as Alcoholics Anonymous. (p. 1245–1249)

In comparing findings found in a charismatic religious group to those found in AA, also a "quasi-therapeutic" large group where consensual belief is important, Galanter (1980) writes:

> Persons who maintained a long-term membership in AA, rather than dropping out after an initial affiliation, were found to have greater need to establish social affiliations. For a religious sect . . . a greater isolation from previous ties accompanies membership. The relative balance between affiliation to members and to old associates therefore becomes important. (p. 1575)

In addition, the technique of mixing group veterans with initiates in conjoint group experiences promotes modeling and group identification. This mixing may be seen in contemporary self-help programs.

In discussing the findings related to charismatic groups and their implications for substance dependence treatment, Galanter (1981) writes:

> One thing we may certainly learn from the religious cults is the importance of sustaining a mutually accepted system of norms and beliefs for the treatment personnel and those who are treated. In recent years, for example, we have found that many of those who were successfully taken off illicit opiates by means of methadone maintenance again become addicted to a variety of other agents. These patients were alienated from the social establishment at the outset of treatment, and limited, if any, support was provided to engage them in the value system of the general population. . . . To treat the substance abusers in isolation from addressing their value systems is to wage a steep uphill battle. (pp. 65–69)

Creative Therapies

Affect change and the prerequisite alteration of brain neurotransmission may be solicited by creative therapies. Dance, music, art, movement, and drama are included in this mode. Movement therapies may include exercise, aerobic dancing (Auer 1980), and stretching (Anderson 1980). These modes can elevate mood and promote relaxation. They can provide the individual with an intuition of the feeling state attached to the gestalt, the essence of a body moving, and an understanding of the possibilities for modulating the movement to produce communication (Fink et al. 1984).

Music arouses specific feelings and emotions that may provide the individual with the opportunity to experience relations with others without the fear of harm or hurt associated with verbal experiences (Frye 1986b). Positive affective arousal may result from small deviations in perceived complexity from the level to which the listener is adapted. It is unclear whether musical meaning lies in the perception of musical form or whether music conveys extramusical feelings, concepts, and meanings (Risset 1978). I favor the latter explanation. Music may imitate natural sounds in the environment. Music also may bring remembrance of sounds that in the past prompted alteration of consciousness and produced changes in feelings, emotions, moods, and temperament. A survey conducted more than half a century ago (with twenty thousand verbal reports) indicated that affective reactions to music are strikingly similar for a majority of listeners regardless of training, age, or experience. Some affective experiences related to music also may be learned—for example, the association of the minor mode with sadness is frequent only for Western listeners (Risset 1978).

Listening to certain types of music can have a positive effect on the physiological and emotional well-being of patients in a hospital setting. In a recent study of intensive care and surgery patients by Phyllis Updike (Eicher 1987), patients listened to music for thirty minutes through earphones that permitted nurse-patient communication. The music had a regular rhythm or meter and predictable dynamics. Upon listening to the music, physical indicators such as blood pressure, heart rate, respiratory rate, and oxygen consumption improved. For some patients, the music evoked memories of twenty years or more, when the patients were better able to cope with stress and pain. Such memories helped these patients to accept their current pain and stress. The judicial use of music within a treatment program for addiction may be one way to modulate consciousness and provide a measure of the natural high that addicts should be encouraged to seek.

Suggestion

It appears that the affective system in humans can be activated by suggestion. Ideas can then lead to direct, immediate, reflexlike corresponding behaviors. Weitzenhoffer (1978) writes, "I am of the opinion today . . . that suggestions can bring about remarkable effects in highly suggestible individuals, including physiological changes" (p. 202). He states that the classical hypnosis effect is the enhancement of classical suggestibility. Hypnotic action occurs with the lessening of volitional participation (or the spreading of automatism).

Marsh (1977) points out that the most common light-trance induction technique in our culture is a television commercial. Humans allow themselves to be hypnotized by the commercial and subsequently follow its suggestions. He writes, "The building blocks of the hypnotic effect seem to be part of the basic equipment of ordinary awake consciousness; the capacity to become completely absorbed in something outside ourselves and the capacity to follow suggestions made to us by another person" (p. 138). Marsh sees meditation, trance, and self-hypnosis as variants of daydreaming. He notes that individuals under the influence of hypnosis seem to have a greater capability for fantasy production and for recalling long-forgotten memories.

Suggestion and the strategic use of trance phenomena are used in Ericksonian psychotherapy, which also uses strategic interventions with complex embedded metaphors. This modality uses resistance, symptom prescription, and paradoxical double binds (Erickson 1980). An Ericksonian induction includes the establishment of a conscious/unconscious dissociation in which the client's attention is dissociated and polarized by using dissociation language, including the use of anecdotes and education about the function of the unconscious thought processes. Lankton and Lankton (1982) provide examples of conscious/unconscious dissociation language:

> Your conscious mind is listening to and hearing my words and your unconscious mind is doing something else. Your conscious mind may be interested in learning one thing and your unconscious mind is concerned with what is relevant. Your conscious mind may have that doubt and your unconscious mind develops its own line of thought. Your conscious mind is probably curious and your unconscious mind isn't even interested. Your conscious mind operates linearly and your unconscious mind thinks globally. Your conscious mind won't do much that's interesting as your unconscious mind has its own idea of what you need. Your conscious mind may be interested in one depth of trance as your unconscious mind develops the proper depth of trance. Your conscious mind can focus on one spot while your unconscious mind is really doing a lot for you. Your conscious mind is sorting, categorizing, and pigeonholing just as your unconscious mind understands the context. (p. 3)

In the course of an Ericksonian induction, an embedded metaphor structure is used. After the client is oriented to the trance and a conscious/unconscious dissociation is established, a metaphor is introduced to provide an altered frame of reference, which allows the client to entertain novel experiences. A diagnostic assessment and contracted therapy goals determine what experiences are needed. These goals are then elicited with indirect suggestion, anecdotes, and binds. The dramatic metaphor parallels the problem situation. The story line is left unresolved. The experiences that are elicited may be arranged into a network of associations that can help the client form a perceptually and behaviorally based map of conduct. The matching metaphor may include retrieval of resources and stimulate patterns of feeling, thinking, and behavior that the client needs to deal with the problem. A variety of characters, anecdotes, and indirect suggestions may occur. The metaphor may abruptly end without an obvious solution, and the end may be surprising or humorous. The client is then reoriented, and posthypnotic suggestions may be given to continue, for example, learning, remaining in a relaxed state, or feeling optimistic. Paradox or confusion may also be used at this stage, as can an increasing reference to the here and now.

The issue of client resistance seems to me to be a natural connection between Ericksonian psychotherapy and substance dependence treatment (McGarty 1985). Rather than resistance in a client, the preferred mode may be surrender. This is used quite effectively in AA's "surrender to a higher power." In Ericksonian psychotherapy, techniques were developed to bypass resistance. These techniques allow the therapist to instill hope in and create a rapport with the client while bypassing conscious resistance. Questions may be used to focus, suggest, and reinforce, and the final question may be in the form of a suggestion. McGarty (1981) provides an example: "Would you like to sit down? Would you like things to improve? And how soon will you begin to notice the freedom that will come when you have finally settled into this decision not to use alcohol?" (p. 149). McGarty feels that this type of indirect technique is useful with clients who are weary, used to failure, tentative, and unable to meet significant expectations in their lives. A recent development, Neuro-Linguistic Programming,™ is based on Ericksonian techniques and may solicit affective and behavioral changes (Grinder and Bandler 1981).

Group Marathon Therapy

Marathon therapy may produce changes in intrapsychic or interpersonal dynamics and may provide a multivariable experience for both staff and clients in substance dependence programs. The intensity, duration, and length of the marathon help to break down psychological defenses such as intellectualization, denial, and isolation. Trust and cohesion, both aspects of the group process, may be molded and strengthened. Consciousness may be modulated, and individuals often feel that they have gone through a unique experience that makes them special (Cohen and Rietma 1980). Active mechanisms that can promote altered affect include sleep deprivation, stimulus intensity (such as light or sound), shared group closeness or cohesion, and emotional release (Hoag and Gissen 1984; Frye, Hammer, and Burke 1981). A marathon encounter may provide an opportunity for the use of multiple affective modes and produce a memorable moment of affective change for clients.

A group marathon may be referred to as an extended encounter, a stew, or a dissipation (of anger) (Hampden-Turner 1976). Planning is necessary to provide structure to the marathon, and goals may be set (both staff and clients participate in the planning). A marathon may have a theme, such as Village South's "life and death" marathon (Hoag and Gissen 1984), in which the marathon took clients through death to rebirth and hope.

Experiential Narrative. On the day after Valentine's Day in 1986, a conjoint marathon titled "A Time Dissipation" was about to commence in Denver, Colorado, with two Denver area TCs—the University of Colorado Therapeutic Community, Peer I, and the Denver Veterans Administration Therapeutic Community, Ayrie. Ayrie served as the host program, and the marathon started at the Ayrie facility, called Park Place, a two-story building with numerous group rooms and a large central meeting room. The building is equipped with two kitchens, rest rooms, and two recreation areas with a pool and table tennis equipment, television sets, and dart boards. The building also has a public address system.

Since both programs are related insofar as they share a common ancestor, Denver's Independence House Family, their ideology and therapeutic tools are similar. Both use the confrontation-sensitivity (C-S) group (Frye, Hammer, and Burke 1981), a variation of the [Synanon and Mendocino Game] (Brewster and Garrigues 1974; Yablonsky 1965). There is no therapist or leader in this type of encounter. In each group, there is a senior games player, the person with the most experience in C-S, who starts and stops the group and may suspend the group if there is an emergency or if one of the group's two rules (no chemicals and no physical violence or threats of violence) are broken.

Except for the two rules, clients may do anything they wish. They may yell, cry, laugh, lie, confess, remain silent, or talk seriously. Policies or suggestions include the following:

1. Talk to only one person at a time, and do not carry on separate conversations; focus all attention on the person in the "hot seat."
2. Support the probe or group focus on an individual.
3. Do not defend the individual in the hot seat, even if you feel sorry for him or her.

Participants may use a variety of techniques, ranging from engrossment of behavior or feelings to righteous indignation to belittlement (making something big appear inconsequential). Catharsis, indicting, projecting, and data running are all modes of participation. The C-S group was to be the basic marathon activity.

The goals of this marathon were to encourage catharsis, dissipate anger, promote trust, and provide optimism for the future. It was decided that after the marathon was over, participants should feel pleasantly exhausted and "cleansed." "Time" would be the theme.

To generate anticipation, a valentine was sent to each client (marked "confidential"), inviting him or her to a "Time Dissipation" beginning at 8 A.M. on February 15. At the appointed time, Ayrie and Peer I clients and staff assembled at Park Place and were given an orientation. They were told that they would experience the past, which would lead to the present and then on into the future. The lights were dimmed, and two marathon candles (one for each program) were lighted by the senior members. The candles would burn throughout the marathon.

As the participants relaxed on large, overstuffed pillows, a one-hour music encounter began. The music was designed to set the tone and to stimulate memory. The music was originally recorded for use at a Peer I marathon in 1981 and started with a Peer I marathon tradition: a recording of "The Journey of the Sorcerer," played by the Eagles, a soft-rock group.

After the music encounter, the fifty participants gathered around two television sets to watch a motion picture, *Somewhere in Time,* starring Christopher Reeves. The movie is based on the novel *Bid Time Return* by Richard Matheson (1975), who wrote: "This idea of the Great Time haunts us in many ways. . . . Man thinks constantly of 'going back,' away from all worldly pressures; to neighborhoods which never change where boymen play forever" (p. 57). The motion picture is a romantic fantasy in which a man goes back in time to meet the love of his life. He can stay only briefly, however, and then must return to the present, leaving his love with a penny dated half a century in the future.

After the motion picture was shown, the Ayrie staff described the marathon concept to the participants (Frye, Hammer, and Burke 1981) and showed a one-hour videotape of a prior marathon. At 2:45 P.M., all the participants convened as the C-S large group. The clients were encouraged to remain in the past, run data concerning the past and their drug-influenced lives, experience catharsis, and get ready for the present. At 5 P.M., participants took a "grazing break" during which they could eat light, high-energy snacks. The participants were then randomly divided into three smaller groups to facilitate individual participation. These small groups met throughout the night, with participants changing groups as desired. At times, the groups broke for special encounters, facilitated by the staff and senior residents, on cooperation and imagery.

At 7 A.M. the next day, the clients were taken in vans to a high-rise overlooking Denver's Cheesman Park. They took the elevator up to the penthouse (a party room with a large outside deck) and prepared for a sunrise encounter. A senior Ayrie resident led the participants through stretching exercises on the deck. After a light breakfast, an Ayrie staff member led the participants through an imagery or fantasy encounter. At 11:30 A.M., the residents returned to Park Place and reformed into their C-S groups. Containers of ice water and towels were available so that they could ward off sleepiness by wiping their faces with the cold water. During breaks, a recording of the "Variations on the Kanon" (by Johann Pachelbel) played by pianist George Winston was broadcast over the public address system in an attempt to maintain the mood.

At 9 P.M., after a light snack, all the participants returned to the large room for a final group session. Those who had not yet "worked" (been in the hot seat) were given an invitation to do so. "George," who had been rather quiet and restrained during the marathon, volunteered. He talked about his past. He said that he had always felt out of place and had tried various fads to fit in. He had been a "biker" (a motorcyclist) and had been in the military, but he had never found a sense of belonging. He talked about his alcohol and cocaine problems and how he had wounded his brother with a shotgun blast while under the influence of drugs. George said that he felt that he was not fitting into the treatment program and that he had found it hard to express his feelings. George cried and made a commitment to express his emotions more openly. The group gave George verbal support and advised him that he could not change the past. What was important was the present. By using the present, the group advised, George could change his future.

"Rose," who had volunteered for the hot seat early in the marathon, said that she wanted it again. During the early work, Rose had been indicted for using sexual manipulation to "come on" to various male residents. Some participants said she had a provocative posture and demeanor. Rose had stoutly denied that she intentionally acted provocatively and said that everyone had imagined it. Rose now wanted to "confess" that she had indeed tried to use sexual manipulation to get her way. She said that in the past, she had been successful in getting her way by being "sexy" and that she had gotten cocaine by offering sexual favors to cocaine suppliers. The group congratulated Rose on her honesty. Rose told the group that she did not want to act that way in the future and asked the group to help her get rid of this habit.

After everyone who wished to participate had done so, preparation for the final encounter commenced. The participants assembled in the large group room. Each client was given a piece of paper, a small candle, and a colored plastic egg. The clients were then asked to think of the future and to write down three goals that they wanted to fulfill. Participants were encouraged to share their goals with others in the group. The participants were asked to open their eggs, one at a time, and examine the contents. Each egg contained a fortune cookie with an upbeat fortune that predicted the future. Each egg also contained a penny from the past (to relate back to the film *Somewhere in Time*). Each participant read his or her fortune to the group, examined the penny, and told the group its date. Finally, the lights were extinguished (except for the marathon candles). The senior residents lighted their own individual candles from the marathon candle and went around the group lighting the individual candles of the participants. As the room grew bright, the participants spoke of their concern for each other. They expressed positive feelings and warmth. The candles were extinguished, and the end of the marathon was announced. It was 1 A.M.; the marathon had lasted forty-one hours.

Charles Hampden-Turner (1976) expressed his feelings this way after participating in a marathon at the Delancy Street Foundation:

> So it's over . . . and I can barely stand. . . . I have always known intellectually—I have even taught—that one must face death with people to appreciate life, encounter deformity to really marvel at perfection, and comfort the despairing to rejoice fully in one's own good fortune. I have known it but not experienced it with the force I now feel. . . . For the next week or so, moods of extreme tenderness will suddenly overwhelm me. . . . The Dissipation certainly has a permanent effect on those who went through it together. We embrace whenever we meet. To some twenty residents I will never be a stranger nor they to me. (pp. 228–33)

Conclusion

The goal of the affective modalities is to train the client to achieve an affective experience, or vicissitude of consciousness, that results in pleasurable feelings, emotions, moods, and temperament. Like psychoactive chemicals, these experiences result in self-induced changes in neurotransmission in the human brain. Unlike psychoactive substances, these experiences and activities are less likely to produce problem behaviors and afford relief from discomfort and stress. The use of affective modalities in substance dependence treatment programs may lead to more vibrant programming and teach clients how to find a natural high, which may help fill the experiential void and help them to live a life without drugs.

In addition to "saying no to drugs," people also can "say *yes* to natural highs." The objective of a national conference held in Boulder, Colorado, in October 1987 was to promote a reawakening in adults and continued enjoyment by children of natural highs. Harvey Milkman, the conference director (1987) writes:

We are guided by natural impulses to become aroused, relax, and to imagine. The unaffected interplay of these experiences can lead to profound sensations of pleasure and fulfillment. During the transition from childhood to adolescence, spontaneous expression becomes increasingly inhibited by comparison between ourselves and others. Drugs and alcohol become preferred means to achieve temporary relief from discomfort and stress. Alternatively, life enhancing means for feeling good and reducing stress may be promoted by the family, school and media.

In addition to the family, school, and media, I suggest that substance abuse treatment programs also can benefit from this perspective.

References

Anderson, B. 1980. *Stretching*. Bolinas, Calif.: Shelter Publications.
Auer, B.A. 1980. *Aerobic Dancing*. New York: Gencom.
Benson, H. 1984. "The Relaxation Response and the Treatment of Anxiety." In *Psychiatry Update*, edited by L. Grinspoon, Washington, D.C.: American Psychiatric Press.
Brewster, J.T., and C. Garrigues. 1974. "The Mendocino Game: Rules, Policies, Modes and Techniques." *Drug Forum* 4 (1): 15–29.
Carper, J. 1986. "If You're Going to the Hospital—Read This." *U.S. News and World Report* 100 (14): 64–65.
Carrington, P. 1978. "The Uses of Meditation in Psychotherapy." In *Expanding Dimensions of Consciousness*, edited by A.A. Sugerman, and R.E. Tarter, New York: Springer-Verlag.
Charlesworth, E.A., and D. Dempsey. 1982. "Trait Anxiety Reduction in a Substance Abuse Population Trained in Stress Management." *Journal of Clinical Psychology* 38 (4): 764–68.
Cohen, E.S., and K. Rietma. 1980. "Utilizing Marathon Therapy in a Drug and Alcohol Rehabilitation Program." *International Journal of Group Psychotherapy* 31 (1): 117–23.
Eicher, D. 1987. "Music Positive Force in Hospital, Research Suggests." *Denver Post*, August 20.
Erickson, M.H. 1980. *The Collected Papers of Milton H. Erickson on Hypnosis*. New York: Irvington Publishers.
Fehmi, L.G. 1978. "EEG Biofeedback, Multichannel Synchrony, Training, and Attention." In *Expanding Dimensions of Consciousness*, edited by E.A. Sugarman and R.E. Tarter, New York: Springer Verlag.
Fink, P.J., M.R. Levick, R. Hays, D.R. Johnson, D. Dulicai, and C.A. Briggs. "Creative Therapies." In *The Psychiatric Therapies*, edited by T.B. Karasu. Washington, D.C.: American Psychiatric Association.
Frye, R.V. 1976. "Concept: Changes." Unpublished manuscript.
———. 1980a. "The Sociobiologic Paradigm: A New Approach to Drug Using Behavior." *Journal of Psychedelic Drugs* 12 (1): 21–25.

———. 1980b. "Why Is Sugar Sweet?" Drug Abuse: A Sociobiologic Approach." In *Drug, Problems of the 70's*. edited by R. Faulkinberry. Lafayette, La.: Endac Enterprises.

———. 1981a. "Drug Using Behavior: An Approach from Behavioral Biology." *Stress* 2 (2): 5–9.

———. 1981b. "Sociobiology and the Therapeutic Community." In *Drug Dependence and Alcoholism: Biomedical Issues*, edited by A. Schecter. New York: Plenum Press.

———. 1984a. "Editor's Introduction." *Journal of Psychoactive Drugs* 16 (1): 1–7.

———. 1984b. "The Therapeutic Community: A Sociobiologic Study." *Journal of Psychoactive Drugs* 16 (1): 27–33.

———. 1985a. "A Multimodality Approach to Addiction Treatment." In *The Addictions: Multidisciplinary Perspectives and Treatments*, edited by H.B. Milkman and H.J. Shaffer, 175–182. Lexington, Mass.: Lexington Books.

———. 1985b. "A Multimodality Approach to Programming in the Therapeutic Community." Paper presented at the Ninth World Conference of Therapeutic Communities, San Francisco, September 1–7.

———. 1986a. "Editor's Introduction." *Journal of Psychoactive Drugs* 18 (3): 191–97.

——— 1986b. "To Fill the Void: Heterodox Programming in Drug Free Residential Treatment for Addiction—Utilizing a Theoretical Position from Evolutionary Biology." *Journal of Psychoactive Drugs* 18 (3): 267–75.

Frye, R.V. In press. "Vicissitudes of Consciousness: Affective Modalities in Addiction Treatment." *Journal of Psychoactive Drugs*."

Frye, R.V., M. Hammer, and G. Burke. 1981. "The Confrontation-Sensitivity (C-S) Group." In *Drug Dependence and Alcoholism: Biomedical Issues*, edited by A. Schecter. New York: Plenum Press.

Galanter, M. 1978. "The 'Relief Effect': A Sociobiological Model for Neurotic Distress and Large-Group Therapy." *American Journal of Psychiatry* 135 (5): 588–91.

———. 1980. "Psychological Induction into the Large-Group: Findings from a Modern Religious Sect." *American Journal of Psychiatry* 137 (12): 1574–79.

———. 1981. "Sociobiology and Informal Social Controls of Drinking." *Journal of Studies on Alcohol* 42 (1): 64–79.

———. 1982. "Charismatic Religious Seets and Psychiatry: An Overview." *American Journal of Psychiatry* 139 (12): 1539–47.

Goleman, D. 1976. "Meditation Helps Break the Stress Spiral." *Psychology Today*, February 1976.

m———. 1977. *The Varieties of the Meditative Experience*. New York: E.P. Dutton.

———. 1984. *Mind/Body Savers—Meditation and Muscle Relaxation*. Cassette tape. New York: American Health.

Grinder, J., and R. Bandler. 1981. *Trance-formations: Neurolinguistic Programming and the Structure of Hypnosis*. Moab, Utah: Real People Press.

Hampden-Turner, C. 1976. *Sane Asylum*. New York: William Morrow.

Hoag, J., & J.P. Gissen. 1984. "Marathon: A Life and Death Experience." *Journal of Psychoactive Drugs*, 16 (1): 47–50.

Mandell, A.J. 1985. "Interhemispheric Fusion." *Journal of Psychoactive Drugs* 17 (4): 257–66.
Marsh, C. 1977. "A Framework for Describing Subjective States of Consciousness." In *Alternative States of Consciousness*, edited by N.E. Zinberg. New York: Free Press.
Matheson, R. 1975. *Bid Time Return*. New York: Viking Press.
McGarty, R. 1985. "Relevance of Ericksonian Psychotherapy to the Treatment of Chemical Dependency." *Journal of Substance Abuse Treatment*, 2:147–51.
Milkman H. 1987. "Natural Highs—New Directions for Mood Alteration." In *A Conference on New Directions* (conference brochure), edited by H. Milkman and A. Hunter. Boulder, Colo.: Center for Interdisciplinary Studies and Boulder District Attorney's Office.
Milkman, H., and S. Sunderwirth. 1987. *Craving for Ecstasy*. Lexington, Mass.: Lexington Books.
Risset, J.C. 1978. "Musical Acoustics." In *Handbook on Perception*, edited by E.C. Carterett and M.P. Friedman. New York: Academic Press.
Rohsenow, D.J., R.E. Smith, and S. Johnson. 1985. "Stress Management Training as a Prevention Program for Heavy Social Drinkers: Cognitions, Affect, Drinking and Individual Differences." *Addictive Behaviors* 10:45–54.
Rothschild, B. 1987. Personal communication. February 1.
Selye, H. 1975. Introduction. In H.H. Bloomfield, M.P. Cain and D.T. Jaffe, eds. *TM: Discovering inner energy and overcoming stress*. New York: Delacourte Press.
Shapiro, D. 1977. "A Biofeedback Strategy in the Study of Consciousness." In *Alternative States of Consciousness*, edited by N.E. Zinberg. New York: Free Press.
Smith, T.M. 1982. "Specific Approaches and Techniques in the Treatment of the Gay Male Alcohol Abuser." *Journal of Homosexuality* 7 (4): 53–69.
Steinbroner, P.J. 1985. *The Haight-Ashbury Cocaine Film*. Manhattan Beach, Calif.: Cinemed.
Weil, A.T., and W. Rosen. 1983. *Chocolate to Morphine*. Boston: Houghton Mifflin.
Weitzenhoffer, A.M. 1978. "Hypnotism and altered states of consciousness." In *Expanding Dimensions of Consciousness*, edited by A.A. Sugarman, and R.E. Tarter. New York: Springer.
Wesson, D.R., and D.E. Smith. 1985. "Cocaine: Treatment Perspectives." In *Cocaine Use in America: Epidemiological and Clinical Perspectives*, edited by M.S. Kozel and M.S. Adams, NIDA Research Monograph, no. 61. Rockville, Md.: NIDA.
Yablonsky, L. 1965. *The Tunnel Back: Synanon*. New York: Macmillan.

18
Family Therapy Approaches to Substance Abuse with a Special Focus on Alcohol Issues

Victor A. Harris

In writing about family therapy approaches to substance abuse, it is first necessary to step back and briefly examine the central concepts of *substance abuse* and *family therapy*. This task is particularly difficult with regard to substance abuse because the underlying conceptual framework—the field of addiction—is currently in chaos.

That conceptual confusion and conflict exist and perhaps the reason that this is so has been documented by Shaffer (1986). He argues that the confusion and lack of clarity stem from the fact that the addiction field is in a preparadigm phase of theory development. Since a clear, universally accepted paradigm does not exist, there are "intensely conflicting and polarized explanations . . . and few 'facts.'" (Shaffer 1986, p. x). This state of affairs has direct relevance for the practice of substance abuse treatment. "For the clinician, the assessment and diagnosis of addiction [substance abuse] is a direct function of the models and frameworks that guide and influence the evaluation process" (Shaffer, 1985).

To be more concrete, we have only to compare the divergent perspectives on alcoholism, which range from those that view it as a primary disease process to those that view it as a learned behavior with dysfunctional consequences. Which view one holds clearly colors one's treatment strategies and goals. The heated confrontation between Sobell and Sobell (1976; 1984) and Pendery, Maltzman, and West (1982) regarding the issue of controlled drinking by alcoholics is perhaps the best example of this divergence and its consequences. This divergence applies not only to addictions but also to family therapy.

Within family therapy approaches to substance abuse, this divergence appears as a conflict between perspectives that view *all* problems, including addiction, as family problems and perspectives that admit the idea of individual etiology—that is, that view families as an adjunct to the problems of the identified patient (IP) and that view the IP and his or her problems as merely symptomatic of family problems. This divergence becomes more dramatic when the specific issue of alcoholism is raised. Many family therapy practitioners regard the family as having a critical role in "supporting" the drinking. The concept of enabling and the writings of Wegscheider (1980) are examples of this view. Other family therapists have chosen to examine the role of the drinking in "supporting" the family. Most notable among these is Steinglass (1979; 1985).

Despite the dramatic nature of this divergence, it can be seen on closer examination that both views are valid. As Bateson (1971) has stated with regard to other such apparent conflicts, it is not "either/or" but "both/and". To effect change, we must look not only at how the family is enabling the drinker but also at how the drinker is enabling the family. For practitioners who have had extensive professional or personal experience with the pain and suffering related to alcoholism, the notion that drinking is in some way critical to the functioning of the family is difficult to accept.

Steinglass (1985) has presented an elegant overview, which, by examining the interplay of pressures for stability and those for change, demonstrates how the family can be traumatized by the consequences of alcoholism and yet find alcoholism essential to its functioning. More importantly, Steinglass provides a developmental perspective that looks at families through time and shows how the introduction of alcoholism into the family system is "resolved."

In Steinglass's formulation, there are four possible long-term outcomes for alcoholic families. These outcomes are defined by choices regarding continuation or discontinuation of drinking (wet or dry) and focusing or not focusing on alcoholism as a central issue (alcoholic or nonalcoholic). They are as follows:

1. Stable dry "alcoholic"
2. Stable dry nonalcoholic
3. Stable controlled drinking nonalcoholic
4. Stable wet alcoholic

Steinglass notes that the stable controlled drinking nonalcoholic outcome is both less common and controversial. These longer term outcomes will become of particular interest when we examine therapy approaches that focus on the family independent of the drinker.

In addition to this view of the "resolution" of the alcoholism, Steinglass also provides a clear presentation of how the intoxicated behavior (in the short term) has a stabilizing influence on family functioning and how this short-run stabilization is part of a longer term unstable/dysfunctional system. It is this phase in family development—unstable wet or dry—that is the focus of most family therapy approaches. The instability is often either the result or the cause of a crisis. And it is often a crisis of some sort that triggers a family's involvement in therapy.

Typology of Treatment Approaches

The conflict between behavioral and disease concepts of alcoholism and its effect on family therapy approaches can best be clarified by classifying family therapy approaches based on the primary focus of the therapist(s).

Type 1—the focus is primarily on the needs of the addict or alcoholic and secondarily on the needs of the family.

Type 2—the focus is on the needs of the addict or alcoholic in conjunction with the needs of the family.

Type 3—the focus is on the needs of the family independent of those of the addict or alcoholic.

The first two types, although having different approaches, are both directed at resolving the addiction or alcoholism, while the third type is concerned with the family and not the addict or alcoholic. Thus, the first two approaches agree that the addiction or alcoholism is a situation deserving of attention while disagreeing about methods, whereas the third approach is not concerned with the addiction or alcoholism but with the consequences for the family of currently having or of having had an addicted or alcoholic member. This third approach derives from the recent emergence of codependence as a focus of therapy as well as from concern about the potential for intergenerational transmission of dysfunctional behavior.

Type 1 Approaches

These approaches are most commonly associated with addiction or alcoholism treatment programs, perhaps this association defines their perspective. They start with an implicit definition of the problem as "alcoholism," which is a disease located within an individual. Nace et al. (1982) provide a clear explanation of this therapeutic model and its assumptions. According to these authors, family therapists should not neglect the strength of the need for the sedative properties of alcohol in the alcohol-dependent person. They propose a sequential model of treatment, first focusing on the alcoholic and getting him or her sober and then switching to a study of how the drinking affects the family and in turn how the family may contribute to the drinking. This approach has value in that it simplifies the therapist's tasks by separating and sequencing the problems.

The Type 1 approach for involving the family is educational first and psychotherapeutic second. The program consists of a number of components:

1. Family group—a weekly group for family members while the IP is in residence
2. Transition group—focus on posthospitalization adjustment for the family and the IP
3. Family education hours—film and discussion
4. Al-Anon—weekly meetings
5. Children's group
6. Couples consultations—selected IPs and spouses are seen for two to four sessions
7. Outpatient groups (spouses and couples) for a recommended six-month period

Although a significant amount of activity is focused on family members (six to eight hours per week) while the IP is hospitalized, it is important to keep in mind that this is all adjunctive to the full-time treatment of the IP. Other inpatient treatment settings deal with the family through "family weeks" during which the family joins the IP at the facility for five to seven days. Although either of these approaches to family involvement is an advance over inpatient treatment focusing solely on the addict or alcoholic, both still give priority to the addict or alcoholic. They are based on the belief that addiction or alcoholism is an individual disease exacerbated by familial and societal concerns.

Type 2 Approaches

These approaches are what most people might envision under the label *family therapy*. However, among proponents who agree that addiction or alcoholism is a family problem, there is still disagreement about whether the addict or alcoholic must first obtain abstinence or even whether one needs to focus on the substance abuse in order to resolve it. Those practitioners who are most strongly committed to a family systems approach view the addiction or alcoholism as secondary to the dysfunction in the family. As Bowen (1978) has stated; "When it is possible to modify the family relationship system, the alcoholic dysfunction is alleviated, even though the dysfunctional one may not have been part of the therapy (p. 260).

An example of this "lack of concern" for the alcoholism on the part of some family therapists appears in Waldo and Guerney (1983), who report that by focusing on training a couple in a variety of interpersonal competence skills and providing supervision of the application of these skills, the husband (who had a thirty-six-year history of alcohol abuse and had failed in both AA and individual substance abuse therapy) achieved and maintained sobriety. While this case report is an example of the treatment of the couple/family without regard to the issue of substance use, many practitioners believe that a focus on abstinence is a basic prerequisite for meaningful family therapy (Davis 1980).

Whether or not to focus on abstinence as an immediate goal is a critical issue in family therapy, as such an effort could place the therapist in the same position vis à vis the addict or alcoholic as is the family—that is, demanding that the use stop. To the extent that the therapist becomes yet one more person ineffectively demanding a change in behavior that the addict or alcoholic is unable or unwilling to make, the process is doomed to failure. If the therapist chooses to make abstinence a requirement, he or she also must be willing to accept a high dropout rate on the part of families. The task is potentially easier in cases where there are legal sanctions against use and external constraints that support either chemical constraint (Antabuse) or monitoring (urinalysis). The successful use of urinalysis in family therapy focusing on drug abuse was clearly documented by Stanton, Todd, and Associates (1982). In their ten-session treatment program, they used urinalysis as a way to monitor the drug user and to reestablish the family hierarchy by placing the parents in charge of the addict.

Berenson (1979) clearly delineates the problems involved in dealing with actively drinking alcoholics and provides a clear description of how to avoid getting caught in the trap of being one more person demanding change. He notes, "The first move, therefore, in restructuring or recontexualizing alcoholic systems is not to pursue the alcoholic." He suggests that one way to accomplish this task is for the therapist to place himself or herself in the role of consultant to the family. This clearly defines the problem as the family's and not the therapist's. As an example, Berenson cites a situation in which the alcoholic attends the session drunk and how the therapist defines this not as his problem but the spouse's. Following this definition, Berenson explores how the drunkenness alters the dynamics between the spouses. This is in some ways parallel to Stanton, Todd, and Associates' (1982) placing the responsibility for clean urinalysis on the parents. The difference is that in one case, the focus is on reestablishing hierarchy, while in the other, it is on making relationship patterns explicit. This difference is appropriate, considering that Stanton, Todd, and Associates' study involved working with families of origin, while most work with adult alcoholics involves families of procreation. Berenson does reserve the right to terminate the session if the alcoholic is too disruptive. His position is that the therapist is in charge of the therapy's structure, while the family is in charge of the behaviors.

Pittman (1980) outlines a more direct approach to dealing with families.

He irreverently characterizes substance abuse as "a sport the whole family gets to play". His seven-step approach to alcoholism is as follows:

1. *Emergency response.* When families bring the alcoholic to the therapist in either binge or withdrawal crisis with the expectation of hospitalization, he prefers to negotiate a commitment to outpatient treatment, including the use of Antabuse.
2. *Family involvement.* Pittman notes that if there is a family crisis directly related to alcohol, involvement is often straightforward; if there is no such crisis, then the family will produce one (depression, threat of divorce or suicide, and the like) to generate the impetus for treatment. (This corresponds to the unstable wet alcoholic family in Steinglass's 1985 model.)
3. *Defining the problem.* In Pittman's framework, there are four types of alcoholism—compulsive, situational, developmental, and habitual. He provides specific criteria for determining the type and describes how an alcoholic would interact differently with the family depending on type.
4. *General prescription.* This is the core concept in Pittman's approach to treating alcoholic families and clearly highlights the unique contribution of family therapy:

   > Perhaps the most important thing that happens in treating an alcoholic's family is the opportunity for everyone in the family to actually talk about the alcoholism as well as about the process of living and the crises of life. Family therapy rather offhandedly repeals the rules against noticing and talking about the drinking or about talking about things that might cause the drinking or upset the drinker. Therapy for alcoholic families has sometimes been successful when it consisted of nothing more than that. (Pittman 1980, 274)

5. *Specific prescription.* The alcoholic is told not to drink. The family is instructed to deal with the alcoholic only when sober and is given support in accomplishing this goal.
6. *Negotiating resistance.* Pittman describes various instances that arise for both alcoholics and families and notes that "family therapy can proceed whether the alcoholic stops drinking or not."
7. *Termination.* Pittman has a unique position on this issue. He states that "an alcoholic family never terminates therapy. They step back into old patterns and try out new therapists sometimes, but they never get well." Thus, in his view, the outcome of "stable dry nonalcoholic" family identified by Steinglass does not exist.

What makes Pittman's approach so interesting is his combination of directness—that is, "stop drinking"—coupled with his sensitivity to the needs of the family.

For Type 2 approaches, despite differences in the directness with which the addictive or alcoholic behavior is approached—from not at all (Waldo and Guerney 1983) to with caution (Berenson 1979) to directly (Pittman 1980)—the focus is still squarely on the family and its dynamics rather than on the individual addict or alcoholic and his or her disease.

Type 3 Approaches

These approaches are different from the previous ones in that the focus is on the family independent of the addict or alcoholic. This issue of concern is not the addict or alcoholic but "codependence." The concern is for the children in families where the addiction or alcoholism has led to divorce, as well as for those families characterized by Steinglass as "stable dry alcoholic" and "stable wet alcoholic." In both of these situations, the problems of familial interaction may well predispose the children to recreate their family of origin. This recreated family may be a direct replica—that is, one involving addiction or alcoholism—or a variation involving enmeshment in relationships. These consequences have been strikingly documented by Peele and Bradshaw (1975); Norwood (1985); and Schaef (1986). From this perspective, the traditional alcohol treatment approaches tend to "replicate the alcoholic family system. The alcoholic is the center of attention, the co-alcoholic is viewed as either the supporter or provider, and the children are neglected" (Greenleaf 1981). Even in Type 2 approaches, it may be difficult for family members to realize that they have value in and of themselves, irrespective of their relationship to the addict or alcoholic.

There has been an increasing interest and concern with adult children and codependence issues (Cork 1969; Wegscheider 1980; Greenleaf 1981; Ackerman 1983; Cermak 1986; Schaef 1986). Some of these writers have accepted the disease analogy and argue that codependence is a primary disease, like alcoholism, while others view codependence as a learned behavioral dysfunction—the same distinction that tends to separate the Type 1 and Type 2 approaches. From my perspective, codependence is a learned behavioral dysfunction that needs to be addressed directly in its own right.

A Model for Type 3 Family Therapy

Two assumptions undergird this model. The first is that the key to better lives for codependents lies in education about *their own* process, clarification of *their own* values and goals, and an exploration of *their own* issues—in short, that they have value independent of their relationship to the addict or alcoholic. This assumption is the core of the Type 3 approaches. The second assumption is more pragmatic—that is, that many of the needs of the family can be met by a structured short-term (six-session) program. Stanton, Todd, and Associates' (1982) success with a ten-session treatment model for heroin addicts provides empirical support for this concept.

The specific model is shown in figure 18–1. The process includes an assessment and treatment planning phase based on a Quality of Life (QOL) questionnaire as well as a therapist's interview. The QOL[1] questionnaire was developed using portions of three devices already in use: the Marital Roles Inventory (Orford et al. 1976), the Family Assessment Device (Epstein, Baldwin, and Bishop), and the Beck Depression Inventory (Beck 1980). Each was revised to suit the current design. The Marital Roles Inventory (MRI) was abbreviated to six questions. Its use as a measurement of the spouse's role participation was expanded to include role positions for children and extended family members, and "current" and "ideal" situations were offered to identify current dissatisfactions and goals for the future. Twenty-six questions from the Family Assessment Device (FAD), including the general functioning scale, were used in the questionnaire, and six questions were taken from the Beck Depression Inventory (BDI). Added to these were eleven demographic questions regarding education, employment, children, length and status of relationship to drinker, and perceived seriousness of problem in terms of the relationship.

Responses to items on this questionnaire are used by the therapist in planning goals for each family as well as in providing a baseline for treatment outcome research. As part of the assessment process, where other primary problems are identified (such as significant mental illness or addiction or alcoholism separate from that of the IP), families are referred to appropriate treatment. The majority of families that the therapists in this program have encountered are appropriate for the short-term treatment model.

The therapy is designed to address both the educational and supportive needs of the family in a straightforward manner. As noted earlier, people are generally more open to receiving information, support, and therapy during a crisis; in this case it is the crisis of the addict or alcoholic voluntarily or involuntarily entering treatment. The specific content of each session is outlined in detailed protocols[2] so that the experiences of the family are consistent throughout the program independent of the particular therapist. Further, since confusion about received messages, relationships, and giving and receiving help are often issues for codependents, and since coming in for treatment is often a frightening experience, the protocols help the therapists to provide clear, direct, uncomplicated, and consistent information and communication.

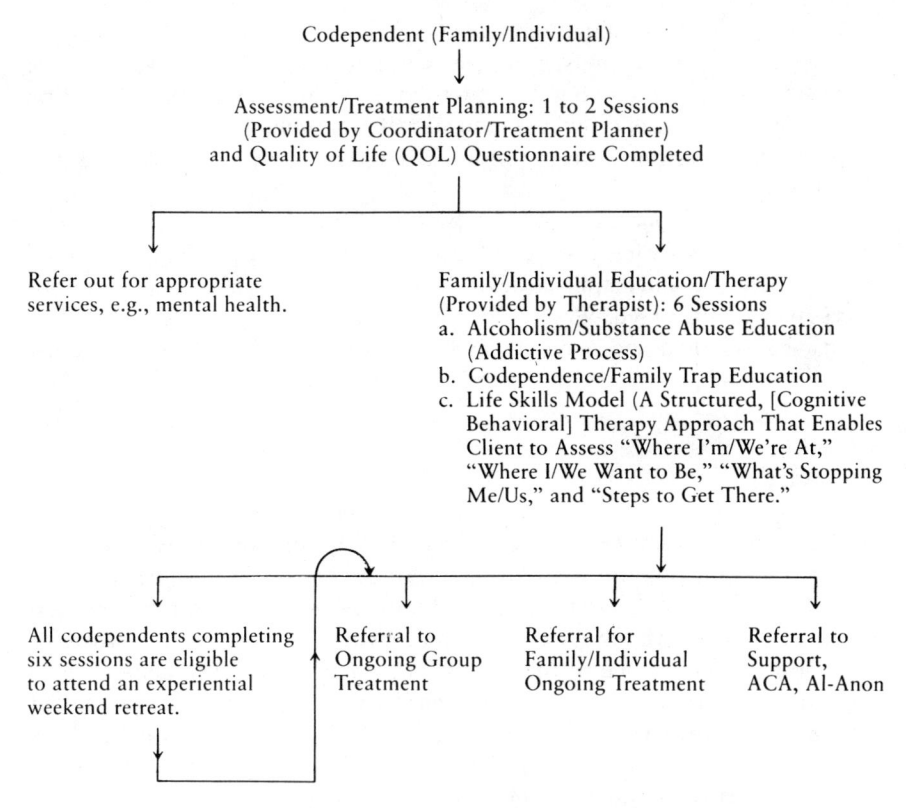

```
                    Codependent (Family/Individual)
                                │
                                ▼
          Assessment/Treatment Planning: 1 to 2 Sessions
              (Provided by Coordinator/Treatment Planner)
          and Quality of Life (QOL) Questionnaire Completed
                                │
                ┌───────────────┴───────────────┐
                ▼                               ▼
Refer out for appropriate          Family/Individual Education/Therapy
services, e.g., mental health.     (Provided by Therapist): 6 Sessions
                                     a. Alcoholism/Substance Abuse Education
                                        (Addictive Process)
                                     b. Codependence/Family Trap Education
                                     c. Life Skills Model (A Structured, [Cognitive
                                        Behavioral] Therapy Approach That Enables
                                        Client to Assess "Where I'm/We're At,"
                                        "Where I/We Want to Be," "What's Stopping
                                        Me/Us," and "Steps to Get There."
                                                │
   ┌────────────────┬──────────────────┬────────┴────────┐
   ▼                ▼                  ▼                 ▼
All codependents    Referral to        Referral for      Referral to
completing six      Ongoing Group      Family/Individual Support,
sessions are        Treatment          Ongoing Treatment ACA, Al-Anon
eligible to attend
an experiential
weekend retreat.
```

We expect that many families will need only support groups
after their program experience.

Figure 18–1. Flowchart of delivery design/treatment protocol.

Source: V.A. Harris, J. Bacon, and T.C. Carleton, "A Short-Term Approach to Family Treatment/Codependence," paper presented at ? Treatment Choices in Substance Abuse, Conference Denver, Co. ? June 3–4, 1988. Reprinted with permission.

In addition to the specific steps outlined in figure 18–1 and detailed in the treatment protocols, clients are encouraged to sharpen their ability to describe events, experiences, and people at three levels: the external descriptive level, the expressive emotional level, and the internal mental, or "view of the world," level. This trilevel descriptive system, called "body, speech, and mind,"[3] helps to ground the participants, cut through anxiety-generated responses, and take, in Berenson's (1979) terms, a "nonreactive" approach to their own lives, much as the therapist strives to do.

After six weeks, the families have a number of options for further work, if appropriate. The foremost option is the use of an experiential retreat. This type of experience is valuable because of the emotional nature of the core codependent issues of low self-esteem, self-defeating behavior, and the lack of a sense of self. The timing of the retreat after the six sessions is based on the therapists' experience, which indicates that until the family has had some help in becoming self-observant/nonreactive, the retreat experience is too threatening.

This model is one example of how one might develop a Type 3 family therapy approach with specific emphasis on issues of codependence. As noted earlier, there are other approaches to codependence, although they are not necessarily family based. Wegscheider (1980), for example, has developed an intensive residential approach, and Schaef (1986) has developed an ongoing group approach, coupled with intensive experiential retreats.

Summary

Where do we stand after our wanderings through different models and approaches to addiction or alcoholism and families. First, we have been able to examine the interface between theories of addiction and treatment approaches. Second, we have seen how approaches can be classified based on their primary focus. One of the points that emerges from this classification process is that it is difficult to make hard and fast distinctions. As noted earlier, some codependence practitioners (classified as Type 3) take a theoretical (disease-oriented) position that aligns them with Type 1 practitioners. That this level of complexity and blurring of distinctions exists is not surprising if we take seriously Shaffer's (1986) views stated earlier in the chapter.

We also have seen how conflicting views are applied in different styles of family practice—from Type 1 approaches, which involve sequencing conflicting perspectives, to Type 2 approaches, which thrive on the paradox of working with conflicting perspectives simultaneously. Perhaps the most important idea, regardless of theoretical perspective, is that there is a rich variety of approaches to the problems of addiction or alcoholism and the family. In addition to the examples provided in the text, the following annotated bibliography describes a number of books that explain in detail family therapy approaches to alcoholism and drug abuse.

Annotated Bibliography

Andersen, C.M., and S. Steward. *Mastering Resistance*. New York: Guilford Press, 1983. This is an excellent "cookbook" on how to deal with the various types of resistances offered by families. It is a must for beginning family therapists regardless of orientation.

Hoffman, L. *Foundations of Family Therapy.* New York: Basic Books, 1981. This book, although somewhat heavy going, offers a thorough discussion of the conceptual origins of family therapy and the relationships among the various schools.

Kaufman, E., and P. Kaufman, eds. *Family Therapy of Drug and Alcohol Abuse.* New York: Guardian Press, 1979.

Kaufman, E., ed. *Power to Change.* New York: Gardner Press, 1984. These two edited volumes provide both theory and case studies of family therapy for various models with a variety of substance abuse problems.

Kaufman, E. *Substance Abuse and Family Therapy.* New York: Grune & Stratton, 1985. This book is both a review of current substance abuse literature and a presentation of the author's views on family therapy with substance abusing families.

Lawson, G., J.S. Peterson, and A. Lawson. *Alcoholism and the Family.* Rockwell, Md.: Aspen Publishers, 1983. This very readable introduction to the topic includes a concise outline of the different theories of alcoholism and a summary of different schools of family therapy and their distinct approaches to alcoholism.

Minuchin, S. *Families and Family Therapy.* Cambridge, Mass.: Harvard University Press, 1974. This is a classic text on how to do family therapy.

Pittman, F.S. *Turning Points.* New York: W.W. Norton, 1980. Pittman presents a systematic seven-step model for approaching families in crisis and transition. He includes detailed case material and writes in a refreshing conversational style that makes the concepts readily accessible.

Stanton, M.D., T.C. Todd, and Associates, eds. *The Family Therapy of Drug Abuse and Addiction.* New York: Guilford Press, 1982. This comprehensive report of ground-breaking work presents a brief (ten-session) family therapy approach used with heroin addicts. The book includes detailed case examples as well as information on the conceptual model, research issues, and outcome data.

Notes

1. Copies of the QOL Questionnaire and protocols are available from Victor A. Harris, Boulder County Health Department, 3450 Broadway, Boulder, CO 80304.

2. Shown in Appendix A, these protocols were developed by Jeri Bacon, codependence project coordinator.

3. The "body, speech, and mind" system was developed by Dr. Antonio Wood and other faculty of the psychology department of the Naropa Institute, Boulder, Colorado.

References

Ackerman, B.J. 1983. *Children of Alcoholics.* 2d ed. Holmes Beach, Fla.: Learning Publications.

Bateson, G. 1971. *Steps toward an Ecology of Mind.* New York: Ballantine Books.

Beck, A.T. 1980. "Depression Inventory." In *Feeling Good*, edited by D. Barns, 31–33. New York: Academic Press.

Berenson, D. 1979. "The Therapist's Relationship with Couples with an Alcoholic Member." In *Family Therapy of Drug and Alcohol Abuse*, edited by E. Kaufman and P. Kaufman. New York: Guardian Press.

Bowen, M. 1978. "Alcoholism and the Family." In *Family Therapy in Clinical Practice*, edited by M. Bowen, 259–68. New York: Jason Arinson.

Cermak, T.L. 1986. *Diagnosing and Treating Codependence*. Minneapolis: Johnson Institute.

Cork, R.M. 1969. *The Forgotten Children*. Markham, Ont.: Paperjacks.

Davis, D.I. 1980. "Alcoholics Anonymous and Family Therapy." *Journal of Marital and Family Therapy* 6:65–73.

Epstein, N.B., L.M. Baldwin, and D.S. Bishop. *The Family Assessment Device*. Providence, R.I.: Brown University/Butler Hospital Research Program.

Greenleaf, J. 1981. *Co-Alcoholic, Para-Alcoholic*. Los Angeles: The 361 Foundation.

Nace, E.P., M. Dephause, M. Goldberg, and C.C. Cammorata. 1982. "Treatment Priorities in a Family-Oriented Alcoholism Program." *Journal of Marital and Family Therapy* 8:143–50.

Norwood, R. 1985. *Women Who Love Too Much*. Los Angeles: Jeremy P. Tharcher.

Orford, J., E. Oppenheimer, S. Egert, C. Hensinon, and S. Guthrie. 1976. "The Cohesiveness of Alcoholism-Complicated Marriages and Its Influence on Treatment Outcome." *British Journal of Psychiatry* 128:318–39.

Peele, S., and A. Bradshaw. 1975. *Love and Addiction*. New York: New American Library.

Pendery, M.L., I.M. Maltzman, and L.J. West. 1982. "Controlled Drinking by Alcoholics? New Findings and a Reevaluation of a Major Affirmative Study." *Science* 217:(4555)169–74.

Pittman, F.S. 1980. *Turning Points*. New York: W.W. Norton.

Schaef, A.W. 1986. *Codependence: Misunderstood, Mistreated*. Cambridge: Mass: Harper & Row.

Shaffer, H.J. 1986. "Conceptual Crises and the Addictions: A Philosophy of Science Perspective." *Journal of Substance Abuse Treatment* 3:285–96.

Shaffer, H.J. "Introduction: Crisis and Conflict in the Addictions." In *The Addictions: Multidisciplinary Perspectives and Treatments*, H. Milkman and H. Shaffer, eds. Lexington Books, 1985. pp. ix–xvii.

Sobell, M.B., and L.C. Sobell. 1976. "Second Year Treatment Outcome of Alcoholics Treated by Individual Behavior Therapy: Results." *Behaviour Research and Therapy* 22:413–40.

———. 1984. "The Aftermath of Heresy: A Response to Pendery et al.'s (1982) Critique of 'Individualized Behavior Therapy for Alcoholics.'" *Behaviour Research and Therapy* 22:413.

Stanton, M.D., T.C. Todd, and Associates, eds. 1982. *The Family Therapy of Drug Abuse and Addiction*. New York: Guilford Press.

Steinglass, P. 1979. "The Alcoholic Family in the Interaction Laboratory." *Journal of Nervous and Mental Disorders* 167:428–36.

———. 1985. "Family System Approaches to Alcoholics." *Journal of Substance Abuse Treatment* 2:161–67.
Waldo, M., and B.G. Guerney, Jr. 1983. "Marital Relationship Enhancement Therapy in the Treatment of Alcoholism." *Journal of Marital and Family Therapy* 9:321–23.
Wegscheider, S. 1980. *Another Chance*. Palo Alto, Calif.: Science and Behavior Books.

Appendix 18–A: Codependency Project Protocols for Therapy Sessions

Purpose

These six sessions are intended to provide substance abuse, addictive process, family trap/roles, and codependency information, and to help each family/individual to use this information to identify their own issues and work with these issues more successfully.

These six sessions will also utilize a family change model using four questions which will help families to examine their circumstances and develop ways to change their lives and work toward goals.

Policy

These sessions will be highly structured for two reasons: (1) so that we will have the time necessary to deliver and discuss the material; (2) so that we can model and explore ways of dealing with chaos, which is often rampant in dysfunctional families.
    A) Practice as foundation
    B) Body, speech, and mind

Procedure

Session I

Session I is a time for the therapist to connect with the family. Any information from the assessment session could be discussed and fleshed out.

A. Get everyone in the family to express his/her individual perception of the situation.
    1. Ask the kids what they like and dislike about their family.

2. Model curiosity (rather than discomfort) about differences between members.
B. Talk with the family about these four questions:
   1. Where are you now?
   2. Where do you want to be?
   3. What steps do you need to take to get there?
   4. What gets in your way?
C. Ask about changes that could be made in the family.
   1. Emphasize smaller changes, the need for realism, and not setting oneself up to fail. Stress that practicing small changes makes big changes possible eventually. *Be specific.* Focus on process-oriented changes—*doing* differently. Be sure client writes down goals. One copy goes in chart; one goes to client.
   2. Elicit a small goal for next week from each member. Ask them to notice what gets in the way of their meeting that goal. Try to model curiosity about obstacles rather than blame. Don't be afraid to make suggestions. Emphasis in this session could be on disciplines which are self-referenting; i.e., keeping a journal, relaxation/meditation exercises, spending time alone, pampering self, etc.
   3. Another alternative is to ask them to *notice* when something occurs: anger, irritation, confusion, some pattern which bothers them; not to do anything about it but notice it and talk about it next time.

After the session, ask yourself:

A. Where is this family in terms of:
   1. Process in the room-communication patterns with you and others.
   2. Issues that need to be dealt with: anger, sadness, etc.
      a. Denial—what can be worked with and how?
      b. How can you work with these issues *within* the structure of the session?
B. Where does this family need/want to be?
   1. How can their perception of their needs and your perception of their needs combine and be worked with concurrently?
C. What steps does this family need to take to get to where it wants to be?
   1. What skills does the family need to learn and practice?
      a. Boundaries?
      b. Building intimacy?
      c. Flexibility?
   2. How could those skills be practiced with you in the room using your relationship?
   3. How could those skills be practiced by this family outside of the session, using current relationships to others and the world?
D. How will substance abuse information fit with this family?

Session II

A. Ask about goals from previous week.
   1. What got accomplished?
   2. What didn't get accomplished?
      a. What did it feel like to accomplish goal—ask for both positive and negative feelings.
      b. What did it feel like to *not* accomplish goal—ask for both positive and negative feelings.
      c. Talk about what got in the way, steps leading up to obstacle; try to verbally identify small steps to obstacles.
B. Give substance abuse information.
C. Talk with the family about how this information relates to their lives.
   1. In terms of women and alcohol.
   2. In terms of relatives and friends and self.
   3. How does each member of the family use substances addictively? TV, food, work.
   4. How does each member of the family relieve tension?
D. Get goals for next week. These could be involved with:
   1. Interactions with drinker
   2. Use of substances—work, TV, smoking, food, relationships
   3. Ways of relieving tension
   4. Might in some way be an expansion or extension of goals for week one

After the session, ask yourself:

A. What was the process in the room?
B. Are there particular things that you notice that could be useful in terms of the family's practice?
C. Look for parallel process in your way of meeting goals in the session and their way of meeting goals for themselves. Consider how you might articulate this for their own purposes; what analogies can you make to their own situation?
D. Does this family pull any of your own personal issues? Do you feel yourself "stuck" in a particular attitude or response to this family? How can you use this response as a tool to help the family work through their dilemma?

Sessions III and IV

A. Ask about goals from previous week, as in Session II.
B. Give family trap information regarding family rules and family roles.
   1. Emphasize that dysfunctional does not necessarily mean that alco-

hol has to be involved. Can be addictions/problems with other "substances" such as work, food, relationships, rigidity, inability to tolerate expression of feelings, etc.
C. Talk with the family about how this information relates to their lives.
1. Ask what rules and roles were in family of origin and in current family. Use process in the room as information, if possible. Discuss positive and negative consequences of rules and roles. Emphasize "don't talk, don't trust, don't feel," and how members might manifest these rules.
2. Ask what needs to be changed in this family in terms of rules and roles.
3. Ask about and discuss what would be painful about making changes. What would each have to give up?
D. Get goals for next week. These could be involved with:
1. Listing explicit and implicit rules.
2. Making or changing a specific rule
3. Changing one behavior that is particularly role-oriented

After the session, ask yourself:

A. How do the rules and roles manifest in the session?
B. How could you help the family to experiment with modifying these in the session, either with you or among themselves?
C. What are the individual styles of the family members? Where are the triangulations and cutoffs? What helps each individual to feel flexible?

Session V

A. Ask about goals from previous week, as in Session II.
B. Give codependency information.
C. Talk about characteristics of codependency as they relate to this family and family of origin. Emphasize that these needs actually are not "selfless" at all, but serve to meet the needs of the codependent to control others.
D. Discuss difficulty of giving up old relationship to drinker; implications for codependent; fears and concerns.
E. Discuss self-acceptance, risk taking in terms of personal change.
F. Get goals for next week. These could be involved with:
1. Practicing changing one specific behavior around a particular codependent characteristic.
2. Getting a need met in a different way.
G. Briefly discuss termination next week. Ask people to think about how they "end" relationships.

H. Ask client(s) to think about four goals for next week:
   1. Two Personal Life Goals—things that you want to do with or change about your life or an aspect of your life. Be specific about how you will meet this goal.
   2. Two Personal Therapeutic Goals—things that you want to work on further or change in terms of your relationship to yourself, others, or the world. Be specific about how you will work on these issues. (Talk with client(s) at this point about other therapy options in this agency and outside, and ask them to think about continuing work.)

After the session, ask yourself:

A. How do I feel about terminating with this family?
B. How can I help myself and them to terminate properly?
C. What do I appreciate about this family?
D. What have been their successes?
E. How could they proceed further in their work?

Session VI

A. Ask about goals from previous week, as in Session II.
B. Ask about their particular styles of "ending."
C. Talk about your appreciation for this family.
D. Review with them their process through the sessions—goals and gains.
E. Ask them to fill out questions and goals. You can help them—reassure them that this is not a test.
F. Discuss weekend retreat.
G. Discuss options for continued therapy. If they want to continue with this agency, see if you can introduce them to the proper person to continue with.

19
Therapy with Families of Adolescent Substance Abusers

M. Duncan Stanton
Judith Landau-Stanton

More and more, adolescents who develop substance abuse problems are being treated within the context of their families. This makes sense for a number of reasons, a major one being that most adolescents either live, or have regular contact, with their families. It is usually not difficult to justify inclusion of the family in treatment when family members are involved in the problem in an intense and ongoing way. There are also instances in which family involvement is indicated despite the appearance that members are "out of the picture." They can and invariably do have an impact even though they have been distant for many years.

> Jack, a thirteen-year-old, was admitted to an inpatient service for regular polydrug abuse, stealing, school suspension, and physically abusing his mother. His parents had divorced when he was three, and he had only vague memories of his father. During treatment, he successfully sabotaged every attempt by the therapists (Jehoshua Kaufman, M.A., and Judith Landau-Stanton) and other treatment staff to support his mother and put her in charge, growing violent when she visited him or tried to discipline him. He was noisy, hyperactive, and belligerent on the unit and tried to dominate every social situation with which he came in contact.
> Despite the family's resistance, Jack's father was eventually tracked down by staff and his aid solicited. He was astounded to learn that anyone thought he could help. He showed a true concern for Jack and was relieved that he might have a chance to reduce his guilt over leaving his six kids. Jack responded to his father's caring and discipline by behaving better with staff and peers. However, he still disobeyed his mother and threatened to use drugs again upon discharge. After much persuasion, Jack's parents were finally talked

---

This chapter is an expansion of a paper that appeared in *Focus on Alcohol and Drug Issues* 6:2(1983).

into meeting in conjoint sessions with their children. This was done by convincing them that they needed to work together as parents even though their marital relationship had long ended. A month after his father's first appearance in conjoint therapy, Jack's behavior had improved markedly. He was (1) treating his mother and other authority figures with respect, (2) concentrating well on his schoolwork, (3) getting along well with peers, and (4) showing determination to remain drug free.

Family Life Cycles Issues

It is common for substance-abusing families not to have adequately negotiated certain family life cycle stages. In some cases, generation after generation has repeated the same problematic patterns; conflicts have been perpetuated around similar points of transition (Landau 1982; Landau-Stanton 1985). One may see cross-generational coalitions, with grandparents parenting grandchildren and parents failing to become competent. Frequently, the stages of growing up, leaving home (Haley 1980), getting "permission to marry" (Stanton 1981a), and becoming competent parents to an adolescent are not adequately achieved in these families. The therapeutic task is one of helping the family through the transition.

In other families, the precipitating life cycle crisis may be of a less chronic nature. For instance, a parent may recently have lost his or her job or be facing retirement, or a serious or life-threatening illness may have incapacitated a family member. Bereavement also is a common source of sudden exacerbation of difficulties in such families (Coleman and Stanton 1978; Stanton and Coleman 1980). For example, the death of a grandparent may result in both grandchild and parent losing effective parenting at the same time. In such cases, suicidal behavior on the part of the adolescent is not uncommon (Landau-Stanton and Stanton 1985). Sometimes treatment, particularly in the middle and later phases, must essentially evolve into a process of helping the family to grieve properly in order to move on in life.

The development issues affecting the adolescent must not be overlooked. Adolescence is fraught with physical, emotional, and sexual changes that in themselves provide new and difficult stresses in any family. However, some families have not effectively navigated the onset of adolescence in previous generations, thereby passing down a tradition of inordinate turmoil when any member reaches this phase.

While adolescents in foster and group homes, in adopted families, or in stepfamilies face many of the same issues noted above, it is easy to be misled into believing that the life cycle and developmental problems they encounter are different because the youngster has not grown up at home with his or her "own" family. Frequently, these adolescents face a composite of the problems of differentiation and development that have not been resolved either in their own or in their surrogate families. It can thus be extremely useful to involve both natural and surrogate systems in the therapy—a task that can be effected by an enthusiastic, energetic, and committed therapist. The cost of the effort is usually compensated for by a greatly improved long-term prognosis.

Seventeen-year-old Terry was an "orphan." He had been raised in a series of foster homes, orphanages, and correctional facilities. He had a serious behavior problem, having been heavily abusing drugs and running away over the previous five years. He also was incorrigible in his inpatient unit, including requiring constant monitoring and attention. He was verbally abusive, physically threatening, destructive of property, and continually attempting to run away. He stole whenever he could, including on one occasion stealing the unit director's grocery money.

When the director of the unit (Judith Landau-Stanton) and the primary therapist (Lynn Brown, M.S.N.) asked the staff who should be invited to Terry's family sessions, the staff members replied that he "had no family." Not satisfied with this response, the director and therapist pushed the staff to find out who, including helping professionals, was presently involved with Terry. After a bit of investigation, it was discovered that no less than thirty-six foster parents, therapists, teachers, and other professionals of various sorts were still actively involved with him. Terry may not have had a biological family, but he certainly had accumulated a large "family" of a different sort. Many of its members maintained an interest in him and continually sought information about his progress. In addition, it was discovered that Terry had been given away by his mother at age two and had not seen her since.

All thirty-six of the surrogate family members were contacted, some with extreme difficulty. They were asked if they would attend a network session regarding Terry. A few of them—generally overloaded caseworkers—had written Terry off and preferred not to attend but asked to be kept informed. The majority wished to come, but scheduling difficulties prevented all but nine from actually attending. The remainder also wished to be kept informed. The nine who attended were all currently involved with Terry. They included his most recent foster parents, his probation officer, a social worker who had been involved with him since his early childhood, a caseworker from youth services, and three social workers and a counselor from Terry's previous placements. In addition, the network included four staff members from his current inpatient unit: the therapist, his primary nurse, his social worker, and his activities therapist.

The therapist's primary intentions for this first network session were to (1) determine what the goals, direction of treatment, and future placement should be, and (2) resolve the cutoff between Terry and his mother. Much of the meeting revolved around determining which of the thirty-six people should remain involved with Terry and in what capacity. All of them were astounded to learn of the magnitude of the following that Terry had collected, and it became clear to all that there were way too many cooks stirring this broth. The network members decided to prune down the number of community professionals and helpers currently involved with Terry's case. They elected to retain five people: the two foster parents, the probation officer, Terry's long-term social worker, and the youth services caseworker. These, plus the inpatient staff and Terry, became the core working team.

When these decisions were conveyed to the other twenty-seven surrogate "family" members after the session, most of them felt relieved to be let off the hook. Not knowing of their counterparts, they had stayed involved with Terry in great part because they thought he had no one else. A few had closed their records and no longer wished to be involved. The remainder all agreed to support the treatment and to abide by the decisions of those who had been present.

By boiling the aggregate down to a core group composed of those whose relationship with Terry would be likely to continue, long-term, after his discharge, a true working group had been distilled. Compared with the large collective, this consensus "family" was much better able to set and enforce guidelines for Terry and to negotiate differences among themselves, if and when these arose.

The above actions proved to be a relief to Terry. He said he felt he had been getting too many instructions from too many adults and that it was especially frustrating because many of these instructions conflicted. He was pleased that they were getting their act together.

Regarding Terry's cutoff from his biological mother, several network members knew of her existence. Because she was a heroin addict and prostitute and had given Terry away, however, they had not thought about reconnecting her with her son. When the therapist suggested a reconnection, there was much resistance. The members viewed the mother as neglectful, abusive, unloving, and potentially damaging to Terry. Nonetheless, the therapist was able to persuade them to allow the mother to be invited to the next meeting.

The biological mother showed up at the second network meeting. The group was surprised and impressed by her. They could see that she had truly loved her son and had given him up only because she thought it was best for him. The group succeeded in persuading her to continue her contact with Terry in whatever limited way she was able. The most she would commit to was a birthday telephone call and a letter once a year. She did not feel capable of visiting him at all. Even then, the contact she did promise (1) required an enormous effort on her part, (2) was more than she had ever managed before, and (3) made a huge difference to Terry. Eventually, he was able to absolve his mother of blame for giving him away and never contacting him and to realize the sacrifice that she had made for his welfare.

To the amazement of the network, once the biological mother had been included in treatment, the team was able to locate the biological father. Because Terry was illegitimate, it had not occurred to people that they should even try to identify his father, much less bring the man in. Upon being contacted, however, the father agreed to join the therapy. The network negotiated with him and obtained his promise to support Terry until the boy turned eighteen.

Soon Terry's behavior began to shift. He ceased being a problem on the ward and enthusiastically embraced the direction that he and his "family" had decided to take. This included planning his schooling, living arrangements, and vocational training. He felt so good about himself and the work of the network that he abandoned his disdain for the inpatient program and began to view it with favor. In fact, he was even elected to the patient government. He was discharged six weeks later and started working on his general equivalency diploma (GED). From discharge on, he was boarded by his father in a room close to where the father and his wife and children lived. A one-year follow-up indicated that Terry was performing satisfactorily in school, was succeeding socially, and had discontinued his drug taking and other behavior problems.

Dealing with the Parental Subsystem

In treating adolescent substance abusers and their families, it is crucial that the authority and responsibility of the adolescent's parents (or parental figures/surrogate parents) be recognized and respected. After all, it is they, not the therapist, who have borne the child and shared with him or her their lifeblood, love, and resources. The therapist who ignores this fact, perhaps by succumbing to an adolescent's ostensible invitation to become a better parent than the adolescent's own, is courting therapeutic failure. While it is sometimes easy to blame parents for not managing their son or daughter better, the question of who will take over when therapy ends invariably arises. Unless the therapist intends to purchase a larger house and legally adopt all of his or her clients, the latter will usually return to their families. This is as it should be. Consequently, if therapy is to succeed in the long term, the therapist would be better advised to help parents to become competent with their own children. This is done by empowering the parents, building on their strengths, and letting any successes that occur be seen as successes of the parents, not the therapist (Stanton 1981b).

It has frequently been observed that a disproportionate percentage of substance-abusing adolescents have parents or other family members such as grandparents, aunts, uncles, or surrogate parents who abuse alcohol or prescription or street drugs. This is certainly not true in every case, but when it is, therapists and counselors may find themselves inclined to attend to the substance abuse problem of the adult, especially if the adult is a parent and is not currently in treatment. Such a problem will, of course, have to be dealt with. However, it is usually wiser to maintain a focus on the person with the presenting problem, the adolescent, rather than immediately shifting to the parent. If the therapist is drawn too soon into attempting to deal directly with a parental problem (be it substance abuse, marital disharmony, depression, or whatever), the family will commonly opt for premature termination of therapy before anything can be accomplished with the adolescent, much less with another family member (Haley 1980; Stanton, Todd, and Associates 1982). Therefore, it is better if the therapist at least temporarily sidesteps the issue, earnestly acknowledging the problem and agreeing to attend to it. As soon as possible thereafter—when the therapist has thoroughly joined the parents and the first signs of improvement are noted in the adolescent—the parents' problems should be addressed. In the case of a chemically dependent parent, both parents should be actively encouraged to attend Al-Anon or Nar-Anon. This step will facilitate what should be the therapist's next agenda, which is to get the addicted parent into Alcoholics Anonymous (AA). If this can be achieved, the chances for the adolescent's recovery will be improved considerably.

While marital issues between parents sometimes arise early in treatment, these also should not be dealt with until well into the course of therapy, if at all. Indeed, issues of parenting the adolescent should remain the focus (Haley 1976). The therapist will need to support the parents, helping them gain confidence around tasks at which they can succeed, however small. (It is surprising how a seemingly inconsequential change, such as helping a parent make the child take his or her feet off a chair, can be a turning point in the therapeutic process.) If there is an inequality between the parenting figures—one appearing ineffective and the other overly competent—it is essential to build up the one who is regarded, or regards himself or herself, as less competent or less worthy. Until this is done, the parents cannot function as an effective team, tending instead to operate as if one were a parent and the other an adolescent. Therapy cannot commence successfully until the "incompetent" parent is elevated (rather than blamed) and the boundary between the parental and sibling generations is established and reinforced (Minuchin 1974). Sometimes this can take the form of placing the less competent parent completely in charge of disciplining the children.

Unlike family therapy with young adult drug abusers, in which the problem is often one concerning the physical separation of leaving home, or "launching," treatment of adolescents and their families is directed more toward transformation of the family system *within the existing composition* (Fishman, Stanton, and Rosman, 1982; Stanton, Todd, and Associates 1982). While the family may initially be pushing to expel the adolescent, such as attempting to place him or her in an institution or foster care setting, therapy is better aimed at keeping the adolescent within the family fold—changing and stabilizing rather than disintegrating. One way of achieving this is to get the parents to be mutually supportive in "holding the line" against their son or daughter's misbehavior and manipulations.

> Gillian, age seventeen, had been using drugs heavily for several years and was disobedient at home and school, although she was academically fairly competent. She ran away from home regularly and battled viciously with her mother, at one point even pulling a knife during one of their arguments. This behavior escalated every time her father left home on one of his frequent business trips. Her parents had been excessively tolerant of her behavior, in great part because her school had labeled her as "sick" and "emotionally disturbed."
>
> In treatment, the parents' efforts were supported vigorously by the therapists (the authors), and the parents' values as to what was correct behavior were strongly reinforced. Eventually they were given the choice of deciding whether they wanted to continue to see Gillian as "sick" or whether she could be regarded as a "normal" and therefore "disobedient" girl. After much soul-searching, combined with encouragement by Gillian's two younger sisters, they chose to see her as responsible for her own behavior. They established a program around privileges and punishments appropriate to her actions and together began to reinforce it.
>
> Gillian naturally tested their resolve. When they stuck together through several incidents, with neither parent backing down, Gillian's behavior began to change dramatically. She dropped her drug contacts, ceased her violent behavior, and actually showed relief. Soon thereafter the father took the mother on an overseas holi-

day, but not before the two of them had drawn up contracts for all three girls pertaining to what was expected of them before, during, and after the parents' absence.

Sibling Factors

Siblings can play an important role in the maintenance of symptomatology such as substance abuse. For instance, a nonsymptomatic sibling may supply a hospitalized patient with drugs. Another may alternate symptomatic behavior with the patient, such as developing a problem of his or her own when the patient improves. This may continue until the therapist realizes what is happening in the system and helps the family stop the repeating pattern.

In Gillian's case, no sooner had she improved than her younger sister started to act out. The therapists, spotting this pattern early, paradoxically praised the "new" patient for bailing out her sister. In addition, they challenged the parents in a teasing way, questioning whether this new alignment of daughters would be able to "whip" them. The parents reared up, denying that they were or would be beaten, and put the recalcitrant daughter in her place. Therapy ended soon thereafter.

Grandparents

Parent's own parents can have a major impact on the therapeutic effort. As mentioned previously, sometimes they are more involved with the index patient than the parents themselves. This could be manifested in a struggle between the two adult generations over who "owns" the child. The therapist who is not sensitive to this possibility—who does not investigate it early on—may see an initial success collapse into failure as the grandparents assert their authority. Essentially, the therapist may be unwittingly working against what the grandparents consider to be their own or the adolescent's best interests, and, consciously or not, they sabotage the treatment. For example, elevating a singe-parent mother so that she can take charge of and control her substance-abusing fifteen-year-old may be doomed to failure if she is still being treated like a child by her own mother. A better strategy is to join initially with the grandmother, make her an ally, and assist her in encouraging her daughter to parent adequately. The therapist may first need to recognize the authority and love of the grandmother and reassure her about her own "parenting" or grandparenting skills in order to free her up to coach her daughter and give the daughter true "permission to parent." In a sense, by respecting the grandmother, the therapist would be going with the system rather than directly opposing it.

> Seventeen-year-old Billie was named after his paternal grandfather. In addition, his father, his paternal aunt, and his maternal uncle were named Billie. Two years after he was born, his paternal grandfather died suddenly, and Billie became elevated as a sort of replacement for this man. His grandmother gave him special care, treated him as a confidant, and called him her "pride and joy." When he ran away from home (which he had been prone to do in recent months), he did not run to the street; he ran away to his grandmother's house.
>
> Billie had engaged in some drug and alcohol use as a sixteen-year-old, but he did not get heavily into chemical dependence until after his twenty-year-old cousin Jack (the grandmother's other favorite grandson) was killed by a car while hitchhiking. Jack was a heavy drug abuser and was suspected of having been fairly heavily drugged at the time of the accident. He had been hitchhiking while running away to grandmother's winter home in Florida.
>
> Billie's grandmother's boyfriend had left her shortly before Billie and his family entered therapy. One of the precipitating processes for therapy was a conflict between Billie's mother and grandmother. The grandmother wanted Billie to leave school and move to Florida to live with her. Billie's mother opposed this.
>
> When the nuclear family appeared for therapy, very few of the above facts were known to the therapist (M. Duncan Stanton). The going was initially very tough with this family. In the first session, the therapist found it difficult to get any change started. It was not until the therapist learned of the grandmother's role in Billie's life, and consequently invited her (and Billie's paternal aunt) to the sessions, that movement started to occur. Once a program and a set of goals that the grandmother could endorse were established, things began to happen. When a vehicle was found upon which the various adults in the system could agree (Billie's partying and late hours) and consequences were established that all would endorse, Billie's behavior began to shift. Within a few weeks, he became drug and alcohol free and stopped running away from home. Probably none of this would have happened if the therapist had continued to ignore both the importance of Billie's grandmother and the untapped potential she had for helping to turn the situation around.

Other Systems

It is always necessary to evaluate the substance-abusing adolescent and his or her family within their total context. Other systems with which they commonly interact are the school, peer group, church, welfare system, and court. Further, many such adolescents and their family members are involved with self-help groups (such as AA, NA, or Al-Anon) or other treatment systems. Unless these multiple systems are taken into account and incorporated into the treatment plan, the therapist may find himself or herself swimming upstream. Often such systems have their own agendas and approaches, and these may not be entirely consonant with the family therapy effort. The therapist needs to join with these systems by enlisting their assistance in empowering the parents and other family members to identify common goals and make the changes necessary for elimination of the problem. In a sense, we are talking not only about a therapy of families but also about a therapy of *interpersonal systems*.

References

Coleman, S.B., and M.D. Stanton. 1978. "The Role of Death in the Addict Family." *Journal of Marital and Family Therapy* 4:79–91.

Fishman, H.C., M.D. Stanton, and B.L. Rosman. 1982. "Treating Families of Adolescent Drug Abusers." In *The Family Therapy of Drug Abuse and Addiction*, edited by M.D. Stanton, T.C. Todd, and Associates, 335–57. New York: Guilford Press.

Haley, J. 1976. *Problem-Solving Therapy*. San Francisco: Jossey-Bass.

Haley, J. 1980. *Leaving Home*. New York: McGraw-Hill.

Landau, J. 1982. "Therapy with Families in Cultural Transition." In *Ethnicity and Family Therapy* edited by M. McGoldrick, J. Pearce, and J. Giordano, 552–72. New York: Guilford Press.

Landau-Stanton, J. 1985. "Adolescents, Families, and Cultural Transition: A Treatment Model." In *Handbook of Adolescents and Family Therapy*, edited by M.P. Mirkin and S.L. Koman, 363–81. New York: Gardner Press.

Landau-Stanton, J., and M.D. Stanton. 1985. "Treating Suicidal Adolescents and Their Families." In *Handbook of Adolescents and Family Therapy*, edited by M.P. Mirkin and S.L. Koman, 309–28. New York: Gardner Press.

Minuchin, S. 1974. *Families and Family Therapy*. Cambridge, Mass.: Harvard University Press.

Stanton, M.D. 1981a. "Marital Therapy from a Structural/Strategic Viewpoint." In *Handbook of Marriage and Marital Therapy*, edited by G.P. Sholevar 303–34. New York: S.P. Medical and Scientific Books.

———. 1981b. "Who Should Get Credit for Change Which Occurs in Therapy?" In *Questions and Answers in the Practice of family Therapy*, edited by A.S. Gurman, 519–22. New York: Brunner/Mazel.

Stanton, M.D., and S.B. Coleman. 1980. "The Participatory Aspects of Indirect Self-Destructive Behavior." In *The Many Faces of Suicide,* edited by N. Farberow, 187–203. New York: McGraw-Hill

Stanton, M.D., T.C. Todd, and Associates, eds. 1982. *The Family Therapy of Drug Abuse and Addiction.* New York: Guilford Press.

20
Interventions with the Substance-Abusing Nurse

Vernice Griffin Hills

"A registered nurse suspected of stealing large amounts of narcotics from patients at a Denver hospital during the last twelve months is the latest person questioned in a two month investigation by Denver police into widespread drug theft by nurses." This statement appeared in a column in the Denver *Rocky Mountain News* on December 31, 1981. According to national figures, the number of substance-abusing nurses is estimated to be between 10 to 20 percent. Sixty-seven percent of all disciplinary cases presented to the state boards of nursing are drug related (Kelly 1982). In Colorado alone, that translates into approximately four hundred to eight hundred nurses who may be involved in drug abuse. Referrals of nurses to the Halsted Clinic for substance abuse treatment have often come as a result of investigations and charges for possession, theft, and use of controlled substances. Other nurses have referred themselves in response to fear generated by such investigations.

When a nurse is reported to the Colorado Nursing Board (CNB) for suspected drug use, the usual course of action involves an investigation by the nursing board followed by a board hearing. The nurse may then be placed on probation and given a set of stipulations to follow to maintain his or her license. Stipulations mandated by CNB depend on the severity of the drug-related charge and generally require that the nurse become involved in some type of drug treatment and provide a specific number of urine samples to be screened for drugs of abuse. Nurses also may be mandated into drug treatment as a result of legal charges for drug possession, use, or theft. Drug-related charges are usually deferred and dropped if the nurse successfully completes a drug program.

A serious problem exists in the lapse of time between the investigation by the nursing board and the board hearing for drug-related charges, which often continues for as long as two years. Another problem is that in some

---

I would like to thank Raymond Conover, Ph.D., Carol Atkinson, Ph.D., and Thomas J. Crowley, M.D., for assisting with this chapter.

cases, nurses confronted by their supervisors are subsequently fired and never reported to the nursing board or legal authorities. This allows them to change their work settings and continue their patterns of abuse (Mereness 1981).

According to nurses treated at the Halsted Clinic, many employers are reluctant to report a suspected nurse-abuser for fear of their own liability. Lack of education regarding treatment for substance abuse and denial that the problem exists in the nursing profession also prohibit nurses from seeking treatment. In addition, there is resistance by the professional abuser to seek treatment because of the stigma, fear of close scrutiny by colleagues, and risk of losing employment or his or her nursing license.

Patient Dynamics and History

This chapter reports on the treatment of twenty-three nurses evaluated and admitted for treatment at the Halsted Clinic between April 1981 and April 1983. Twenty-one were non-Hispanic Caucasians, one was Hispanic, and one was black. Eleven were single, seven were married, and five were divorced. The population included ten with associate's degrees in nursing (ADNs), ten with bachelor's degrees in nursing (BSNs) two diploma nurses, and one licensed practical nurse (LPN). Six were self-referred, five were transferred or referred from another treatment facility, five were referred by probation officers, two by employers, two by attorneys, one by the nursing board, and two by hospitals. Twenty-two of the patients were employed as nurses when they entered drug treatment. In addition, eleven nurses had been employed on the evening shift of work, six on evening/night rotation, four on the night shift, and two on the day shift. Eighteen abused opiates, three amphetamines, and two tranquilizers as their primary drugs of abuse.

All the nurses studied viewed the threatened loss of their professional licenses as a primary motivating factor in seeking treatment. As treatment progressed, four major themes emerged as problems for these nurses:

1. Conflicts in relationships
2. Dysphoria and anxiety
3. Financial problems
4. Medical problems that may have had psychosomatic origins

Turbulent relationships with significant others—boyfriends, girlfriends, spouses, and parents, primarily the mother—were prominent. Many patients described their mothers as dominant, overbearing, and hypercritical. Several nurses viewed themselves as unable to cope psychologically without the use of drugs and labeled themselves "mentally ill." These nurses denied having a drug problem. Of all the nurses evaluated at the Halsted Clinic, only one was identified as not having a drug problem and was referred for psychiatric treatment. Financial difficulties were considered a major concern in approximately one-third of the nurses studied. Drug-related issues contributed to poor money management and absences on the job, which often led to termination of employment. Medical problems and symptoms varied from migraine headaches to backaches and were not necessarily identified as organic in nature. These nurses attributed their drug use in part to their medical problems; they rationalized taking drugs to relieve physiological pain. In most instances, these nurses did not seek proper medical attention for their somatic complaints.

More than two-thirds of the nurses studied were reared in upper-middle-class and middle-class families. Most relocated in Colorado as adults from other areas of the United States. They described their childhoods, for the most part, as stable and traditional in nature—that is, mother as the homemaker and father as the breadwinner. In addition, the patients commonly described their mothers as being the dominant household figure, while their fathers took on a more passive role. Only four of the nurses reported their childhoods to have been extremely unstable, characterized by significant losses, such as divorced parents, and/or subjection to physical and/or sexual abuse. Only three of the nurses reported an immediate family history of drug abuse; approximately one-third reported a history of alcohol abuse.

The nurses described their current lifestyles as quite isolated, with few friends, poor support systems, and limited social contacts. Daily patterns of living consisted mainly of work—often double shifts—domestic chores, and errands.

More than 75 percent of the nurses were the primary wage earners of their households. Very few possessed other job skills that would enable them to support themselves or their families at the same level outside the nursing profession.

More than two-thirds of the nurses studied began their abuse of substances as adults, with minimal sporadic nonopioid recreational use in adolescence. The two male nurses studied began opiate use while serving in the armed forces during the Vietnam War.

The drugs most frequently abused were Demerol and morphine, followed by Dilaudid, codeine, amphetamines, and tranquilizers. The opiate abusers said that they would substitute any opiate but codeine for their drug of choice. The three amphetamine abusers all used opiates to come down from their drug highs. The tranquilizer abusers substituted alcohol followed by opiates for their drug of choice. Figure 20–1 shows the breakdown of the nurses' primary drugs of abuse.

Twenty-one of the nurses studied were multiple substance abusers but identified only their primary drug of abuse to be a problem if they admitted

Amphetamines 13%

Tranquilizers 9%

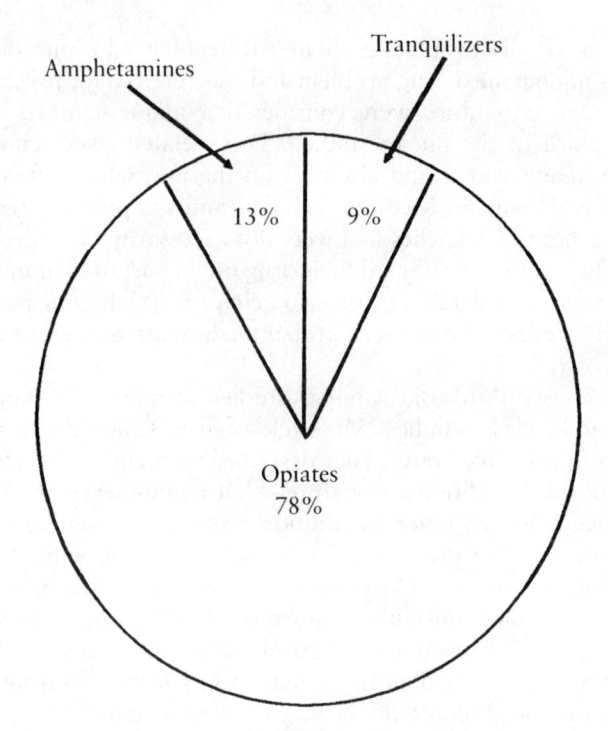

Opiates 78%

Figure 20–1. Primary drugs of abuse.

to a drug problem. Most frequently abused secondary drugs in descending order were cocaine, marijuana, and alcohol. Secondary drugs of abuse were reported to be used "occasionally and recreationally," but the nurses' descriptions of use ranged from weekly to binges lasting one week to several months.

The most common route of administration was intramuscular followed by intravenous. Cocaine was most often administered intravenously. Ten of the twelve nurses working in a specialized setting—intensive care unit, critical care unit, or emergency room—used the intravenous route of administration.

The nurses reported their use of opiates to be confined to the work setting, self-administered, solitary, and taken from the hospital or patient supplies. Two of the primary amphetamine abusers procured their drug of choice from private physicians but also resorted to street procurement when their regular supplies were not available. One nurse traded hospital supplies of opiates for street amphetamines. Tranquilizer abusers also procured drugs from private physicians as well as from hospital or patient supplies. The nurses altered their documentation of medications administered to patients to account for the missing narcotics.

The three nurses treated with methadone followed a pattern of the general addict population whereby they procured drugs by "doctor shopping" and forged prescriptions when their hospital or patient supplies were not available. Two of the three nurses maintained on methadone reengaged in opiate use when they discontinued methadone treatment. The nurses who reported unstable family histories had less favorable treatment progress.

Narcotic drug doses taken for self-administration were reported to range from 25 to 800 milligrams of Demerol per day. Frequency of use ranged from three times a week to three times a day, and length of use ranged from four months to seven years. Only four nurses studied reported withdrawal symptoms after discontinuing their use of narcotics, even though their histories warranted potential addiction. These nurses were generally uninformed regarding the symptoms associated with withdrawal from opiates. In addition, reported drug histories proved to be inconsistent as treatment progressed.

Throughout treatment, all the nurses reported that they did not deprive their patients of adequate care while using drugs and in fact described feeling more efficient while under the influence. The nurses also reported that their coworkers and supervisors did not suspect a drug problem and that these same colleagues were surprised to find out that a valued employee was taking drugs for self-administration.

Two major reported reasons for taking narcotics were (1) to increase energy and (2) to calm down in order to perform efficiently. Eight of the nurses described paradoxical stimulating affects of narcotics after a pattern of addiction was established. More than 75 percent expressed having experienced extreme fear that they would not make it through their shifts without drugs. The nurses also said that they feared the easy access to narcotic substances would make it more difficult to resist the temptation to use. They expressed a deep sense of guilt about engaging in drug use and felt unable to seek the help they needed for their drug problems.

Treatment

During treatment, the nurses were provided protection under strict federal confidentiality regulations. Each nurse was evaluated and had an individualized treatment plan established. All of the nurses studied were seen on an outpatient basis in weekly individual or family sessions. Brief inpatient hospitalization was available through the University of Colorado Health Sciences Center Hospital, although it was only used twice. Psychological testing and medical services were provided through the hospital clinic by staff psychologists and physicians when appropriate. Vocational services also were available for nurses under license suspension to explore alternative job skills.

Each nurse provided urine samples that were screened for drugs of abuse, including opiates, tranquilizers, amphetamines, alcohol, barbiturates, cocaine, and marijuana. Typically, a staff person randomly observed the patient passing the urine specimen into the collection bottle at the Halsted Clinic. Samples were collected on specified days (Monday, Wednesday, and Friday) or according to a random schedule whereby the patient called into the clinic each Monday, Wednesday, or Friday to find out if he or she needed to provide a urine sample.

Length of treatment ranged from one month to one year, with the average treatment lasting seven months. Two of the nurses continued providing urine specimens randomly after discharge from the outpatient counseling program.

Treatment involved counseling and education to help the nurses stop their reliance on drugs. In addition, the nurses were provided the option, when appropriate, to use medication and/or "contingency contracting" to decrease the possibility of reengaging in drug abuse.

Three of the nurses included used methadone maintenance and/or detoxification. Methadone is a synthetic opiate that has a longer duration of action than other narcotics, lasting up to twenty-four hours, thereby permitting administration once a day. It is almost as effective when administered orally as by injection and is controlled, prescribed, and carefully monitored (Crowley 1983).

One nurse was prescribed Antabuse to dissuade alcohol ingestion. Eight nurses chose to use contingency contracts. The various reinforcing or punishing events that predictably follow a given behavior are called contingencies of that behavior. A contingency contract between therapist and patient is a formal agreement that the therapist is to respond predictably to certain patient behaviors with specified reinforcements or punishments.

Eight of the nurses studied deposited with the Halsted Clinic a letter to the CNB or to his or her nursing supervisor surrendering his or her nursing license. Each nurse directed the clinic to mail that letter whenever a urine specimen contained a drug of abuse or a scheduled specimen was not given. The contract made immediate and certain a result of drug abuse that would otherwise be uncertain or delayed. Although nurses referred to the clinic by the legal or regulatory agencies had contingencies in operation, the expected outcome or event was much less immediate and certain than that of the contingencies drawn up at the clinic.

The eight nurses in the study who entered into a written agreement with the Halsted staff agreed to provide urine specimens each Monday, Wednesday, and Friday for one month at the Halsted Outpatient Clinic. A staff member observed the nurses passing of the urine specimen into the collection bottle. Each specimen was split in half; one half was sent to the Colorado Health Department for analysis, and the other half was stored at the outpatient clinic. The second half was submitted for analysis if the first half tested positive for drugs of abuse.

For the next four months after signing the contract, the nurses called into the clinic each Monday, Wednesday, and Friday to find out whether he or she needed to provide a urine sample. A random urine schedule allowed for a two-thirds risk on each Monday, Wednesday, and Friday that the nurse would have to provide a sample. For two more months, nurses remained on a random schedule that allowed a one-third risk of having to provide a urine sample each Monday, Wednesday, or Friday. If the patient was sick when a urine examination was scheduled, he or she was still required to provide a specimen. If he or she was so sick that hospitalization was required, the sample was obtained at the hospital. If he or she was scheduled to take a vacation or be out of town, the urine program was suspended—with proper advance notification and verification—during his or her absence.

As mentioned earlier, the clinic had on file a letter from each nurse to the CNB or to his or her nursing supervisor. The clinic staff was directed to mail the letter if both halves of a urine sample tested positive for drugs of abuse or if the nurse failed to make a scheduled urine examination. If the urine sample provided by the patient was too small for a double analysis as described above, the staff was directed to mail the letter if a single sample tested positive for drugs of abuse. If a medical condition required the patient to take an abusable drug and a copy of a legitimate prescription was provided to the staff, the appearance of that drug in the urine would not trigger mailing of the letter.

Most of the compounds from the drugs tested for in urinalysis can be detected within forty-eight hours. However, two of the nurses reported using drugs on days that they did not provide a urine sample, and these drugs went undetected. These nurses were then placed on a more frequent call-in schedule.

Six of the nurses who used contingency contracts were referred by probation officers or employers, and two were self-referrals. The patients selecting this type of treatment may have been highly motivated compared to the patients treated by noncontingency methods. These patients practiced behaviors in their daily lives to sustain abstinence. With abstinence and counseling, the nurses worked toward recognizing the rewards of a drug-free lifestyle that outweighed the benefits of resuming drug use (Crowley 1983). In counseling, the nurses developed more appropriate ways of improving their work performance and skills in dealing with turbulent relationships as well as medical, psychological, and financial problems. Simultaneously, the nurses were encouraged to develop more realistic expectations and to increase their socialization and support systems. Another significant aspect of counseling was to focus attention on the client's family dynamics and history and to draw relationships between these factors and their abuse behavior. Increasing a patient's awareness of his or her behavior patterns and motivational processes increased the sense of control over chemical use. This also helped to diminish and stop destructive cycles of guilt and perfectionism.

Results

The results concerning noncontingency and contingency patients are shown in figure 20–2. Of the nurses without contingency contracts, 33 percent remained in treatment longer than three months, whereas all of the nurses engaged in contingency contracts remained in treatment for a minimum of four months. Results of urine screens for noncontract patients indicated that 51

Noncontingency Patients

1	2	3	4	5	6
100%			33%		
51%				60%	

Contingency Patients

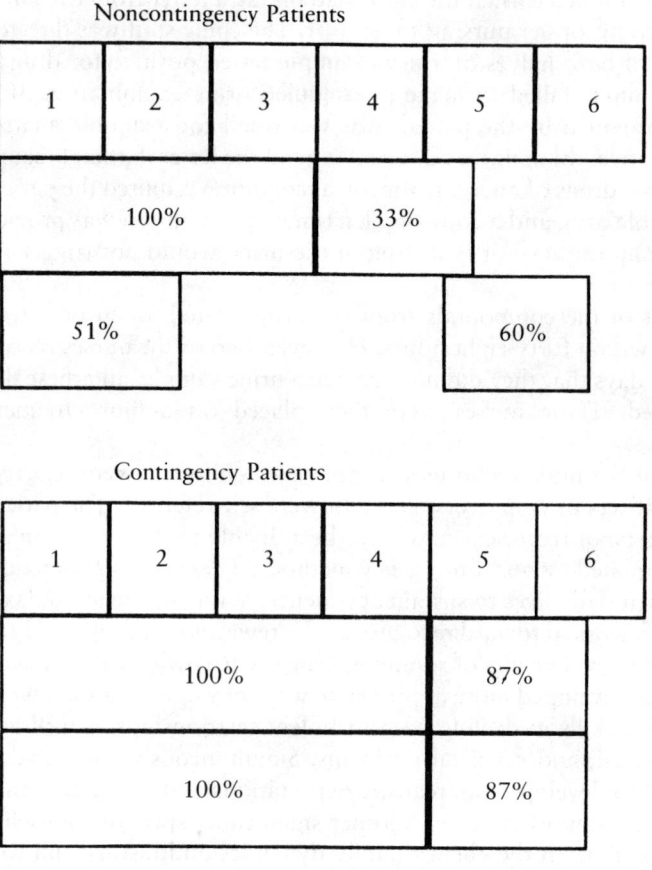

1	2	3	4	5	6
100%				87%	
100%				87%	

Figure 20–2. **Noncontingency versus contingency patients.**

percent remained abstinent during the first four months, while 87 percent of the contract patients did so.

Conclusion

Nurses abusing drugs and alcohol on and off the job has become a substantial problem. These nurses need treatment, and their patients need protection. Obstacles that prevent their engagement in treatment can be reduced with the awareness and recognition that such a problem exists in the nursing profession and will continue to exist. We also must acknowledge that nurses are at increased risk for substance abuse. They have access to highly addictive drugs and have been taught that these drugs relieve pain perceived as both psychological and physical. Nurses also believe that since they are knowledgeable about drug actions, side effects, and therapeutic dosage, they are immune to the addictive process. Therefore, drug availability, social modeling, social reinforcement, and pharmacologic optimism are special risk factors in the nursing profession that warrant considerable attention.

We must acknowledge that drug abuse is a pathologic process that often can be treated, like most other illnesses, while the patient is employed. One effective method of treatment that enables a patient to remain abstinent while a viable member of the nursing profession is through the use of contingency contracting. In turn, contingency contracting as a treatment tool offers a viable solution to the drug abuse problem in the nursing profession.

The medical community can facilitate treatment through educational programs on the process of addiction and referral to appropriate treatment programs. Seven known programs are currently available in the United States, but many more are needed. In addition, continued studies of the substance abuse problem within the nursing profession is paramount in understanding and rehabilitating this special patient population.

Suggested Readings

Bissell, L., and R.W. Jones. "The Alcoholic Nurse." *Nursing Outlook* 29 (2): 96–101 (1981).
Buxton, M., M. Jessap, and M. Landry. "Treatment of the Chemically Dependent Health Professional." In *The Addictions Mulidisciplinary Perspectives and Treatments,* edited by H. Milkman and H. Shaffe, pp. 131–145. Lexington Mass.: Lexington Books, 1985.
Darity, M. "Drugs: Facing up to a Problem on Your Staff." *RN* 42 (11): 20–26 (1979).
"Help for the Helper." *American Journal of Nursing* 572–87 (1982).
"Helping the Nurse Who Misuses Drugs." *American Journal of Nursing* 74 (9): 1665–71 (1975).

Levine, D.G., P.A. Preston, S.G. Lipscomb, and W.F. Ross. "A Special Program for Nurse Addicts." *American Journal of Nursing* 74 (9): 1672–73 (1974).

Pierce, S.M. "When the Addict Is a Nurse. *AORN Journal* 24 (4): 655–64. (1976).

Poplar, J.F. "Characteristics of Nurse Addicts." *American Journal of Nursing* 69 (1): 117–9 (1969).

Redding, W. "Drug Diverson—The Addicted Nurse. *Oklahoma Nurse* 26 (1): 6 (1981).

References

Crowley, T.J. "1983 Contingency Contracting Treatment of Drug-Abusing Physicians, Nurses, and Dentists." *NIDA* Research *Monograph Series.* 46:68–83.

Kelly, L. 1982. "Are Nurses Dipping in Demerol? *New Jersey Nurse* 12 (4): 18–19.

Mereness, D. 1981. "Protect Your Patients from Nurse Addicts." *Nursing Life* 1 (1): 70–73.

Epilogue:
Integrating Treatment Choices

Howard J. Shaffer
Blase Gambino

If the adage "Practice follows theory" is correct, then for an integrated and comprehensive theory of practice to be adopted, a conceptual paradigm must emerge (Kuhn 1970; Shaffer 1986a). In this epilogue, we do the following:

1. Move beyond the disease model toward individualized, prescriptive treatment—a position more compatible with clinical science

2. Present a model of natural change (Shaffer and Jones 1989) that describes how "addicts" become free of addiction[1]

3. Examine how a stage change model can integrate the prescriptive choice of treatment methods

4. Discuss some integrative treatment trends of the future.

The Disease Controversy

For the substance abuse[2] field to move toward a prescriptive model of treatment, it is necessary to begin to resolve one of the most hotly debated issues of our time: Is addiction a disease? The debate surrounding addiction as disease reflects the fact that the study of the addictions is in a preparadigmatic stage of scientific development (Shaffer 1986a). While this controversy centers primarily on alcoholism, the repercussions have been felt throughout the other addictions.

The idea that alcoholism is a disease has been with us for many decades.

We would like to thank Chad Emrick, Harvey Milkman, Lloyd Sederer, and Sharon A. Stein for their helpful comments on earlier drafts of this chapter. Preparation of this chapter was supported in part by a contract (no. 2322905893) from the Massachusetts Department of Public Health. Requests for reprints should be sent to Howard J. Shaffer, Ph.D., Center for Addiction Studies, Harvard Medical School, The Cambridge Hospital, 1493 Cambridge Street, Cambridge, MA 02139.

Room (1983) described the evolution of this perception. Between 1946 and 1951, 20 percent of the public said that alcoholism is a disease. From 1955 to 1960, about 60 percent of the American population said that alcoholism is a disease. By 1989, between 85 and 90 percent said that alcoholism is a disease (Foreman 1989).

Alcoholism as disease represents the use of a metaphor gone astray. Some proponents believe that alcoholism *is* a disease. Others see it as *like* a disease. In the first instance, theorists have taken the metaphor far beyond constructive use and committed a major error of logical types; they have confused the map with the territory and the menu with the meal (Shaffer 1985).

Definitions and Agreement

The application of the disease label to the addictions generates confusion and disorder rather than clarity and structure. The lack of consensual agreement about the definitions of *alcoholism* and *addiction* further complicates this debate. These terms have not demonstrated their usefulness as scientific or treatment concepts.

The concept of disease itself is ambiguous. Applying the disease concept to specific cases often produces disagreement among both the public and physicians (Campbell, Scadding, and Roberts 1979; Shaffer 1987). This confusion leads some diagnosticians to propose that treatment providers refer to the "target disorder" rather than to the disease (Sackett, Haynes, and Tugwell 1985).

The clinical issue, as opposed to the conceptual debate, is not now, nor has it ever been, whether alcoholism (or addiction) is a disease or the result of a disease process. The issue from a clinical perspective involves establishing a diagnosis or working formulation. These clinical devices permit clinicians to select treatment methods that offer patients a favorable prognosis given knowledge of the disorder and patient.

There is little or no value in diagnosing any individual as diseased unless it permits clinicians to choose a treatment plan that will maximize the health status of the patient. "[Put more formally], the act of clinical diagnosis is classification for a purpose: *an effort to recognize the class or group to which a patient's illness belongs so that, based on prior experience with that class, the subsequent clinical acts we can afford to carry out, and the patient is willing to follow, will maximize that patient's health*" (Sackett, Haynes, and Tugwell 1985, 4, emphasis added).

The value of the concept of an addictive disease, then, is dependent on the extent to which an *individual patient* benefits from its application. While diagnosis is dependent on comparison with groups, choice of treatment must remain prescriptive in application. Prescriptive treatment requires consideration of three interactive domains:

1. That of the physician (for example, medical management strategy)
2. That of the patient (for example, compliance with rules and expectations of care and concern)
3. That of society (for example, social mores and attributions of responsibility)

Together these domains define the "sickness" that is to be treated (Kleinman 1988).

Explaining the Contradiction of Disease and Morality

These three dimensions of sickness explain the seeming contradiction of the public and physicians holding both a medical and moral view of many diseases (Blum, Roman, and Bennett 1989). Shaffer (1987), in the only factor analytic study on this subject, established that a New England subject sample did not view addictive behaviors (such as alcoholism, cocaine abuse, alcohol abuse, and heroin dependence) as being similar to other disorders that are widely accepted as diseases (such as AIDS, lung cancer, diabetes, measles, and tuberculosis). Taken together, these studies reveal that the public has a high level of ambivalence about the disease concept. They are willing to designate certain addictive behaviors as diseases, but they hold on to their judgments of behavioral excess as a moral weakness.

Fuzzy Thinking

To date, disease model proponents (such as Johnson 1986; Scott 1987; Talbott 1983) and opponents (such as Peele 1984; Peele 1987) are guilty of fuzzy thinking that is fracturing the addictions field. Both groups have failed to define their concept of disease without invoking tautologies. It is no wonder, then, that they cannot resolve their differences or put their positions to an empirical test. They simply apply the concept of disease as they see fit in order to make sense out of the existing data.

Defining the concept of disease is not an easy task (Campbell, Scadding, and Roberts 1979; Shaffer 1987). The *Oxford English Dictionary* (*OED*) defines *disease* as an absence of ease, discomfort, or annoyance. Would Peele suggest that delirium tremens and narcotic withdrawal do not meet the requirements of this definition? Similarly, the *OED* defines *disease* as an evil affection or tendency. Would those proponents of the addictive disease model who are trying to get a "better deal" for addicted patients accept this definition?

To make sense of this controversy and escape the dilemma of yes-it-is versus no-it-isn't, we have to raise the discussion to another level of analysis.

On this plane, we can see that *addictive disease* is a convenient metaphor. Disease as metaphor (Blum 1985; Payer 1988; Shaffer 1985; Shaffer 1987; Sontag 1979; Sontag 1989) permits a culture to make sense out of behavior patterns that are difficult to understand. Alcoholism, like athletic skills, has a biogenetic component. We are willing to call one a disease but not the other. Both activities place participants in potentially dangerous situations; both can lead to social isolation. Both endeavors appear to have a large perceptual component of drive, need, or self-determination. The alcoholic, like the slumping professional athlete, may be held in disdain by observers.

It is time to stop using metaphors promiscuously. To comprehend drug use, abuse, dependence, and addiction, we have to understand the nature of drug users, abusers, and addicts. We must stop destroying them in our continuing war on drugs and begin to grasp their motives, beliefs, interests, and desires.

The disease model rests more on faith than on scientific evidence (Sobell and Sobell 1984). There is little doubt that many people have been helped by the disease model. When people believe that addiction is a disease, a clear path to recovery emerges. However, when patients are without this conviction, the addiction treatment specialist, guided by the disease model, has had little to offer. Often these clinicians accuse the skeptical patient of being in denial, as if it were a place that has no escape.

Alternatively, an individualized, prescriptive treatment approach rests on an empirical base (Marlatt et al. 1988; Sobell and Sobell 1984). The following section reviews some of the historical evidence that serves as a foundation for individualized approaches to addiction treatment. This chapter is not intended as a review of the literature. Marlatt et al. (1988) accomplished that task most ably. Instead, we briefly examine addiction treatment theory and research from the 1980s. More specifically, we attempt to identify any common threads that converge toward a paradigm for research and theory on the treatment of the addictions.

Treatment Choices: A Review of Recent Trends

Where We Were

At the end of the seventies, we examined the field of addiction treatment (Gambino and Shaffer 1979; Shaffer and Gambino 1979). We observed the lack of a guiding scientific paradigm that could direct investigations and treatment of these disorders. We concluded that the scientific study of the addictions field was in a preparadigmatic state (Gambino and Shaffer 1979).

As we enter the final decade of the twentieth century, it seems appropriate to examine the past ten years and assess the extent to which advances in theory, research, and practice in the addictions reflect the emergence of a paradigm. Alternatively, the field may still remain in a preparadigm stage of development.

Paradigms and the Addictions

The Value of Paradigms. Scientists apply the concept of paradigm to help understand the knowledge generation and acceptance process that occurs within professional disciplines (Kuhn 1970; Shaffer and Burglass 1981). Paradigms determine how scientists conduct research, which methods they choose, and how they interpret their findings. Boneau (1974) succinctly described the value attendant to the adoption of a paradigm in reference to the emergence of cognitive-behaviorism:

> Paradigms ... relate to one another the major pieces of a science. The interconnections among the pieces become visible; prerequisite skills to enhance understanding are made apparent; strategies for teaching the discipline as a whole are evolvable; the material becomes easier to learn when it ties together; the important is delineated from the trivial; the field becomes easier to understand and to use as a basis for advancement of knowledge. In retrospect, some obvious substantive advances may fall quickly and simply out of fresh paradigms, or complex formulations may become simplified. (p. 298)

Paradigms and Treatment. A paradigm also may be thought of as a miniature world view that shapes a practitioner's understanding of the phenomena to be assessed and treated. An operating paradigm serves as an a priori template through which clinicians view patients and their problems. This template organizes information and suggests which questions to ask and which data are important. Paradigms focus attention. As a consequence of this concentration, clinicians use evidence they obtain to direct their interventions. Paradigms are responsible for clinicians seeing only those things for which they are looking.

A Lack of Agreement between Theory and Treatment. At the beginning of this decade, we maintained that "there is little agreement between theorists as to the etiology of addiction and somewhat less agreement as to the course of proper treatment" (Shaffer and Gambino 1979, 299). Has this situation changed during the past decade? Sederer (1988) notes:

> To set foot into the field of psychiatry [or the addictions] is to encounter an overwhelming mass of clinical data, hypothetical notions, and theoretical constructs. Dopamine mingles with denial, and serotonin with symbiosis. Defenses and divorce appear as meaningful, and influential, as gamma ami-

nobutyric acid and the endorphins. Urban drift, ego-deficits, and ventricular enlargement may be found rubbing conceptual shoulders. (p. 71)

A Crisis of Concepts. Shaffer (1986a) suggests that

> a crisis of concepts and categories exists in the body of knowledge associated with the phenomena of the addictions. This crisis is characterized by the absence of an accepted paradigm, the consequent paucity of facts, and the lack of integration between research, theory, and practice.... In the absence of a paradigm, it is difficult to agree on what are the important parameters of addiction. Furthermore, the research intended to support constructs such as addiction, abuse, dependence, etc. is clouded because experts in the field of addictions have great difficulty agreeing as to what comprises the important data. These conditions ... impede our understanding of addictive behavior and serve to block efforts at teaching, training and the acquisition of knowledge relevant to treatment interventions. (pp. 294–95)

Signs and Symptoms of an Emerging Paradigm?

Coping and Addictive Behavior. Despite the observations of Sederer and Shaffer, there are signs of consensus. During the past ten years, clinicians and researchers increasingly recognized the individual as a purposive being seeking to gain control of his or her fate. "People play a major role in directing their own behavior ... towards certain ends ... [for example] drugs [as] a viable coping mechanism" (Gambino and Shaffer 1979, 212). This recognition marked a shift away from reactive models (addiction as disease) toward proactive models ("addictive behavior as a habitual maladaptive means of coping with stressors"). In this view, the addicted person is seen as "an active agent of change rather than a helpless victim of uncontrollable forces" (Marlatt 1985, 367–68).

Motivation and Coping Mechanisms. A major determinant of coping is individual motivation (Marlatt 1985). As clinicians increasingly came to study and elaborate on the role of motivational factors, theorists developed more complex and sophisticated models. Some of these models capture, in rich detail, the complex tapestry of motivational processes and their relation to drug use and abuse: "[We present] a motivational model of alcohol use that takes into account *all* the variables that are known to affect drinking and show how these variables are interrelated" (Cox and Klinger 1988, 177–78, emphasis added). This research also demonstrates the need to understand how both negative affect reduction and positive affect gain are involved in goal-seeking behavior and how these may be revealed through the disclosure of expectancies (Niaura et al. 1988).

Expectancies and Drug Effects. In the eighties, important research focused on the effects of the substances people ingest. Investigators sought to clarify the relationships among drug action, psychological set, and social setting (Shaffer and Jones 1989; Zinberg 1984). As Zinberg (1984) demonstrated, however, it may be impossible to separate the role of expectancies as a modifier in order to reveal the "pure" effects of a substance. There are two major types of expectancies (Marlatt et al. 1988). The first are outcome expectancies. Beliefs that alcohol is a "magic elixir" (Marlatt 1987) that will produce a number of desired effects is an example of this type of expectancy. The second type are self-efficacy expectations (Bandura 1977). Self-efficacy is a measure of an individual's confidence that he or she will be able to succeed at a task or at least control events in a favorable way. The use of substances to enhance efficacy judgments can be an important motivational device in some circumstances (Shaffer and Jones 1989). The expectancy concept has provided a greater understanding of substance use and abuse and offers greater potential for effective intervention (Marlatt and Gordon 1985; Shaffer and Jones 1989). The use of the *abstinence violation effect* to explain relapse is the most notable example of the value of the concept of expectancies. Indeed, it has been shown to be a powerful integrative concept that helps us understand common processes among addictions (Brownell et al. 1986; Shaffer and Jones 1989).

Explanations and descriptions of coping strategies (Shiffman and Wills 1985), motivational mechanisms (Cox and Klinger 1988), and expectancies (Cooper, Russell, and George 1988; Niaura et al. 1988) converge to provide an integrated view of substance use and abuse. While necessary to explain much of what is observed, these scientific models of addiction and relapse are not, in themselves, sufficient to serve as the structure of an operative treatment paradigm. Next we consider some of the additional components that are needed.

Components for Treatment Intervention

Individual Differences. At the beginning of the 1980s, many theorists did not demonstrate a thorough understanding of how to incorporate individual differences into their explanations of addiction (Gambino and Shaffer 1979). Theorists relied on simplistic laws of interaction. They usually applied these principles universally for all situations. Further, addiction theorists expressed "a belief in the unity of human personality which assumes that any individual actor will behave the same, given his personality style, regardless of the contextual situation within which activity occurs" (Gambino and Shaffer 1979, 212).

Researchers gained considerable progress in addressing individual differences since we made our original observations. In no small part, this reflects a combination of the steady accumulation of important knowledge (Marlatt et al. 1988) and the increasing sophistication of theory, research design, and statistical analyses (for example, the use of survival analysis by Curry et al. 1988). "These improved measures . . . and more sophisticated analytical techniques represent the major achievement [in the treatment of substance abuse] of the past 5 years" (Jaffe 1984, 15). When properly focused, statistical methodology is a powerful tool in the identification of patient, treatment, and environmental variables that are indicators of risks and benefits associated with specific classes or types of patients. This type of research is a requirement for the matching of patient to treatment.

Patient-Treatment Matching. The concept of patient-treatment matching is another sign that things are indeed changing. When clinicians enter characteristics of patients, including background and history, into the treatment-outcome equation, they can derive important treatment advances (Krantz and Moos 1988; Gambino 1989). "The identification of meaningful subgroups is theoretically and clinically important, especially to match patients more adequately to the most effective treatments" (Marlatt et al. 1988, 236).

Efforts to discover key individual difference variables that will serve as indicators of beneficial treatment outcome have not been spectacularly successful (Dance and Neufeld 1988). Nevertheless, the need for research exploring the concept of treatment-patient matching has become a standard comment in research and clinical discussions (Marlatt et al. 1988). After years of discussion about the need for prescriptive intervention (Shaffer 1986b; Shaffer and Gambino 1979), clinical scientists are only now beginning to make prescriptive research a priority. "Researchers have but barely begun to ask, much less answer, approximations to the proper therapy outcome question: Which treatment procedures, administered by which therapist to which patient, with which specific problems are predicted to yield which outcomes" (Goldstein and Stein 1976, 3).

Marlatt (1988) reviewed the literature on matching patients to treatment. This evidence suggests that patient-treatment matching must be an integral part of treatment planning and evaluation. Even in the absence of strong evidence from clinical trials (see chapter 15 in this book), making a choice of treatment strategy conditional on patient characteristics will lead to the design of better clinical programs. This will occur because treatment matching requires clinical staff to articulate their implicit clinical assumptions.

Consider the following simplified example of an implicit treatment strategy that clinicians might articulate. Patient John Doe is actively denying substance abuse as a meaningful factor in his life despite deteriorating health and multiple accidents. Some clinicians think that successful psychotherapy can occur only after a patient detoxifies from methadone maintenance. In this case, however, clinical staff decide that his ego strength is sufficient to withstand confrontational techniques. They choose group psychotherapy as an adjunct to John Doe's individual counseling.

Taxonomy of Situations. A discussion of individual differences and patient-treatment matching flows naturally into a consideration of situational specificity. "We must develop a taxonomy of situations that describes the vast variety of contexts and conditions within which people use substances to alter their perceived experience" (Gambino and Shaffer 1979, 213). What do environments that encourage, precipitate, or inhibit drug taking have in common? What are the differences? Two excellent examples indicate the value of taxonomies for treatment. The Inventory of Drinking Situations (Annis and Davis 1988) provides an important and insightful model of efforts to identify situations specific to drug use and abuse. For purposes of relapse prevention, this instrument provides a measure of potential drinking behavior within high-risk situations. Another instrument also important for treatment planning is the Situational Confidence Questionnaire (Annis and Davis 1988). This questionnaire measures self-efficacy and helps guide treatment interventions by identifying the variety of situations in which the client will have difficulty coping.

Integrating Theory and Treatment Models

A Confusion of Voices and Models

"The existence of numerous and often conflicting models and theories of the disorders that are treated has been a long standing and continuing problem in the mental health professions. Furthermore, decisions to choose among different models or theories can rarely be made on an empirical basis" (Maisto and Connors 1988, 424).

Substance abuse treatment specialists perceive current models to have little relevance to clinical practice (if they are aware of them at all). This is the primary reason that clinicians make little use of research, although there are many other reasons as well (see for example, Gambino and Shaffer 1979; Shaffer and Gambino 1984). This situation will change only if theorists can develop a theory of practice that is consistent with the way in which practice actually operates. Clinical scientists often forget that science must be relevant to real-world problems. Theorists are often too preoccupied with their own particular theoretical interests and too little concerned with the problems confronted by the practitioner.

Models of Treatment and Addiction

The reasons why most theoretical models are not useful in practice—although some stimulate exciting and important research (Marlatt and Gordon 1985; Prochaska and DiClemente 1985)—are both simple and complex. We believe that one major reason resides in the failure of researchers and clinicians to recognize that what has been lacking historically are not models of addiction but models of treatment practice. For example, practitioners and theorists alike fail to recognize the implications of the distinction between models of addiction, such as disease and learning, and models of treatment, such as abstinence and controlled drinking. Each of the latter is an approach in which the goal—abstinence or controlled drinking—is confounded with the treatment (for example, the imposition of abstinence or the teaching of controlled drinking). These treatment choices reflect the strategic assumption that the etiology of the addictive disorder is either the result of a disease or learned behavior.

Abstinence (refraining from drinking) and controlled drinking (or controlled drug use) are behaviors or activities (means) not outcomes or goals (ends). We must not put controlled drinking in the same category as the instrumental positive consequences of drinking provided by social reinforcement from peer approval (White, Bates, and Johnson in press) or the motivational value of a self-image consistent with the individual's need for belonging to a group that defines drinking as a preferred activity under certain sanctioned circumstances (Vuchinich and Tucker 1988).

This emphasis on measures of abstinence or controlled drinking diverts attention from the critical question "What is the relative risk of controlled drinking treatment compared to abstinence treatment (where abstinence represents the current gold standard)?" Clinicians are often convinced, naively, that treatments are benevolent. Often they forget that every treatment contains some element of risk. For example, when we define risk solely in terms of relapse, the implication is that relapse is the end point of interest—that is, the primary outcome of concern. Rarely do we limit our clinical interest to such behavior. More typically, clinicians and patients are concerned with lapse and relapse as intermediate markers toward major negative outcomes, such as additional morbidity, incarceration, or death. Similarly, abstinence as a treatment outcome tells us little about the quality of life for patients. Abstinence does not preclude the risk of depression and suicide. This caution holds equally true for treatments that promote controlled drinking.

Change Processes and Stages of Change

Until recently, there has been a lack of meaningful integration of theory, research, and practice (Tims and Leukefeld 1986; Niaura et al. 1988). Marlatt

(1988) and other observers (see, for example, Maisto and Connors 1988; Shaffer and Jones 1989) describe the emergence of a significant theoretical movement: the evolution of the concept of *stages of change* to understand and explain the entire addiction process. Prochaska & DiClemente (1985) stimulated this movement by giving theoretical substance and empirical sustenance to the idea of discrete developmental stages of addiction. The stages of change concept has had a powerful heuristic effect on the development of models of addiction (Marlatt 1988; Marlatt et al. 1988), the evaluation and understanding of treatment (Maisto and Connors 1988), and the understanding of natural recovery (Shaffer and Jones 1989). Some theorists (e.g., Goldfried, 1980) have gone so far as to conclude that "a zeitgeist has emerged in which therapists from different systems are searching for common processes of change" (Prochaska et al. 1988, 520).

Shaffer offers a model that extends the theory of stages of change to an account of the "natural recovery" process reported by "cocaine quitters" (Shaffer and Jones 1989). In the following section, we outline this model as a prototype of a common set of processes that may explain recovery from any addiction whether or not it occurs within the framework of formal treatment. While the model has much in common with earlier models—for instance, it describes stages similar to those of precontemplation, contemplation, and action (Prochaska and DiClemente 1985)—it provides a more detailed emphasis on the role of events and states in the transition from addiction to recovery.[3] Such a view is more consistent with epidemiological concepts and descriptions of the natural history of a disorder. It is also more useful for treatment providers than is an immediate process view. The treatment provider has numerous alternative strategies to induce events, such as short-term objectives and long-term treatment goals, or to help the patient move from state to state, such as improved treatment status.

A Model of Change and Recovery

Natural recovery from substance abuse, such as quitting cocaine, cannot be considered spontaneous; the use of this terminology is clearly a misnomer. Quitting is the consequence of undergoing a sequence of events that tend to correlate with the recovery of self-control. Shaffer and Jones (1989) found that natural cocaine quitters recover their independence through a sequence of phases comprising identifiable activities. The major events associated with quitting are observable and thus can be made explicit.

It appears that all successful quitters pass through these phases, though at different rates. It does not follow, however, that if a person goes through these phases, he or she will be assured of breaking the habit. Systematic research is necessary to confirm that conclusion or to determine the circumstances under which the sequence of quitting phases proves to be insufficient for recovery. At present, we suggest that identification of these phases, and recognition that they are an integral part of the quitting process, holds great promise for those who desire more effective behavior change skills.

Cocaine quitters—those who have descended to the depths of despair and then ascended back from dependence—have a great deal to teach us about addiction. Perhaps most importantly, cocaine quitters reveal that addiction does not reside in drugs. It resides in human experience. The presence of a substantial number of cases of natural recovery from cocaine, alcohol, opiates, and tobacco *all* serve to remind us that, in spite of the physiological dependence that may be one consequence of drug use, addiction is not inevitable. Furthermore, neither physiological dependence nor behavioral addiction imply that death is inevitable. It is possible to recover and regain one's independence. In order to recover from addiction, however, a sequence of well-defined events must occur. The intensity and duration of each milestone in the sequence will vary from person to person, but the basic sequence will be common to all.

Stage 1: The Emergence of Addiction

Phase 1: Beginning Cocaine. It is obvious that in order to become a successful quitter from any activity, one must participate in it at some point. Everyone who uses cocaine, however, does not become a cocaine abuser or addict. In fact, the vast majority of those who have tried the drug do not become addicted to it. We identified a set of precipitating factors, or catalytic events, that exacerbate the need for the effects that once resulted from the addictive behavior of choice, such as use of cocaine. These catalysts—for instance, the loss of a loved one—explain why beginning users may become abusers; they may serve as the gating event to addiction. In addition, these catalysts explain some of the reasons why quitters may remain abusers once initiated to drug use.

Phase 2: The Activity Produces Positive Consequences. If the activity is not associated with some positive consequences, it will not be continued. Positive effects can be a direct result of the pharmacologic properties of the drug or the psychological reinforcement (for example, relief of depression or sexual inhibition) obtained by its use. The consequences also can be positive in a more indirect manner. For example, some cocaine users experience more social rewards, are held in higher esteem, and have more to do when they are using cocaine. Without some positive consequences, any activity or drug use would not be continued to the point that addiction could emerge.

Phase 3: Adverse Consequences Develop but Remain out of Awareness. Cocaine use or any other activity must be, by definition, associated with adverse consequences if it is to be considered an addictive behavior. The essence of addiction is that it continues to provide some of the positive consequences while simultaneously producing adverse consequences that begin to weigh more heavily. Addictive behaviors serve while they destroy. The reason they can be so destructive rests on the notion that the addict is not fully aware that the adverse effects of their addictive behavior are, in fact, the results of that behavior.

An epicycle of this nature can escalate without regulation because the cybernetic or feedback channels are impaired.[4] The addict perceives others as the source of his or her problems. During this phase, addicts believe that their behavior has little to do with their suffering. The urging of friends and family to reduce or stop the addictive behavior is of little consequence; in fact, their pleading can become fuel that energizes the addictive behavior so that the pattern intensifies further. Bean-Bayog (1988) called this type of denial a focused delusional system. At this level, addicts are capable of making sense of their world, with one exception: They cannot make any causal association between their addictive behavior and the life problems they have to endure. To minimize the discomfort associated with these problems, addicts persist in engaging in the behavior that previously produced positive consequences—that is, the addictive behavior—and the cycle continues. Prevailing beliefs have suggested that there is no escape from this epicycle unless it is interrupted from the outside. More often than not this is true. The natural recovery from addictive behavior, however, stands as a scintillating contradiction.

For some addicts, such as natural quitters, the adverse consequences enter their awareness, and their lives take a turn. This *turning point* into awareness, or insight, has often been considered the end of denial. More accurately, it is a reclaiming of the projections that characterize phase 3. No longer are the addict's problems the result of external events; no longer can he or she continue to claim victimization. The adverse consequences associated with addictive behavior now are experienced as the addict's own. This is the beginning of an epistemological shift. The addict is confronted by his or her own recognition of the causal connection between drug-using behaviors and problems such as poor health, financial difficulty, and family disintegration. He or she now realizes that those behaviors are not anomalous and without adverse effect. Often experiencing this as a life crisis, the addict recognizes that his or her lifestyle must change if he or she is to regain control. The addict begins to recognize that he or she must give up the positive consequences of the drug-using behavior while he or she gains access to the negative outcomes that are connected with the addictive behavior pattern. The event or events associated with turning-point experiences mark the beginning of stage 2, the evolution of quitting.

Stage Two: The Evolution of Quitting

Phase 1: Turning Points. A turning point represents a shift from unencumbered cocaine use to the realization that cocaine abuse is responsible for the presence of profoundly negative life circumstances. The thought of quitting or controlling cocaine first appears prior to the actual turning point. Drug abusers begin to express a wish that they want to quit. Increasing levels of self-observation are involved. The abusers now begin to realize that the costs of their addictive behavior exceed the benefits. Cocaine is explicitly identified as the major[5] destructive agent in their lives. It is at this point that quitters often asks friends and significant others to help them stop. Before a turning point, the burden of self-control had been delegated more to others than to themselves; *the acceptance of personal responsibility* represents the actual turning point.

A turning point is not simply a transition. It is actually the end of a complex thought process about cocaine (or other addictive behavior). We consider it an end point even though abstinence and recovery might be months or years away. The experience of a turning point does not produce instantaneous results. Commonly experienced turning points have been described as periods of dissonance associated with feelings of self-loathing or a deterioration of personal values. Other turning point perceptions include the recognition that cocaine abuse begins to exacerbate rather than diminish intrapersonal and interpersonal conflict. An extremely important yet commonly reported turning point centers on the recognition that one's deteriorating physical condition is related to cocaine abuse. This is experienced as a do-or-die situation: If cocaine is used, the user believes that he or she may die as a result. Other turning points that are less extreme but no less important involve the recognition that a person may lose what is important to him or her—for example, his or her job or a special relationship—because of cocaine use.

Phase 2: Active Quitting Begins. Once a turning point is experienced, the process and task associated with active quitting can begin. Two basic approaches to quitting have been identified: tapered quitting and cold turkey quitting. It is possible that a successful quitter will mix these approaches in order to find a method that works. The majority of quitters, however, fall predominantly or entirely into one style or the other. Few successful quitters mix their stopping strategies.

The notion of *active* quitting is important. Successful quitters make observable changes during this second phase of the stopping stage of addiction.

The methods for quitting cocaine include energetic attempts to avoid the drug, gain social support for personal change, and engage in some form of self-development. Thus, this phase is characterized neither by thoughtfulness nor ambivalence. It is identified by important and marked behavioral change and lifestyle reorganization. New activities are elevated to a position of prominence; they gain intrapersonal and interpersonal value. Old behaviors become devalued and less meaningful.

Phase 3: Relapse Prevention. Very few individuals who stop their drug use remain totally abstinent from that moment on. Marlatt and Gordon (1985) examine how slips—that is, single episodes of drug use—can lead to full-blown relapse. Biological, psychological, and sociological factors interact to influence the risk of relapse for any individual. The final phase of quitting involves the maintenance of new skills and lifestyle patterns that promote positive, independent patterns of behavior. The integration of these behaviors into regular day-to-day activities is the essence of relapse prevention.

The experience of natural quitters suggests that having a number of strategies and tactics to draw on is essential to maintaining abstinence from cocaine. Successful quitters substitute a variety of behavior patterns for their old drug-using lifestyle. For example, they become regularly involved in physical exercise. At times, these substitute patterns also become excessive; this risk is most probable when (1) excessive behavior patterns serve as anodynes to uncomfortable affective states, and/or (2) self-observation skills are weak and poorly developed. Flights into spiritual or religious conversions also help many individuals sustain their abstinence. For some, it takes the shape of entry into formal treatment. Others occasionally substitute other drugs that they consider less troublesome than cocaine. The use of pharmacologic substitution is extremely risky and often backfires. The results of drug substitution can be as devastating and destructive as the original cocaine abuse.

In sum, six phases describe the cycle of addiction. The first three phases compose the natural history stage of addiction, while the last three are associated with quitting or the treatment history of the addictive disorder. The first stage serves as groundwork for the second stage and thus must not be ignored in the therapeutic process.

Toward Clinical Integration

Clinical Applications of a Stage Change Model[6]

According to a perspective of stages of change, clinicians should base treatment choices on a determination of which method of care for which patient should be applied at which specific time during the process of recovery. This is not as complicated as it first appears. For example, consider the third phase of our model. When adverse consequences develop but remain out of the addict's awareness, most people do not seek treatment for addiction. Others (family, friends, a doctor or lawyer) often entreat or coerce phase 3 addicts into a clinical setting. When treatment is available, confrontation and clarification are the most useful clinical interventions at this point in the sequences of phases. A substance abuser needs to be held responsible for the adverse consequences of his or her drug abuse. During this period, enablers or co-dependents unwittingly help the addict keep these negative effects out of his or her awareness. Consequently, family and systems treatments offer the greatest utility. Group therapy is very helpful if the patient is willing to participate. One addict's denial is another's irritation. Behavioral and psychodynamic treatments are of little assistance during this phase of addiction.

During a turning point, when an addict wants to stop, psychodynamic treatments can be very useful. These techniques help the patient to make sense out of chaotic emotions. In addition, dynamic therapies help manage the growing awareness of adverse consequences and mobilize the executive functions of the personality to regain control. During this phase of change, behavioral treatment is still premature. Once the patient becomes sufficiently organized to consider actively changing, however, behavior therapy becomes the most appropriate treatment of choice.

During the active change phase, patients need to learn new behavior patterns and get support for testing their ability to carry these out; in particular, they must have the option of failing and resolving associated negative affect. Consequently, behavior, psychodynamic, family or systems, and group therapies all can be applied judiciously and effectively. Passive, nondirective therapies have little value at this point unless they serve to help the patient integrate the emotional experience of actively changing.

During the relapse prevention phase, both behavioral and psychodynamic treatments are essential. Behavioral approaches help the patient learn how to avoid or cope with risky situations, determine the cues that begin a sequence of events that threaten his or her sobriety, and successfully manage negative thoughts. The majority of incidents involve negative emotional states, however, and can benefit from psychodynamic techniques. New research emphasizes the importance of behavior change (Svanum and McAdoo 1989). This work reveals that for nonpsychiatric patients who are substance abusers, those who sustain a regimen of physical exercise are less likely to relapse. Psychodynamic and pharmacologic treatments are most helpful for psychiatric patients during this phase of addiction treatment. These methods help patients to manage the emotional turmoil that often predicts substance abuse relapse (see, for example, Marlatt and Gordon 1985; Svanum and McAdoo 1989).

The question may arise as to whether therapists must cultivate a sufficiently broad base of clinical skills to provide continuous care or whether they should direct patients to other clinicians during the course of treatment. Both possibilities are acceptable. Throughout the field of medical practice, the idea of a primary care provider as case manager is common. For the therapist whose range of clinical skills is narrow, the clinical task is to coordinate treatment interventions prescriptively. This therapist need not deliver every treatment personally. He or she should, however, remain sensitive to the shifting needs of the patient throughout the course of recovery and try to provide or access specialty treatments when appropriate.

It is crucial for addiction treatment specialists to determine how patients envision their place in the sequence of addiction phases. This process helps patients engage and remain in the therapeutic process. In addition, it aids both therapist and patient in accessing a useful rationale for the treatment program that will follow. If the treatment rationale is in conflict with the patient's perception of his or her problem, the patient will often drop out of treatment. When therapy follows a formulation that is consistent with the patient's view, treatment compliance is common. In short, the patient's perception of the change process is essential to determining which clinical method should be applied.

Assessing the Patient's Perception

The most important view of addictive behavior for the drug treatment specialist is the patient's. The patient's perception of his or her disorder will determine when, how, and to what treatment provider, if any, he or she will go. Understanding a patient's perception of his or her substance abuse permits the clinician to negotiate and navigate treatment interventions.

To develop an integrated model of substance abuse treatment, clinicians need to begin to learn how to *access* and then to *assess* the patient's view of addiction. While it may be possible to impose a clinical model on some patients, most patients bring their own view of addiction with them when they enter treatment. When the provider and patient see things similarly, treatment can go well. However, most clinicians recognize that the majority of substance abusers find it difficult to engage in treatment. As we mentioned before, this has historically been a patient problem: Many treatment specialists blame the patient and his or her "disease of denial." More likely, however, this situation results when the patient's view does not match the therapist's opinion.

Kleinman (1988) and Pfifferling (1980) discuss the importance of examining a patient's perspectives for the treatment of psychiatric disorders in general. Their work is particularly relevant for the addictions, since excessive behaviors can be understood from a multiplicity of views. Aside from cross-

dynamics of the methods by which society attempts to effect changes in individuals (Boyanowsky 1977). Social and cultural factors operate in two directions to transmit values. On the one hand, these influences can encourage an individual to assume a preemptive identity—from user to abuser to addict. On the other hand, social factors can assist addicts to shift their identity from addict to recovering person. We need to continue research on ethnic minorities and other cultural groups whose special traditions and lifestyles are known to influence levels of drug use and patterns of risk. An understanding of the mechanisms by which social and cultural processes influence behavioral change holds great promise for developing efficient treatment methods (Gambino and Shaffer 1979).

Lifestyle. In one form or another, treatment providers will have to come to terms with the definition and meanings of the concept of lifestyle (see, for example, Shaffer et al. 1983). A stage change approach requires clinicians to assess and influence a recovering patient's lifestyle in order to maintain treatment gains. In the same way that therapists attend to shifts in how patients think and feel, they need to assess the changes in how people live and behave. Psychometric research must be conducted to operationalize this construct and develop coordinating definitions between the conceptual system and the empirical referents.

Lifestyle will no doubt be found to be a multifactorial construct. This will force us to make distinctions among cultural, social, and other normative factors. Researchers will examine how consistently an individual behaves (lifestyle) in diverse environments and activities such as home, work, leisure, social, community, athletic/exercise, avocational, and intellectual/cultural/educational pursuits. Perhaps of particular importance will be the measurement of lifestyle behaviors that reflect the propensity for risk taking and health-promotion/disease-prevention activities. Lifestyle measurement will be important for another reason. The cycle of drug use—that is, the waxing and waning of the popularity of different drugs (Shaffer 1985)—is no doubt related to changing cultural influences as one generational cohort succeeds another.

Psychoanalysis and the Unconscious. Some unexpected changes are occurring in the field of substance abuse treatment. Behaviorists are beginning to pay attention to the contributions of the psychoanalytic and psychodynamic traditions of therapy. In the past, behaviorists failed to acknowledge the systematic study of the "organized" complexity of unconscious processes and the structure of the unconscious. Researchers will soon discover the relationship between the unconscious and the selective attention process. The experimental study of perception without awareness will contribute to this understanding. The psychodynamicists, however, will need to devise measurement systems that reflect and bring into focus the meaning of these concepts. As these workers articulate the essence of their concepts, clinicians will be able to use these methods as part of an operative paradigm (Shaffer and Gambino 1979). Some individual researchers have broken new ground in this area and have thus provided a legitimate methodological foundation for scientific research by showing the application of neuroscience to the study of the unconscious (Miller 1986).

Theory, Research, and Practice

Clinical Tasks and Relevance. Treatment and research in the addictions remain separate domains. Researchers and clinicians alike are guilty of maintaining this separation. Theorists fail to specify the implications of theory for practice. When they do address implications for treatment, it is rarely in a form useful to the practitioner (Maletzky 1981). Theorists (and practitioners) forget that ultimately what is important is not good theory but good practice.

Treatment Protocols. The collection of valid and reliable data on multiple variables under conditions that do not take up a great deal of the clinician's task are fundamental at this level of the development of theories of practice. This requires the development of "clinician-friendly" information systems for collecting data. For example, self-reports validated by significant others often produce practical and pragmatic results (Gambino 1989). To establish the biopsychosocial data base necessary to serve as the foundation of effective practice (Galanter 1989), we must establish procedures for defining treatment protocols (Sederer 1988).

These protocols will permit clinicians to replicate the conditions under which other therapists successfully work. This is one area in which the empirical measurement perspective of behavior therapy has demonstrated its worth. Reliance on measurement must be adopted by theorists of other persuasions. One researcher stated it in the form of an axiom and a corollary: If you cannot measure the problem, it does not exist; if you cannot measure the problem, you cannot treat it (Hudson 1978).

Practitioners need to develop methods of making *systematic* observations in practice. Clinical researchers can use these contentions to generate further ideas and hypotheses. The generation and application of this information comprises the cyclical process that characterizes an ideal linkage between theory, research, and practice (Shaffer and Gambino 1984). For example, systematic evaluation of treatment in practice can lead to practice-generated research. Relevant research can lead to theory refinement, which in turn can guide more efficient practice. The end result is an integration of treatment choices.

Notes

1. In the more general sense, this model describes the process of recovery from *any* harmful lifestyle.
2. Throughout this chapter, we use the terms *substance abuse* and *addiction* interchangeably. These concepts are not equivalent, but we substitute them freely as a matter of convention and because the treatment principles we examine apply to both sets of behaviors. Addiction is a higher level construct than substance abuse. While chronic substance abusers are often addicts, many addicts are not substance abusers (for example, pathologic gamblers).
3. Readers interested in this transition should see Shaffer and Jones (1989) for a more thorough discussion of this stage change.
4. This circumstance is similar to a furnace that continues to heat an excessively warm house because the thermostat is malfunctioning and cannot send a message back to the furnace telling it to stop.
5. They may be involved addictively with other substances or activities.
6. Much clinical evidence and experience support the clinical application of a stage change model as described in this section. Systematic research, however, is necessary to clarify the complex causal influences that affect treatment outcome.

References

Annis, H.M., and C.S. Davis 1988. "Assessment of Expectancies." In *Assessment of Addictive Behaviors:* edited by D.M. Donovan and G.A. Marlatt, 84–111. New York: Guilford Press.

Bandura, A. 1977. "Self-Efficacy: Toward a Unifying Theory of Behavioral Change." *Psychological Review* 84:191–215.

Battjes, R.J., and C.L. Jones. 1986. "Implications of Etiological Research for Preventive Interventions and Future Research." In *Etiology of Drug Abuse: Implications for Prevention,* edited by C.L. Jones and R.J. Battjes, 269–76. NIDA Research Monograph, no. 56. Washington, D.C.: GPO.

Bean-Bayog, M. 1988. "Psychotherapy and Alcoholism." Paper presented at the symposium *Treating the Addictions,* Harvard Medical School, March 3–4.

Blum, A. 1985. "The Collective Representation of Affliction: Some Reflections on Disability and Disease as Social Facts." *Theoretical Medicine* 6:221–32.

Blum, T.C., P.M. Roman, and N. Bennett. 1989. "Public Images of Alcoholism Data from a Georgia Survey." *Journal of Studies on Alcohol* 50:5–14.

Boneau, C.A. 1974. "Paradigm Regained: Cognitive Behaviorism Restated." *American Psychologist* 29:297–309.

Boyanowsky, E.O. 1977. "The Psychology of Identity Change: A Theoretical Framework for Review and Analysis of the Self-Role Transformation Process." *Canadian Psychological Review* 18:115–27.

Brownell, K.D., G.A. Marlatt, E. Lichtenstein, and G.T. Wilson. 1986. "Understanding and Preventing Relapse. *American Psychologist* 41:765–82.

Campbell, E.J.M., J.G. Scadding, and R.S. Roberts. 1979. "The Concept of Disease." *British Medical Journal* 2:757–62.

Cooper, M.L., M. Russell, and W.H. George. 1988. "Coping, Expectancies, and Alcohol Abuse: A Test of Social Learning Formulations." *Journal of Abnormal Behavior* 97:218–30.

Cox, W.M., and E. Klinger. 1988. "Motivational Model of Alcohol Use." *Journal of Abnormal Psychology* 97:168–80.

Curry, S., G.A. Marlatt, A.V. Peterson, Jr., and J. Lutton. 1988. "Survival Analysis and Assessment of Relapse Rates." In *Assessment of Addictive Behaviors*, edited by D.M. Donovan and G.A. Marlatt, 454–73. New York: Guilford Press.

Dance, K.A., and R.W.J. Neufeld. 1988. "Aptitude-Treatment Interaction Research in the Clinical Setting: A Review of Attempts to Dispel the Patient Uniformity Myth." *Psychological Bulletin* 104:192–213.

Foreman, J. 1989. "Attitudes Shifting on Alcohol Abuse." *Boston Globe*, February 21.

Galanter, M. 1989. "Subspecialty Training in Alcoholism and Drug Abuse." *American Journal of Psychiatry* 146:8–9.

Gambino, B. 1989. "The Search for Prescriptive Interventions." In *Compulsive Gambling: Theory, Research, and Practice*, edited by H.J. Shaffer, S. Stein, B. Gambino, and T. Cummings, Lexington, Mass.: Lexington Books.

Gambino, B., and H. Shaffer. 1979. "The Concept of Paradigm and the Treatment of Addiction." *Professional Psychology* 10:207–23.

Goldfried, M.R. 1980. "Toward the Delineation of Therapeutic Change Principles." *American Psychologist* 35:991–99.

Goldstein, A.P., and N. Stein. 1976. *Prescriptive Psychotherapy*. New York: Pergamon Press.

Hudson, W.W. 1978. "Notes for Practice: First Axioms of Treatment." *Social Work* 23:65.

Jaffe, J.H. 1984. "Evaluating Drug Abuse Treatment: A Comment on the State of the Art." In *Drug Abuse Treatment Evaluation: Strategies, Progress, and Prospects*, 13–28. Washington, D.C.: GPO.

Johnson, V.E. 1986. *Intervention: How to Help Someone Who Doesn't Want Help*. Minneapolis: Johnson Institute.

Kleinman, A. 1988. *The Illness Narratives: Suffering, Healing and the Human Condition*. New York: Basic Books.

Kramer, M.S. 1988. *Clinical Epidemiology and Biostatistics: A Primer for Clinical Investigators and Decision Makers*. New York: Springer-Verlag.

Krantz, S.E., and R.H. Moos. 1988. "Risk Factors at Intake Predict Nonremission among Depressed Patients." *Journal of Consulting and Clinical Psychology* 56:863–69.

Kuhn, T.S. 1970. *The Structure of Scientific Revolutions*. 2d ed. Chicago: University of Chicago Press.

Maisto, S.A., and G.J. Connors. 1988. "Assessment of Treatment Outcome." In *Assessment of Addictive Behaviors*, edited by D.M. Donovan and G.A. Marlatt, 421–53. New York: Guilford Press.

Maletzky, B.M. 1981. "Clinical Relevance and Clinical Research." *Behavioral Assessment* 3:283–88.

Marlatt, G.A. 1985. "Coping and Substance Abuse: Implications for Research, Prevention, and Treatment." In *Coping and Substance Use*, edited by S. Shiffman and T.A. Wills, 367–86. Orlando, Fla.: Academic Press.

———. 1987. "Alcohol, the Magic Elixir: Stress, Expectancy, and the Transformation of Emotional States." In *Stress and Addiction*, edited by E. Gottheil, K.A. Druly, S. Pashko, and S.P. Weinstein, New York: Brunner/Mazel.

———. 1988. "Matching Clients to Treatment: Treatment Models and Stages of Change. In *Assessment of Addictive Behaviors*, edited by D.M. Donovan and G.A. Marlatt, New York: Guilford Press.

Marlatt, G.A., J.S. Baer, D.M. Donovan, and D.R. Kivlahan. 1988. "Addictive Behaviors: Etiology and Treatment." *Annual Review of Psychology* 39:223–52.

Marlatt, G.A., and J.R. Gordon, eds. 1985. *Relapse Prevention: Maintenance Strategies in the Treatment of Addictive Behaviors*. New York: Guilford Press.

Miettinen, O.S. 1985. *Theoretical Epidemiology: Principles of Occurrence Research in Medicine*. New York: John Wiley & Sons.

Miller, L. 1986. "In Search of the Unconscious." *Psychology Today*, December, 61–64.

Moos, R.H. 1985. "New Perspectives on Coping and Substance Use." In *Coping and Substance Use*," edited by S. Shiffman and T.A. Wills, xiii–xix. Orlando, Fla.: Academic Press.

Niaura, R.S., D.J. Rohsenow, J.A. Binkoff, P.M. Monti, M. Pedraza, and D.B. Abrams. 1988. "Relevance of Cue Reactivity to Understanding Alcohol and Smoking Relapse." *Journal of Abnormal Psychology* 97:133–52.

Payer, L. 1988. *Medicine and Culture*. New York: Henry Holt and Company.

Peele, S. 1984. "The Cultural Context of Psychological Approaches to Alcoholism: Can We Control the Effects of Alcohol?" *American Psychologist* 39:1337–51.

———. 1987. "A Moral Vision of Addiction: How People's Values Determine Whether They Become and Remain Addicts." *Journal of Drug Issues* 17:187–215.

Pfifferling, J.H. 1980. "A Cultural Prescription for Medicocentrism." In *The Relevance of Social Science for Medicine*, edited by L. Eisenberg and A. Kleinman, 197–222. Boston: D. Reidel.

Prochaska, J.O., and C.C. DiClemente. 1985. "Common Processes of Self Change in Smoking, Weight Control, and Psychological Distress." In *Coping and Substance Use*, edited by S. Shiffman and T.A. Wills. San Diego, Cal.: Academic Press.

Prochaska, J.O., W.F. Velicer, C.C. DiClemente, and J. Fava. 1988. "Measuring Processes of Change: Applications to the Cessation of Smoking." *Journal of Consulting and Clinical Psychology* 56:520–28.

Room, R. 1983. "Sociological Aspects of the Disease Concept of Alcoholism." In *Research Advances in Alcohol and Drug Problems*, vol. 7, edited by R.G. Smart, F.B. Glaser. 47–91. New York: Plenum Press.

Sackett, D.L., R.B. Haynes, and P. Tugwell. 1985. *Clinical Epidemiology: A Basic Science for Clinical Medicine*. Boston: Little, Brown.

Scott, N. 1987. "Putting an End to the Disease Concept." *Alcoholism and Addiction*, May/June, 5.

Sederer, L. 1988. "An Organization Model for Those Entering the Field of Psychiatry." *Journal of Psychiatric Education* 12:71–81.

Shaffer, H.J. 1985. "The Disease Controversy: Of Metaphors, Maps and Menus." *Journal of Psychoactive Drugs* 17:65–76.

———. 1986a. "Conceptual Crises and the Addictions: A Philosophy of Science Perspective." *Journal of Substance Abuse Treatment* 3:285–96.

———. 1986. "Assessment of Addictive Disorders: The Use of Clinical Reflection and Hypothesis Testing." *Psychiatric Clinics of North America* 9 (3): 385–98.
———. 1987. "The Epistemology of 'Addictive Disease': The Lincoln-Douglas Debate." *Journal of Substance Abuse Treatment* 4:103–13.
Shaffer, H.J. and M.E. Burglass, eds. 1981. *Classic Contributions in the Addictions*. New York: Brunner/Mazel.
Shaffer, H.J. and B. Gambino, 1979. "Addiction Paradigms. Part 2: Theory, Research, and Practice." *Journal of Psychedelic Drugs* 11:299–304.
Shaffer, H.J. and B. Gambino, 1984. "Addiction Paradigms. Part 3: From Theory-Research to Practice and Back." *Advances in Alcohol and Substance Abuse* 3:135–52.
Shaffer, H.J. and S.B. Jones. 1989. *Quitting Cocaine: The Struggle against Impulse*. Lexington, Mass.: Lexington Books.
Shaffer, H.J., S. Stein, B. Gambino, and T.N. Cummings, eds. 1989. *Compulsive Gambling: Theory, Research, and Practice*. Lexington, Mass.: Lexington Books.
Shaffer, J.W., N. Wegner, T.W., Kinlock, and D.H. Nurco. 1983. "An Empirical Typology of Narcotic Addicts." *International Journal of the Addictions* 18:183–94.
Shiffman, S. and T.A. Wills. 1985. *Coping with Substance Use*. San Diego, Cal.: Academic Press.
Sobell, M. and L.C. Sobell. 1984. "The Aftermath of Heresy: A Response to Pendery et al.'s Critique of 'Individualized Behavior Therapy for Alcoholics.'" *Behavior Research and Therapy* 22: 413–40.
Sontag, S. 1979. *Illness as Metaphor*. New York: Vintage Books.
———. 1989. *AIDS and Its Metaphors*. New York: Farrar, Straus & Giroux.
Svanum, S. and W.G. McAdoo. 1989. "Predicting Rapid Relapse Following Treatment for Chemical Dependency: A Matched-Subjects Design." *Journal of Clinical and Consulting Psychology* 57:222–26.
Talbott, G.D. 1983. "The Disease of Chemical Dependence: From Concept to Precept." *Counselor*, July/August, 18–19.
Tims, F.M. and C.G. Leukefeld. 1986. "Relapse and Recovery in Drug Abuse: An Introduction." In *Relapse and Recovery in Drug Abuse*, edited by F.M. Tims and C.G. Leukefeld, 1–4.
NIDA Research Monograph, no. 72. Washington, D.C.: GPO.
Vaillant, G.E. 1966. "A Twelve Year Follow-up of New York Narcotic Addicts. Part 2: The Natural History of Chronic Disease." *New England Journal of Medicine* 275:1282–88.
Vuchinich, R.E. and J.A. Tucker. 1988. "Contributions from Behavioral Theories of Choice to an Analysis of Alcohol Abuse." *Journal of Abnormal Psychology* 97:181–95.
White, H., M. Bates, and V. Johnson. 1987. "Alcohol Consumption as a Social Reinforcer." In *Why People Drink: Parameters of Alcohol as a Reinforcer*, edited by W.M. Cox. New York: Gardner Press.
Zinberg, N.E. 1984. *Drug, Set, and Setting: The Basis for Controlled Intoxicant Use*. New Haven: Yale University Press.

Appendix: Counseling Interest Inventory

The purpose of the Counseling Interest Inventory is to guide people to the systems of counseling and psychotherapy that are consistent with their life philosophies and personal beliefs. The inventory has demonstrated utility in matching a patient's world view with particular treatment choices widely used within the contemporary health care network.

COUNSELING INTEREST INVENTORY

Read each of the statements that follow. Mark the box next to the concept that best represents your point of view. If you are unsure or feel equally strong about both extremes, reread the question and try to choose the phrase that is most appealing. Ignore the letters below each box, as they are for scoring purposes only. Take your time and remember that there are no correct or incorrect answers.

Example: I prefer to discuss family problems:
- ☐ With all members of my family present. (F)
- ☒ With one family member at a time. (I)

1. A person is most likely to bring constructive change to his or her life by:
   - ☐ Setting goals and making positive decisions. (B,C)
   - ☐ First understanding, then resolving, internal conflicts. (D)

2. To alter a negative pattern an individual should:
   - ☐ Change his or her self-defeating beliefs. (C)
   - ☐ Become aware of his or her emotions. (E,D)

3. When involved in a project or task, I prefer to:
   - ☐ Work alone or with one other person. (I)
   - ☐ Work with several others. (F)

4. Which phrase best describes your view of humanity?
   - ☐ Humans are basically rational and fundamentally good. (E,G)
   - ☐ Humans are often irrational and basically programmed for their own survival. (D)

Reprinted, with permission, from H. Milkman and S. Sunderwirth, *Craving Ecstasy: The Consciousness and Chemistry of Escape*, Lexington, Mass.: Lexington Books, 1987.

5. A person may alter a maladaptive quality of his or her life by:
   - [ ] B — Modifying his or her behavior.
   - [ ] C — Modifying his or her beliefs and expectations.

6. I feel most comfortable when engaged in conversation with:
   - [ ] I — One person at a time.
   - [ ] F — Several people at a time.

7. The most important cause of human suffering may be attributed to:
   - [ ] E,G — Spiritual disharmony and confusion about the meaning of life.
   - [ ] A,D — Environmental stress that triggers chemical imbalance resulting in mental illness.

8. To help a person who is experiencing emotional problems, it is most important to:
   - [ ] D — Understand how he or she has been influenced by the past.
   - [ ] B — Focus on the behavior that is causing current problems.

9. People are best able to experience more fulfillment in life when they:
   - [ ] C,E — Change their thoughts and feelings about themselves.
   - [ ] B — Change the behaviors that are causing problems.

10. My life seems most fulfilled when:
    - [ ] G — I follow my religious convictions.
    - [ ] E,C — I am able to live according to my personal values and innermost feelings.

11. The people who have been most able to help me with personal problems:
    - [ ] C,D,E — Spoke at length about my thoughts and feelings.
    - [ ] A,B — Prescribed medicine or suggested activities to overcome the problem.

12. When I'm with a group of people, I usually pay most attention to:
    - [ ] I — The person I'm talking to at the moment.
    - [ ] F — All people in the room including the person I'm talking to.

13. The majority of people with moderate to severe emotional problems are most effectively helped by:
    - [ ] I — A form of individual counseling or psychotherapy that does not require medication.
    - [ ] A — A combination of effective counseling and an appropriate level of prescribed medication.

14. Most psychological problems originate from:
    - [ ] E,G — Absence of purpose and fear of nonbeing.
    - [ ] B — Learned habits that have negative consequences.

15. An effective psychotherapist will focus most intensively on:
    - [ ] B,C,I — The client's behavior and belief system.
    - [ ] D,F — The client's relationship and feelings within his or her family or social group.

16. When something is wrong, I would be most likely to seek the advice of:
    - [ ] A,I — My personal physician or a psychiatrist.
    - [ ] G,F — A group of people who understand my spiritual or religious values.

17. With regard to problems in living, the people most equipped to be of help are:
    - [ ] A — Physicians or other scientists who have studied the origins and treatment of mental disorder.
    - [ ] G — People who have experienced similar problems and have discovered the spiritual meaning of their lives.

18. The opinions and ideas that seem to influence me the most are:
    - ☐ I — Highly confidential communications from my most intimate associates.
    - ☐ F — Observations about my behavior which are substantiated by group consensus.

19. All things being equal, I would tend to seek help from:
    - ☐ A — My personal physician.
    - ☐ G — A person qualified to offer spiritual guidance.

20. When I have been most anxious or upset the cause seems to have been:
    - ☐ A — A physical problem.
    - ☐ F — Disharmony in my family.

Scoring:
Count the numbers of As, Bs, etc., that correspond to the answers you have given. Record the letters that occur four or more times in the adjacent box: ☐ These letters correspond to the counseling and psychotherapy approaches listed below:

A—biomedical   B—behavioral   C—cognitive
D—psychodynamic   E—existential/humanistic F—family/group
G—spiritual   I—individual

The letters that appear most frequently are likely to represent counseling and psychotherapy approaches that are compatible with your personal philosophy and beliefs.

Index

Abstinence, 368; in family therapy, 313
Abstinence violation effect, 103, 274, 357
Abuse: dimensions of in U.S., 95–97
Accidents: and alcohol use, 96
Acquired Immunodeficiency Syndrome (AIDS), 153
Addictable personality, 18
Addiction, 8; assessing patient's perception, 367, 368; cycle of, 362–365; definitions and agreement, 352, 353; disease controversy, 351–354; medical management of, 46; as moral weakness, 353; occurrence of, 202–204; and paradigms, 355, 356; risk factors in, 202, 203; treatment choices, 354–359; treatment intervention, 357–359
Addiction models, 360
Addiction Severity Index, 242
Addictive Behavior Research Center, 74
ADDS program: evaluation of, 118, 119
Adolescent substance abuse: impact of other systems, 338; role of grandparents, 336, 337; sibling factors, 336
Adolescent substance abusers: family life cycle issues, 330–333; parental subsystem, 333–336
Adoptees: causation studies of, 13
Adoption: alcoholism studies, 15, 16
Adventures in Change, 227
Affective disorders, 47, 166, 168–170
Affective modalities: goal of, 304
Affective modes, 290, 291; biofeedback, 295, 296; charismatic group therapy, 296, 297; group marathon therapy, 300–304; meditation, 293–295; stress management training, 291–293; suggestion, 298–300
Aftercare: in EAP program, 152
Age: minimum drinking, 101
Aggression: against women, 184–186
Alcohol, 5; concurrent psychiatric disorders, 53, 54; control of availability, 100, 101; craving, 52, 53; detoxification, 49–52; effect on human system, 75–78; inhibitors of metabolism, 51, 52; mechanism of action, 48, 49; young adult intervention, 102, 103
Alcohol abuse: costs of, 95; familial, 15; impact on society, 95–97; and tobacco use, 19
Alcohol and Drug Abuse Division (ADAD), 109
Alcohol and Drug Evaluation Specialist (ADES), 109; eligibility requirements, 110, 111; evaluation procedures of, 111–115; state certification of, 111
Alcohol dependence: intervention measures, 102–105; treatment outcomes, 97, 98
Alcohol Drug Driving Safety (ADDS), 109
Alcohol Expectancy Questionnaire (AEQ), 276
Alcohol treatment: controlled vs. uncontrolled studies, 253, 254; effectiveness, 260–262; myths of, 254–256; specific modalities, 256–259
Alcohol Use Inventory (AUI), 275

Alcoholic families: long-term outcomes, 310, 311
Alcoholic hepatitis, 49
Alcoholics: anemia in, 84; factors in recovery of, 206, 207; nutritional assessment of, 83, 84; relapses of, 202
Alcoholics Anonymous (AA), 177, 201, 202, 206, 207, 239, 240, 242, 258
Alcoholism, 47; adoption studies on, 15, 16; alcohol-suppressing strategies, 256, 257; broad spectrum treatment strategies, 257, 258; client-treatment matching, 259, 260; and depression, 82; evaluation of, 84, 85; family studies on, 14, 15; and malnutrition, 73–78; study on twins, 16; traditional treatment strategies, 258, 259; types of, 314; Type 3 approaches, 315–318; Veterans Administration definition of, 74
Aldehyde dehydrogenase, 51
Alleles, 10
ALL-STARS, 128
Alternative lifestyle: in juvenile treatment, 227, 228
Amantadine, 55
Amantadine hydrochloride, 55
American Drug and Alcohol Survey, 132
American industry: substance abuse costs in, 143
American Medical Association (AMA): definition of alcoholism, 74
Amitriptyline, 53
Amphetamine, 31; similarity with norepinephrine, 27
Anemia: in alcoholics, 84
Anhedonia, 54, 55
Animals: genetic studies in, 19, 20
Antabuse, 206
Anticonvulsants, 58
Antidepression, 38
Antisocial personality, 47, 171, 173, 174, 190, 191
Anxiety, 38, 53, 54, 66, 82; and nutritional deficiency, 82
Anxiety disorders, 47, 61, 64, 67, 166, 170
Anxiolytics, 58

Arapahoe County Residential Center (ACRC), 242
Arapahoe House, 241, 242
Arousal: determinants of, 31; and synaptic chemistry, 30–32
Aspen treatment program, 239, 240
Assessment process, 227
Association of Junior Leagues, 187
Attention deficit disorder (ADD), 53, 57, 58; residual type, 170
Attributions, 274, 275
Aversion therapies, 256

Barbiturates, 5
Beck Depression Inventory, 277, 278, 316
Behavioral: approach, 288; marital therapy, 257; responses in withdrawal, 9; self-control training, 256
Benzodiazepines, 5, 48; detoxification, 60, 61; mechanism of action, 58, 59; substitution therapy, 61; withdrawal symptoms, 59
Berkson's law, 165
Beta-blockers, 50
Biochemical factors: genetic influences on, 9
Biochemical processes: effect of drugs on, 7
Biofeedback, 295, 296
Bipolar affective disease, 67
Bipolar disorder, 57, 168–170
Blood alcohol concentration (BAC), 110
Borderline disorder, 171, 172
Brain, 28–30; effect of alcohol on, 77, 78; effect of substance abuse on, 176
Bromocriptine, 55, 57

CAGE test, 188, 189
Campus-based prevention programs: college, 100
Carbimide, 51, 52
CARE of Colorado, 130
Causation: model for, 164, 165
Central nervous system (CNS), 31, 43; effect of alcohol on, 48, 50, 77; opiate effect on, 44, 46
Challenge Program, 228

Change: stages of, 360, 361
Charismatic group therapy, 296, 297
Chemical Abuse Addiction Treatment Outcome Registry (CATOR), 194
Child care services: barrier to treatment, 189
Children's Awareness Theater (CHAT), 131
Chloral hydrate, 49
Chlordiazepoxide, 49, 50
Clonidine, 45
Cocaine, 19, 20, 31; concurrent psychiatric disorders, 57, 58; management of withdrawal, 55, 57; mechanism of action, 54
Cocaine abuse: treatment modalities, 288
Code of Hammurabi, 3
Codependence, 154, 155, 315, 316, 318; in women, 193, 194
Coercion: impact on treatment, 214
Cognition: effect of nutrient deficiency on, 82
Cognitive approach, 288
Cognitive-behaviorial therapy, 249
Cognitive-behaviorial treatment: assessment tools, 275–278; behavioral factors in, 266, 267; cognitive factors in, 268, 269; description of, 275–282; expectancies, 268, 269; intervention strategies, 278–282; lapses during, 282; social factors in, 267, 268; theory, 266, 267; therapist role in, 266; vs. disease concept, 265, 266
Cognitive function: and diet, 81, 82
Colorado: drunk driver treatment system, 237, 238; evaluation of school programs, 132; model for rehabilitation, 241–244; school prevention programs, 123; traffic offender laws and legislation, 109
Colorado Alcohol and Drug Abuse Division (ADAD), 225, 237
Colorado model: clinical observations, 244, 245; failure/success of groups, 244; phases of, 242, 243; preliminary results of, 244; programmatic observations, 244, 245

Colorado OSAP Project, 225–227; client selection, 228, 229; evaluation plan, 230–232
Colorado Teen Institute, 131
Community: drug education of, 129; reinforcement approach, 257
Community transition: for juvenile treatment, 228
Comorbidity, 164
Comprehensive Drinker Profile, 276
Concordance: study of twins, 14
Concurrent psychiatric disorders: treatment of, 47, 48, 53, 54
Conditioned withdrawal, 204
Confidentiality: in EAP programs, 146, 147
Confrontation-sensitivity (C-S) group, 301
Conviction: and punishment, 218, 219
Coping mechanisms: and addiction, 356; and motivation, 356
Coping resources: in alcohol treatment, 277–282
Corrections: and treatment, 238–241
Court Proceduress for Identifying Problem Drinkers, 111
Craving: control of, 52, 53
Creative therapies, 297, 298
Crime: and alcohol use, 95; deterrents to, 212; and drug abuse, 97; effect of drug use, 217; and intoxicant use, 211, 212; need for reeducation programs, 212, 213; new treatment methods, 213
Criminals: problems in treatment of, 213–215
Cyclothymic disorder, 57

DBI, 5
Death: and alcohol use, 95, 96
Death penalty: vs. rehabilitation, 221
Deficiency: folic acid, 79; magnesium, 81; niacin, 80; nutrient, 82; riboflavin, 80; thiamine, 78, 79; vitamin B(6), 80; vitamin B(12), 79, 80; vitamin C, 81
Delirium tremens, 50, 51
Delta opiate receptor, 43
Denial, 177, 250, 363, 367
Denver Veterans Administration Therapeutic Community, 301

Denver's Independence House Family, 301
Dependence: causes for, 9
Depression, 26, 33, 53, 57, 61, 62, 64, 168, 169; and alcoholism, 82; and opiate addicts, 169; in women, 190–193
Desipramine, 55, 57
Deterrence: general and specific, 92; reason for punishment, 220
Detoxification: alcohol, 49–52; benzodiazepine, 60, 61; methadone, 46; nicotine, 63; opiate, 44, 45; polydrug, 66
Diagnostic Interview Schedule (DIS), 188
Diazepam, 50
Diphenylhydantoin, 50
Disease model: of alcoholism, 249, 250
Disulfiram, 48, 257
Dopamine, 33, 34
Dopamine agonists, 58
Dopamine-deficient state, 58
Doxepin, 48, 53
Dopaminergic blocker, 50
Drinking/Drug History Questionnaire (DDHQ), 111–113
Driving under the influence (DUI): background of, 25, 235
Driving while intoxicated (DWI), 236
Drug: definition of, 7
Drug abuse: and crime, 97; economic costs of, 96; environmental variation in, 11; genetic variability in, 10; heritable factors, 12, 13
Drug Free Schools and Communities Act (DFSCA), 123
Drug screening, 152, 153
Drug use: factors correlated with delinquency, 226; impact on crime, 217
Drugs: avidity, 12; dependence, 7–9; reinforcement, 12
Drunk drivers: Colorado rehabilitation model, 237–245; scope of problem with, 235, 236
DSM: II, 161; III, 162; III R, 161
DSM III-R: Axis I, 166–170; Axis II, 166, 170–174; Axis III, 166
DSM-III-R Axis disorder, 163
DSM-III-R Axis II disorder, 163

Dual diagnosis: in alcoholic women, 190–193; discussion of, 174–178; importance of, 177, 178; models of, 164, 165
Dysthymic disorder, 168

EAPs: codependency, 154, 155; confidentiality, 146, 147; and cross-addictions, 155; effectiveness of, 147; future role of, 155, 156; history of, 144; impact on health costs, 154; information resource, 153–155; models, 145, 146; referrals by supervisors, 148–151; relationship with unions, 153, 154; role in aftercare, 152; role in drug screening, 152, 153; self-referrals, 150, 151; treatment information resource, 151
Education program: Level I, 237, 238
Ego regression: in substance abusers, 176, 177
Elliott causal model, 227
Emetine, 52
Employee assistance program (EAP) See EAPs
Endorphins, 5, 27, 34, 38, 43
Enkephalin, 5, 34, 38, 43, 48
Environmental causation: in adoptees, 13
Environmental factors, 11, 12
Environmental influences: on alcoholism, 15; on smoking, 17
Environmental variation: in drug abuse, 11
Enzyme expansion theory, 33
Enzymes, 7, 9
Epidemiological Catchment Area study, 190, 191
Ericksonian induction, 299
Ethanol, 48–52; See also Alcohol
Ethanol withdrawal syndrome, 49
Euphoria, 9, 38
Euphorogenic chemicals, 34
Exercise: effect on mood, 38, 39
"Exercise euphoria", 38
Expectancies: alcohol, 275–277; alcohol-efficacy, 273, 274; in cognitive-behavorial treatment, 268, 269; and drug effects, 357; evidence for alcohol outcome, 270, 271;

evidence for alcohol outcome-direct, 271, 272; evidence for alcohol outcome-indirect, 270, 271; self-efficacy, 272, 273; sources of alcohol outcome, 269
Experiential narrative: in group marathon therapy, 301–304

Familial alcoholism, 15
Families: genetic causation in, 13; life cycle, 330–333
Family Assessment Device, 316
Family therapy: abstinence in, 313; model for Type 3, 315, 316
Family therapy approaches: and substance abuse, 309, 310; typology of treatment, 311–315
Fetal alcohol syndrome, 99, 189
Folic acid deficiency, 79
Food and Drug Administration (FDA), 46
Fort Logan Drinking History Scale, 112
Funding: of prevention programs, 98, 99

Gamma-aminobutyric acid (GABA), 5, 48, 58
Gastrointestinal tract: effect of alcohol on, 77
Genetic causation: in adoptees, 13
Genetic factors, 11, 12; influence on biochemical factors, 9
Genetic influences: on alcoholism, 15; animal studies on, 19, 20; detection of, 13–15; on substance abuse, 14
Genetic variability: in drug abuse, 10
Genetics: and alcoholism, 14–16; and polysubstance use, 18, 19; and smoking, 16–18
Grandparents: role in recovery, 336, 337
Group marathon therapy, 300–304

Haloperidol, 50
Halstead Clinic, 346, 347
Harrison Act, 45
Hepatic metabolism: of ethanol, 51
Hepatic microsomal activity, 53
Hepatic toxicity, 47
Heritability, 17, 18
Heroin, 34, 44

Heroin addiction, 43, 44
Heroin addicts: recovery in, 207; relapses of, 202
Heterodox approach, 288, 289. See also Multimodality approach
Highway Safety Research Institute, 112
Hormone, 7
Humanistic/existential approach, 288
Huntington's disease, 33
Hyperactivity. See Attention deficit disorder
Hypnosis, 299

IMPACT training, 130
Insomnia, 53, 54, 66
Integrated Social Psychological Model, 226
Intervention, 97, 98; cognitively based, 104; efforts involved in, 102; programs in Colorado schools, 123, 129–132; programs in industry, 148–153; strategies involved in, 92, 93; young adult misusers, 102, 103
Inventory of Drinking Situations, 359
Ion channels, 8, 9

Jail sentences: treatment method for DUI offenders, 238–241
"Just Say No" campaign, 26
Juvenile delinquency: and drug use, 226–228

L-dopa, 55
Law of Romulus, 184
Laws: impact on alcohol consumption, 100, 101; used as coercion, 214
Legislation: and traffic offenders, 109
Level I education program, 237
Level I programs: for traffic offenders, 115, 116
Level II programs: for traffic offenders, 116–118
Level II theraputic education, 237
Level II treatment program, 237
Levo-alpha-acetylmethdadol (L-AAM): advantages of in withdrawal, 47
Life structure: impact on recovery, 205
Limbic system, 43
Lithium, 48, 53, 54
Liver: effect of alcohol on, 76

Longwood treatment program, 239–241
Lorazapam, 50

Magnesium deficiency, 81
Major affective disorders, 67
Malnutrition: and alcoholism, 73–78; treatment for alcohol-related, 84
Mania, 33, 191
Manic-depression. See Bipolar disorder
Marital Roles Inventory, 316
Medications: traditional treatment strategy, 258, 259
Meditation, 293–295
Mental illnesses: major categories of, 167–170
Methadone, 44–46
Methadone maintenance programs, 66; federal regulation of, 46
Methylphenidate, 58
Metropolitan Life Foundation, 124, 126
Michigan Alcohol Screening Test (MAST), 112, 188
Mile High Council on Alcohol and Drug Abuse, 131
Millon Clinical Multi-Axis Inventory, 242
Minnesota Multiphasic Personality Inventory (MMPI), 112, 277
Modifier model, 165
Molecules: in brain, 28–30; exogenous opiate, 27; mood-altering, 25; psychoactive, 25, 26
Mood alterations, 26–28; effects on, 35, 38, 39; need for, 26, 27
Morphine, 34, 44
Morphine Maintenance Clinics, 45
Mortimer-Filkins test, 112, 113. See also Court Procedures for Identifying Problem Drinkers
Mothers Against Drunk Driving (MADD), 101, 235
Motivation: for treatment, 104, 105
Multimodality addiction treatment, 287–289
Multimodality approach, 288
Multiple DUI offenders: treatment objectives for, 241
Multiproblem patients: description of, 163

Naloxone, 47
Naltrexone, 47
Narcissistic personality, 171–173
Narcotics Anonymous (NA), 207
National Highway Traffic and Safety Administration (NHTSA), 236
National Institute on Alcohol Abuse and Alcoholism (NIAAA), 187
National Institute on Drug Abuse, 143
National Institutes for Mental Health, 39
Natural high, 27, 31, 290, 304; concept, 128, 129; ways of achieving, 291
Nerve cells, 28
Neurochemistry, 27–30
Neurons, 28
Neurotransmission, 30, 32
Neurotransmitter receptors, 7, 8; interaction, 29, 30
Neurotransmitters, 25, 28–31
Niacin deficiency, 80
Nicotine, 19; antagonists to, 64, 65; detoxification, 63, 64; mechanism of action, 62, 63; pharmacologic deterrents, 65; replacement therapy, 64; withdrawal symptoms, 62
Nonfamilial alcoholism, 15
Norepinephrine, 27, 34, 35, 38
Nurses: patient dynamics and history, 342–345; treatment of, 345–348; treatment results, 348, 349
Nutrients, 75; depletion of, 78; effects of alcohol on, 75; specific deficiencies in, 78–81
Nutritional assessment: applied to alcoholics, 83, 84
Nutritional deficiency, effects on cognition, 82
Nutritional status: cognitive and psychological function, 81, 82
Nutritional therapy, 74

Obsessive-compulsive disorder, 192
Occam's razor, 161
Offenders: drug-involved, 221, 222
Office of Substance Abuse Prevention (OSAP), 225
OMNI Research and Training, 231
Omnibus Drug Bill of 1988, 196

Opiate addicts: and depression, 169; pharmacologic stabilization of, 45–47; psychiatric disorders in, 47, 48
Opiate-binding receptors, 43
Opiates, 34, 43–48; antagonists, 47; detoxification, 44, 45; effect on central nervous system, 44; mechanism of action, 43, 44
Opioid peptides, 43
Opioids: endogenous, 5
Opium, 43
Organic mental disorders: substance-induced, 166
Oxazepam, 50

Pancreas: effect of alcohol on, 77
Panic disorder, 192
Paradigms: and addictions, 355, 356
Paraldehyde, 49
Parallel disorders, 164
Parental subsystem, 333–336
Parents: drug education of, 129; role in adolescent abuse treatment, 333–336
Parkinson's disease, 33
Patient-treatment matching, 358, 359
Pellagra, 80
Peptides, 38
Personality: antisocial, 47, 171, 173, 174, 190, 191
Phenocopy, 15
Phenonmena: relapse-related, 103, 104
Phenotypic variance, 4
Phobia, 192
Phobic disorder, 191
Phoenix South Community Mental Health Agency, 240
Physical dependence, 9, 13
Physiological processes: effect of drugs on, 7
Physiological responses: in withdrawal, 9
Pittman, F.S.: approach to alcoholism, 313–315
Polydrug abuse: concurrent psychiatric disorders, 66, 67; detoxification, 66; patient management, 66, 67; patterns of use, 65
Polysubstance use: and genetics, 18, 19
Postsynaptic membrane, 30

Power motivational training (PMT), 236
Prescriptive treatment, 250, 251
Prevention, 97, 98; campus-based, 100; Colorado schools, 123; funding of, 98, 9; laws and regulations, 100, 101; programs in industry, 148–153; public education programs, 99; school-based programs, 99, 100; strategies involved in, 92, 93
Primary prevention, 148
Prince George treatment program, 239
Profile of Mood States, 278
Promiscuity: related to drinking, 185, 186
Propranolol, 50
Prosecutors: goals beyond conviction, 218, 222, 223
Psychedelic drugs, 27
Psychiatric disorders: treatment of concurrent, 47, 48, 53, 54, 57, 58, 66, 67
Psychoactive molecules, 25, 26
Psychoactive substances: early history of, 3; factors influencing use, 4, 5
Psychodynamic approach, 288
Psychological function: and diet, 81, 82
Public education: role in prevention, 99
Punishment: reasons for, 219–223

Quality of Life (QOL) questionnaire, 316

Reagan administration: prevention attempts by, 98, 101
Receptors, 9
Recidivism, 241; in ADDS program, 118, 119; rates of, 238
Recovery, 201, 202, 289; model of, 361–365; natural, 251; pathways to, 206, 207; steps in, 289
Regulations: impact on alcohol consumption, 100, 101
Rehabilitation: Colorado model for, 237, 238; of drunk drivers, 236; reason for punishment, 220, 221; vs. death penalty, 221
Relapse: cognitive therapy used, 104; nutrient deficiency, 82; prevention of, 201, 202; rates of, 204, 205

Relaxation: response instruction, 291–293; and synaptic chemistry, 34, 35
Remove Intoxicated Drivers (RID), 235, 236
Restitution, 219, 220
Restraint: means of punishment, 221, 222
Retribution, 219, 220
Rhomberg balance, 110
Riboflavin deficiency, 80
Risk model: in multiproblem patients, 165
Roman society: norms for women in, 183, 184
"Runner's high", 38

Schizophrenia, 33, 166–168
School-based programs: role in prevention, 99, 100
School Health Education Evaluation (SHEE), 124, 126
School Team Approach Training Effort (STATE), 129
Schools: drug and alcohol policies, 126; health curriculum, 126, 127; intervention procedures, 123, 129, 130; staff development in, 127, 128
SCL-90, 277
Secondary prevention, 148
Sedative-hypnotics, 58
Self-efficacy, 272, 273
Self-referrals: in EAP programs, 150, 151
Sensitivity, 12
Sensory stimuli: relationship with body chemistry, 5
Serotonin, 35
Siblings: role in recovery, 336
Situational Competence Test, 277
Situational Confidence Questionnaire, 359
Smoking: factors influencing, 16–18
Social control theory, 226
Social learning theory, 226
Social perception: importance of, 368
Social skills training, 257
Stages of change: clinical applications of, 365–369
Strain theory, 226
Stress, 26

Stress management strategies, 257
Stress management training, 291–293
Student assistance program (SAP), 130
Students: alternative activities for, 128, 129
Students Against Drunk Driving (SADD), 101, 128
Students Taking a New Direction (STAND), 128
Substance abuse: animal studies in, 19, 20; cost to industry, 142, 143; effects on brain, 176; effects on ego, 176, 177; environmental and genetic influences on, 7–19; impediments to recovery, 174–178
Substance use: genetic influences on human, 14–19
Suggestion, 298–300
Supervisors: training of, 148–151
Synanon model, 46
Synapse, 28
Synaptic chemistry, 26, 30–32; and relaxation, 34, 35
Synaptic homeostasis, 32, 33
Synaptic junction, 28

Taxonomy: of situations, 359
Tertiary prevention, 148
Theory: integrating with treatment models, 359–361; vs. practice, 371
Thiamine deficiency, 78, 79
Tolerance, 9, 12
Tourette's syndrome, 33
Toxicity, 9
Traditional behavioral therapy: role of therapist in, 266
Traffic offenders: background information, 111, 112; classification of, 114, 115; Drinking/Drug History Questionnaire, 112; education and therapy of, 115–117; evaluation procedures, 111–115; legislation, 109; Mortimer-Filkins Test, 112, 113; referrral of, 114, 115
Traynor v. Turnage, 4, 74
Treatment: alcohol-related malnutrition, 84; and corrections, 238–241; for drunk drivers, 236; future trends in, 369–371; for juveniles, 227, 228; motivation for, 104, 105; programs in industry,

148–153; protocols, 371; staging, 178
Treatment alliance: impediments to, 177
Treatment models, 360; integrating with theory, 359–361
Treatment staging, 178
Tricyclic antidepressants, 53–55
Twins: concordance in, 14; studies of, 13, 14
Type 1 approaches: to family therapy, 311, 312
Type 2 approaches: to family therapy, 312–315
Type 3 approaches: to alcoholism, 315–318

Unions: EAP relationship with, 153, 154
United States: dimensions of abuse in, 95–97
University of Colorado Health Sciences Center Hospital, 345
Universiy of Colorado Therapeutic Community, Peer I, 310

Valium, 5
Variances: environmentally determined, 4; genetically determined, 4, 5; phenotypic, 4

Verbal invocation: in meditation, 294, 295
Veterans Administration: definition of alcoholism, 74
Vitamin B(6) deficiency, 80
Vitamin B(12) deficiency, 79, 80
Vitamin C deficiency, 81

Weekend Intervention Program, 236
Wernicke-Korsakoff syndrome, 78
Wilderness experience, 227
Withdrawal, 12
Withdrawal syndrome, 9, 13; alcohol, 49–52; benzodiazepine, 60, 61; cocaine, 55; nicotine, 63; opiate, 44, 45
Woman to Woman program, 187, 189
Women: aggression toward, 184–186; assessment failures, 193; attitudes concerning drinking, 183–184; barriers to treatment, 187–190; codependence issues, 193, 194; implications for prevention, 186, 187; mortality rates for, 195; old attitudes toward, 183, 184; special problems of, 190–193; treatment outcomes for, 194, 195; as victims, 185, 186

Zinc malabsorption, 80, 81

About the Contributors

Gregory A. Aarons
Metropolitan State College
Denver, Colorado

Sheila B. Blume, M.D., C.A.C.
Medical Director
Alcoholism, Chemical Dependency, and Compulsive Gambling Programs
South Oaks Hospital
Amityville, New York
Director
The South Oaks Institute of Alcoholism and Addictive Behavior Studies
Amityville, New York
Clinical Professor of Psychiatry
State University of New York at Stony Brook
Stony Brook, New York

Judy Brown
Outpatient Coordinator
Arapahoe House
Denver, Colorado

Dave Christiansen
Adventures in Change
Denver, Colorado

Carole Christianson
Records and Program Evaluation Manager
Arapahoe House
Denver, Colorado

Allan C. Collins
School of Pharmacy and Institute for Behavioral Genetics
University of Colorado
Boulder, Colorado

Christopher M. de Fiebre
School of Pharmacy and Institute for Behavioral Genetics
University of Colorado
Boulder, Colorado

Chad D. Emrick, Ph.D.
Veterans Administration Medical Center
Denver, Colorado

William A. Frosch, M.D.
Professor of Psychiatry
Cornell Medical College
New York, New York

Robert Vaughn Frye, M.S., C.A.C. III
Denver Veterans Administration Medical Center
University of Colorado School of Medicine
Denver, Colorado

Blase Gambino, Ph.D.
Center for Addiction Studies
Harvard Medical School and Department of Psychiatry
The Cambridge Hospital
Cambridge, Massachusetts

Carol J. Garrett, Ph.D.
Division of Youth Services
Denver, Colorado

Carol L. Hacker, Ph.D.
Employee Assistance Program Director
Jefferson County Schools
Golden, Colorado

Victor A. Harris, Ph.D.
Services Coordinator
Boulder County Health Department
Boulder, Colorado

Vernice Griffin Hills, R.N., C.A.C. II
Veterans Administration Medical Center
Fitzsimons Psychophysiology Lab
Chronic Pain Research
Aurora, Colorado

Alexander M. Hunter
Boulder County District Attorney
Boulder, Colorado

Judith Landau-Stanton, M.B., Ch.B., D.P.M.
Associate Professor of Psychiatry and Family Medicine
Director of Training and Clinical Services
Division of Family Programs
Department of Psychiatry
University of Rochester School of Medicine
Rochester, New York

Steven P. Merrefield
Correctional Resources, Inc.
Denver, Colorado

Harvey B. Milkman, Ph.D.
Professor of Psychology
Metropolitan State College
Denver, Colorado

William R. Miller, Ph.D.
Professor of Psychology and Psychiatry
Director of Clinical Training
University of New Mexico
Albuquerque, New Mexico

Lee Ann Mjelde Mossey, M.S.W.
Consultant and Lecturer
Colorado Springs, Colorado

Peter E. Nathan, Ph.D.
Vice President for Academic Affairs
University of Iowa
Iowa City, Iowa

Robert A. Pudim, M.S.
Office of the District Attorney
Boulder, Colorado

John A. Renner, Jr., M.D.
Assistant Chief
Psychiatry Service
VA Outpatient Clinic
Associate Professor of Psychiatry
Boston University School of Medicine
Boston, Massachusetts

Robin Room, M.D.
Alcohol Research Group
Medical Research Institute of San Francisco
San Francisco, California

Lloyd I. Sederer, M.D.
Assistant General Director
McLean Hospital
Assistant Professor of Psychiatry
Harvard Medical Schjool

Howard J. Shaffer, Ph.D.
Director
Center for Addiction Studies
Assistant Professor
Harvard Medical School at The Cambridge Hospital
Cambridge, Massachusetts

Phillip G. Sidoff
Corrections Program Coordinator
Arapahoe House
Denver, Colorado

M. Duncan Stanton, Ph.D.
Professor and Director
Division of Family Programs
Department of Psychiatry
University of Rochester School of Medicine
Rochester, New York

Susan L. Stein, Ph.D.
OMNI Research and Training, Inc.
Littleton, Colorado

Stanley G. Sunderwirth, Ph.D.
Department of Chemistry
Indiana University-Purdue University at Indianapolis-Columbus
Columbus, Indiana

Boris Tabakoff, M.D.
Scientific Director
National Institute on Alcohol Abuse and Alcoholism
National Institute of Health Clinical Center
Bethesda, Maryland

David S. Timken, Ph.D.
Clinical Services Coordinator
Alcohol and Drug Abuse Division
Colorado Department of Health
Denver, Colorado

George E. Vaillant, M.D.
Department of Psychiatry
Dartmouth Medical School
Hanover, New Hampshire

Mary VanderWall
Senior Health Education Consultant
Colorado Department of Education
Denver, Colorado

Norman E. Zinberg, M.D.
Clinical Professor of Psychiatry
Harvard Medical School at The Cambridge Hospital
Cambridge, Massachusetts

About the Editors

Harvey B. Milkman, Ph.D. received his doctorate in 1974 from Michigan State University and is currently professor of psychology at Metropolitan State College. He is founder and director of the Center for Interdisciplinary Studies in Denver. From 1969 to 1972 he conducted research with William Frosch at New York Bellevue Psychiatric Hospital on the drug user's choice of drug. Dr. Milkman's theory of drug preferences was subsequently adopted by the National Institute on Drug Abuse as a major contribution to the literature. In 1980–81, he studied addictive behaviors in Africa, India and southeast Asia; in 1985–86 he was recipient of a Fullbright-Hays Lectureship award at the National University of Malaysia. Recently he has represented the United States Information Agency as a consultant and featured speaker in Brazil, Iceland, Australia and The Netherlands.

Dr. Milkman is also co-editor (with Howard Shaffer) of *Addiction: Multidisciplinary Perspectives and Treatments*, Lexington Books, 1985 (winner of the Choice Award for outstanding academic books). His multidisciplinary model for addiction, "The Chemistry of Craving," written with Stanley Sunderwirth, was featured in the October 1983 issue of *Psychology Today* and fully developed in *Craving for Ecstasy: The Consciousness and Chemistry of Escape*, Lexington Books, 1987.

Lloyd I. Sederer is an assistant general director, McLean Hospital; assistant professor of psychiatry, Harvard Medical School; president-elect of the Massachusetts Psychiatric Society; and a fellow of the American Psychiatric Association. He has authored and edited *Inpatient Psychiatry: Diagnosis and Treatment*, a textbook on the hospital care of psychiatric patients, which is entering its third edition. He has also written and lectured extensively on the treatment of problem patients and on administrative, historical and economic aspects of psychiatry.